Democracy in Austria

Günter Bischof and David M. Wineroither, eds.

CONTEMPORARY AUSTRIAN STUDIES | VOLUME 28

UNO PRESS

innsbruck university press

Printed in the United States of America

Cover photograph ©Parlamentsdirektion/Bernhard Zofall
Book design by Allison Reu and Alex Dimeff

Published in the United States by
University of New Orleans Press
ISBN: 9781608011742

UNO PRESS

Published and distributed in Europe
by Innsbruck University Press
ISBN: 9783903187542

iup

Publication of this volume has been made possible through a generous grant by the Federal Ministry of Science, Research and Economy through the Austrian Academic Exchange Service (ÖAAD). The Austrian Marshall Plan Anniversary Foundation in Vienna has been very generous in supporting Center Austria: The Austrian Marshall Plan Center for European Studies at the University of New Orleans and its publications series. The College of Liberal Arts at the University of New Orleans, as well as the Vice Rectorate for Research and the International Relations Office of the University of Innsbruck provided additional financial support.

Bundesministerium
Bildung, Wissenschaft
und Forschung

Federal Ministry
Republic of Austria
Education, Science
and Research

Contemporary Austrian Studies

Sponsored by the University of New Orleans and University of Innsbruck

Table of Contents

IV. REVIEW ESSAY

V. BOOK REVIEWS

Democracy in Austria

Preface

Günter Bischof
David M. Wineroither

I. On the Global State of Democracy

Some nearly thirty years ago, the influential work of two scholars appeared to make somewhat antagonistic sketches of global political trends. One, more optimistic, proclaimed "the end of history."[1] The author, Francis Fukuyama, predicted no less than universal or quasi-universal acceptance of core liberal-democratic values across cultural hemispheres. The other, Samuel P. Huntington, decidedly more pessimistic both in looking forward and looking back, anticipated rounds of "clashes of civilizations."[2]

Whatever the precise (shifting) nature of political conflicts and systemic competition around the globe, the share of the world population governed democratically has been growing somewhat more slowly since the early 1990s. Proliferation of democratic rule has always been characterized by ebb and flow, rapid advancement and painful setbacks. The Arab Spring movement describes just the latest example. In this vein, Huntington famously coined the term "waves of democratization."[3]

We currently do not experience a wave of de-democratization. But matters are worse than stagnating numbers of democratic countries indicate. There currently is, from a European geographic perspective, a tightening autocratic ring of fire stretching from Murmansk at the Barents Sea to the Atlas Mountains that glimpse the Atlantic Ocean. While the Bertelsmann Foundation in a bi-annual comparison found the numbers of democracies and autocracies stable, the share of defective democracies among all democracies was rising, and so was the share of hardcore oppressive dictatorship among all non-democracies.[4] Similarly, in its latest 2019 release, Freedom House

1 Francis Fukuyama, "The End of History?", *The National Interest* 16 (Summer 1989): 3-18.

2 Samuel P. Huntington, "The Clash of Civilizations?", *Foreign Affairs* 72, no. 3 (1993): 22-49.

3 Samuel P. Huntington, *The Third Wave: Democratization in the Late Twentieth Century* (Norman: University of Oklahoma Press, 1993).

4 Bertelsmann Stiftung,"Schwierige Zeiten für demokratischen Wandel: BTI 2016, accessed March 15, 2016, https://www.bertelsmann-stiftung.de/de/themen/aktuelle-meldungen/2016/februar/schwierige-zeiten-fuer-demokratischen-wandel/.

"recorded the 13th consecutive year of decline in global freedom."[5] In accordance with BTI and other more comprehensive indices of quality of democracy, these developments occur within both the group of liberal (consolidated) democracies and the set of countries governed in authoritarian ways.

Developments in Europe

Even in Europe, "democracies with adjectives" are spreading. In selected post-socialist countries of Central Eastern Europe, recent political developments cast doubt on democratic stability and maturity. These setbacks serve as a reminder that only two generations ago, a majority of countries that are now EU member states had been ruled autocratically. Some of them had virtually never experienced democratic rule before the system change took place in the late 1980s.

Will signs of an authoritarian backlash translate into hybrid regimes, thereby locking-in EU-members in semi-democratic polity?[6] As an interesting aside, such development curiously contrasts with fears held by many — elites and citizens alike — in older Western European countries that the combined effects of globalization and supranationalism would eradicate national identity. In fact, scholars have found some evidence in support of the convergence hypothesis when it comes to democratic practice. But these trends are by no means universal, nor are they unconditional in polities where they can be observed. National peculiarities are far from disappearing—for better and worse.

Across the spectrum, individual rights seem in retreat. The reasons for that are manifold but not entirely disconnected from each other: the "war on terror" launched in the aftermath of 9/11, social disenfranchisement facilitated by the international financial crisis of 2008/9, and shifting public sentiment over the migration challenge that peaked in 2015 all contributed and continue to contribute. In several democracies, governments got swept into office that show dedication to a toxic mix of targeting minority rights, media freedom, and separation of powers. Textbook cases in that regard are to be found in Northern America and Southern, Central, and Eastern Europe.

Some challenges are faced by all liberal democracies, including rising degrees of political polarization at the elite *and* mass level, while not all

5 Freedom House, "Democracy in Retreat: Freedom in the World 2019," accessed Feb. 5, 2019, https://freedomhouse.org/report/freedom-world/freedom-world-2019.

6 Jacques Rupnik, "From Democratic Fatigue to Populist Backlash," *Journal of Democracy* 18, no 4 (2007): 17-25 (here 19).

changes with a profound impact upon the state of democracy are unequivocally of negative influence. Populism in such reading may also help to hold political elites accountable and to ensure effective representation of most voters. Some worries that various sets of problems would necessarily solidify into systemic crisis then appear overstated. The prominent example of public trust in politicians and political institutions comes to one's mind: It has indeed reached notoriously low levels in many democracies while it poorly serves those interested in uncovering the actual state of democracy.

Functioning democracies educate their citizens to critically evaluate the performance of a polity's key actors and institutions. Hence, it does not come as a surprise that the operation of democracy in the UK, the motherland of parliamentarianism, is viewed significantly more negatively when compared to the level of (dis)satisfaction found in notoriously fragile and defective democracies by the respective national population.[7] The BREXIT case, on the other hand, promoted citizens' belief in the benefits of sustained EU membership in the remaining countries. In Austria, public support of the country's EU membership reached an all-time high in early 2019![8] Finally, forecasts into vote choice in the upcoming European parliamentary election predict modest gains for Eurosceptic right-wing parties.[9] The two large mainstream establishment party families, social democrats and Christian democrats/conservatives, falling short of a majority, seems likely at this point, merely mirrors trends of diversification to be found in national party systems.

The State of Democracy in Austria

Austrian democracy as a (former) outlier of late-coming democratization and neutralization during the Cold War has come a long way in terms of convergence—denoted by the label of de-Austrification.[10] As in other Western European power-sharing polities, consociationalism—and

7 Oscar W. Gabriel and Fritz Plasser, "Deutschland, Österreich und die Schweiz im europäischen Vergleich," in *Deutschland, Österreich und die Schweiz im neuen Europa: Bürger und Politik*, ed. Oscar W. Gabriel and Fritz Plasser (Baden-Baden: Nomos, 2010), 265-30 (here 290).

8 https://orf.at/stories/3111973/, accessed Feb. 20, 2019. See also http://www.europarl.europa.eu/austria/de/aktuell-presse/meldungen/meldungen-2018/oktober-2018/pr-2018-oktober-7.html, accessed Feb. 19, 2019.

9 https://www.faz.net/aktuell/politik/ausland/umfrage-zur-europawahl-evp-weiter-staerkste-kraft-16047351.html, accessed Feb. 19, 2019.

10 Anton Pelinka, "Die Entaustrifizierung Österreichs: Zum Wandel des politischen Systems 1945-1995," Österreichische Zeitschrift für Politikwissenschaft 24 (1995): 5-16.

neo-corporatism in particular[11]—contributed to stable economic growth and low unemployment rates. Social peace got preserved past the golden age of welfare state expansion well into the 1980s. According to comparative studies, this non-majoritarian type of democracy would qualify as "better, kinder, and gentler."[12]

On the downside, critiques pointed out a tendency of power-sharing political systems to prioritize output performance over procedural aspects of the quality of democracy. Remnants of party and consensus democratic features in contemporary Austria are in fact tied to rather unwelcome and negative consequences in that regard, as emphasized also in several contributions to this volume. Most prominently, as Reinhard Heinisch has pointed out, there is a causal link running from consociational features to the strong presence of a right-wing populist party in parliament.[13] The levels of clientelism and corruption remain notoriously high in comparison with post-industrial democracies elsewhere despite some retreat over past decades.[14]

Such ambiguities are closely reflected in the country's political culture. Fritz Plasser and Gilg Seeber recently summarized a stable, deeply anchored democracy coupled with declining trust in political elites and rising levels of polarization within the wider society.[15] While authoritarian ideas of strongman leadership are still not resonating with an overwhelming majority of voters, the recent representation of the far-right Freedom Party as junior partner in government spurs worries as the party does not clearly demarcate itself from extremist groups and activists.

Austrian has not approached European average by losing its adjectives of party democracy and neo-corporatism. In other words, on a range of issues, various sets of countries (peers) have themselves moved towards Austrian practice (i.e. due to rising party membership in newer democracies in Eastern Europe, grand coalitions in Germany and coalition government

11 Klaus Armingeon, "The Effects of Negotiation Democracy: A Comparative Analysis," *European Journal of Political Research* 41, no. 1 (2002): 81-105.

12 Arend Lijphart, *Patterns of Democracy: Government Forms and Performance in Thirty-Six Countries*, 2nd ed. (New Haven: Yale University Press, 2012), chapter 16.

13 Reinhard Heinisch, "Demokratiekritik und (Rechts-)Populismus: Modellfall Österreich?," in *Die österreichische Demokratie im Vergleich*, ed. Ludger Helms and David M. Wineroither, 2nd ed. (Baden-Baden: Nomos, 2017), 449-477 (here 451).

14 David M. Wineroither and Herbert Kitschelt, "Die Entwicklung des Parteienwettbewerbs in Österreich," in *Die österreichische Demokratie im Vergleich*, ed. Ludger Helms and David M. Wineroither, 2nd ed. (Baden-Baden: Nomos, 2017), 251-285 (here 256-9).

15 Fritz Plasser and Gilg Seeber, "Politische Kultur und Demokratiebewusstsein in der Zweiten Republik im internationalen Vergleich", in *Die österreichische Demokratie im Vergleich*, ed. Ludger Helms and David M. Wineroither, 2nd ed. (Baden-Baden: Nomos, 2017), 337-364 (here 355).

in the UK). In terms of fostering the quality of democracy, the challenge is to create viable hybrid systems by combining the best of two, if not many, worlds of liberal democratic rule.

Summary of Volume

The parliament of the Austro-Hungarian Monarchy closed in March 1914. Three years, two months, seventeen days after its adjournment, the *Reichsrat* reopened in May 1917 in the middle of World War I. John Deak and Jonathan Gumz conclude in their essay on the *Reichsrat* role in World War I that "[by] returning to the path that this constitutional state had laid, the *Reichsrat* first positioned itself as the defender of individual rights guaranteed by the constitution as it had existed in Cisleithania since the 1870s." Minister-President Karl Graf von Stürgkh adjourned parliament in 1914 to strip the elected MPs of their immunity during mobilization for the war. Without parliamentary control, the government also proclaimed a state of emergency that furthered the military's takeover of the justice system and the suspension of trial by jury. As the war went on and nine MPs were convicted by military courts and the former MP Cesare Battisti was executed for treason, there was more and more pushback against these emergency laws. When Karl became emperor after Francis Joseph's death in November 1916, he curtailed the military's independence, abolished the emergency decrees beyond the front lines, and called the *Reichsrat* back into session. Constitutionalism was reasserted.

Erin Hochman, the author of the recent prize-winning *Imagining a Greater Germany*, makes a plea for more openness in interpreting the failure of Austrian democracy after World War I. She strongly argues that there were good democrats in the large Socialist and the smaller liberal camps who wanted democratic governance to survive in both Austria and Germany. Like in the case of Weimar democracy, the democratic regime after the Great War was crisis-ridden but not bound to fail in Austria. In fact, the Socialist *Republikanischer Schutzbund* made common cause with the German veterans' association *Reichsbanner Schwarz-Rot-Gold* to support democratic governance in common patriotic celebrations and political symbolism. Support of the "Anschluss" was a *grossdeutsch* strategy on both sides of the border in support of democracy and republicanism: "The unity of the German *Volk* can only be realized on the basis of democracy and the republic." Socialists like Julius Deutsch made a big effort to reach across the political divide but found fewer and fewer allies as the Christian Social Party turned more authoritarian.

The turn of the Christian Socials after 1929 towards a more authoritarian ideology is the subject of Janek Wasserman's essay. Wasserman, the author of *Black Vienna: The Radical Right in the Red City, 1918-1938*, traces the Catholic authoritarian, anti-democratic, and anti-Semitic ideology of the Christian Socials back into the late 19th century. Leading intellectual lights and the *Vordenker* of "Black Vienna" ideology in the Christian Social Camp, such as Othmar Spann and Joseph Eberle, saw concurrent arcs of crisis in democracy, capitalism, and socialism and advocated a "*völkisch* revolution by cultural German rooted in Christian values" in publications such as *Das neue Reich* and *Schönere Zukunft*. With the radical turn towards an authoritarian solution after 1929 and the crisis of Austrian democracy in 1933, Dollfuss getting rid of parliament in March 1933, only five weeks after Hitler and the National Socialists seized power in Germany, did not come as a surprise. Now a growing number of intellectuals in "black Vienna" welcomed Nazism in Germany and the authoritarian corporate state in Austria. Was this the "better future" they had hoped for?

The renowned Austrian political scientist Anton Pelinka penned a book on "the failed" First Austrian Republic on the occasion of the 100th anniversary of the formation of the Republic of Austria in November 1918. In his essay on the reestablishment of Austrian democracy in 1945 after World War II in this volume, he sees continuities with the First Republic: the same principal political camps (only with the German Nationals now discredited), the Constitution of 1920, and Karl Renner as *pater patriae*. But the beginnings of the Second Republic, he argues, took a markedly different turn from the First Republic. The big difference was that Austria was occupied after World War II. With the "Moscow Declaration" of 1943, the great powers set the parameters for Austrian statehood after the war. Austria would be treated as a "liberated" country after the war, in spite of having fought on the side of Nazi Germany after the "Anschluss" (Germany was treated as a "defeated" country). Internally, the Christian conservatives (now called ÖVP), who had undermined Austrian democracy in the First Republic, now decided to work with the social democrats (SPÖ) in forming a coalition government after the November election of 1945. In an "informal understanding," these two parties decided to exclude the Communist Party (KPÖ), which was also part of the governing coalition. Unlike the First Republic, the two principal political camps, ÖVP and SPÖ, agreed to "power-sharing" arrangements after 1945. The "external" pressure from the Western occupation powers, then, was crucial for the blossoming of Austrian democracy after the war.

The "grand coalition" of the ÖVP and SPÖ would survive until 1966 only to be replaced by an ÖVP government in 1966 and then an SPÖ government in 1970. As Reinhard Heinisch shows in his essay, the realignment of the Austrian party system happened in the 1980s with the rise of populism in the new FPÖ and the formation of the Green Party in 1986. The iconic young leader Jörg Haider took over the leadership of the FPÖ, which had represented the old nationalist camp—with a liberal wing—up until that time. Haider's populist new strategy of "verbal aggressiveness, gross exaggeration, and blatant disinformation" would meet a string of electoral successes and make the FPÖ the second strongest party by 1999 to enter a coalition government with the ÖVP in 2000—the first time a populist party entered the government in Western Europe. At the same time, the different strands of various alternative movements (ecological, anti-nuclear, life style, etc.) came together over a massive protest, stopping the building of a nuclear power plant on the Danube (Hainburg) to form a new party with changing names: the "Greens." Both the FPÖ and the Greens had success with attacking the old corruption and influence-peddling system of "*Proporz*" in the Grand Coalition and transformed the Austrian political system after 1986.

In his contribution, David M. Wineroither highlights a unique ability of the Austrian polity to switch back and forth between predominantly majoritarian and consensual features in the practice of democracy in recent decades. Challenges to core foundations of consociationalism seem more pronounced today than they were during the first black-blue coalition (2000-7), the so-called "*Wende*"-government. The zeitgeist of today represents a widespread acceptance of conflictual mechanisms of political decision making and an adversarial style of political communication. In key areas of democratic practice, Austria converged towards an all-European average, for example, with regard to party-state related features and the ideological composition of the party system. In a few notable instances, the latecomer has advanced to become a trendsetter (i.e. voting age of sixteen).

Martin Dolezal's analysis locates the profile of political participation in Austria within his peer group of older Western European democracies. Based on a rich trove of individual-level data, he asserts a gradual shift away from party-state characteristics to unconventional, bottom-up forms of civic engagement over the past forty years. His data also challenge conventional wisdom that claims protest activity used to be below average in comparative perspective during the 1970s. Altogether, the empirical results represent mixed evidence in favor of the movement society thesis with (more) unconventional forms of participation supplementing (more) conventional ones. Notably, Austria observes the disappearance of a once strong gender gap in political activism that addresses a more diverse range of topics than ever seen before.

Hannes Richter's essay takes note of the fact that both in the United States and Europe, a substantial decline in support for democracy as the preferred form of government has been recorded over time. More recently, millennials have been receiving scholarly attention ranging from their policy preferences to their social media habits, but at the same time, a continuation of the ongoing decline in support for democracy has also been recorded among this age cohort. Richter investigates millennials' support for democracy and democratic institutions in Austria compared to their older peers and finds evidence that this age group indeed shows less support for democracy and its institutions than previous generations.

Karin Liebhart and Petra Bernhardt's essay deals with the 2016 presidential election campaigns of Norbert Hofer and Alexander Van der Bellen as the first political campaigns in Austria, which were mainly fought online. Placing emphasis on social media communication enabled the run-off candidates to directly address target groups, influence the agenda for traditional media coverage, and bypass the gatekeeper function of journalists. The contribution reconstructs how Van der Bellen's campaign turned the notion of *Heimat* (homeland), an until then exclusionary concept "owned" by the far-right political opponent, into an inclusive one through linking it with the candidate's biography and thus introducing it as a political vision represented by the candidate. The focus is on visual and verbal references to the reframed "homeland"-story in the candidate's social media posts on Facebook, Twitter, and Instagram.

The comparative evaluation of the quality of democracy in contemporary Austria is dealt with in David Campbell's study. Assessment includes EU member states and OECD countries. In line with more recent attempts of finely calibrated measurement across institutional and cultural settings, the conceptual framework presented here systematically addresses the input and procedural dimensions, as well as output related and sustainability aspects. According to Campbell's findings, the Nordic states of Scandinavia and Switzerland form a benchmark of outstanding democratic performance. While Austria ranks above the average, it fails to obtain consistently high scores across all dimensions. Specifically, it scores rather poorly in areas of migrant integration, corruption, and accessibility of citizenship.

Dirk Rupnow's essay on 2018 as a big commemorative year deals with contemporary Austrian historical memory issues. In the surfeit of 2018 commemorations, he sees a major disconnect between contemporary Austrian political discourses about refugees and the bathetic speeches delivered by the politicians of the ÖVP-FPÖ governing coalition in historical commemoration events. Particularly the right-wing FPÖ, undermining the Austrian human rights traditions in its policies vis-à-vis refugees, constitutes a threat to core values of Austrian democracy. He also recognizes the instrumentalization of contemporary Holocaust memory in anti-migration discourses, where, in the process, Holocaust memory has shifted from the center to the margins.

Apart from our main focus on the permutations of 100 years of Austrian democracy, this volume offers Florian Wenninger's historiographical essay on the Berkeley historian of Austria Charles Adams Gulick (1896-1989). The Texas-born Gulick, a progressive and supporter of the New Deal, became a historian of Austria in the 1930s. During a sabbatical in Vienna in 1936/37, he collected numerous documents on the Austrian labor movement and became friends with leading politicians in the Socialist movement (many of them in the underground during the "Austrofascist" era). He published his results after World War II in his two-volume, 2,000 page study of the First Republic, *From Habsburg to Hitler* (1948). Blaming the Christian Socials for the demise of Austrian democracy in 1933/34 (like Wasserman does in his essay in this volume), he became the darling of the SPÖ. They had "the Gulick" translated and published in a five-volume edition (Gulick was not happy with the error-ridden translation). People in the conservative camp responded with the "anti-Gulick" to set the record straight. Heinrich Benedikt edited the *Geschichte der Republik Österreich*, published in 1954, which became a classic in its interpretation of Austria's political camps (*Lager*). However, to the chagrin of the conservative camp, it did not upend Gulick's analysis of 1933/34. The American historian Gulick thus left a lasting contribution to the writing of the history of the First Austrian Republic.

A roundtable discussion of Manfred Flügge's bestseller *Stadt Ohne Seele: Wien 1938* dissects this book's dramatic rendition of the "Anschluss" and the expulsion and flight of the Jews in 1938 from a number of different perspectives. Two review essays—one on new literature of 1938 exiles and another on the history of the Green movement and party in Austria—and a number of book reviews complete this volume.

Acknowledgements

The year 1918 was a major one for historical anniversaries in Austria. We have taken note of this and dedicate the topical essays of this volume to the anniversary of the foundation of the Austrian Republic in November

1918. We thought that the changing fortunes of democratic governance in Austria over the last hundred years would be a fitting contribution to this anniversary's discourses. With our Roundtable on Manfred Flügge's *Stadt Ohne Seele: Wien 1938* (2018), we also want to contribute to the eightieth anniversary of the "Anschluss."

A number of people have been instrumental in making the completion of this volume possible. We are sincerely thankful to all the contributing authors for submitting their essays in a timely fashion and responding favorably to all editing suggestions from our production team. Vicko Marelić, the 2018/19 Austrian Ministry of Education, Science, and Research Dissertation Fellow at UNO and PhD student in the Department of Eastern European History at the University of Vienna, has done a fine job in tracking every manuscript through both the copyediting and proofreading processes and towards final publication. He also has been relentless in correcting and aligning footnotes with our style sheet and humoring authors toward completion of their manuscripts. At the final stages of the project, Hans Petschar and Michaela Pfunder from the Picture Archives of the Austrian National Library helped secure the picture for the cover of this volume from the Austrian Parliament. We are grateful to Bernhard Zofall from the director's office of the Austrian Parliament for granting us the copyright to use this picture.

We would also like to thank our anonymous outside peer reviewers for their thorough and timely assessments.

Lauren E. Garcia at UNO Press put her enthusiasm into the final round of copyediting the individual manuscripts; Alex Dimeff skillfully typeset the final text of the volume and designed the cover. G.K. Darby and Abram Himelstein, the leadership team at UNO Press, have been hugely supportive to spirit this volume through to final publication. At Center Austria: The Austrian Marshall Plan Center for European Studies, Marc Landry, the Associate Director, was helpful with sage advice. Gertraud Griessner, with the help of Raphaela Fischnaller, conducted the Center's daily business with superb efficiency to allow the coeditor to work on managing the completion of this volume. Without the dedicated teams at Center Austria and UNO Press, there would be no CAS series. At Innsbruck university press, Birgit Holzner was helpful with the production of the cover, the final round of proofreading, and then producing the volume for the European market. Cooperating with her has become a big bonus in the production of these volumes. We would like to thank Bernhard Zofall from the director's office of the Austrian parliament (*Parlamentsdirektion*) for providing us with a high-resolution copy of the cover photo and Hans Petschar and Michaela

Pfunder from the Picture Archives of the Austrian National Library for facilitating the receipt of this picture.

As always, we are happy in acknowledging our sponsors and supporters for making the publication of the *Contemporary Austrian Studies* series possible at all, not a small matter in the age of diminishing budgets for higher education in general and the social sciences and humanities in particular. At the Universities of Innsbruck and New Orleans, our thanks go to Vice *Rektor* for Research Sabine Schindler for a grant towards the printing of this volume, and Matthias Schennach, Barbara Tasser, Gerhard Rampl, and Janine Köppen in the New Orleans Office. At UNO, Kim Long, the Dean of the College of Liberal Arts and Education, and Robert Dupont, the chair of the History Department, have given us green lights and much support whenever needed. We are also grateful to President John Niklow and *Rektor* Tilmann Märk for their support of the entire UNO-University of Innsbruck partnership agenda, including its publication series. In the Federal Ministry of Economics, Science, and Research and its student exchange office, Österreichischer Auslandsdienst (ÖAD), we are grateful to Barbara Weitgruber, Christoph Ramoser, Felix Wilcek, Josef Leidenfrost, and Florian Gerhardus. Markus Schweiger, the executive secretary, Ambassador Wolfgang Petritsch, the chairman of the board, as well as the board members of the Austrian Marshall Plan Foundation have been our strongest supporters for more than a decade now. It is a great pleasure and privilege to work with them all and acknowledge their unwavering support of Center Austria: The Austrian Marshall Plan Center of European Studies at UNO and its activities and publications.

New Orleans/Budapest, February 2019

I. Democracy in Trouble (1918-1933)

The Reichsrat in 1917/18 and the Beginning of the First Republic

John Deak
Jonathan E. Gumz

Opening of Parliament, 30 May 1917

The Austrian Parliament opened to little fanfare on May 30, 1917. Hunger and war-exhaustion tempered the spirits of the population. Uncertainty abounded in the meeting rooms of the party clubs and in the government halls. Emperor Karl's decision to open parliament had left the government of Minister-President Count Heinrich Clam-Martinic in an exposed and friendless position. Only months before, Clam's government had been involved with drafting legislation that would centralize education and make German the official language of the Austrian half of the empire. That legislation would be released by decree, or *Octroi,* to please nationalist German parties. The negotiations for the *Octroi* had collapsed in April, but the damage had been done. Karl's government thus entered parliament having alienated many of the German liberal parties and the Czechs. Even the Poles, once a mainstay of parliamentary majorities, abandoned Clam; war weariness and national aspirations for a reconstituted Poland dominated the thoughts of the Polish Club.[1]

Clam thus entered parliament with a governmental minority. And in the weeks leading up to the opening of parliament, this kept him busy with all of its technical aspects. Divided into two houses, the *Herrenhaus,* whose members were appointed, and the House of Representatives, whose members were last elected in 1911, the parliament had been adjourned since 4:40 P.M. on March 13, 1914. It was supposed to resume four days later, but Minister-President Karl Graf von Stürgkh had closed the house in order to avoid unseemly behavior in parliament: obstruction.[2] The declaration of war on July 26, 1914 had kicked

1 For an excellent assessment of the political situation in 1917, see Christopher Brennan, "Reforming Austria-Hungary: Beyond His Control or beyond His Capacity? The Domestic Policies of Emperor Karl I, November 1916 - May 1917." (Ph.D. Thesis, London School of Economics and Political Science, 2012); Lothar Höbelt, *"Stehen oder Fallen?" Österreichische Politik im Ersten Weltkrieg* (Vienna: Böhlau Verlag, 2015).

2 Fussek, Alexander, "Ministerpräsident Karl Graf Stürgkh und die parlamentarische Frage," *Mitteilungen des Österreichischen Staatsarchivs* 17/18 (65 1964): 51–53; John W. Boyer, *Culture and Political Crisis in Vienna: Christian Socialism in Power, 1897-1918* (Chicago: University of Chicago Press, 1995), 294; Lothar Höbelt, "Parteien und Fraktionen im Cisleithanischen Reichsrat," in *Die Habsburgermonarchie*, ed. Helmut Rumpler and Peter Urbanitsch, vol. VII/1 (Vienna: Verlag der Österreichischen Akademie der Wissenschaften, 2000), 994–96.

the proverbial can further down the road. Parliament remained definitively closed, and military administration quickly followed.

The long closure of parliament (three years, two months, seventeen days) made its reopening in May 1917 resemble the awkwardness at the beginning of an alumni reunion. The war had changed everyone's lives. Everyone was older and looking hungry, haggard, and tired. Twenty-four MPs had died. Two more had resigned. Ten had their mandates stripped, and one of those, Dr. Cesare Battisti, had been executed for treason the previous year. Joseph Redlich describes in his diary entry for this day that no one on the government bench made a good impression: "the gentlemen sat there, half of them looking trampled, half of them all puffed up."[3] Clam himself made a bad impression too. As the bell rang to open parliament, Clam awkwardly began to "introduce" his government to parliament—a government that had been formed six months before! And as Clam ceded the floor to the most senior member of the floor, Dr. Viktor von Fuchs, the awkwardness continued. Fuchs pointed directly to the long duration of parliament's closure and the intervening years of "woe and inner pain."[4] This was not a celebration of the return of democracy to Cisleithania.

In fact, the parliamentarians themselves had more questions than answers when they entered parliament. And a central question would be not only how to return to a parliamentary system but how to make parliament work in the crucial moment of the war, a war that everyone from Emperor Karl to the average peasant or proletarian wanted to end. And what role would parliament have in the crisis of war and internal exhaustion? As the *Neue Freie Presse* articulated in their lead article on the opening of parliament, "The *Reichsrat* must choose to follow a difficult path, through crisis, that will lead to power. [...] The *Reichsrat* must get to work."[5] The *Reichsrat* (and its House of Representatives elected by universal manhood suffrage since 1907) would follow a path shaped by an attempted return to constitutional governance within Cisleithania. The vision of constitutionalism here was not one of extreme parliamentary sovereignty as imitators of British parliamentary sovereignty might have it.[6] Rather it was a general

3 Josef Redlich, *Schicksalsjahre Österreichs: Die Erinnerungen und Tagebücher Josef Redlichs 1869-1936*, ed. Fritz Fellner and Doris Corradini, 2nd ed., Veröffentlichungen der Kommission für neuere Geschichte Österreichs 105 (Vienna: Böhlau, 2011), ii, 300 (entry for 30 May 1917).

4 Stenographische Protokolle über die Sitzungen des Hauses der Abgeordneten des österreichischen Reichsrates XXII. Session [hereafter SP], 1. Sitzung (30 May 1917), 11.

5 *Neue Freie Presse* [Hereafter NFP], Nr. 18954 (Morgenblatt, 30 May 1917), 1.

6 This is not to say that parliamentary sovereignty was completely unchecked in the British case, but it was curious that so many written constitutions in the 19th century looked to the United Kingdom, a country without a written constitution, as a model. See Linda Colley, "Empires of Writing: Britain, America, and Constitutions, 1776-1848," *Law and History Review* 32, nr. 2 (2014): 237-266.

reassertion of the *Reichsrat* in the vision of a balanced constitutional state between centralized and localized power, between administration and parliamentary authority, anchored in a vision of law that provided limited but recognizable constraints on the state while grounded in individual rights.[7] In returning to the path that this constitutional state had laid, the *Reichsrat* first positioned itself as the defender of individual rights guaranteed by the constitution as it had existed in Cisleithania since the 1870s.

War Regime and the closing of parliament.

Parliament's task of "getting to work" in the late spring and summer of 1917 was made all the more challenging by the scope and depth of events that had passed since the declaration of war and the accompanying state of emergency in July 1914. In a session of the Council of Ministers on July 23, 1914, the Austrian government prepared for war. The cabinet meeting discussed two critical points on this day. The first regarded the Austrian Parliament. Karl Graf von Stürgkh, the Minister-President at the time, reminded his fellow ministers that parliament had merely been adjourned, not dissolved. The parliamentary session was therefore still in effect and, importantly, the members of parliament still enjoyed immunity from prosecution. Stürgkh thought it best to close the session and thereby strip the elected MPs of their immunity. "In the event of mobilization," Stürgkh added, "where it would be the task of the criminal justice system to counter all obstacles to military measures through the energetic use of the law, the privileged position of the members of parliament could possibly be a great impediment; it would therefore be prudent to remove this privilege through the closing of the session."[8] At this point, however, Interior Minister Karl von Heinold-Udynski intervened, suggesting that shuttering parliament and ending MPs' immunity was not so simple. There were permanent standing committees of parliament, particularly those that administered social insurance, that would remain open even if parliament was dissolved. The members of these committees would still have immunity. Moreover, he added, there also was the question of the crownland assemblies, eight of which were still in session and which had their own permanent committees that would provide immunity for their members between sessions. Heinold

7 See John W. Boyer's elegant description of this state's creation in the late 1860's in, John W. Boyer, "Power, Partisanship, and the Grid of Democratic Politics: 1907 as the Pivot Point of Modern Austrian History," *Austrian History Yearbook* 44 (2013), 149-153.

8 Österreichische Staatsarchiv [hereafter ÖstA], Allgemeines Verwaltungsarchiv [Hereafter AVA], Inneres, Ministerratspräsidium [hereafter MRPräs, Ministerratsprotokolle [herafter MR Prot] Akten [herafter A] 28, Nr. 30: 23.VII.1914.

suggested that if they were really to close all the crownland assemblies and the parliament, as well as shut down the standing committees, they would need to seek an imperial sanction. The Cabinet voted to present the emperor with such a request, though it appears that no proclamation was released. In the meantime, the parliamentarian and scholar of politics and administration Joseph Redlich remarked in his diary—in the midst of excited reporting about the war and mobilization—simply, "The post offices are permanently open; the state of exception has been declared."[9] Austria's parliament had been shuttered without notice or attention as the war began.

That state of exception, or state of emergency, formed the second important matter that the Austrian cabinet discussed on July 23, 1914. Specifically, the cabinet was presented with no less than seventeen war emergency measures that were to accompany the event of mobilization and war. These measures had been discussed between civilian and military officials periodically since 1906; they were published in confidential service manuals that were to be opened in the event of mobilization. The latest edition of the service manual, titled as an "Orientation-Guide for Exceptional Decrees in the Event of War," was published in 1912.[10] The guide contained pre-written legislation that was to be enacted by decree and use of the emergency paragraph § 14, which allowed the government to temporarily enact legislation while parliament was not in session.[11] The emergency measures laid the groundwork, or —so the officials thought, —for a frictionless mobilization and prosecution of a short war. These laws regulated the more mundane aspects of war mobilization, including aspects of passport inspections, the possession and confiscation of weapons, the handling of communications (including mail inspection and post and telegraph communications, as well as the use of carrier pigeons), and the necessity of secrecy regarding military positions and activity. But these emergency laws also began a process

---

9 Redlich, *Schicksalsjahre Österreichs (2nd ed.)*, i, 617 (entry for 26 July 1914).

10 *Orientierungsbehelf über Ausnahmeverfügungen für den Kriegsfall für die im Reichrate vertretenen Königreiche und Länder*, 3. Auflage (Vienna: Hof- und Staatsdruckerei, 1912). For an account of the successive discussions of these service manuals, see Tamara Scheer, *Die Ringstraßenfront: Österreich-Ungarn, das Kriegsüberwachungsamt und der Ausnahmezustand während des Ersten Weltkrieges*, Schriftens des Heeresgeschlichten Museums 15 (Vienna: Republik Österreich, Bundesministerium für Landesverteidigung und Sport - BMLVS, 2010), 15–27.

11 For more on § 14, see Gernot D. Hasiba, *Das Notverordnungsrecht in Österreich (1848-1917): Notwendigkeit und Missbrauch eines "Staatserhaltenden Instrumentes,"* Studien zur Geschichte der Österreichisch-Ungarischen Monarchie 22 (Vienna: Verlag der Österreichischen Akademie der Wissenschaften, 1985). For the use of § 14 in this situation, see Gernot D. Hasiba, "Inter arma silent leges? Ein Beitrag über die rechtlichen Grundlagen der österreichischen Verwaltung im 1. Weltkrieg," in *Modell einer neuen Wirtschaftsordnung. Wirtschaftsverwaltung in Österreich 1914-1918*, ed. Wilhelm Brauneder and Franz Baltzarek, Rechtshistorische Reihe 74 (Frankfurt am Main: Peter Lang, 1991), 21–27.

in which the military encroached upon civilian affairs and, importantly, civil rights guaranteed by the constitution. Laws were released, spelled out in the service manual, for the subordination of civilian officials to military authority (Nr. 156); for the criminal prosecution of civilians for disturbing the public peace or interfering with supplies (Nr. 155); and for the prosecution of civilians accused of crimes against the war-making power of the state in military courts (Nr. 164). The reach into the administration of justice was quick and deep. Law Nr. 163 suspended trial by jury in the province of Dalmatia. But Dalmatia was only the first domino to fall. The military takeover of justice would only grow as the war deepened with a series of disastrous military reverses against Serbia and Russia in August and September 1914 and as Italy came into the war in May 1915.[12]

Two points are worth making here. The first is that the emergency legislation and the closure of parliament were intended and agreed upon by civilian officials because they thought a war would be short. They, like many officials from the combatant states, would be sorely disappointed. By December 1914, not only was it clear that everyone was in for a long war, but that, secondly, the Habsburg Monarchy would be involved in a major conflagration for its very existence. In short, all the emergency legislation that was meant to accompany mobilization and provide for an easier prosecution of the war, —including the closure of parliament, —not only was not lifted after a few months but was intensified by military elites in their struggle to win the war under increasingly challenging conditions. Often enough, this meant expanding military justice to regions well into the hinterland of the empire, resulting in a direct confrontation between local commanders and Austria's civilian officials, judges, as well as parliamentary members. In fact, the political activities of Austrian citizens and the constitutional rights that guaranteed those activities became legal liabilities as Austria-Hungary's general staff led investigations and smear campaigns against judges, officials, and local officials for their activities *before the war*.[13]

Members of parliament were also targets of military justice. An internal report from November 1916 states that nine MPs were convicted for crimes against the war-making powers of the state, four more were convicted for minor infractions, and several others were "interned" or "confined." Others

12 On the further expansion of military legal authority over civilians for a wide range of offenses across large portions of the empire, see, *Reichsgesetzblatt für die im Reichsrate vertretenen Königreiche und Länder* [hereafter RGBl.] Nr. 307, November 4, 1914.
13 John Deak and Jonathan E. Gumz, "How to Break a State: The Habsburg Monarchy's Internal War, 1914–1918," *The American Historical Review* 122, no. 4 (October 2017): 1105–36, https://doi.org/10.1093/ahr/122.4.1105.

had avoided prosecution by fleeing the empire.[14] One of the latter, Cesare Battisti, whose name now adorns street signs and piazzas all over Italy, was executed by a military court for treason after he reentered Austria-Hungary to spy on military positions. His fellow Tyrolian, Karl Niedrist, was expelled from Tyrol and "confined"—kept from meeting his erstwhile constituents or even reentering the province.[15] Niedrist had come under the watchful eye of the commander of the SW Front, Archduke Eugen, and his older brother, the titular commander of the Imperial and Royal Armed forces Archduke Friedrich. In a letter to Minister-President Stürgkh from March 1916, Friedrich complained that the closure of parliament was due to the unstatesmanlike and disloyal behavior of the parliamentarians themselves. He singled out Niedrist for having a negative influence on officials in Tirol. In particular, Eugen and Friedrich hated Niedrist's *Plauderstunden*, informal meetings between Niedrist and his constituents at taverns and pubs in his district.[16]

The situation of politicians like Niedrist was merely the tip of the iceberg. In Slovene-speaking areas, the military police and justice system launched a systematic attack against members of the Slovenian intelligence. In the early days of the war, Slovenian priests, active local politicians, and teachers and other types of public, educated peoples were targets for observation and arrest. Many were arrested as a result of denunciations from Austro-Germans in the mixed language provinces of Carinthia and Styria.[17] By the middle of October 1914, Minister-President Stürgkh complained to Archduke Friedrich that the arrests among the loyal population had created bitterness against the authorities there. Friedrich passed the buck, saying that since Styria was not a military zone, Stürgkh would have to write to the War Ministry, but clearly the arrests had caught Austria's civilian government on its back feet.[18] Damage to the state's reputation was widespread and not just among the Slovenes. In Bohemia, the food crisis and the military's use of force under the provisions of the War Requirements Act of

14 ÖStA AVA Inneres MRP Präs A 290, Pr Nr. 5707 / 1916.

15 Höbelt, "Parteien und Fraktionen," 208.

16 See the letter from Archduke Friedrich to Minister-President Stürgkh (28 March 1916, Org. K. Nr. 6685, "Abgeordnete, Einmischung in militärische Angelegenheiten,") in KA MKSM (1916) 69-10/1-1 and the correspondence of Archduke Eugen on Niedrist's political activities, dated from February 1916 in ÖStA Kriegsarchiv [herafter KA] Zentralstellen [hereafter Zst] Kriegsministerium [hereafter KM] Präs (1916) Karton 1900, 54/21-1.

17 The persecution of Slovenes in the province of Styria has received detailed attention in the work of Martin Moll. See, above all, Martin Moll, *Kein Burgfrieden: Studien zum deutsch-slowenischen Nationalkonflikt in der Steiermark vor dem und im Ersten Weltkrieg* (Graz: Studien Verlag, 2002). Moll counted between 770 and 951 persons who were politically persecuted in Southern Styria alone. See, ibid., ch. 13.

18 Stürgkh to Archduke Friedrich (19 October 1914), ÖStA AVA Inneres MR Präs A 235 (1914) Z. 5958.

1912 (*Kriegsleistungsgesetz*) had by 1916 created a demoralizing dynamic in which men under arms forced starving people to work.[19]

The war had made everyone weary. And the old emperor, Franz Joseph, had isolated himself both from politicians and from the army, which had increasingly taken on the reins of state. His death on November 21, 1916, however traumatic for the many citizens who had only known one emperor, brought with it the hope of change. Karl I's first steps was to curtail military independence. He quickly asserted himself as the supreme commander of the armed forces, subordinating Archduke Friedrich and the Army High Command under his personal authority.[20] This meant, according to an administrative communication from the emperor's military chancellery, that the new emperor was in control of the internal political situation and held the supreme command of the armed forces. "Therefore it is no longer necessary for those possessing military authority to transfer such authority to the civilian administration." Karl was stripping the military of their ability to intervene in domestic politics without supervision. He abolished the emergency decrees of July 25 and 31, 1914 beyond the front lines, which were still directly under military control.[21] Especially important here were laws that subordinated civilians under the control of military law and government offices under military command (Nr. 153 and 164/1914 and Nr. 156/1914, respectively).

Likewise, Karl informed military leadership that he would exercise his civilian and governmental authority through the responsible civilian government. His chancellery prepared another statement to military commanders, stripping them of the power to promulgate laws in territories under their jurisdiction. All laws must be sanctioned by him. Karl further reined in the AOK by ordering it, against Field Marshall Franz Conrad von Hötzendorf's wishes, to move from Teschen/Těšín/Cieszyn in Silesia to Baden bei Wien. Karl

---

19 On the War Requirements Act see Pogány, Ágnes: War Requirement Acts, in *1914-1918-online. International Encyclopedia of the First World War*, ed. by Ute Daniel et al., issued by Freie Universität Berlin, Berlin 2014-10-08. [Accessed 3 January 2019]. DOI: 10.15463/ie1418.10302. For the enforcement of the act in Bohemia, see Rudolf Kučera, *Rationed Life: Science, Everyday Life and Working-Class Politics in the Bohemian Lands, 1914-1918* (New York: Berghahn, 2016); Peter Heumos, "'Kartoffeln her oder es gibt eine Revolution': Hungerkrawalle, Streiks und Massenproteste in den böhmischen Ländern 1914-1918," *Mitteilungsblatt des Instituts zur Erforschung der europäische Arbeiterbewegung* 23 (2000): 148 76; John David Robertson, "Calamitous Methods of Compulsion: Labor, War, and Revolution in a Habsburg Industrial District, 1906-1919" (Ph.D. Thesis, University of North Carolina at Chapel Hill, 2014), chap. 5.

20 See the draft of Karl's decrees to the military in AT-OeStA KA Allerhöchster Oberbefehl [hereafter AhOB] Militärkanzlei Seiner Majestät [herafter MKSM] (1916) Hauptreihe [hereafter HR] A 1250, 68-8/8-1,2,3,4,5,6.

21 Draft of an imperial order, concerning the state administration in war zones, in AT-OeStA/KA AhOB MKSM (1916) HR A 1250, 68-8/8-4. The law would be published as the "Kaiserliche Verordnung vom 9. Jänner 1917, womit die Übertragung von Befugnissen der politischen Verwaltung and den Armeeoberkommandanten, beziehungsweise Höchskommandierenden aufgehoben wird," in RGBl. Nr 18, 1917.

would be able to sit at the table with his generals, reining in their capacious definition of how to propagate war in the multinational empire.[22]

Reasserting Constitutionalism: The *Reichsrat*, §14 Decrees, and Law

Politics would quickly change in Austria, but it took more than six months before Karl would be able to stand in a reopened parliament in May 1917. But for Karl, his hopes to lead a renewal of the empire depended in part on the goodwill of the peoples and their representatives—and that goodwill by May 1917 had largely been spent. When the *Reichsrat* was called back into session, its reappearance was, in the eyes of Karl and his advisors, to be choreographed for external as well as internal political purposes. The Entente's assault on what it viewed as autocracy was made more potent by the fall of the Tsarist regime and the advent of the Provisional Government, which in the late spring of 1917 seemed to herald a wave of democratization. In such an environment, the charge of "autocracy" stung more than usual for the empire, but it especially hurt given the spectacular trial of Friedrich Adler, which was reported on in detail in the daily press. Moreover, the unstable and combustible mix of slogans favored by the Entente, with its portrayal of Germany as an autocratic regime that subordinated Parliament and undermined international and domestic law, created dangers for Austria-Hungary as its ally. Parliamentary governance in multinational Austria was a real possibility, though how this would look remained an open question. When it convened, Parliament turned back to the roots of the nineteenth-century constitutional state to regain a voice and to maintain itself as a public institution in the Habsburg state. One can read the decision to call the *Reichsrat* back into session as an attempt to generate symbolic separation from Germany, while at the same time testifying to Austria-Hungary's commitment to constitutionalist rule and the rule of law.

Yet calling the *Reichsrat* back into session placed a premium on a careful choreography of support once that session actually took place. The initial choreography of the *Reichsrat's* opening stumbled as Karl attempted to straddle the line between committing to constitutional rule and binding his freedom of maneuver through an oath of allegiance to the present constitution. Beyond this, managing the *Reichsrat* fell to successive Minister-Presidents Heinrich von Clam-Martinic and Ernst von Seidler, though it became quickly apparent that this would be a very difficult task, exceeding the political skills of either leader.[23]

---

22 On the move of the Army High Command to Baden bei Wien, see Bernhard Wenning, "Das k.u.k. Armeeoberkommando (AOK) im Ersten Weltkrieg," in *Baden: Zentrum der Macht, 1917-1918* (Wien: Almathea, 2018), 53–73; Helmut Hoyer, *Kaiser Karl I. und Feldmarschall Conrad von Hötzendorf: Ein Beitrag zur Militärpolitik Kaiser Karls* (Wien: Verl. Notring, 1972), 69–89.

23 See the assessment regarding the difficulty of doing this by Felix Höglinger in, *Heinrich Graf Clam Martinic*, Studien zur Geschichte der Österreichisch-Ungarischen Monarchie, vol. 2, ed. Hugo Hantsch (Graz: Böhlau, 1964), 204-205.

In turn, many historians have portrayed the *Reichsrat* as an institution out of control, whose members independently pursued a range of ever more radical, nationally blinkered solutions to the Monarchy's perceived problems and became an anti-Monarchy mouthpiece from within the heart of the government itself. Manfried Rauchensteiner argues that these early sessions of the *Reichsrat* foreshadowed the breakup of the Monarchy and the coming of the successor states.[24] In contrast, we would argue that the *Reichsrat* should be viewed as a leading element in the reassertion of constitutionalist rule and the *Rechtsstaat* within the Empire. When seen through this lens, the *Reichsrat* was far less fractured than the ethnicized version of it would have it. In the *Reichsrat* debates of these final years, one witnesses the reassertion of nineteenth-century constitutionalism in a variety of guises. For the purposes of this article, that reassertion was nowhere stronger than in discussions among *Reichsrat* deputies over the reauthorization of §14 decrees for military legal jurisdiction over civilians and the suspension of trial by jury.

This issue was closely linked to an amnesty issued by Karl for a range of offenses for which people were convicted by military courts, most notably Czech politicians such as Karel Kramář. The precise timing of and reasons for the amnesty, plus the positive and negative reactions it provoked, disappointed many German nationalist politicians and absorbed the attentions of certain prominent contemporaries such as Josef Redlich and Josef Baernreither, as well as that of later historians.[25] In turn, the amnesty has obscured the other measures still related to the amnesty that the government wanted the *Reichsrat* to authorize. The government proposed a straight authorization

---

24 Manfried Rauchensteiner, *Der Erster Weltkrieg und das Ende der Habsburgermonarchie* (Vienna: Böhlau, 2013), 734-738.

25 See, Redlich, *Schicksalsjahre Österreichs*, ii: 309-13 (entry for 5 July 1917); Josef Maria Baernreither, *Der Verfall des Habsburgerreiches und die Deutschen: Fragmente eines politischen Tagebuches, 1987-1917*, ed. Oskar Mitis (Wien: Holzhausen, 1939), 231-237; Alfred Optiz and Franz Adlgasser, eds., *"Der Zerfall der europäischen Mitte": Staatenrevolution im Donauraum, Berichte der Sächsichen Gesandtschaft in Wien, 1917-1919*, Quellen zur Geschichte des 19. und 20. Jahrhunderts, Fritz Fellner, ed., vol. 5 (Graz: Neugebauer, 1990), 55-59. More positive with regard to the amnesty, but still largely looking past the attempt to reauthorize military legal jurisdiction and the suspension of jury trials were close confidants of Karl. See, Karl Freiherr von Werkmann, *Deutschland als Verbündeter: Kaiser Karls Kampf um den Frieden* (Berlin: Verlag für Kulturpolitik, 1931), 97-110; Arthur Graf Polzer-Hoditz, *Kaiser Karl: Aus der Geheimmappe seines Kabinettchefs* (Vienna: Amalthea Verlag, 1980), 421-433, 439-448. An Austrian dissertation provides insights into some of the assumptions regarding the amnesty. See, Christine Kosnetter, "Ministerpräsident Dr. Ernst Ritter von Seidler," (Diss., University of Vienna, 1963), 32-42. Manfried Rauchensteiner focuses on the timing of the amnesty along with the disappointment it provoked within the Army and German nationalist parties. See, Manfried Rauchensteiner, *Der Erster Weltkrieg*, 777-779. See also Felix Höglinger's assessment that the Clam-Martinic's reluctance to support a general amnesty contributed to his dismissal as Minister-President, in, Höglinger, *Ministerpräsident Heinrich Graf Clam-Martinic*, 203.

of military legal jurisdiction over civilians and the suspension of jury trials, measures that had been previously authorized by article 14 of the Austrian constitution. The government's proposals were immediately referred to parliamentary committees for justice and the constitution. Moving to military trials for civilians for a range of crimes, including §327—the elastic charge of "crimes against the war making power of the state,"—had to be done quickly in late July 1914. Due to the "suddenness" with which the war began, it could not, so the government argued in 1917, be authorized through the *Reichsrat*. The government justified the suspension of jury trials through a causal chain that began with the unreliability of juries in Dalmatia due to infiltration by Serb subversive groups, made a similar argument for areas near the Galician border with proximity to Russia, and then simply expanded the argument to the whole of the Austrian half of the Empire. What was striking about these arguments was the degree to which they continued to rely upon the notion of suddenness and potential disorder at the beginning of the war to carry through into what was almost a full third year of conflict. Notably, both governments' proposals made reference to "mobilization," though this term was itself tightly bound up with the immediate entry into war and the transition from peace to war.

The Justice Minister Hugo von Schauer, who was sent forward to defend the government's proposals, found it difficult to defend the process through which they were enacted. The use of §14 was wrong, and he pointed out that he stood in agreement with both committees on this issue. From here, however, he pointed to a number of technical and contextual challenges that prevented the removal of military jurisdiction over civilians and a return to jury trials. Immediately withdrawing military courts jurisdiction over civilians from some areas would leave certain areas close to the front without any functioning courts at all. Reconstituting juries would be difficult, Schauer explained, because the general dislocation of the war had left parts of the male population scattered across the Empire, and local authorities assembling jury lists would be consumed with this task, thus creating lists full of inaccuracies. In turn, the justice system would cease to exist in some areas, and in others, massive delays would result with some of the accused spending an inordinate amount of time in protective custody.[26]

Schauer's attempt to argue on behalf of the government's proposal was met with a wall of opposition from a range of *Reichsrat* deputies. Over three days, one deputy after another stood up relating hair-raising stories of abuses by military courts and decrying the years of non-parliamentary

26 SP, 13. Sitzung, Statement of Justice Minister Hugo von Schauer, July 3, 1917, 589-590.

rule under Stürgkh.[27] These were not all focused statements to be sure. Some veered in the direction of nationalist politics, others wandered into questions concerning the future constitution of the Empire, while some, such as the denunciation of large scale speculators by the Christian Social deputy Johann Wohlmayer, seemed to embody a palpable and almost incoherent rage of the *Reichsrat* against the government, a kind of explosion of repressed resentments that had gathered over the previous three years.[28] Yet, a consistent line appeared that denounced the government's legal overreach as a grave breach of the constitution and the *Rechtsstaat*, positioning the *Reichsrat* as restoring key elements of the nineteenth-century constitutionalist state through rejecting the government's barely warmed over proposals.

It was not simply a question of one hair-raising tale after another of encounters between civilians and the military courts during the war, though there were certainly plenty of these stories to go around, and deputies from South Tyrol, Dalmatia, or Galicia were prepared to provide them. It was a question not only of how jurisdiction over civilians or the suspension of jury trials came about and how fundamental rights derived from the constitution came to be lost. The report from the Justice Committee back to the *Reichsrat* on military legal jurisdiction over civilians made this very clear. First, the committee explained that the decree for this, like all the other decrees from the war, were released using the argument that their "urgency" meant that the *Reichsrat* could not be recalled to vote them into law. This "urgency" argument hardly applied for the whole of wartime, and it was clear, according to the report by the Justice Committee, that Stürgkh's government simply did not want the *Reichsrat* to have any part in governance.[29] Beyond that, the Justice Committee argued that a central element of the constitutionalist state was the assurance that justice would be independent. The independence of the judiciary was a "bulwark of citizens' freedom." The constitution had provided for that independence, and judges were appointed for life to help guarantee that independence. They were "sworn

27 Perhaps one of the most dramatic examples of this was when Dr. Stanislaus Dnistriańskyj, a deputy from the Ukrainian club, related a story of a priest in Galicia condemned to death and hanged in September 1914, when another deputy screamed out that he had nearly been hanged himself at the same time at the same time. See, SP, 13. Sitzung, Statement of Dr. Stanislaus Dnistriańskyj, 614.

28 SP, 13. Sitzung, Statement of Johann Wohlmeyer, July 4, 1917, 667-670.

29 As a later speaker, the Social Democratic deputy Engelbert Pernerstorffer, noted, the original animating force behind §14 was to make it possible for the government to intervene in instances of natural catastrophe when time was of the essence, not as a routine governing mechanism through simply not recalling the *Reichsrat* for years on end. See, SP, 13. Sitzung, Statement of Engelbert Pernerstorffer, July 3, 1917, 600-601.

to observe the fundamental laws of the state without exception." Moreover, "justice and administration were, in all instances, separate." Such separation and independence were precisely not what a trial through military trial procedures offered. Here, the Justice Committee's report contended, judges were anything but independent. They were not lifelong appointees. They could be removed at the will of the commanding officer. The key figure in a trial, according to military legal procedure, was the commanding officer who ordered the investigation and the trial, not an independent judiciary. And if one had any doubt as to a judge's vulnerable position in the military legal system, the Justice Committee turned to an order from the Army High Command from 1915, which threatened military judges who demonstrated excessive leniency with dismissal since such leniency "showed they were unfit to be officers." Finally, military legal procedure's entire purpose was directed towards the maintenance of discipline within the Army, not towards securing the fundamental rights of citizens.[30] Both committees recommended that the *Reichsrat* withhold its approval for both of the government's proposals. In the Justice Committee, the recommendation was unanimous.

Over three days, arguments put forth by one speaker after another came back again and again to the basic breach of the fundamental laws of the Austrian half of the Empire that lay behind the suspension of trial by jury and military legal jurisdiction over civilians. One could, if one wanted, put a kind of ethnic grid over the opposition to these government proposals. Deputies from Ruthenia concentrated on abuses there, those from South Tyrol focused on abuses as a result of these laws there, while the few German nationalist deputies that spoke noted with far less vehemence problems in their own districts while acknowledging the clear constitutional violations associated with these imperial edicts. Almost every speaker touched on the illegality of the government's actions, how that illegality functioned in ways that eroded the basic rights of citizens, or the incompatibility between these basic rights and the military trial process. Legality and moving toward the restoration of the nineteenth-century constitutionalist state was at the heart of this discussion, and the *Reichsrat*, with some room for difference,

30 SP, "Bericht des Justizauschusses über die Regierungsvorlagen Nr. 34 und 35 der Beilagen, betreffend die kaiserlichen Verordnungen vom 25. Juli 1914, RGBl. Nr. 156, und vom 4. November 1914, RGBl. Nr. 307," June 28, 1917, Beilage 378. The Constitutional Committee examined the abolition of trial by jury and found that this had similarly violated the Constitution in that it was done by decree and renewed each year by decree when such renewals of decrees were explicitly forbidden by a law from May 20, 1873. Further suspensions could only be authorized by law, not by decree. See, SP, "Bericht des Verfassungsausschusses über die kaiserlichen Verordnungen betreffend Einstellung der Geschworenengerichte," June 27, 1917, Beilage 379.

operated out of a basic consensus on these issues. With the statement on behalf of the Justice Committee, Julius Ofner surgically dissected the legal and constitutional problems that the government had created for itself by turning to §14 for these measures since the beginning of the war. Imperial decrees were used to undermine constitutional rights, and the argument of "urgent necessity" was repeatedly used over the years to extend those decrees, often flagrantly contradicting the plain letter of the law. Not only this, Ofner argued, but turning civilians over to military jurisdiction through §14 was the equivalent of using an imperial edict to undermine citizens' basic constitutional rights. For Ofner, the independence of the judiciary rested at the heart of the constitutional order. "The dispensation of justice through independent and autonomous judges," he exclaimed, "is the best defense for citizens against state power that is excessive and oversteps its boundaries."[31] This central building block of the constitution, as the Bohemian Social Democrat Lev Winter argued, "was felt in the bones" of nearly everyone in the country.[32] On this issue, Thaddeus Tertil of the Polish Club explained, that of all the §14 measures, those used to alter procedures around justice "cut the most deeply into life, honor, freedom,… and into public order" in Cisleithania. As a legislative body, the *Reichsrat* had to compromise as part of its remit, but there could be no "compromise between the constitution and the breaking of the constitution."[33]

What was interesting about many of these arguments was the degree to which some speakers stressed that this could not simply be portrayed as a military legal system by raging over what it perceived as widespread, subversive activities in particular areas. Many speakers were quite ready to concede that the military legal system contained a large number of well-trained and dedicated judges. It was the way in which the military legal system interspersed itself into a functioning constitutional order and warped its basic assumptions that made it so problematic. As Ofner asked in a series of rhetorical questions: "Are military judges appointed for life? Can military judges not be replaced or transferred? Have military judges sworn to uphold the fundamental laws of the state? In military courts, is justice sealed off from the decision-making power of state officials?"[34] Because all of these questions would be answered in the negative, it was clear that there was no way that military jurisdiction over civilians could

31 SP, 13. Sitzung, Statement of Dr. Julius Ofner, July 3, 1917, 586.

32 SP, 13. Sitzung, Statement of Lev Winter, July 3, 1917, 597. See also, SP, 13. Sitzung, Statement of Dr. Adolf Groß, July 3, 1917, 616; SP, 13. Sitzung, Statement of Eduard Koerner, July 4, 1917, 638.

33 SP, 13. Sitzung, Statement of Thaddeus Tertil, July 4, 1917, 642.

34 SP, 13. Sitzung, Statement of Dr. Julius Ofner, July 3, 1917, 586.

continue to exist without undermining the fundamental rights of citizens as constructed in the nineteenth-century constitutionalist state. The principle of "subordination" and the need to uphold discipline formed the understandable goals of the military legal system, but it clashed with a broader political order that had the rights of citizens at its center according to Dr. Stanislaus Dnistriańskyj, a Ukrainian deputy from Galicia.[35] The vulnerable position of military legal officers on military courts was also stressed by Lev Winter, a Czech Social Democrat, who noted that legal officers were frequently outranked by other officers on these courts.[36]

Even one German nationalist deputy from Bohemia, who spoke in the debate over parliamentary authorization of these decrees and most of whom were deeply disappointed by Karl's amnesty decree, expressed deep concern over the way in which parliamentary power had been undermined in the first three years of war. Even though Rudolf von Lodgman was sympathetic on one level to the pragmatic arguments of the Justice Minister, he also openly acknowledged the illegal nature of the decision to suspend trial by jury through the use of §14, as well as the extension of military legal jurisdiction to civilians. Both of these measures were, in Lodgman's words, "clear violations not only of the law, but violated the fundamental constitutional laws of the state."[37] Lodgman clearly had elements from the Bohemian German agenda in mind throughout his talk, but he also articulated the need for the *Reichsrat* to take on greater responsibility in the Austrian state, reminding people that even for German nationalists, the years of "absolutism" in the war were abhorrent. He "was far from wanting to defend its excesses."[38]

The entire discussion of these proposals was marked by concerns not only typical of nineteenth-century constitutionalism in Cisleithania but those typical of the nineteenth-century constitutionalist project as a whole. Law always rested at the heart of these concerns, but it went to issues such

35 SP, 13. Sitzung, Statement of Dr. Stanislaus Dnistriańskyj, 612. Also on the problematic subordination of officers on military courts, see, , 13. Sitzung, Statement of Dr. Hermann Liebermann, July 4, 1917, 672; SP, 13. Sitzung, Statement of Dr. Ivo Benkovič, 622-623. Benkovič, himself an Army legal officer in Ljubljana / Laibach for part of the war, argued that though there had been a reform of military legal procedures in 1912 to try to ensure that legal officers had more independence, subordination characterized the typical reality of a legal officer during the war and these reforms were largely ignored.

36 SP, 13. Sitzung, Statement of Lev Winter, July 3, 1917, 596.

37 SP, 13. Sitzung, Statement of Dr. Rudolf Lodgman, July 3, 1917, 605.

38 SP, 13. Sitzung, Statement of Dr. Rudolf Lodgman, July 3, 1917, 610. Alexander Dobernig, another Bohemian German nationalist deputy, chose in his speech to focus on Karl's amnesty, which he grudgingly accepted, and referred little to the broader constitutional issues posed by reauthorization of the proposals at hand. See, SP, 13. Sitzung, Statement of Dr. Rudolf Lodgman, July 4, 1917, 650-651.

as fear of despotic power and the need for structures, in this case legal ones, that would help constrain such power. Czech deputies laid out this case in a document requesting the release of a Czech deputy interned through military courts. Such a measure was emblematic of "despotic" use of §14, not its "legal" use.[39] Going even further, Adolf Groß, a member of the Polish Club, maintained that the military courts often were engaged in "completely despotic" acts that were actually "not legal procedures."[40] Such sentiments were reflective not only of a particular moment in wartime Cisleithania but of a primary anxiety that surrounded and propelled the liberal constitutionalist project forward over the nineteenth century and into the twentieth. This anxiety focused in particular on the way in which structurally determined conflicts of interest could emerge at points high and low in various polities and sought to counteract such conflicts of interest through opposing structures, which themselves were often rooted in emerging legal frameworks. As Lauren Benton and Lisa Ford have argued in the case of the British Empire of the first half of the nineteenth century, concern abounded in the British Empire about the despotic exercise of power, whether it be over the treatment of slaves, the use of convicts, or the arbitrary power exercised by imperial governors. Such arguments "focused largely on the need for a superintending authority, one that could control arbitrary justice and bring colonial subjects with different sets of rights into a single legal imperial order."[41] While the British Empire of the early nineteenth century was in the process of forming that legal order, for Cisleithania in 1917, the reconvened *Reichsrat* looked back to a finished touchstone of the December Constitution and the rights associated with it to reassert itself and rebalance the state against what it understood as three years of military despotism. We should also note that constitutionalism and empire were by no means opposed to one another over the course of the nineteenth century.[42] Moreover, the centrality of law to constitutional

39 SP, 13. Sitzung, "Antrag der Abgeordneten Dr. Stranśky und Genossen betreffend der Enthaftung des Abgeordneten Wenzel J. Klofáč," Beilage 180.
40 SP, 13. Sitzung, Statement of Dr. Adolf Groß, July 3, 1917, 616. Groß later exclaimed: "a state is only viable when it is a *Rechtsstaat*, not a despotic state." SP, 13. Sitzung, Statement of Dr. Adolf Groß, July 3, 1917, 620.
41 Lauren Benton and Lisa Ford, *Rage for Order: The British Empire and the Origins of International Law, 1800-1850* (Cambridge, Mass.: Harvard University Press, 2016), 54. See also, Mary Sarah Bilder, *The Transatlantic Constitution: Colonial Legal Culture and the Empire* (Cambridge, Mass.: Harvard University Press, 2004); R.W. Kostal, *A Jurisprudence of Power: Victorian Empire and the Rule of Law* (Oxford: Oxford University Press, 2008).
42 This connection between constitutionalism and empire could appear in the most unexpected places in the 19th century. See, for example, Daniel Hulsebosch, *Constituting Empire: New York and the Transformation of Constitutionalism in the Atlantic World, 1664-1830* (Chapel Hill, N.C.: University of North Carolina Press, 2006)

and imperial projects meant that it was a key territory that framed debates in a polity like the Habsburg Empire.

While this discussion was a forceful reassertion of the Austrian constitutional state in the face of three years of assaults, elements of it also subtly and not-so-subtly rewrote the history of that constitutional state in a way that made it appear more fragile than the increasingly robust force that it actually had become prior to the war. A series of speakers portrayed that state as undermined since its inception, with little more than a shallow grounding in society and continually vulnerable to the machinations of the government. Thus, the longtime deputy Adalbert Pernerstoffer characterized the constitution as little more than a "decoration" for the absolutist regime of Franz Josef.[43] Dnistriańskyj and other deputies focused on what they believed was a pattern of constitutional subversion through Stürgkh and other Minister Presidents who preferred to use §14 to subvert the *Reichsrat* already prior to the war.[44] Such supposed fragility, however, was belied by the very strength and near unanimity of the *Reichsrat's* response to the §14 decrees concerning military justice and suspension of trial by jury. This response demonstrated the extent to which the *Reichsrat* represented the leading force in a reassertion of nineteenth-century constitutionalism in the context of Cisleithania. It helped demonstrate, moreover, the degree to which Cisleithania had become a constitutional state with a considerable level of commitment to the constitutional exercise of power across key elements of the polity.

Conclusion

Seen within the frame of the First World War, this return to nineteenth-century constitutionalism might seem to have been a deft opening intended to hit with perfect pitch the notes of resurgent claims for democracy across the European continent and the world. Certainly, there were indications during these discussions that some in the *Reichsrat* thought that was the case.[45] Forcefully rejecting proposals for military jurisdiction over civilians and the suspension of jury trials would again place Cisleithania in line with other belligerents who, according to one deputy, had refused to take such measures. Yet following this line of thinking would be to draw too straight of a line between what John Horne has called the war's "second mobilization," which took hold by 1917, and moves toward democratic

43 SP, 13. Sitzung, Statement of Adelbert Pernerstorffer, July 3, 1917, 600.
44 SP, 13. Sitzung, Statement of Dr. Stanislaus Dnistriańskyj, 611-612.
45 SP, 13. Sitzung, Statement of Dr. Hermann Liebermann, July 4, 1917, 671.

or constitutional rule. Especially for the Habsburg Empire, a return to its constitutional framework was likely to inspire accusations of "unworkable" government, obstructionism, and "muddling along" in search of impossible solutions to intractable problems. These were already long established tropes prior to 1914 for constitutionalism in the Habsburg context, especially in its Cisleithanian variant. It also meant that the reconvened *Reichsrat*, with its insistence on a return to constitutionalism, looked like anything but a state mobilizing behind a newly invigorated war effort. From this perspective, it was the perception among the Entente of Imperial Germany's very lack of constitutional checks that made this state appear as such a formidable opponent later in the war. As discussions of constitutional rights and the limits of the wartime state rolled out from time to time in the *Reichsrat*, Cisleithania's parliamentary life looked ever more fractured and disunited, though it merely looked like the nineteenth-century constitutional project that it was.

But nonetheless, the opening of parliament in 1917 had a number of important implications. The reassertion of parliamentary authority worked to end military absolutism in the Austrian half of the monarchy. Moreover, these very debates in 1917, when deputies called out the government to justify its complicity with the military, show the commitment of deputies to reassert constitutionalism and the rule of law in a place and at a time when this was far from simple. Austria-Hungary was still at war, and even as the deputies railed against the parliament, the Italians were still pressing hard at the Isonzo. The reopening of parliament was also meant by Kaiser Karl to show his openness and magnanimity. But quickly, the emperor was pushed to the side. Once the doors of parliament were opened in May 1917, its members rushed in and took possession not only of the building but the attention of the public.

Moreover, one should remember in the history of the Austrian republic that parliamentary rule—and the assertion of parliamentary sovereignty—began not as a national, Austrian project but as a multinational one. Czech national politicians, Italians, Slovenes, Poles, Ukrainians, and Dalmatian Croats led the charge against military excesses and cited constitutional law against the excesses of military authority. When those delegates left the chambers of parliament on the Franzensring in 1918, the remaining delegates of German-Austria would stand in the wake that they left. As the Ring in front of Parliament building would be renamed the *Ring des 12. November*, commemorating parliament's role in the new state, the Austrian parties would wrestle with one another for control of the Austrian state. Parliamentary sovereignty was supreme. But who controlled it? That would be a discussion that would continue into the First Republic.

The Failed Republic, 1918-1933?

Erin R. Hochman

After trekking through the snow, Julius Deutsch, injured and dirty, reached the border of Czechoslovakia in February 1934.[1] As a leading figure in the Social Democratic Workers' Party of Austria (SDAPÖ), he had fled to the neighboring country after Engelbert Dollfuss, a politician from the rival Christian Social Party (CSP), crushed the socialists and established a one-party Austrofascist dictatorship. Deutsch's flight from Austria, at first glance, would seem indicative of the failure of the First Republic. After all, Deutsch had been the head of the *Republikanischer Schutzbund*, the paramilitary arm of the SDAPÖ. Through this organization, which he created in 1923, he sought to defend the democratic republic against the twin threats of monarchism and fascism. He devoted considerable energy to this endeavor not only in Austria but also throughout Central Europe by creating a partnership with the *Reichsbanner Schwarz-Rot-Gold*, the pro-republican veterans' group in Germany. In both Austria and Germany, he travelled extensively to give lectures on the fight against fascism and to deliver speeches at mass rallies and celebrations that called for an *Anschluss* (a union with Germany) to create a *großdeutsch* (greater German) republic and a unified German *Volk*.[2] Although Deutsch's efforts drew large and enthusiastic crowds in the two countries, fascists were able to seize power in Germany in 1933 and Austria in 1934.

In a pamphlet published in the months following his escape and in a memoir published almost thirty years later, Deutsch reflected on the reasons for the fascists' victory. It is notable that he did not see the outcome as inevitable; this was not a case in which the First Austrian Republic was doomed to fail. He did admit that bourgeois circles had become increasingly interested in fascism by the 1930s. Yet, he continued, the main representatives of fascism in Austria, the *Heimwehr*, had been weak until 1933.[3] He also explained that he had friendly relationships with members of bourgeois parties, including the CSP, the socialists' main opponent. Indeed, he noted that a number of prominent Christian

1 Julius Deutsch, *The Civil War in Austria: A First-Hand Account from Eye-Witnesses and Participants*, trans. David Berenberg (Chicago: The Socialist Party, National Headquarters, 1934), 75-77.

2 Erin Hochman, *Imagining a Greater Germany: Republican Nationalism and the Anschluss Idea* (Ithaca: Cornell University Press, 2016), Chapter 4.

3 Deutsch, *Civil War*, 10.

Socials—Leopold Kunschak, Franz Hemala, Josef Schlegel, Franz Rehrl, Julius Raab, and Josef Reither—had also been supporters of the democratic republic and opposed any collaboration with the Heimwehr. Unfortunately their position continually weakened due to the "fascist ideology gripping this epoch."[4] Nonetheless, he concluded, parliament "had performed its duties without any particular difficulty, and which—it is essential to say—had done its work well, taking into consideration the tremendous economic difficulties it faced."[5]

The end of the republic, in Deutsch's estimation, was wholly contingent on the events that were transpiring in Germany at that moment and the actions of Engelbert Dollfuss, who had assumed the chancellorship in 1932. Hitler's seizure of power in Germany cast a pall over Austria, for as Deutsch wrote in his memoir, there was a "close interdependence of the fate of Austria with that of the German Reich."[6] It left much of Austria surrounded by fascist or authoritarian dictatorships. In this context, Dollfuss, who at the time had a weak parliamentary majority, saw a chance to strengthen his hand and get rid of the parliament when a procedural mistake caused its three presidents to resign in March 1933. This outcome, according to Deutsch's 1934 pamphlet, was entirely Dollfuss's making: "The government could easily have overcome the ensuing parliamentary crisis had it wished to do so. But Dollfuss did not wish it."[7] Disparagingly describing Dollfuss as an "abnormally small, almost dwarfish man,"[8] Deutsch clarified in his memoir that the chancellor "overcompensated ... for his inferiority complex. He became dictator because his nervous oversensitivity did not tolerate criticism, which constituted the essence of democracy."[9]

Deutsch's accounts are interesting, for they upend the common explanations advanced by scholars about why the First Republic ceased to exist. Much of the secondary literature on this period provides a bleak assessment of Austria's first experience with a full-fledge democratic state. Indeed, this has to do with the fact that researchers studying interwar Austrian democracy have focused on the reasons for the republic's demise and fascism's success. As the historian Ernst Hanisch explained in his sweeping work on twentieth-century Austria: "In the field of view of research on contemporary Austrian history, the question has always been: why did democracy fail in the First Republic?"[10]

4 Julius Deutsch, *Ein weiter Weg: Lebenserinnerungen* (Vienna: Amalthea Verlag, 1960), 186-7; Deutsch, *Civil War*, 9-10.
5 Deutsch, *Civil War*, 11.
6 Deutsch, *Ein weiter Weg*, 176.
7 Deutsch, *Civil War*, 11.
8 Deutsch, *Ein weiter Weg*, 184.
9 Deutsch, Ibid., 188.
10 Ernst Hanisch, *Der lange Schatten des Staates: Österreichische Gesellschaftsgeschichte im 20. Jahrhundert* (Vienna: Verlag Carl Ueberreuter, 1994), 279.

Scholars and other observers have thus focused on identifying the problems with Austria's first democratic government, paying particular attention to the circumstances surrounding the creation of the republic and the hardened divisions within Austrian society. It was, according to the secondary literature on this period, a "state that no one wanted;" [11] it experienced economic difficulties that caused its inhabitants to question its viability, lacked a clear national identity in an era of nation-states, and was riven by hatred between the Marxist and anti-Marxist *Lager* (sociopolitical camps) that prevented the consensus necessary for democracy to function. In diagnosing these ills of the First Republic, some scholars have assumed a deterministic outlook. For instance, the political scientist Norbert Leser stated that "the shock of being reduced from a great empire to a small state" had a "fatal influence on the further development of the republic." This "natal trauma" was then compounded by the inability of the parties to develop "a minimum of consensus, mutual conviction, and common values," which "doomed [the state] to ultimate failure."[12]

Other scholars haven taken a more nuanced and less fatalistic view, but they too remain concerned with the reasons why the republic failed and the fascists came to power. While they recognize the role of human agency in the republic, their focus remains on the "crises" caused by political divisiveness, economic problems, and an "identity crisis."[13] Some of these studies have approached the question of democratic collapse by elucidating the active role played by the right wing of the CSP, the Heimwehr, and Austrian Nazis in abolishing the republic.[14] Even works examining the one group that consistently championed democracy, the SDAPÖ, still

---

11 Hellmut Andics, *Der Staat den keiner wollte: Österreich 1918-1938* (Vienna: Verlag Herder, 1962).

12 Norbert Leser, "Austria between the Wars: An Essay," *Austrian History Yearbook* 17 (1981): 127–142 (here 129).

13 Ernst Hanisch, "Einleitung: Das politische System Erste Republik," in *Handbuch des politischen Systems Österreichs: Erste Republik, 1918-1933*, ed. Emmerich Tálos, et. al. (Vienna: Manzsche Verlags- und Universitätsbuchhandlung, 1995), 1-7; Hanisch, *Der lange Schatten*, 279-309.

14 Alfred Diamant, *Austrian Catholics and the First Republic: Democracy, Capitalism, and the Social Order, 1918–1934* (Princeton, NJ: Princeton University Press, 1960); Guenther Steiner, *Wahre Demokratie? Transformation und Demokratieverständnis in der Ersten Republik Österreich und im Ständestaat Österreich, 1918–1938* (Frankfurt am Main: Peter Lang, 2004); Klemens von Klemperer, *Ignaz Seipel: Christian Statesman in a Time of Crisis* (Princeton, NJ: Princeton University Press, 1972); C. Earl Edmondson, *The Heimwehr and Austrian Politics, 1918–1936* (Athens: University of Georgia Press, 1978); Bruce Pauley, *Hitler and the Forgotten Nazis: A History of Austrian National Socialism* (Chapel Hill: University of North Carolina Press, 1981); Martin Kitchen, *The Coming of Austrian Fascism* (Montreal: McGill–Queen's University Press, 1980); R. John Rath, "The Deterioration of Democracy in Austria, 1927–1932," *Austrian History Yearbook* 27 (1996): 213–259; Julie Thorpe, *Pan-Germanism and the Austrofascist State, 1933–1938* (Manchester: Manchester University Press, 2011); Janek Wasserman, *Black Vienna: The Radical Right in the Red City, 1918–1938* (Ithaca, NY: Cornell University Press, 2014).

concentrate on the question of failure. According to the scholarly literature on the party, the achievements of "Red Vienna" became a weakness, for they led the socialists to overestimate their strength, preventing them from stopping the rise of fascism.[15] And although the most recent appraisal of the First Republic by political scientist Anton Pelinka notably acknowledges the "unused potentials" within the republic, its guiding question remains "why the republic failed first before it could be successful."[16] Pelinka labels the First Republic "the failed republic" because the sociopolitical camps' demonization of one another, compounded by the fact that citizens had no clear sense of what it meant to be Austrian, prevented the establishment of a shared republican political culture. Although he states that such an outcome was not predetermined, his work still implies that this conclusion was likely because the republic inherited the "broken" culture and politics of the late Habsburg era.[17]

This scholarship on the First Republic has undeniably helped us to appreciate the monumental hurdles that made the popularization of republican and democratic governance difficult, as well as the reasons why various forms of fascism took root in Austria. However, by approaching the republic primarily from the standpoint of its weaknesses, these works neglect to consider other questions and approaches that may help us appreciate how interwar Austrians understood and engaged with the republic and democracy. Although not an impartial observer, Julius Deutsch suggested that the breakdown of democracy and the fascist takeover were not preordained developments. He also implied that many of the problems identified by scholars—the Austrian "identity crisis" and the rigid divisions between the *Lager*—were not necessarily as harmful as the secondary literature contends.

To see how productive new approaches can be, scholars of Austria can look across the border to the historiography on the Weimar Republic. Like studies on the First Republic, scholars assumed for decades that the Weimar Republic was doomed fail. It was a "republic without republicans,"

15 Anson Rabinbach, *The Crisis of Austrian Socialism: From Red Vienna to Civil War, 1927-1934* (Chicago: The University of Chicago Press, 1983); Anson Rabinbach, ed., *The Austrian Socialist Experiment: Social Democracy and Austromarxism, 1918–1934* (Boulder, CO: Westview Press, 1985); Helmut Gruber, *Red Vienna: Experiment in Working-Class Culture, 1919-1934* (New York: Oxford University Press, 1991); Ernst Hanisch, *Der Grosse Illusionist: Otto Bauer, 1881-1938* (Vienna: Böhlau Verlag, 2011); Wolfgang Maderthaner, "Austro-Marxism: Mass Culture and Anticipatory Socialism," *Austrian Studies* 14 (2006): 21-36.

16 Anton Pelinka, *Die gescheiterte Republik: Kultur und Politik in Österreich 1918-1938* (Vienna: Böhlau Verlag, 2017), 9.

17 Pelinka, *Die gescheiterte Republik*, 55.

or at the very least a republic with only "rational republicans" who were not wholeheartedly committed to democracy.[18] Yet beginning in the late 1980s, historians began to reframe their approach to the republic. In his seminal work on the Weimar period, Detlev Peukert refuted the notion that a German *Sonderweg* (special path) had condemned the republic to failure. Instead, he argued that the republic was an experiment that went awry due to the economic problems created by a "crisis of classical modernity."[19] By the mid-1990s, Peter Fritzsche rephrased the main question animating the study of the Weimar politics. Rather than asking why the republic failed, he urged scholars to ask, "Did the Weimar Republic fail?"[20]

Taking up this question, scholars of the Weimar Republic have increasingly underlined not just the tragic outcome of the republic but also its "promise."[21] A growing body of scholarship has shown that the republic did indeed have enthusiastic supporters who achieved success in generating mass support for democracy.[22] Additionally, Thomas Mergel, in a study on communicative and symbolic practices in the Reichstag, has demonstrated that representatives from rival parties, even the fiercely antidemocratic German National People's Party, socialized, collaborated, and achieved consensus about parliamentary procedures.[23] And Rüdiger Graf, Moritz Föllmer, and Per Leo have gone so far as to question whether the notion of crisis must be understood in a negative sense. The idea of crisis, according to

---

18 Peter Gay, *Weimar Culture: The Outsider as Insider* (New York: Harper Torchbooks, 1968); Ian Kershaw, ed., *Weimar: Why did German Democracy Fail?, Debates in Modern History* (London: Weidenfeld and Nicolson, 1990); Richard Bessel, *Germany after the First World War* (Oxford: Clarendon Press, 1993).

19 Detlev Peukert, *The Weimar Republic: The Crisis of Classical Modernity*, trans. Richard Deveson (New York: Hill and Wang, 1989).

20 Peter Fritzsche, "Did Weimar Fail?", *The Journal of Modern History* 68, no. 3 (1996): 629-656.

21 Eric Weitz, *Weimar Germany: Promise and Tragedy* (Princeton: Princeton University Press, 2007).

22 Bernd Buchner, *Um nationale und republikanische Identität: Die deutsche Sozialdemokratie und der Kampf um die politischen Symbole in der Weimarer Republik* (Bonn: Verlag J.H.W. Dietz Nachf., 2001); Eric Bryden, "Heroes and Martyrs of the Republic: Reichsbanner *Geschichtspolitik* in Weimar Germany," *Central European History* 43, no. 4 (2010): 639-665; Manuela Achilles, "With a Passion for Reason: Celebrating the Constitution in Weimar Germany," *Central European History* 43, no. 4 (2010): 666-689; Nadine Rossol, *Performing the Nation in Interwar Germany: Sport, Spectacle and Political Symbolism, 1926-1936* (Houndmills and New York: Palgrave Macmillan, 2010); Benjamin Ziemann, *Contested Commemorations: Republican War Veterans and Weimar Political Culture* (Cambridge: Cambridge University Press, 2013); Erin Hochman, *Imagining a Greater Germany*.

23 Thomas Mergel, *Parlamentarische Kultur in der Weimarer Republik: Politische Kommunikation, symbolische Politik und Öffentlichkeit im Reichstag* (Düsseldorf: Droste Verlag, 2002).

them, contained within it both destructive and creative potentials.[24] These studies show that there was nothing inevitable about the triumph of the Third Reich over the Weimar Republic. The republic did not simply collapse under supposedly fatal flaws, lack of support, or economic instability. Rather, antidemocratic conservatives and the Nazis had to actively work to undermine and destroy a democratic republic that had garnered legitimacy among a growing number of citizens.

Of course, the First Austrian and Weimar Republics were not identical, even though they had many similarities and connections to one another.[25] After all, no one in Germany questioned the existence or viability of the state itself. This article contends, however, that scholars of the First Republic should follow the lead of Weimar historians in moving beyond the failure paradigm. Instead of viewing the First Republic through the lens of failure, researchers should view it as a grand, open-ended experiment. In doing so, we can ask how Austrian citizens shaped this experiment with democracy and republicanism: How did Austrians understand the relationship among nation, state, and politics in this era? How did people conceptualize themselves as citizens in a democratic state? How did they understand and practice democracy? How and why did their views and practices change over time? Who supported democracy? How did they do so and why? This essay uses such questions to look briefly at three issues often cited by scholars as both the symptoms and causes of failure: the desire for an *Anschluss*, the debate over the state's anthem, and the inability to create a shared republican culture. In doing so, it shows that we need to question some of the assumptions often made about the supposed weaknesses of the democratic republic. Embracing new approaches to the study of the First Republic does not ignore the immense challenges facing it or the fact that the Austrofascist and Nazi movements ultimately prevailed. However, by asking different questions we can develop new insights about Austrians' experience with a democratic and republic form of government, the possibilities for democracy, and the reasons why a fascist dictatorship ultimately supplanted the First Republic.

---

24 Moritz Föllmer, Rüdiger Graf, and Per Leo, "Einleitung: Die Kultur der Krise in der Weimarer Republik," in *Die 'Krise' der Weimarer Republik: Zur Kritik eines Deutungsmusters*, ed. Moritz Föllmer and Rüdiger Graf (Frankfurt am Main: Campus Verlag, 2005), 9–41, here 14; Rüdiger Graf, *Die Zukunft der Weimarer Republik: Krisen und Zukunftsaneignungen in Deutschland, 1918–1933* (Munich: R. Oldenbourg Verlag, 2008).

25 Hanisch, "Einleitung," 6-7; Ernst Hanisch, "Das Fest in der fragmentierten politischen Kultur: Der österreichische Staatsfeiertag während der Ersten Republik," in *Politische Teilkulturen zwischen Integration und Polarisierung: zur politischen Kultur in der Weimarer Republik*, ed. Detlef Lehnert and Klaus Megerle (Opladen: Westdeutscher Verlag, 1990), 43-60 (here 58-60); Hochman, *Imagining a Greater Germany*.

Republicans in a "Republic against its Will"

As the Habsburg Empire dissolved into independent nation-states in the final days of the First World War, German-speaking delegates from the imperial parliament assembled to discuss their response to the events unfolding around them. On November 12, 1918, one day after both the war on the western front ended and Kaiser Karl I relinquished his power, representatives from the SDAPÖ, the CSP, and the precursor of the Greater German People's Party (GDVP) passed a law that began, "German-Austria is a democratic republic. All public authority is established by the people." In the very next line, however, these politicians announced their desire to abolish the very state they had just founded. Article two of the law proclaimed, "German-Austria is a constitutive part of the German Republic."[26] This desire to dissolve their new state and join Germany stemmed from two predominant beliefs at the time: Austrians were members of a German nation and the newly diminished country, cut off from the resources and markets in the other Habsburg successor states, was economically unviable. Even though the arbiters at the Paris Peace Conference prohibited an *Anschluss* the following year, support for it among Austrians remained around 90 to 95 percent, according to contemporary observers.[27]

For scholars, this founding moment encapsulated many of the reasons the republic "failed." The state established that day was simply left over; its citizens had not forged the new state but were merely responding to external circumstances. It was consequently, to use Pelinka's appellation, a "republic against its will."[28] Compounding this problem was the new state's economic instability, which, according to Hanisch, led to a "legitimacy crisis." But "particularly precarious," Hanisch argued, "were the effects of the identity crisis. German or Austrian, German and Austrian, German-Austrian—what were the residents of the First Republic?"[29] Austrians, even those who tried to create a sense of Austrian patriotism, overwhelmingly saw themselves as part of a German national community. Consequently, state and nation did not align in interwar Austria, a problematic situation

26 "Nr. 5/1918, Gesetz vom 12. November 1918 über die Staats- und Regierungsform von Deutschösterreich," in Staatsgesetzblatt für den Staat Deutschösterreich, Jahrgang 1918 (Vienna: Deutschösterreichischen Staatsdruckerei, 1918), 4.

27 Letter from Deutsche Gesandtschaft Wien to Auswärtige Amt, Vienna, 31 March 1925, in Politisches Archiv des Auswärtigen Amts, Berlin (PAAA), R73293, IIOe517; "Christlichsoziale, Republik und Anschluß," *Kölnische Zeitung*, 28 November 1926, in Wienbibliothek (WB), L121260, Band 5, Fasz. IV, Untermappe 13, Nr. 13; Deutsch, *Ein weiter Weg*, 128-29.

28 Pelinka, *Die gescheiterte Republik*, 45.

29 Hanisch, "Einleitung," 5.

in an era when the ideas of the nation-state and of the right to national self-determination became the main organizing principles of European geopolitics. The ongoing desire for an *Anschluss*, according to researchers, therefore pointed to the economic and identity crises that weakened loyalty to the republic and democracy.[30]

However, the desire for an *Anschluss*, i.e. for the dissolution of the Republic of Austria, was not necessarily synonymous with ambivalence about or outright opposition to a republican and democratic form of government. If we want to understand Austrians' attitudes towards the ideas of democracy and a republican system, we need to disentangle support for the Republic of Austria in its interwar geographic form from support for a democratic republic. In other words, we need to investigate the manifold ways that Austrians understood the links among nation, state, and politics. Although today the word "*Anschluss*" is associated with the Nazis and their annexation of Austria in 1938, socialists in Austria and republicans in Germany—consisting of the Social Democratic Party of Germany, the left liberal German Democratic Party, and the Catholic Center Party—were actually at the forefront of the *Anschluss* movement from the end of the Great War until the Nazi seizure of power in Germany.[31] In fact, their calls for an *Anschluss* were central to their endeavor to legitimize democracy and a republican form of government throughout interwar, German-speaking Central Europe. As I have argued elsewhere, Austrian Social Democrats and their allies in Germany used the *großdeutsch* idea, the historical notion that Austria should join Germany, and their interwar commitment to the *Anschluss* cause in order to create a form of German nationalism that was compatible with democracy, international loyalties, and a tolerant understanding of nationhood. By forging their own type of German nationalism, they could demonstrate that they possessed genuine national convictions, thereby countering attacks by the political right that democracy and its supporters were un-German.[32] The basis of the Austrian "identity crisis" was thus actually a vital component of their efforts to popularize democracy.

30 Hanisch, "Einleitung," 5; Evan Burr Bukey, *Hitler's Austria: Popular Sentiment in the Nazi Era, 1938–1945* (Chapel Hill: University of North Carolina Press, 2002), 9; Steven Beller, *A Concise History of Austria* (Cambridge: Cambridge University Press, 2006), 197; Pelinka, *Die gescheiterte Republik*, Chapter 3.

31 Stanley Suval, *The Anschluss Question in the Weimar Era: A Study of Nationalism in Germany and Austria, 1918–1932* (Baltimore: Johns Hopkins University Press, 1974). For more on just the SDAPÖ's support of *Anschluss*, see Helmut Konrad, ed., *Sozialdemokratie und 'Anschluss': Historische Wurzeln Anschluss 1918 und 1938 Nachwirkungen* (Vienna: Europaverlag, 1978).

32 Hochman, *Imagining a Greater Germany*.

German nationalism was critical to the Social Democrats' defense of parliamentary democracy. To fend off the political right's claims that democracy was foreign to the German *Volk*, members of the SDAPÖ insisted that democracy and republicanism were actually at the heart of the German national movements from its beginnings in the nineteenth century. In particular, they focused their arguments on the revolution of 1848 and the Frankfurt Parliament, which had included Austrian representatives and sought to create a united Germany with a parliamentary basis. "Since 1848 the republican idea is already linked with that of German unity," the *Arbeiter-Zeitung*, the socialists' flagship newspaper, asserted in 1919.[33] Citing the revolution of 1848, the newspaper still maintained thirteen years later that the "cause of the *Anschluss*, the cause of German unity has always been the cause of German democracy."[34] This constant refrain enabled socialists to assert that democratic and republican movements were authentically German.

Not only did democracy constitute a German tradition, according to Austrian socialists, but it also would be the only way to accomplish an *Anschluss* in their present day. After all, the Frankfurt Parliamentarians were unable to realize the goal of national unification due to the rivalry between the Habsburg and Hohenzollern monarchies, which had crushed the revolution of 1848 and conducted a war against one another in 1866 that ultimately led to Austria's exclusion from a German nation-state. "Monarchy means the dismemberment of the German *Volk*; republic means the possibility of a united Germany," declared Julius Deutsch in a 1925 article written for the one-year anniversary celebration of the Reichsbanner in Magdeburg.[35] Moreover, socialists argued that the opponents of democracy in the present would, for similar reasons, prevent an Austro-German union. During a Reichsbanner visit in 1929 to the Vienna housing complex named for the German Social Democrat Friedrich Ebert, Deutsch argued that "Heimwehr fascism, which embodies the reactionary forces in our country, is ... also an obstacle to the national development of the entire *Volk*" because, like the monarchies, the Heimwehr promoted "that particularism which does not allow the German *Volk* to achieve inner unity." Deutsch concluded his speech by repeating an argument often advanced by republicans in both countries: "The unity of the German *Volk* can only be realized on the basis of democracy and the republic."[36] By supporting

33 "Das Bürgertum und die Republik," *Arbeiter-Zeitung* (AZ), 14 November 1919, in WB, Tagblattarchiv (TA), Nationalfeiertag (12. November).
34 „Die Reaktion gegen den Anschluss," *AZ*, 17 July 1932, in WB, TA, Anschluss 1932-38.
35 "Gruß aus Deutschösterreich," *Das Reichsbanner*, 1 March 1925, 1-2 (here 2).
36 "Eine Anschlußkundgebung im Ebert-Hof," *AZ*, 23 May 1929, in WB, L121260, Band 19.

an *Anschluss*, socialist leaders endeavored to make democracy and republicanism (as well as themselves) appealing to the overwhelming majority of Austrians who supported union with Germany.

The Social Democratic belief in the *großdeutsch* and *Anschluss* ideas also enabled them to forge a partnership with republicans in Germany, which powerfully showed the expansiveness and vitality of the republican movement. At the heart of this alliance were the two organizations created to defend the democratic republics: the Austrian socialists' Schutzbund and the Reichsbanner, the republican veterans' group consisting of socialists, left liberals, and Catholics in Germany. Their leaders served on each other's executive committees, and their members invested their time and money to attend numerous rallies and celebrations on the other side of the border. The largest of these visits included the 1,500 Schutzbund members who participated in the Reichsbanner's 1929 Constitution Day festivities in Berlin and the 4,000 Reichsbanner members who travelled to Vienna for the Workers' Gymnastics and Sport Festival in 1926.[37] The Schutzbund's aim for these cross-border rallies was to "declare one's belief in German democracy and in the community all Germans who shared a common fate" and to show the Schutzbund's adversaries that it stood "in solidarity with the republicans in the German Reich in the fight against violent fascism and spiteful chauvinism," as Hans Lagger, the leader of the Schutzbund in Carinthia, explained ahead of a trip to the 1931 Reichsbanner Constitution Day celebration in Koblenz.[38] Such events drew large and enthusiastic crowds, illustrating the popular appeal of the intertwined republican and *großdeutsch* ideas.[39] Moreover, these rallies were effective in showcasing the strength of the republican cause; conservative and right-wing radicals were so worried about this relationship that they spread multiple lies about the Schutzbund and Reichsbanner in an attempt to sever their bonds.[40]

Indeed, it was two of the main opponents of a democratic republic—the Heimwehr and the right wing of the CSP—that sought to create a stronger sense of Austrian patriotism and, in many instances, maintain the country's independence. Although these groups saw Austrians as part of a larger German nation, they argued that Austrians constituted a special people within a German national community. Ernst Rüdiger Starhemberg, a leader of the Heimwehr, noted in a 1932 speech, "We need no instruction

37 Hochman, *Imagining a Greater Germany*, Chapter 4.
38 Hans Lagger, "Warum fahren wir nach Koblenz?," *Das Reichsbanner*, 8 Aug 1931, 250.
39 Hochman, *Imagining a Greater Germany*, Chapter 4; Erin Hochman, "Staging Socialism, Staging Nationalism," Rethinking the *Festkultur* of the Social Democratic Workers' Party in the First Austrian Republic," *Austrian Studies* 25 (2017): 181-197.
40 Hochman, *Imagining a Greater Germany*, 156-168.

from other German tribes about true Germanness. We thereby prove to be the best Germans in that we do not renounce our Austrianness."[41] For the Heimwehr and its Christian Social supporters, Catholic and Habsburg traditions were the defining characteristics of Austrianness. They consequently reintroduced the use of Habsburg melodies and medals to the army, reestablished Haydn's melody for "God Preserve, God Protect Our Emperor, Our Country" as the legal anthem of the country, and organized massive celebrations for the dual occasions of the 1933 German Catholic Day and the 250th anniversary of the Battle of Vienna. This commemoration, which included Catholic masses and rallies by the Christian-Social-led government and the Heimwehr, provided a preview of the Austrofascist *Ständestaat* that was to fully emerge months later. Following these events, the *Reichspost*, the newspaper aligned with the right wing of the CSP, declared that "Austria has awakened. … A new Austria, which builds on all of the proven values of a better past, should be built; the Christian, social, German state of Austria should become a reality, the state of corporative harmony."[42] The attempt to create Austrian patriotism thus entailed the establishment of an authoritarian state, where a corporatist, one-party system replaced a parliamentary one, and power came from God instead of the people.

It was the proponents of Austrian pride and sovereignty that worked to dismantle democracy, while one of the most vocal advocates of an *Anschluss*, the SDAPÖ, worked to bolster democracy and republicanism. Julius Deutsch could therefore proclaim at a match between Austrian and German socialist soccer clubs that "*we gladly commit this suicide [of the Austrian state]*" without seeking to undermine a democratic and republican system of governance. After all, the very next line of his speech was, "*we want to join the German republic.*"[43] The Social Democrats wanted to eventually do away with the rump state and the Republic of Austria in order to create a more expansive republic, a "great social, free, German republic," as Paul

41 "Die große Wiener Kundgebung," *Oberösterreichische Morgenblatt*, 4 December 1932, in WB, L121260, Band 51.

42 "Neues Oesterreich," *Reichspost*, 12 September 1933, 1. On the attempts to create a stronger sense of Austrianness, see Hanns Haas, "Staats- und Landesbewußtsein in der Ersten Republik," in *Handbuch des politischen Systems Österreichs: Erste Republik, 1918–1933*, ed. Emmerich Tálos et al. (Vienna: Manz Verlag, 1995), 472–487 (here 479-481); Suval, *The Anschluss Question*, Chapter 12; Michael Steinberg, *Austria as Theater and Ideology: The Meaning of the Salzburg Festival* (Ithaca: Cornell University Press, 2000); Anton Staudinger, "Austrofaschistische 'Österreich'-Ideologie," in *Austrofaschismus: Politik—Ökonomie—Kultur, 1933–1938*, ed. Emmerich Tálos and Wolfgang Neugebauer (Vienna: LIT Verlag, 2005), 28-52; Hochman, *Imagining a Greater Germany*, Chapters 2 and 3.

43 "Wir wollen als Deutsche spielen!", *Vorwärts*, 17 December 1928, in Bundesarchiv Berlin, R72/914, Bl. 55. Emphasis in original.

Speiser, a Social Democratic city councillor and member of the Bundesrat, declared in 1926.[44] Scholars should therefore disentangle support for the Austrian state from support for democracy. In the end, the basis of the "Austrian identity crisis," Austrians' identification with Germanness, was central to the energetic efforts to defend and popularize democracy and republicanism.

Active Citizens and Political Participation in the First Republic

In 1932, around one thousand adolescents gathered for a *Völkisch* Rally of the Catholic German Middle School Youth in Graz. Throughout the evening, a group of about 100 Nazi youths tried to disrupt the proceedings. At first they began by coughing but grew bolder when it was time to sing Austria's official anthem, "Be Blessed without End." This song, which used Haydn's tune from the Habsburg anthem with lyrics by the priest Ottokar Kernstock, had become the official anthem in late 1929 as part of the CSP's endeavor to bolster Austrian patriotism and to reform the constitution to strengthen executive authority. But, instead of singing Kernstock's lyrics, the Nazi students chose to sing "*Deutschland, Deutschland über alles*," which used the same Haydn melody, while giving the Heil-Hitler salute.[45] This was not a singular occurrence after 1929; right-wing students also interrupted a host of other events.[46] On the other end of the political spectrum, the Social Democrats began to publish articles that also criticized the new legal anthem, which they called "the song of reaction."[47] To protest the anthem further, the socialist chairman of the Viennese school board, Otto Glöckel, ordered that "*Deutschland, Deutschland über alles*" be sung at school celebrations. Unlike the Nazis, his goal was to "cultivate the national and republican education of the youth" in accordance with the SDAPÖ's understanding of nationalism explored in the previous section of this essay.[48] Such incidents left Christian Social leaders angry that these groups took

44 "Der Abschied der Freien Typographia," *AZ*, 23 July 1926, in WB, L121260, Band 4, Fasz. III, Untermappe 8, Nr. 35.

45 "Gestrige Sicherheitswachekommandierungen: 1/48, Frührapport der Abteilung I am 13. November 1931," in Steiermärkisches Landesarchiv, Zeitgeschichte Sammlung, Karton 132, Polizeidirektion Graz: Vorfallenheitsberichte, Versammlungen, Veranstaltungen, 1.6.1931-31.5.1932.

46 Johannes Steinbauer, *Land der Hymnen: Eine Geschichte der Bundeshymnen Österreichs* (Vienna: Sonderzahl, 1997), 102-106; Hochman, *Imagining a Greater Germany*, 82-84.

47 "Das Volk pfeift die 'Volks'hymne aus," *AZ*, 15 May 1930, 4.

48 "Wenn schon Haydn – dann das Deutschlandlied," *AZ*, 13 February 1930, 1.

"a position that opposes that political direction that seeks to strengthen Austria's faith in itself."[49]

Like the declaration of the republic, the anthem debate appears only to highlight the very ills that scholars have diagnosed as damaging the First Republic's chances. As Ernst Hanisch has written, "the confusion [about the anthem] was an accurate reflection of the political fragmentation as well as the divided national identity in Austria."[50] It is certainly the case that disagreements about whether Austria should have a *Staatshymne*, an anthem fostering support for the rump state, or a *Nationalhymne*, an anthem recognizing Austrians' Germanness,[51] were indicative of Austrians' "identity crisis" and inability to form a shared symbol that could help to legitimize the new state.

Yet, if we only look at instances such as the anthem debate through the lens of failure, we neglect to ask other questions that can help us to better understand how Austrians experienced democracy. For instance, beyond showing the divisions in Austrian society and the difficulties with defining Austrianness, the anthem debate also provides a window into political and civic engagement in the First Republic. We can take the advice of Graf, Föllmer, and Leo to look at the notion of crisis as a destructive process that provides the space for new, creative possibilities.[52] In the case of the Austrian anthem, the disappearance of imperial authorities opened up a vacuum that allowed citizens to shape the debate and choice of an important state symbol. They voiced their opinions in manifold ways: creating new songs, writing to the government with song suggestions, and singing or shouting their views like the right-wing students mentioned above.[53]

The most notable example of this civic engagement was actually the development and promotion of "Be Blessed without End" before the 1929 decision by the CSP to institute it as the official anthem. In 1919, when

---

49 "Die deutsche Studentenschaft Wiens und die Bundeshymne," *Welt-Blatt*, 4 February 1930, in ÖStA, AdR, Parteiarchive, GDVP, Zeitungsausschnitte, Mappe 24a, 02/c.

50 Hanisch, "Das Fest," 45-6 (here 46). Also see Ernst Hanisch, "Politische Symbole und Gedächtnisorte," in *Handbuch des Politischen Systems Österreichs: Erste Republik, 1918-1938*, ed. Emmerich Tálos et. al. (Vienna: Manz Verlag, 1995), 421-430; Franz Grasberger, *Die Hymnen Österreichs* (Tutzing: H. Schneider, 1968); Steinbauer, *Land der Hymnen*, 7-106; Gustav Spann, "Fahne, Staatswappen und Bundeshymne der Republik Österreich," http://www.demokratiezentrum.org/media/data/staatswappen.pdf.

51 Steinbauer, *Land der Hymnen*, 21; Hochman, *Imagining a Greater Germany*, Chapter 2.

52 Föllmer, Graf, and Leo, "Einleitung."

53 On the various anthem proposals, see Steinbauer, *Land der Hymnen*, 7-106; Grasberger, *Die Hymnen Österreichs*; Eckart Früh, "Gott erhalte? Gott bewahre! Zur Geschichte der österreichischen Hymnen und des Nationalbewußtseins zwischen 1918 und 1938," Österreich in Geschichte und Literatur mit Geographie 32, no. 5 (1988): 280-315; Hochman, *Imagining a Greater Germany*, Chapter 2.

other individuals were sending in their compositions to the government, the People's Council-Working Group for the Preservation of the Homeland in Graz enlisted Kernstock's help to write lyrics that could "save the wonderful melody of our former Kaiser's anthem."[54] The song that would legally become Austria's anthem thus originally came about due to the private initiative of a local, civic-minded organization.

A few years later, a Viennese schoolteacher by the name of Louise Pibus began a concerted campaign to make this song Austria's anthem. By this time, Austria had a de facto anthem, "German-Austria, thou Magnificent Land" by composer Wilhelm Kienzl and the socialist politician Karl Renner, but the government never enshrined it into law and it remained unpopular. Therefore, individuals like Pibus continued to try to shape the search for an anthem by writing to the government with their own suggestions. Even though she had gained political rights only a few years earlier, she showed political savvy in trying to transform the Haydn-Kernstock song into Austria's official anthem. Beginning in 1922, she began writing to the federal government, asking them to instate "Be Blessed without End" as the anthem.[55]

When her initial letters did not produce the desired outcome, she then looked into other constitutional means to make "Be Blessed without End" the official anthem. Showing an awareness of the new role played by citizens in a democratic republic, she reached out to her "dear national comrades" in 1923 and to federal authorities in 1925, explaining that she would try to use article 41 of the constitution, which stated that parliament had to address any petition campaign able to collect the signatures of 200,000 voters or half of all voters in three provinces, to prompt the government to take action.[56] To whip up popular support for her campaign, she wrote to newspapers, contacted numerous municipal governments and provincial school officials, and produced postcards for the population at large.[57] As she tried to gather signatures, she continued to implore federal authorities in 1925 to adopt the song, explaining that she had received many enthusiastic responses to her proposal, which "proves the participation of the population." She urged the government to recognize the Kernstock-Haydn song as the legal anthem, arguing that "the old melody was never legally superseded by a new one" and that its reintroduction would foster unity

54 Quoted in Steinbauer, *Land der Hymnen*, 59.
55 For reprints of many of her letters, see Steinbauer, *Land der Hymnen*, 63-73.
56 Steinbauer, *Land der Hymnen*, 66-68.
57 Steinbauer, *Land der Hymnen*, 63-73. For the postcard, see "Die neue Volkshymne," in Österreichiches Staatsarchiv (ÖStA), Allgemeines Verwaltungsarchiv (AVA), Unterricht Allgemein (U. Allg.) 3258, 12733/1926.

among Austrians.[58] The following year, she wrote to the government that she was halting her campaign but included the signatures of about 350 people who had signed petitions.[59] Although her efforts were not immediately successful, they provide a view into the new roles that citizens adopted in a full-fledged democracy. She studied the constitution, wrote to a variety of authorities hoping that they would listen to her, and sought to mobilize public opinion behind her cause.

Thus, rather than solely viewing the anthem debate as a window into the problems of the First Republic, we can also use it to study the practices and subjective experiences of citizenship. Scholars can apply this approach to other aspects of the First Republic—from electoral campaigns to the act of voting to political rallies and celebrations—to understand how Austrians were "practicing democracy," to use historian Margaret Anderson's phrase. After all, the First World War, as Maureen Healy has shown in her work on wartime Vienna, had expanded the possibilities for political participation and agency—particularly with regard to women—and created a closer relationship between the state and its citizens.[60] With the establishment of a democratic state system after the war, citizens could take advantage of the new political situation not only to support the parliamentary republic but also to undermine it. By using this approach, we can view the First Republic as an experiment whose outcome was not predetermined but was rather shaped by its citizens in multiple and contradictory ways.

Under a Big Tent? The Divisions between the *Lager*

A week before the fifteenth anniversary of the republic, a legal holiday since 1919, the *Arbeiter-Zeitung* and the *Reichspost* traded barbs. The *Arbeiter-Zeitung* explained how a number of other "bourgeois republics," including Czechoslovakia and Turkey, had recently held popular, joyous celebrations on the occasion of the founding of their states. Yet Dollfuss's government had banned any such festivities in Austria that year; it prohibited public marches and ordered that no commemorative activities should occur in the schools. Not only had the bourgeois government forbidden celebrations that year, but also in previous years, "the bourgeoisie took no part in the celebration of the republican state," the *Arbeiter-Zeitung*

58 Steinbauer, *Land der Hymnen*, 67-68.

59 The petitions are located in ÖStA, AVA, U. Allg. 3258, 12733/1926.

60 Maureen Healy, "Becoming Austrian: Women, the State, and Citizenship in World War I," *Central European History* 35, no. 1 (2002): 1-35; Maureen Healy, *Vienna and the Fall of the Habsburg Empire: Total War and Everyday Life in World War I* (Cambridge: Cambridge University Press, 2004) and Healy, "Becoming Austrian."

contended. This attitude and lack of action contrasted with "the Austrian working class," who "every year on November 12 expresses its loyalty to the republic, its belief in the republican state in giant marches and festive celebrations." "It was," the article continued, "not our fault that we remain alone at these celebrations."[61] The *Reichspost* rebuffed such claims, arguing that "Social Democracy burdens the republic and state holiday with far too many unbearable things" and therefore "only it is guilty for the state holiday not being able to become a popular celebration and for our *Volk* never properly being able to be happy in the republic."[62] These accusations, made on what turned out to be the final anniversary of the republic, reflected the divisive discourse used in previous years of the commemoration.[63]

The anniversary of the founding of the republic is but another example that scholars highlight to demonstrate the sharp cleavages between the Marxist and anti-Marxist *Lager*.[64] This theory that Austrian society was rigidly divided into sociopolitical camps that developed their own worldviews and governed people's lives from birth to death has been central to the scholarly interpretations of the First Republic ever since historian Adam Wandruszka developed the idea in the 1950s.[65] According to the political histories of the First Republic, these *Lager* fostered an us-versus-them mentality that made compromise difficult and hampered the functioning of democracy.

However, in a study on Linz in the first half of the twentieth century, historian Evan Burr Bukey questions the conventional approach and interpretation of political culture in the First Republic. He argues, "[The] republic did not collapse overnight: it was prone to political violence and civil war, but it prevailed for over a decade, managing change and demonstrating considerable vitality. Given the centrifugal drives of the system, historians

61 "Staatsfeiertage," *AZ*, 4 November 1933, in WB, TA, Nationalfeiertag (12. November).
62 "Staatsfeiertag und Sozialdemokratie," *Reichspost*, 5 November 1933, in WB, TA, Nationalfeiertag (12. November).
63 Ernst Hanisch, "Das Fest"; Hanisch, "Politische Symbole"; Gustav Spann, "Der österreichische Nationalfeiertag," in *Der Kampf um das Gedächtnis: Öffentliche Gedenktage in Mitteleuropa*, ed. Emil Brix and Hannes Stekl, (Vienna: Böhlau Verlag, 1997), 145–170; Hochman, *Imagining a Greater Germany*, Chapter 3.
64 Ibid.
65 Adam Wandruszka argued there were socialist, Catholic and German nationalist *Lager*. More recently, scholars have proposed that there were two camps: the socialist and the anti-Marxist *Lager*. Adam Wandruszka, "Österreichs politische Struktur: Die Entwicklung der Parteien und der politischen Bewegungen," in *Geschichte der Republik Österreich*, ed. Heinrich Benedikt (Vienna: Verlag für Geschichte und Politik, 1954), 289-485; Hanisch, *Der Lange Schatten des Staates*, 117–153; Diamant, *Austrian Catholics*, 73–80; Edmondson, *Heimwehr*; Julie Thorpe, *Pan-Germanism*; and Wasserman, *Black Vienna*; Pelinka, *Die gescheiterte Republik*.

have been hard put to explain its relative durability."[66] Bukey importantly reframes the approach to the politics of the First Republic. Instead of asking why the republic failed or even asking why it was destroyed, he asks how and why it was able to survive given the inauspicious circumstances. In doing so, he finds that the existence of opposing *Lager* did not preclude cooperation across parties. Already in the late imperial period, the leaders of the Christian Socials and Social Democrats in Upper Austria cooperated with one another to democratize the provincial voting system. This commitment to democracy and willingness to reach across party lines continued into the interwar period, particularly under the leadership of the Christian Social provincial governor, the prelate Johann Hauser, and the socialist mayor of Linz, Josef Dametz. Their shared democratic principles and cooperation helped to dampen enthusiasm for the Heimwehr and the Nazis in the area. According to Bukey, this political situation amounted to a "consociational or concordant democracy," just like that found in the successful Second Republic.[67] By investigating the First Republic from an unconventional angle, he shows that the outcome of the democratic experiment was far from determined.

Following Bukey's lead, we should ask whether other politicians from the opposing *Lager* remained completely siloed. Julius Deutsch's recollections mentioned at the beginning of this essay suggest that the answer is no. Notably, Deutsch acknowledged supporters of democracy from the rival parties. Moreover, he recounted numerous instances of socializing and attempting to negotiate with leaders from the other *Lager*. He warmly remembered, for example, his relationship with the priest Adam Hefter in Krems-Klosternueburg. Acknowledging their "political rivalry," he argued that "we got along well personally and were not willing to let the exchanges of opinions … become spiteful."[68] In another instance, he recalled that Julius Raab, a fellow *Nationalrat* delegate and a member of the CSP who had briefly belonged to the Heimwehr, approached him in order to come to an understanding that could avert the chances of a civil war in the early 1930s.[69] Given his pragmatic outlook and willingness to discuss matters with his political opponents, it is not surprising that he supported the 1931 offer by Ignaz Seipel, the leader of the right wing of the CSP, to recreate the Grand Coalition of the early years of the republic, a proposition ultimately rejected by the SDAPÖ for fear of being blamed for the growing economic crisis.[70]

66 Evan Burr Bukey, *Hitler's Hometown: Linz, Austria, 1908-1945* (Bloomington: Indiana University Press, 1986), 39. Also see Hanisch, *Der lange Schatten*, 285.
67 Ibid., 59.
68 Deutsch, *Ein weiter Weg*, 133.
69 Ibid., 187.
70 Ibid., 180.

Deutsch even recalled good relationships with politicians who paved the way for the Austrofascist state and the Nazi *Anschluss*. For instance, according to his memoirs, he and many others members of the SDAPÖ had gotten along well with Dollfuss before he became chancellor.[71] And Deutsch had established such a good relationship with Hermann Neubacher, a middle-class, German nationalist who later became the first mayor of Vienna after the Nazi *Anschluss*, that Deutsch worked to free Neubacher from a Yugoslav prison after the Second World War.[72] Even though he was the head of the Social Democrats' paramilitary organization, Deutsch called attention to his good relationships with members of the opposing *Lager*. Of course, his views of these relationships were probably colored by his decision to return to Austria after the Second World War, when he witnessed the successful collaboration between socialist and Catholic politicians in the Second Republic. However, even in his 1934 pamphlet, he maintained that the parliament had functioned well until Dollfuss dismissed it.[73] Scholars should therefore look beyond the antagonistic relationship between Seipel and Otto Bauer, the SDAPÖ's dogmatic leader, and carry out more investigations of the myriad relationships among representatives from the rival *Lager*. After all, as Mergel showed in the case of the Reichstag delegates in the Weimar Republic, such an approach can reveal surprising results.[74]

And beyond the boundaries of Austria, we have seen how Deutsch and the Schutzbund cooperated with the Reichsbanner, an organization that was dominated by Social Democrats but also included left liberals and the left wing of the Catholic Center Party. The fact that the Schutzbund had to reach across the border to create a sustained cross-party and cross-class republican defense movement does indicate the inability to create a similar partnership on a widespread scale at home. Yet this situation arose because, unlike the Weimar Republic, the First Austrian Republic lacked a liberal party committed to democracy, and the right wing of the Austria's Catholic party had the upper hand. This asymmetrical relationship between the party makeup of the two organizations created some difficulties, but Deutsch repeatedly explained that they were committed to working with non-socialists.[75] Even though Austrians were unable to establish an equivalent to the Reichsbanner, the Schutzbund's partnership with the German

71 Ibid., 184.
72 Ibid., 158. Also see Harry Ritter, "Hermann Neubacher and the Austrian *Anschluss* Movement, 1918–1940," *Central European History* 8, no. 4 (1975): 348–369.
73 Deutsch, *Civil War*, 11.
74 Mergel, *Parlamentarische Kultur*.
75 Hochman, *Imagining a Greater Germany*, Chapter 4.

association is another example of the ways that the impermeability of the *Lager* needs to be rethought.[76]

These three short case studies show that it is fruitful to ask new questions and challenge our assumptions about the First Republic. Reframing our approach does not erase the fact that fascists and their abettors were able to destroy the republic, but it does encourage us to move beyond using the idea of failure as the starting point for explorations of the First Republic. Instead, we should view this period of Austrian history as an open-ended experiment that Austrians of all political stripes influenced. The First Republic was more than just a stepping stone to the Austrofascist and Nazi dictatorships.

76 Hochman, "Staging Socialism".

1933: The Christian Social/German Nationalist Camps and the Collapse of the First Republic

Janek Wasserman

On March 4, 1933, the three presidents of the Austrian national assembly resigned their positions during the course of a procedural vote. This left no one to end the session or call for a new one. Chancellor Engelbert Dollfuss used this opportunity to end parliamentary democracy in Austria by refusing to call for new elections. On March 7, he announced he was invoking the wartime emergency act, which permitted him to rule by decree. He declared that the republic faced a "parliamentary crisis, but not a state crisis." In the name of the Austrian *Volk*, he assumed full executive and legislative power. His first actions were to prohibit all assemblies and demonstrations and to curtail freedom of assembly, freedom of speech, and the freedom of the press. These restrictions supposedly permitted the government to focus its attentions on responding to the ongoing economic emergency that plagued the country. Dollfuss beseeched the Austrian people to set aside petty political squabbles and to behave like a "good family" and help one another out in this dire time. He concluded his announcement with a rallying cry: "Follow us! Help us!"[1]

As scholars like Emmerich Tàlos and Walter Manoschek have noted, the 1933 putsch did not come out of nowhere; a long preparatory period preceded the March events.[2] While these authors highlight late 1932 and early 1933, conservative intellectuals had been paving the way for these developments almost since the inception of the First Republic. By the time of the parliamentary "crisis", conservative politicians and thinkers possessed a comprehensive vocabulary for just such an eventuality. If one turns to the pages of leading newspapers and journals of the "Black Viennese" cultural milieu in March 1933, one encounters neither surprise nor uncertainty about the road ahead.[3] In the first extended editorial in *Die*

1 "An Österreichs Volk!" *Die Reichspost*, 9 March 1933, 1. Translations mine unless otherwise noted.

2 Emmerich Talos and Walter Manoschek, "Zum Konstituierungsprozeß des Austrofaschismus," in Emmerich Talos and Wolfgang Neugebauer, eds., *Austrofaschismus. Politik—*Ökonomie*—Kultur*, 1933-1938, 7th ed. (Berlin: Lit-Verlag, 2014), 6-23.

3 On Black Vienna, see Janek Wasserman, *Black Vienna: The Radical Right in the Red City, 1918-1938* (Ithaca: Cornell University Press, 2014).

Reichspost after Dollfuss's announcement, editor-in-chief Friedrich Funder already had a fully articulated defense not just for authoritarianism but also a rejoinder to critics. He claimed the crisis of parliamentarianism was a long time coming and noted how the *Volk* had long clamored for "reform." He insisted on a new "chamber of estates" (*Ständekammer*) and "corporatist representation" (*berufsständische Vertretung*) based on the 1931 papal encyclical "*Quadragesimo Anno.*" He rejected opponent's fears of dictatorship and fascism as polemical distortions. To forestall civil war, Dollfuss had to restore freedom and autonomy, true democracy, and economic health through authority: "Wise self-limitation and consciousness of its fundamental scope of functions (*ureigentlichen Aufgabenkreis*) are for democracy and parliament in Austria the final saving grace...the motto must be: 'In the name of authority, for a true, lasting, guaranteed freedom and for a purified democracy!'"[4] Invoking conservative Catholic lessons on authority and Austrian conservative views on democracy that owed to figures like Othmar Spann and Ignaz Seipel, Funder distilled the political philosophy of interwar Austrian conservatism into a rousing *Streitschrift*. Dollfuss—and later Kurt Schuschnigg—turned to this playbook to articulate and realize his authoritarian aims.

Obviously, given the *Reichspost*'s closeness to the Christian Social Party, the congruence of its views and Dollfuss's is expected, yet Funder's editorial represented only the best example of a barrage of similar defenses in 1933 and 1934. For example, Gregor Uhlhorn, a spokesperson for the regime, wrote in exactly the same terms in *Die schönere Zukunft*. He believed the parliament had killed itself, opening the way for Dollfuss to save the regime through authoritarian rule: "[The dissolution] is the most obvious proof of the incapacity for survival (*Lebensunfähigkeit*) and fruitlessness of radical parliamentarianism in Austria. The Parliament committed suicide, thereby admitting its inability to master the prevailing emergency conditions."[5] He maintained that Dollfuss was a reform-minded ruler, not a dictator, and the present moment was propitious for the creation of a state along the lines of "*Quadragesimo Anno.*" By accomplishing these changes, "parliamentarianism will be fundamentally reformed to save true Christian democracy and the people's freedoms, grounded in natural law."[6] The editor of *Die schönere Zukunft*, Joseph Eberle, echoed these sentiments, arguing that the shuttering of the parliament permitted the kinds of reforms already seen in Fascist Italy and Nazi Germany:

4 Friedrich Funder, "Heraus aus dem Sumpf!" *Die Reichspost*, 9 March 1933, 1.
5 Gregor Uhlhorn, "Regierungskurs des Reformwillens," *Die schönere Zukunft* 8 (1932/3), 603.
6 Ibid., 604.

> One naturally does not wish to permanently eliminate the parliament's right of codetermination, but only until the creation of a constitution that better assures the selection of representatives, operates above all according to the authoritarian or leadership principal, the true desire of the people, enflamed by the examples of Fascism in Italy and National Socialism in Germany.[7]

This chapter explores the intellectual and ideological origins of this authoritarian conservative consensus as it evolved during the First Republic in venues like the Catholic scholarly society, the *Leo-Gesellschaft*, in intellectual monthlies *Das neue Reich*, *Die schönere Zukunft*, and *Der christliche Ständestaat*, and in the writings of prominent conservative thinkers such as Othmar Spann, Hans Eibl, Johannes Messner, and Dietrich Hildebrand. For these conservatives, the crisis year 1933 was confirmation of their most dire predictions, as well as an opportunity to actualize a more beautiful future. It was the moment when social and political reality seemed to catch up with their own theoretical pronouncements of the previous decades. As events unfolded in Germany and Austria, this consensus frayed, demonstrating the underlying tensions within conservative Austrian thought. Conservatives found themselves caught between two authoritarian solutions: National Socialism and Austrofascism. Thus, it was only in the early 1930s that the *Lager* divisions of interwar Austrian history fully hardened. These divisions informed the disparate reactions to the implementation of the Austrofascist *Ständestaat* and the increasing threat from Nazi Germany.[8]

Origins of Antimodernist Conservative Thought before the Great War

While the most significant political and economic ideas that informed Black Viennese authoritarianism developed in response to postwar considerations, some of the socio-political dimensions of this thinking dated to the late imperial traditions of *Sozialreform* that inspired the radical wing of the Christian Social movement. Between 1895 and 1910, the Christian Social party under Karl Lueger and Albert Gessmann dominated politics and culture in Vienna. With its command of municipal government, it emboldened a younger generation of activists, which impelled Christian

7 Joseph Eberle, "Widergeburt," *Die schönere Zukunft* 8 (1932/3), 805.

8 For the standard account of Austria's *Lager*, see Adam Wandruszka, "Oesterreichs Politische Struktur," in Heinrich Benedikt, ed., *Geschichte der Republik Österreich* (Vienna: Verlag für Geschichte und Politik, 1954), 289-455.

Socialism toward a greater commitment to Catholic social values and political Catholicism. These radicals saw Vienna as a battleground in an ongoing *Kulturkampf* between German Catholics on one side and secularists, Jews, liberals, and socialists on the other.[9] Catholic intellectuals formed the *Leo-Gesellschaft* in 1892 to publicize Christian ideas and challenge modern secular science and social theory.

The *Leo-Gesellschaft* was founded in 1892 by a group of six scholars, led by Franz Schindler, a professor of theology at the University of Vienna and one of the leading ideologues in the Christian Social party. Named after Pope Leo XIII, the founders wanted to establish an Austrian society for Catholic scholars that followed the example of the German *Görres-Gesellschaft*. In addition to its demands that the society be Austrian and scientific, they also stressed the importance of the Catholic faith. Scholars could pursue their own research interests as long as it was in keeping with the ethical foundations of the Church, especially as laid out in the 1891 papal encyclical, "Rerum Novarum." Catholic doctrine did not dictate the objects of investigation; it simply provided the ethical foundation and "Christian spirit" for research.

The *Leo-Gesellschaft* represented a more radical interpretation of recent Catholic teaching, exemplified by the *Sozialreform* movement. This trend would inform Austrian conservatism through the 1930s. In the course of the nineteenth century, two competing interpretations of Catholic social theory emerged: *Sozialpolitik* and *Sozialreform*. Representatives of the former sought incremental change within the existing order. They treated the state and economy as matters of indifference; instead, they focused on spiritual reform. They cooperated with political parties and collaborated with non-Catholic organizations.[10] *Sozialreform*, on the other hand, demanded a return to the structures of the middle ages; namely, a restoration of corporate guilds and the end of capitalism. *Sozialreform* stressed hierarchy and authoritarian leadership, not democracy. The leading representative was Karl Vogelsang, the Catholic publicist and politician, who provided Viennese antisemitism with cultural legitimacy. He was central to the early Christian Social movement, assembling an eclectic group of reactionary Catholics and antisemitic nationalists.[11]

In the decade before the Great War, the Christian Social movement, inspired by *Leo-Gesellschaft* thinkers, evolved in a more dogmatic direction.

9 On the prewar Christian Socials, see John Boyer, *Culture and Political Crisis in Vienna: Christian Socialism in Power* (Chicago: University of Chicago Press, 1995), 298-330, 448-58.
10 Alfred Diamant, *Austrian Catholics and the First Republic* (Princeton: Princeton University Press, 1960), 16-22.
11 John Boyer, *Political Radicalism in Late Imperial Vienna* (Chicago: University of Chicago Press, 1981), 166-80.

The decisive figure was Richard Kralik. He initiated an "integralist" turn in Austrian conservatism that joined reactionary, antimodernist social aims, German nationalism, *Sozialreform* Catholicism, and antisemitism.[12] Kralik believed that Catholics were the defenders of the one true worldview and that they must fight Freemasonry, Judaism, democracy, socialism, and capitalism. Through this *Kulturkampf*, the Catholicism's mission would be achieved. Kralik argued that political, social, and cultural issues could no longer be considered independently; they had to be integrated into a single project. He urged Catholics, ethnic Germans, and conservatives to enter the political fray.[13]

The Postwar Radicalization of the Conservative Project

If the Austrian conservative intelligentsia had arrived at a stable worldview by the first decade of the twentieth century, the Great War shook it to its core. The war destroyed the Habsburg Empire and left a mutilated republic behind. Moreover, the postwar moment found conservatives increasingly anxious about the viability of their worldview. This precipitated a turn to politics and a radicalization of rhetoric. This was more than a simple identification with the Christian socialism, though; it signified a commitment to a form of German nationalism based on ideas of a pan-German Reich in Central Europe.[14] Hans Eibl, a professor of early Christianity, exemplified this Catholic-nationalist synthesis. In his work, he addressed two recurring themes for postwar conservatives: the travesty of the Paris Peace Accords and the historical mission of the German Reich. He eviscerated the peace treaty, calling it "the greatest violation of human rights in history."[15] Eibl advocated for German *Lebensraum* and used *Blut und Boden* rhetoric to present his idealized image of a German-dominated Central Europe, which, as we will see, he identified with the idea of a "Third Reich" in his 1933 *Vom Sinn der Gegenwart*.

The two most significant intellectual figures for the postwar radical conservative turn were undoubtedly Othmar Spann and Joseph Eberle.

12 On Kralik, see Judith Beniston, *Welttheater: Hoffmannsthal, Richard von Kralik, and the Revival of Austrian Drama* (London: W.S. Maney, 1998) 89-93. On *Sozialreform*, see Alfred Diamant, *Austrian Catholics and the First Republic* (Princeton: Princeton University Press, 1960), 41-7.

13 Beniston, *Welttheater*, 91.

14 On *Reichsgedanken* in Austria, see Elke Seefried, *Reich und Stände. Ideen und Wirken des deutschen politischen Exils in Österreich 1933-1938* (Dusseldorf: Droste, 2006).

15 Hans Eibl, "Die Stellung der Nation," *Jahrbuch der österreichischen Leo-Gesellschaft* (1924), 28.

In the summer of 1920, Spann held a series of lectures titled "*Der wahre Staat*," which were published the following year. It became a fixture in discussions about state forms, government, and society for the remainder of the Republic.[16] Spann identified three "crises" to be overcome: a political crisis of democracy and liberalism, an intellectual, economic one of individualism and capitalism, and a crisis of socialism. His solution consisted of a *völkisch* revolution by cultural Germans rooted in Christian values.[17] He ridiculed the "frivolousness" of mass democracy and posited the *Führer* state as its replacement. "The will of the people as political will may only be built through the *Führer*, before it can be expressed as such."[18] For Spann, the *Führer* represented the people and its collective will, standing above contemporary problems.[19]

Der wahre Staat made Spann a star. German nationalist and conservative Catholic students flocked to his lectures. He lectured to the *deutsche Studentenschaft* and participated regularly in the *Akademische Legion*.[20] Spann's circle grew to an impressive size by the 1930s. Conservatively, the *Spannkreis* included several hundred active members in Vienna, most of whom were university educated, often with advanced degrees. Members became involved with several fascist and radical conservative movements in the 1920s and early 1930s. Walter Riehl was the head of the Austrian NSDAP. In the mid-1920s, Walter Heinrich, Spann's most successful student, and Hans Riehl took on leadership positions in the fascist *Heimwehr*. In 1930, Heinrich helped author the Korneuberg oath of the organization.[21]

If the Spann movement was the academic locus of radical conservative Viennese thought, the publications edited by Joseph Eberle served as the journalistic mouthpiece. Eberle made his reputation writing jingoistic essays during the war, which appeared as 1918 books: *Zertrummert die Götzen!* and *Die Überwindung der Plutokratie*. Eberle castigated liberalism and socialism as products of the spiritually-bankrupt Enlightenment and Jewish influence. He rejected the atheistic and materialistic forces of the modern world. He sought an end to capitalism and a return to a German Catholic corporatism, modeled on the Holy Roman Empire. After the war, Eberle cemented his status with a searing repudiation of the Paris Peace Accords, *De Profundis*.[22]

16 Othmar Spann, *Der wahre Staat* (Leipzig: Quelle & Meyer, 1921), 3-4.
17 Ibid., 97-110.
18 Ibid., 111.
19 On Spann's political tendencies, including his Nazi sympathies, see Klaus Jörg Siegfried, *Universalismus oder Faschismus* (Vienna: Böhlau, 1974), 152-3.
20 Siegfried, *Universalismus oder Faschismus*, 64-71.
21 Ibid., 100-53.
22 On Eberle, see Barbara Maria Hofer, "Josef Eberle. Katholischer Publizist zwischen 'Monarchie' und 'Schönerer Zukunft'" (PhD diss., University of Salzburg, 1955).

Das Neue Reich—edited by Eberle, supported by Friedrich Funder and the *Reichspost*, and sustained by contributions from Spann's Richard Kralik's respective circles—had a wide readership from its inception in 1918. Its circulation reached 10,000 by April 1921. In December 1924, the journal reached an all-time high of 15,000 copies. The journal provided a forum for debate over evolving conservative positions. Eberle and *Das Neue Reich* helped establish a relatively unified ideology of Austrian conservatism, one that was Catholic, (Austro-) German nationalist, anti-socialist, anti-democratic, and antisemitic. These positions were more radical than those espoused by members of the Christian Social party or the Greater German People's Party. Over the years, the political parties would have to shift if they hoped to maintain support from increasingly authoritarian conservative thinkers.

In the earliest editions of the journal, radicalized Christian Social authors criticized socialism and democracy and advocated conservative unity. Alois von Liechtenstein, a close political ally of Karl Lueger, proposed an alliance of Catholic conservatives and German nationals in German-Austria in order to prevent socialist domination.[23] Richard Kralik tried to reconcile Catholic conservatives and their secular German nationalist brethren by suggesting they shared a true German mission, rooted in the Holy Roman Empire.[24] Kralik's reactionary, anti-modern tendencies led him not only to criticize the postwar democratic order but to demand a counterrevolution against "sham" democracy (*Mauldemokratie*):

> True democracy, whose name people have unjustly stolen, comprises the whole people and all its social groups (*Ständen*) with the monarch as the head of the social body. All true culture is *Volkskultur*. National culture is based on this alone. The true people, the culture carriers are not the Jewish-organized followers of Jewish power interests under the deceptive name of Social Democracy. The true people, the true democracy, is really its opposite. Everything for the people, everything from the people! The *Volk* is not a class with class prejudices and class hatred; rather, the *Volk* is everything—nation, government, intellectuals, nobility, army, king.[25]

Kralik's invocation of "true democracy" prefigured Chancellor Seipel's famous speech on the subject by ten years, when the latter turned away

23 Alois Liechtenstein, *Das neue Reich* 1 (1918/19), 241-3.
24 Richard Kralik, *Das neue Reich* 1 (1918/19), 249-50.
25 Ibid., 304.

from republicanism and towards fascism. Kralik's attack on parliamentary democracy, along with Spann's, became the cornerstones of conservative Austrian critiques, and they informed the 1933 justifications for Dollfuss's coup.

Eberle extended these positions, pressing his readers to embrace authoritarianism, if not dictatorship. After the first national elections, he cast a jaundiced eye on participatory democracy: "We absolutely must begin to doubt, whether democracy and parliament, whether a ruling form built above all on the will of the masses is capable of leading a people out of the direst emergency and disorganization to order and achievement. We do not believe so. We do not believe in democracy."[26] Eberle questioned whether democracies could deal with crises. This crisis argument become the core of the defense of dictatorship: "Parliaments and accommodating parliamentary committees have never saved the day in extraordinary times, in times of emergency, chaos and revolution. Only strong self-willed individuals have done it and led the people to new heights. Moses was a dictator –Caesar was a dictator." Drawing on the arguments of Carl Schmitt, whom he reviewed favorably, Eberle argued for a strong Führer.[27]

After a falling out with the publisher of *Das neue Reich* in September 1925, Joseph Eberle announced that he was leaving to start a new journal, *Die schönere Zukunft*. Eventually the more radical *Schönere Zukunft* displaced *Das neue Reich* as Central Europe's conservative journal of choice. The media battles between the two papers crystallized the dominant ideological positions within the Viennese conservative intellectual milieu. By the early 1930s, radical authoritarian, corporatist, and antidemocratic ideas carried the day.

After Eberle's departure, *Das neue Reich* rebranded itself as a more moderate offering, but the paper changed only slightly. It represented a distinct "Austrian cultural idea" that stressed German-Christian culture. It supported an independent Austria and rejected *Anschluss*. It declared itself the implacable enemy of capitalism, socialism, and Bolshevism. The editors called for the return of "authoritarian thinking" and the institution of a *völkisch* "true democracy." They repudiated "corrupt" democracy, "weak" pacifism, and "chauvinistic" rationalism in the name of Christian peace between nations. Practically, this meant a call for the end of liberal constitutionalism. Catholic social theory served as the social and economic model. Under Aemilian Schoepfer and Johannes Messner, *Das neue Reich* changed

26 Joseph Eberle, "Nach der Wahlen," *Das neue Reich* 3 (1920/21), 86.
27 Ibid.

its tone, yet its content remained the same. Messner in particular would be pivotal in shaping the post-1933 *Ständestaat*, especially its socioeconomic foundations.[28]

Die schönere Zukunft distinguished itself by embracing a more radical conservatism, at least in tone. The editors, including Eberle, the Spannian Eugen Kogon, and Österreichische *Aktion* founder Alfred Missong, declared war on "bad press," characterized by "Jewish hacks," in the name of the *Volk*. He explained, "The way into the more beautiful future (*schönere Zukunft*) is the way of the crusader." He delineated his paper's main themes: "State, Tradition, Authority, Monarchy, Nobility, Democracy, Parliamentarianism, Republic, Marxism, Plutocracy, Jewishness, Freemasonry."[29]

At the center of this ideological development was *Die österreichische Aktion*, the Austrian analogue to Charles Maurras's *Action Française*.[30] Between 1927 and 1930, *Die Aktion* expanded into a full-fledged movement, recruiting followers in periodicals, organizing youth groups, and establishing connections with Austrian and central European political groups. Alfred Missong ensured his comrades wrote for *Die schönere Zukunft*. Missong published a defense of Catholic antisemitism in 1928 that disavowed racial antisemitism yet demanded a re-Christianization of Europe to resist Judaism, liberalism, and capitalism.[31] Hans Zessner affirmed the role of Austria within the German cultural realm.[32] Wilhelm Schmid not only contributed to the paper, but he also reached out to youth organizations throughout central Europe. He forged ties with Anton Orel's nationalist and antisemitic *Bundesvereinigung der freien christlichen Jugend Österreichs*, *der Bund der deutschen katholischen Jugend Österreichs*, and *der Vaterländische Studentenbund Ostmark*. Schmid's journal, *Das Vaterland*, also established connections to the *Heimwehr*. They consequently established *Die österreichische Aktion* as an official association in 1930.[33] The crisis years of the early 1930s would offer an opportunity for conservatives to offer proposals for the salvation of Central Europe. The more radical solutions of

28 *Das neue Reich* 7 (1924/5), 1210-1.

29 Joseph Eberle, "Die schönere Zukunft," *Schönere Zukunt* 1 (1925/6), 1-2.

30 On the Austrian Action, see Janek Wasserman, "Österreichische Aktion: Monarchism, Authoritarianism, and Unity of the Austrian Conservative Ideological Field during the First Republic," *Central European History* 47, no. 1 (2014): 76-104.

31 Alfred Missong, "Wie Karl von Vogelsang über die Judenfrage dachte," *Schönere Zukunft* 3 (1927/8), 816-19. On Catholic antisemitism, see John Connelly, *From Enemy to Brother: The Revolution in Catholic Teaching on the Jews, 1933-1965* (Cambridge: Harvard University Press, 2012).

32 Hans Zessner-Spitzenberg, "Der österreichische Gedanke und die deutsche Frage," *Schönere Zukunft* 3 (1927/8), 922-4.

33 *Das Vaterland* 1 (1927), 1-21, 37-44, 63-4.

Eberle, Spann, and the *Schönere Zukunft* circle came to seem more appealing as the political systems of Germany and Austria struggled and the world economy collapsed.

The Crisis Years and the Emergent Consensus within Austrian Conservatism

In 1929 and 1930, the debates over the reform of the Austrian constitution, the invocation of Article 48 in Weimar Germany, and the rise of National Socialism suggested that democracy's end and authoritarian's rise were near at hand. Most significantly, Austrian conservatives had to decide where they stood on National Socialism and other fascist solutions. In 1931, Eberle published a gently critical treatise on Hitler and National Socialism. Although he rejected the pagan and anticlerical elements in Nazi ideology, Eberle did not blame the Nazis for their radicalism. He hoped that the Brüning government would radicalize its efforts to combat liberalism, socialism, and Judaism, yet he applauded the Nazis for proposing more radical approaches to these "problems". Missong could not abide these views. Missong began a shadow career, writing under various *noms de plume* in anti-Nazi publications.[34] Eberle and Missong, like their Black Viennese compatriots, evinced the uneasiness of Austrian conservatives with the materialism and racism of the Nazis, yet they also demonstrated how far along the anti-democratic path they had already traveled. The Nazis were the wrong answer to the right political and social questions. The key was finding a better solution.

We see this clearly as Austrian conservatives looked to fascist and authoritarian movements, not to mention Catholic teachings, to challenge the existent order. August Maria Knoll and Ernst Karl Winter, members of the Österreichische *Aktion*, wanted to form a common anti-capitalist and antidemocratic league with Spann, Orel, and others. Authoritarianism and corporatism dominated the thinking in the Catholic conservative and German nationalist camps. When the Vatican published "*Quadragesimo Anno*" in 1931, the update of Leo XIII's "*Rerum Novarum*," it received universal acceptance within Central European conservative circles, even if moderates and radicals interpreted it differently. Othmar Spann interpreted the encyclical as a call for radical social transformation. He rejected the meliorist *Sozialpolitik* of the authors of the encyclical, who had not rooted

34 Alfred Missong, "Mein Leben," in Alfred Missong, Cornelia Hoffmann, and Gerald Stourzh, eds., *Alfred Missong. Christentum und Politik in Österreich* (Vienna: Böhlau, 2006), 30-3.

out their individualistic tendencies, and argued for a "true state" with fascistic elements, rooted in his universalism.[35]

Johannes Messner responded angrily to Spann. In this "fateful hour" of Central European conservatism, Catholic unity was required.[36] Messner rallied notable Catholic theorists to defend Catholic Solidarism—the putative core of "*Quadragesimo Anno*"—and to criticize universalism.[37] These corporatism debates radiated more heat than light, demonstrating that Central European conservatives had already reached a consensus on their anti-capitalist, anti-democratic, and authoritarian program. The merger of *Das neue Reich* and *Die schönere Zukunft* under Eberle confirm this. Messner defended the merger, saying it was necessary for all Catholics to join together to achieve their goals. The *Schönere Zukunft* could now serve as the focal point of German-language conservatism and authoritarianism.[38]

1933

For nearly fifteen years, the ideas of Central European intellectuals had run ahead of political developments. That changed in 1933 with the accession to power of Adolf Hitler and the National Socialists in Germany and Dollfuss's nearly simultaneous March putsch. The dual (and dueling) conservative revolutions of German-speaking Europe rendered intellectuals ecstatic and somewhat breathless. Instead of proposing radical changes, they were left reacting to them. And with two authoritarian or fascist alternatives on offer, there was room for continued disputation. While those more steeped in Catholic social theory stood behind Dollfuss, more nationalistically inclined Austrians hewed ever closer to the Nazi solution.

As we saw in the introduction, writers like Friedrich Funder and Gregor Uhlhorn embraced the Dollfuss putsch unreservedly in March, using the language of Austrian radical conservatism to defend the breach of legality. Other Black Viennese intellectuals were similarly ecstatic. *Schönere Zukunft* editor Alfred Missong portrayed the collapse of parliamentary democracy with delight, identifying the current situation as "salvation" for Austria. While he recognized that rule by emergency decree could not last indefinitely, he welcomed the moment when the state would overcome the "constraints on the construction of a regime, established by the

35 Othmar Spann, "Schicksalsstunde der deutschen Katholiken," *Schönere Zukunft* 7 (1932/33), 565

36 Messner, "Schicksalsstunde," 540.

37 See *Das neue Reich* 14 (1931/2), especially 650-771.

38 Johannes Messner, "*Das Neue Reich* und *Die Schönere Zukunft* vereinigen sich," *Das neue Reich* 14 (1931/2), 1003-4.

parliamentary constitution." He pressed for an authoritarian *Ständestaat* that resembled Fascist Italy and the Estado Novo in Portugal and made use of "*Quadragesimo Anno*" to inform its corporatism.[39]

The young political theorist Erich Voegelin began making his reputation in 1933 with two books on race theory, which attracted a wide readership in Nazi Germany.[40] In addition to these works, he also articulated a defense of Dollfuss, which claimed that it was respect for "true democracy" that mandated the destruction of the existing Austrian system. For him, the Fatherland Front had a responsibility to the country to protect it from the "anti-democratic" Social Democrats and National Socialists: "[T]he democrats [Christian Socials] were under an obligation to cling to the letter of the constitution until the anti-democratic forces [socialists and Nazis] were strong enough to do away with it. ...The 'democratic' contents of the constitution should be the guiding rule for the government, in spite of the fact that there existed no Austrian 'demos.'"[41] In his 1936 *Authoritarian State*, he further elaborated why Dollfuss was justified in ending the postwar republic: The Christian Socials were the sole advocates of democracy in the First Republic. They defended the system as long as it was feasible. In 1933, they were left with no choice but to seize power to save it from the anti-democrats. Voegelin thus had little use for questions of legitimacy or legality, since there was no such thing as an "Austrian people" with a legitimate claim to sovereignty.[42]

While Voegelin focused on the political justifications for Austria's authoritarian turn, Johannes Messner, the former editor of *Neues Reich*, spearheaded the effort to provide a working socioeconomic program. His 1929 *Sozialökonomik und Sozialethik* and, more significantly, the 1934 *Die soziale Frage der Gegenwart* criticized the capitalist economic order and its individualist, rationalist ethos for the impoverishment of contemporary society. Messner attacked the "sham equality" of democratic states and decried the disappearance of "true democracy," which characterized "organic," hierarchical societies. He contrasted "formal" democracy with "real" democracy: "If the common good remains the unconditional norm for state leadership [in authoritarian democracy], in formal democracy the regime is wholly bound to the majority will, which is all too easily corrupted

39 Hugo Diwald, "Staatsgestaltung im Geiste der Quadragesimo Anno," *Der christliche Ständestaat*, December 3, 1933, 15.

40 The books are *Rasse und Staat* and *Die Rassenidee in der Geistesgeschichte*. Voegelin did not deny the centrality of race for human communities, even though he rejected the physiological, deterministic views of the Nazis.

41 Eric Voegelin, "Government and Constitution," in Eric Voegelin, *Published Essays 1934-1939* (Columbia: University of Missouri, 2001,) 104.

42 Eric Voegelin, *TheAuthoritarian State* (Columbia: University of Missouri, 1999), 223-46.

by chance and party egotism. It is in real democracy that the weight of each individual's voice is categorized according to their social responsibility."[43] Messner implied that the Austrian state had reached an impasse that required a fundamental change. A new state had to be established, which prioritized social wellbeing by attending to the needs of the nation's estates and professions (*berufsständische Ordnung*). The only way for such a state to appear would be under a unitary leader.[44]

While primarily oriented toward Austrian affairs, Messner's work suggested ways that Austrian conservatives could reconcile their views with elements of the Nazi program. Messner saw some merit in Nazi economic programs: "Even if the economic picture of National Socialism is only now recognizable in outline, it is nevertheless clear that a thoroughgoing agreement with the fundamental principles of Christian *Sozialreform* exists."[45] Messner's views on race, anti-Semitism, and eugenics also placed him in the mainstream of Central European Catholic racial thinking.[46] Though he denied the Nazis' claims about the purity of the Aryan race and the possibility of pure races at all, he nevertheless believed that lesser races must be prevented from breeding with the *Volk*. Messner called for a "national eugenics" to protect Germandom from corruption. Messner advocated pro-natalist measures and restrictions on procreation for "tubercular, alcoholic, feeble-minded or criminal families."[47] Clear overlaps existed between Messner's views and the German nationalists and Nazis he criticized.

Messner's onetime rival Joseph Eberle also commented on the political crises wracking Central Europe by directing readers to Fascism and Nazism as the roads to a more beautiful future. Initially, Eberle hewed closer to the Italians. After some initial hesitations about Mussolini—particularly about attitudes to the Church and ambitions in the Tirol—Eberle invited positive articles on the movement by the early 1930s.[48] Eberle's support of Nazism followed a similar trajectory. Shortly after the Nazis made parliamentary gains in 1930, Eberle authored a series of admonitory essays. In his 1931 brochure, "*Zum Kampf um Hitler*," he expressed a preference for Brüning over Hitler. He argued that German Catholics had better solutions for the problems of Weimar Germany. He also rejected the "socialist" elements in the Nazi platform. Although he criticized the Nazis, he recognized that

43 Messner, *Die soziale Frage der Gegenwart* (Innsbruck: Tyrolia, 1934), 172.
44 Ibid., 488-90.
45 Ibid., 422. See also 167-84, 556.
46 See Connelly, *From Enemy to Brother*, Ch. 1.
47 Messner, *Soziale Frage*, 557-60.
48 See Joseph Eberle, "Bilanz des ersten faschistischen Jahrzehnts," *Schönere Zukunft* 8 (1932/33), 269.

they were an important force combating Bolshevism, plutocracy, Jewry, and democracy. Eberle's solution to the turmoil in Germany was to provide the Chancellor with more power, which would undercut the Weimar Republic and strip Hitler of his appeal.[49]

Eberle's views on the Nazis softened as Hitler consolidated power. By the "seizure of power" in March 1933, Eberle had adopted a position of tacit endorsement. Instead of focusing on the "un-Christian" and "barbaric" qualities of the movement, Eberle now stressed the reasons why Nazism was a necessary development: "Nazism is therefore a reaction against the inadequacies of the parliamentary system, against the program of western democracy. This does not seem to be a system for Germans...Nazism owes its upswing ultimately to a reaction of natural feelings of the people against the overwhelming Jewification of Germany."[50] Eberle may still have viewed the Nazis as an unsavory symptom of the post-Versailles order, yet he accepted them as superior to the alternatives. While Eberle cautioned the Nazis against excluding German Catholics from the *Volksgemeinschaft*, he characterized Hitler's achievement as "extraordinary" and a first step towards a federated, re-Christianized *Großdeutschland.*

Other German nationalist Austrians were likewise unconcerned about making common cause with the National Socialists, even as they supported Dollfuss in his fight against Judaism, socialism, capitalism, and democracy. Hans Eibl and other members of the *Schönere Zukunft* circle wrote laudatory pieces about both the Nazis and the Dollfuss regime. The Othmar Spann *Kreis* only endorsed the former. It would be up to the anti-Nazis around Dietrich Hildebrand at *Der Christlicher Ständestaat* to resist this drift in German and Central European toward Nazism. Of course, virtually no Austrian conservatives supported the actual conservation of the democratic status quo. The 1933/1934 writings of these thinkers demonstrated that parliamentary democracy had no defenders outside of socialist and some liberal circles.

Hans Eibl articulated a new Central European authoritarian vision informed by recent events. He lauded the emerging German and Austrian states for their anti-Western and anti-modern radicalism. He celebrated their rejection of atomistic individualism for a moral order consisting of "human souls...*a priori* bound up with metaphysical values."[51] Eibl's 1933 book, *Der Sinn der Gegenwart,* demonstrates the possibility of a convergence of authoritarian conservatism with National Socialism through a shared *völkisch* value system. Eibl viewed the German political revolution as part of

49 Joseph Eberle, *Zum Kampf um Hitler* (Innsbruck: Schönere Zukunft, 1931), 3, 19-29.
50 Ibid., 575.
51 Hans Eibl, "Die Scheidung der Geister," *Schönere Zukunft* 9 (1933/4), 142.

a large spiritual rebirth in the form of the "Third Reich": "I have characterized the cultural synthesis, which also belongs as part of the present political struggles of Germans, with the Romantic philosophical term 'The Third Reich'... That the idea of the Third Reich is for me strongly suffused with politics is only natural."[52] For him, the emergence of the National Socialist regime signaled the coming of a new age: "The present world-historical moment is a chosen time, in which a glimpse onto a new, comprehensive order of values is afforded."[53] Eibl called on his compatriots to execute the German mission—by all means necessary. His program consisted of: "1) combating the peace treaty as murderous and morally bankrupt; 2) a struggle for a new legal order; 3) a struggle for a new Kingdom of God."[54] Although his language resonated with Nazi rhetoric, it still reflected Austrian and Catholic conservative beliefs. He called for a crusading zeal in the fight for God and country. Only through the combined efforts of all Germans under the leadership of a strong *Führer* could a spiritualized German nation re-emerge. Germans possessed a messianic mission that had to be brought to surrounding nations through a grand imperial project.[55]

Along with Eibl, members of the notorious *Bärenhöhle* (Othenio Abel, Richard Meister, Oswald Menghin, and Heinrich Srbik) also reconciled National Socialist thought with the nationalist strains in Austrian conservatism.[56] Menghin's 1933 *Geist und Blut* offered a justification on racial grounds for the exclusion of Jews from the German *Volksgemeinschaft*. Allowing Jews to assimilate would only corrupt the character of the German people. He defended the right of German states to discriminate in the name of the *Volk*. He repeated these views in the 1934 articles, *Die schönere Zukunft*. Menghin's "biological turn" introduced racialist discussions into the debates over authoritarianism and Nazism in Austria.[57] While most of the other major contributions by these authors fall outside the scope of this study, they contributed articles and lectures in 1933 that paralleled Eibl's.[58]

52 Eibl, *Von Sinn der Gegenwart* (Vienna: Braumüller, 1933), viii.
53 Ibid., 5.
54 Ibid., 286.
55 Ibid., 380
56 On the *Bärenhöle*, see Klaus Taschwer, "Geheimsache Bärenhöhle. Wie ein antisemitisches Professorenkartell der Universität Wien nach 1918 jüdische und linke Forscherinnen und Forscher vertrieb," *Alma mater antisemitica* (2015), https://www.academia.edu/4258095; Taschwer, *Hochburg des Antisemitismus. Der Niedergang der Universität Wien im 20. Jahrhundert* (Vienna: Czernin, 2015).
57 On Menghin, see Richard Geehr, *The Aesthetics of Horror: The Life and Thought of Richard von Kralik* (Boston: Brill, 2003), 130-39.
58 Key works were: Srbik, *Deutsche Einheit* (1935) and Österreich in der deutschen Geschichte (1936); Hudal, *Rom, Christentum und das deutsche Volk* (1935) and *Die Grundlagen des Nationalsozialismus* (1936).

Othmar Spann and his circle went even further than Eibl and the *Bärenhöhle* crowd to accommodate fascism and Nazism. In fact, they saw their primary audience as German, not Austrian, and they commented far more extensively on German affairs than Austrian ones. Spann introduced *Das ständische Leben* in early 1931 to get his universalist teachings out to a broader audience. He also used the journal as a vehicle for theoretical discussions about radical conservatism and fascism. Spann offered essays on the "inner history" of the German *Volk* and the issues of race and national belonging. He identified a unique German *Geist* that owed to its unique racial lineage. All Germans therefore had to defend their blood from corruption.[59] The journal also invited Benito Mussolini to introduce fascist theory and practice to a German-speaking audience in a January 1933 article.[60]

Walter Heinrich and Ilse Roloff, the journal's editor, went furthest in their overtures to the ascendant Nazis. Heinrich contributed three major articles in 1933, one on Italian Fascism and two about the reconstruction of German society in light of the Nazi "seizure of power" in January.[61] Heinrich offered economic advice to Nazi business leaders within a week of their takeover. The two articles saluted recent German developments and proclaimed the coming of a new corporate order. Heinrich reveled in the advance of authoritarian ideas across Europe. Heinrich quoted Hitler, proclaiming, "The State has become a *Stand* again!" He supported a comprehensive *Gleichschaltung* at all levels of society. Heinrich boasted that Germany had entered a new Golden Age under Hitler.[62]

Roloff developed the ideological similarities between universalism and Nazism in the face of growing opposition from Nazi ideologues. Roloff favorably compared several major features of Hitler and Spann's respective thought. She concluded that Hitler and Spann embodied two vital contributions to the radical transformation of European society: "The German spirit has produced men in the realms of politics and science who have conducted the same fight against the same poisons—of Jewish Marxism, international liberalism and Western, un-German state conceptions. It is in this light that a closer examination of *Mein Kampf* and Othmar Spann's

59 Othmar Spann, "Innere Geschichte des deutschen Volkes," *Ständisches Leben* (1932), 196.

60 Benito Mussolini, "Die Lehren des Faschismus," *Ständisches Leben* (1932), 1-9.

61 Walter Heinrich, "Die Überwindung des Parlamentarismus in Reich, Land, und Gemeinde," *Ständisches Leben* (1933), 191-5; "Die berufständische Wirtschaft im neuen Staat," *Ständisches Leben* (1933), 409-18.

62 Heinrich, "Überwindung," 191, 195, 418.

so-called universalism or *Ganzheitslehre* shows truly striking agreement."[63] Hitler and Spann both rejected Marxism, liberalism, and democracy. They espoused a fundamental anti-Semitism. They believed in the German spirit and the rebirth of *Volk*. Although Hitler was primarily a statesman and Spann a philosopher, they pursued the same end: the true state composed of members of the *Volksgemeinschaft*. Spann and Hitler were therefore brothers-in-arms.

The *Spannkreis* devoted virtually no time to discussion of events in Austria. Despite surface similarities between the corporatist vision of Dollfuss and other Austrian conservatives with Spann's "true state," the social theorist rejected Dollfuss's program categorically. In his 1934 *Kämpfende Wissenschaft*, he dismissed any overlap between the two systems:

> [The new state] has made an eerie carnivalesque joke (*unheimliche Fastnachtsscherz*) out of the corporate order. I raise forceful objection to the intellectual borrowings that the Austrian constitution has made from my lessons. People do not believe that they must understand thoughts in order to successfully borrow them. The May Constitution is a mix of the ideas of 1789 and contemporary corporate ones. I must complain bitterly against this corruption of corporatist ideas.[64]

As he had argued during the "*Quadragesimo Anno*" debates, Austrian Catholic conservatives still held onto too many individualistic beliefs, hence their corporatism was a sham. Too many civil liberties, too many individual rights, and too much capitalism still remained, which corrupted a truly universalistic vision. As such, Spann maintained his distance from Austrian developments, laying his hopes for a revolutionary order with the Nazis.

Spann's derisive comments about Dollfuss and the *Ständestaat* and his Nazi sympathies attracted the ire of pro-Austrian, anti-Nazi conservatives. It was one thing to identify commonalties with the Nazi program, as Eberle, Voegelin, and Messner had done. It was another to endorse the Hitler movement, as Spann, Eibl, *inter alia*, had done. *Der christliche Ständestaat* launched a blistering salvo on the latter group. Otto Maria Karpfen called Spann a dangerous crypto-Nazi elitist who favored a total state like the one "to the north."[65] Aurel Kolnai discredited Spann's philosophy, calling it a

63 Ilse Roloff, "Adolf Hitlers ‚Mein Kampf' im Lichte der Gesellschaftswissenschaft," *Ständisches Leben* (1933), 608.
64 Othmar Spann, *Kämpfende Wissenschaft* (Jena: Gustav Fischer, 1934), 234.
65 Otto Fidelis, "Ist Österreich ein totaler Staat?" *Der christliche Ständestaat*, September 16, 1933, 8-9.

heathen system. Dietrich Hildebrand, editor of the *Christliche Ständestaat*, led the charge. He deplored conservative support for Nazi racism and argued that there was no way for a true conservative to square Nazi racial ideas with Catholic dogma. He identified Spann as part of a dangerous group of Catholics that tacked towards Nazism despite its heretical tendencies. This group included Spann, Eibl, Menghin, and Hudal. All of these men were subjects of lengthy attacks by *Christlicher Ständestaat* authors.[66]

The Dietrich Hildebrand-edited *Christliche Ständestaat* was the primary home for those thinkers. In early 1933, the anti-Nazi Hildebrand fled Germany to avoid arrest. He resettled in Vienna, where he made connections to the Dollfuss government. He chose Austria for he believed the country to be the best hope for a Catholic German state and the last bastion against "economic materialism" (i.e. Marxism) and "materialism of the blood" (Nazism). Hildebrand advanced an "Austrian mission" that warned against the twin evils on the left and right.[67] These ambitions coincided with Dollfuss's, and the paper became an unofficial outlet of Austrian authoritarianism.[68]

Hildebrand presented authoritarian Austria as Europe's hope for a Christian future and a third way between political extremisms. "Europe, the Christian West and true Germandom turn their eyes with expectation on Austria, which has chosen a Christian, German *Ständestaat* as a program. This program goes well beyond the boundaries of politics; it demands a profound, spiritual clarification of worldview. False and erroneous conceptions, economic materialism and materialism of the blood, liberal individualism and heathen totalitarianism (*Staatsomnipotenz*), must be opposed by the great classical formulations of western thought."[69] Hildebrand proffered the "Austrian idea" as a political and spiritual answer to the crises of modern Central Europe. He advocated a "Christian, German" state—preferably, an authoritarian one. In his rejection of party politics and liberal democracy, Hildebrand channeled Dollfuss's own rhetoric defending the *Staatsstrich*: "This paper will serve the ideological conquest of Austria. Outside of all party politics it will help work for...the development of a fully flourishing life, which is captured in the words of the man entrusted with the leadership of the great, truly German, Christian future [Dollfuss]: '*Austriam instaurare in Christo.*'"[70]

66 *Der christliche Ständestaat*, May 20, 1934, 22-3.

67 Rudolf Ebneth, *Die österreichische Wochenschrift "Der Christliche Ständestaat"* (Mainz: Matthias-Grünewald Verlag, 1975), 22-35.

68 Richard Kromar, "Der 'Österreich-Mythos.' Die Funktion der Presse im 'Ständestaat'" (Phd diss., University of Vienna, 2000), 114.

69 Dietrich Hildebrand, "Was Wir Wollen," *Der christlicher Ständestaat* 1 (December 3, 1933), 3.

70 Hildebrand, "Was Wir Wollen," 3.

Hildebrand and the *Christlicher Ständestaat* conservatives expressed a worldview that was distinctively Austrian, anti-Nazi, and anti- "totalitarian", yet it was also antidemocratic and authoritarian, if not outright fascist.[71] They saw themselves as part of a broader European trend away from Enlightenment values, and they believed the time had come for the actualization of their mission. Hildebrand stressed his rejection of parliamentary democracy in favor of strong leadership (*Führertum*): "Not only is it the awareness that democratic parliamentarianism is an unfeasible state form, which must be replaced for a healthy political life to thrive, but it is also a true desire for authority *as such* in the state, because of the virtue and majesty that only true authority can establish."[72] While Hildebrand's authoritarian position seems unremarkable for Austrian Catholic circles, it nevertheless signaled a clear break from the Church on political matters. Just two years earlier in "*Quadragesimo Anno*," the Catholic Church expressed a willingness to work within democratic states for a Catholic social program, and it disavowed any attempts to challenge existing political forms. Hildebrand and others had defended this course at the time. By 1933, however, Hildebrand rejected compromise with liberal democratic forms and offered theoretical justifications for Dollfuss's actions.

Conclusion

This paper has shown a dialectical relationship between Central European conservative ideology and political developments in the years up to and including 1933. From the late nineteenth century, conservative Catholics developed a distinctive anti-modern worldview that was antidemocratic, anti-socialist, anti-capitalist, and antisemitic. It espoused authoritarian and corporatist attitudes and hearkened back to the Holy Roman Empire for ideological inspiration. After the Great War, the dissolution of the Habsburg Empire and the formation of a liberal democratic Republic precipitated the radicalization of this thought. Black Viennese intellectuals dreamed of the end of the current system. With the authoritarian turn of Central European politics in the late 1920s, and especially with the events of early 1933, these thinkers saw an opportunity to put their ideas into practice. They sought confirmation in the actions of Hitler and especially Dollfuss. Hence, we saw a remarkable overlap between the

71 See James Chappel, "The Catholic Origins of Totalitarianism Theory in Interwar Europe," *Modern Intellectual History* 8 (2011): 561-90.

72 Dietrich Hildebrand, "Autorität und Führertum," *Der christlicher Ständestaat*, December 3, 1933, 6.

ideas of the Austrian regime and the leading conservative thinkers of the interwar era. As events unfolded in 1933 and 1934, however, the direction of influence shifted, as intellectuals scrambled to keep up with the changing social and political landscape in Germany and Austria. They now adapted their thought to conditions on the ground. Sharp divides emerged between thinkers of a more German nationalist persuasion and those of a radical Catholic tendency. These fissures characterized the mid-1930s, as Austrofascist and National Socialist supporters vied for dominance. What was clear as early as 1933, however, was that there were virtually no conservative defenders of the First Republic, whether in the *Spannkreis*, *Schönere Zukunft* circle or the Hildebrand crowd. While individuals like Ernst Karl Winter would eventually seek accommodation with socialists and democrats, the First Republic died largely un-mourned in 1933. Rather than the suicide depicted by Gregor Uhlhorn at the beginning of the essay, Austrian parliamentary democracy expired because of willful neglect—if not active assistance—especially from Black Viennese circles.

II. Democracy Embraced in Cold War Austria(1945-1989)

1945: The Beginning of Democracy in the Second Republic

Anton Pelinka

In one particular respect, the history of Austrian democracy is a kind of enigma. When in 1918, in reaction to the military defeat of the armed forces of Austria-Hungary and in response to the establishment of Habsburg Austria's (other) successor states—like Czechoslovakia and the Kingdom of Serbs, Croats, and Slovenians—the members of the 1911 elected parliament of Habsburg Austria declared the "rest" of the old Austria to be a republic. The very name the parliamentarians chose for the "rest" of the empire indicated that this new Austria was in search of a specific narrative. The republic called itself "German Austria" and underlined its unwillingness to be independent. "German Austria" wanted to become part of Germany, of the German Republic, of the Republic of Weimar.

After being forced to stay independent by the powers of the Entente, the Austrian Republic succeeded in passing a democratic constitution—a democratic and republican constitution which, in the meantime, has become the oldest among the still-existing constitutions of Europe. But the constitution should be, more or less, the only great success of the "First Republic", which became replaced by the Dollfuss-Schuschnigg dictatorship before Austria became occupied by Nazi Germany in 1945. The enigma: The republic returned in 1945 re-established by more or less the same political parties, which were unable to sustain democracy before. And as "Second Republic", the democratic republic developed as a stable, liberal (pluralistic, "Western") democracy in the decades since then.

The success story started in 1945: External actors (the Allies) and domestic actors (the founding parties) allowed the democracy to flourish. Austrian democracy after 1945 has been the product of probably more unintended than intended cooperation between global and Austrian interests.

External Factors

The territory, which had been "Austria" between 1919 and 1938, was liberated in April and May 1945 by Soviet, US-American, British, and French troops. It was the authority of the Allied powers, which had to administer Austria in the last weeks of World War II. The Allies governed

Austria during the decisive weeks of April and May. But the Allies followed a script written and signed by the foreign ministers of the USSR, the US, and the United Kingdom in Moscow on November 1, 1943; the Allies had made the restoration of Austria as an independent state their official goal—Austria within the borders of 1937.

The "Moscow Declaration" was the result of the inability of the Allies to prepare a compromise for the Tehran summit concerning the questions seen as the most decisive ones, like the future of Poland and of the need to find a positive compromise at least in a question of lesser significance. Compared to the Polish question, Austria was of secondary importance. Concerning Austria, there was no principal clash of Soviet and Western interests. Restoring Austria became an undisputed objective for the Allies, because Austria was not so important—for the USSR, for the US, and for the UK.

In spring 1945, the Allies felt bound by the consensus of 1943. As a consequence, Austria was treated differently from Germany. Significantly, Austria was occupied—like Germany, but at the same time, Austria was seen as "liberated"—like Belgium or Greece. This created an ambivalence that allowed a significant freedom to manoeuvre politically—freedom for those actors who in 1945 were free again to act on behalf of liberated Austria.

But this freedom had its limits. To give credibility to the claim that Austria had fallen victim to Nazi Germany in 1938, Austria had to start an Austrian-controlled de-Nazification: by putting war criminals on trial (Butterweck 2016), by excluding all Austrians who were registered as (former) members of the NSDAP from voting, and by starting the process of restitution of "aryanized" property, a process lasting for years and years and years.[1]

Besides Germany, Austria was the only European country occupied and liberated by both the USSR and Western powers. This also created an ambivalence allowing Austria, represented since April 27, 1945 by the Provisional Government of SPÖ, ÖVP, and KPÖ, to use the different interests of the Allies for broadening the political choices Austria had to face.

After Germany's "unconditional surrender", the unity between the West and the USSR had started to crumble. It was again Poland, which played a significant role in creating and defining differences among the Allies. Soviet behaviour made the US and the UK suspicious, that the main interest of the USSR was to create pro-Soviet satellites in Central-Eastern

1 Robert Knight, ed., *„Ich bin dafür, die Sache in die Länge zu ziehen": Die Wortprotokolle der österreichischen Bundesregierung 1945 bis 1952 über die Entschädigung der Juden.* (Frankfurt a.M.:Athenäum, 1988); Stuart E. Eizenstat, *Imperfect Justice. Looted Assets, Slave Labor, and the Unfinished Business of World War II* (New York: Public Affairs, 2003), 293-314

Europe—independently from democratic procedures. In Austria, the Provisional Government, led by Karl Renner as "State Chancellor", was recognized first by the USSR. It was in the Soviet occupational zone, where SPÖ, ÖVP, and KPÖ had formed their coalition cabinet and declared Austria's independence, and at the beginning, the USSR had been so only among the Allies, which had recognized officially the Renner government.

It has been the USSR, which promoted the Renner government. Differently from the US, the UK, and France, the Soviet policy in Austria, like in all European countries controlled by the Red Army, favoured the establishment of broad "antifascist" coalitions. The US had a much less clear vision concerning Austria's immediate future.[2] This explains why the Western powers hesitated to accept the Provisional Government, suspecting Renner to play a role designed by the USSR. As soon it became clear that this was far from the reality Renner and the other non-communist coalition partners had in mind, the Western powers changed their attitude towards Renner.

The Western Allies used the Austrian government's interest to become recognized by all the Allies to formulate conditions that had to be fulfilled before the government could be recognized. One important condition was that an Austrian parliament should be elected as soon as possible. This condition was to reduce the possibility that the Austrian government would become too dependent on the USSR and to prevent Austria to follow the path in the direction countries like Poland and Hungary, Romania, and Bulgaria have already started under Soviet pressure.

Austria's secondary problem was solved quite easily: The Moscow Declaration included an ambivalent message. Austria was a victim of Nazi Germany—even the "first victim" of Nazi Germany's aggressive expansionism. But Austria was also declared co-responsible for the war and the war crimes of Nazi Germany. This ambivalence was correct: On the one hand, it was a realistic reflection of the victim's role Austria as a sovereign state was forced into by the military blackmailing on the eve of the "*Anschluss*" of March 1938; and, on the other hand, the enthusiasm of a significant part of Austrian society demonstrated during the invasion of the German troops was widespread in the Austrian population. Moreover, the participation of Austrians in the criminal machinery of Nazism was undeniable.

From the very beginning, from the "Declaration of Independence" of April 27, 1945, the Austrian government (first the provisional under Renner, then the government established after the November elections)

2 Oliver Rathkolb, *Die Paradoxe Republik: Österreich 1945 bis 2005* (Vienna: Zsolnay, 2005).

tried to convince the Allies that the second part of the Moscow Declaration's ambivalent meaning, the formula of "co-responsibility", should play only a secondary role compared to the formula of the "first victim". For that reason, the Austrian government assembled all possible facts and arguments in a document that underlined the "victim" role—and neglected more or less Austrians' "co-responsibility". Austria realized that the Allies needed such a biased line of arguments to treat Austria differently from Germany. Such arguments were not wrong but happened to be one-sided.[3]

And it worked. While Germany was administered directly by the Allies until 1949, Austria had a government two weeks before World War II ended—a government, recognized first only by the USSR, but soon also by the other Allies as well. Austria was treated significantly better than Germany.

Internal Factors

Accepting the Moscow formula of an Austria "within the borders of 1937" did imply an Austria as defined territorially by the State Treaty of Saint Germain—an Austria as one among other successor states of the Habsburg Empire. But this definition did not, automatically and formally, imply the democratic republic as established in 1918 and especially not the democratic republican constitution of 1920. The Austria of 1937 was neither republican nor democratic. It was of the decisive internal decisions that Austria was not only to be re-established within the borders of 1937 but as a democratic republic, based on the constitution of 1920.

Looking back, this had been a surprisingly undisputed decision. One aspect that played a role was Karl Renner's attitude to present himself in his first talks with Soviet representatives as the last President (speaker) of the last freely elected republican parliament.[4] For the coalition partner, Renner was looking from the beginning of his government-building activities in April 1945 for the Catholic Conservative "camp"; the return to the constitution of 1920 was less self-evident, at least on the surface. The Austrian People's Party (ÖVP), which defined itself as the successor of the Christian Social Party, was represented by people who had been active in the transition from the democratic republic to the authoritarian regime of the years 1933–1938. These were people that the political left saw as responsible for

3 *Rot-Weiss-Rot Buch. Gerechtigkeit für Österreich! Darstellungen, Dokumente und Nachweise zur Vorgeschichte und Geschichte der Okkupation Österreichs: Erster Teil (Nach amtlichen Quellen)* (Vienna: Verlag der Österreichischen Staatsdruckerei, 1946); a second volume was never published.

4 Karl Renner, *Denkschrift über die Geschichte der Unabhängigkeitserklärung Österreichs* (Zurich: Europa Verlag, 1946), 9-13.

the destruction of the republican and democratic regime enshrined in the constitution of 1920.

The ÖVP had to acknowledge that the geopolitical conditions of 1945 had been very different from 1933 and 1934, when fascism in its different shades was in the upswing, and liberal (pluralistic) democracy seemed to be on the losing side of history. As it has been the case in 1918, 1919, and 1920, the Catholic Conservative "camp" saw the necessity to compromise with the Socialist "camp", represented by the (renamed) SPÖ, the Socialist Party of Austria, successor of the "Social Democratic Workers' Party", to prevent the "greater evil"; communism. The KPÖ on the other side, visibly allied with the Red Army, had to respect the USSR's strategy as defined by Stalin in that specific period: not to alienate the Western Allies by alienating the other "antifascist" parties.

From its very beginning, the "Second Republic" was characterized by a specific form of ambivalence. There was continuity; the two major political parties, including their leading actors, were coming from the past. The constitution that the Provisional Government accepted as its legal basis was the constitution of 1920 (amended in 1929). The government's basic argumentation was to make the best possible use of the Moscow Declaration. For that reason, Renner, ÖVP leader Leopold Figl and the others acted on behalf of a sovereign state that had fallen victim to German expansionism. Now liberated, it had to be re-established.

But in contrast to this continuity, the kind of democracy that ÖVP and SPÖ were practicing was culturally very different from the democratic understanding prevalent in the years after 1920. ÖVP and SPÖ did not see democracy anymore, like in the past, as a ritual towards defeating as decisively as possible the other party. They understood, under the conditions of 1945, that they had to reconstitute democracy in form of a win-win situation. In a legal, constitutional way, the "Second Republic" was not different from the First. But democracy, as practiced beginning in 1945, was very different from the democracy of the period between 1920 and 1933-34.[5] Renner, Figl, and the other actors had learned that the best option for the Austria of 1945 was to restore the Republic of Austria; but to succeed as a democracy, the political culture, the patterns of political behaviour within the rules of the constitution, had to be a new one.

Soon after the beginning of the "Second Republic", a specific impact of external factors on the working of the three-party coalition became

5 Anton Pelinka, *Die gescheiterte Republik: Kultur und Politik in Österreich, 1918 – 1938* (Vienna: Böhlau, 2017).

important: the building of a coalition within the coalition. SPÖ and ÖVP established a kind of informal understanding, which excluded the KPÖ. The communists had tried, with the help of some of the socialist left wingers, to convince the SPÖ of a merger of the two left parties, a pattern that became a reality in Czechoslovakia and Hungary, Poland and Romania, Bulgaria, and in the Soviet occupation zone of Germany. Under Soviet pressure, socialist "Unity Parties" were formed that were de facto communist parties. In Austria, the SPÖ did not allow this design to be implemented. Soviet pressure could not play an overall decisive role, and in the Western occupation zones of Austria, direct Soviet influence did not exist at all.

The coalition within the coalition played a role in the planning for the period after the elections. With considerable US-American pressure, the first post-war election was planned for November 1945. SPÖ and ÖVP informally agreed that the party that would get the plurality of seats in parliament would be entitled to nominate the head of government, the chancellor, and the other of the two parties would nominate the head of state, the president. This was exactly what happened at the end of 1945: Leopold Figl, chairman of the ÖVP, became chancellor, and Karl Renner moved from the chancellery to the presidency.

The way ÖVP and SPÖ reacted to the November elections underlined the difference between the "First" and the "Second" Republic. When the elections of 1920 allowed the parties of the right, the "*Bürgerblock*", to govern alone, there was no significant tendency to keep the "socialist camp" in the government. According to the rules of a Westminster-style democracy, the Social Democrats became an opposition party, never to return to government until the very end of the "First Republic". When the elections of 1945 offered a similar chance for the ÖVP to form a cabinet alone, the party opted to go on with the power-sharing arrangement within a coalition government.

The three-party-coalition survived the November elections, despite the significant defeat of the KPÖ, which was able to win only five percent of the votes. And despite the overall majority, the ÖVP did win. But when the beginning of the Cold War changed the global framework of post-1945, Europe, and especially Austria's neighbours, became sucked either into the Western or into the Eastern bloc system. Austria, despite the still existing four-power-occupation, sent a strong signal indicating a Western orientation. By accepting the US offer to participate in the Marshall Plan, Austria opted indirectly for the West, as Czechoslovakia, still governed by a broad coalition, opted for the East. In Czechoslovakia, the USSR-pressure to abstain from participating in the Marshall Plan, the road towards a

Soviet-style, one-party system, became irreversible. In Austria, the KPÖ left the three-party-coalition.[6]

The way ÖVP and SPÖ followed from the beginning was a kind of de facto "Switzerization" of Austria: a democracy based on free and competitive elections but also on power sharing between the major parties, as well as by the organized interests of business and labour, by "social partnership". Differently from the years after 1918, the Austria of the "Second Republic" tried to become a second Switzerland—even before 1955, when the window of opportunity, opened by global politics, allowed Austria to become a second Switzerland even in the field of international politics. By opting for a Western political and economic system, without directly confronting the USSR, the policies of the coalition governments between 1945 and 1948 allowed the option of 1955: military neutrality combined with Western democracy.

"Consociationalism" was the way Austria defined liberal democracy, beginning in 1945: political culture that went beyond the "winner takes all" culture that had overshadowed the "First Republic".[7] The "Second Republic's" democracy, as exemplified by the long lasting power-sharing arrangements between ÖVP and SPÖ and between organized labour and organized business, was significantly different from the "First Republic". And, also following the Swiss model, Austria had lost the temptation to follow the example of major empires—may it be the lingering shadows from the past (like the shadow of Habsburg), or may it be the focus on everything coming from Berlin. The "Second Republic", from its beginning, had accepted its status as a small country.

Karl Renner: Bridging All the Gaps

Austria was able to make the best of the situation of April and May 1945. To allow the success story to begin, it was necessary to bridge different gaps, to overcome external as well as internal contradiction. For bridging the gaps, a master bridge builder happened to be there—at the right moment, in the right place—Karl Renner.

Karl Renner represented continuity. As member of the democratically elected Chamber of Representatives ("*Abgeordnetenhaus*") of the k.k.

---

6 Günter Bischof, Anton Pelinka, Dieter Stiefel, eds., *The Marshall Plan in Austria* (Contemporary Austrian Studies, vol.8) (New Brunswick: Transaction Publishers, 2000); Günter Bischof and Hans Petschar, *The Marshal Plan since 1947* (Vienna: Brandstätter, 2017), 63-69.

7 Pelinka, *Die gescheiterte Repubkik*, 33-34.

Empirical Council ("*Reichsrat*"), he symbolized the democratic potential of the old empire. As chancellor of the republic's first (provisional) government, he stood for the democratic beginnings of this republic, including the acceptance of the dictated treaty of St. Germain, which Renner had signed in 1919. As the speaker ("President") of the 1930 elected National Council ("*Nationalrat*"), he represented Austria's democracy before the Dollfuß government started its way on the slippery slope leading, first, towards authoritarian dictatorship and, then, to the annexation to totalitarian Germany. He was able speak for the respectable side of Austria's recent history—respectable especially for the Allies.[8]

Renner experienced the Red Army's march to victory in his Lower Austrian home town, Gloggnitz (an hour south of Vienna), in the first days of April 1945. He contacted Soviet officers and through them got in touch with Josef Stalin by exchanging letters.[9] It was Stalin himself who decided to make Renner the key figure in an attempt to implement the Moscow Declaration by forming an Austrian government. This created the impression that Renner was following the Soviet script of establishing a "*fait accompli*", excluding the interests of the Western Allies. It needed some weeks to convince the Western powers that Renner was not Stalin's puppet. It was Stalin who had become Renner's instrument.

The result of the bridges Renner built was a paradox. Countries, liberated by the Allies from Nazi Germany's occupation, which had been represented during the war by internationally-recognized governments in exile like Poland and Czechoslovakia, had much less to manoeuvre politically after 1945 than Austria, which was never represented by a government in exile. Countries, occupied by Nazi Germany against the protest and the opposition of the Allies (Czechoslovakia and Poland), fared much worse in 1945 and the following years than Austria.

Of course, this was first and foremost the result of the military and geographic conditions of 1945. But Renner's, and the following government's, bridge building succeeded in convincing the Allies that treating Austria favourably was in their own interest; in the interest of the US, the UK, and France, to prevent Austria from becoming dependent on the USSR; and in the interest of the USSR, which had to realize that the only alternative to Austria's indirect tendency towards the West (as expressed in accepting Marshall Plan aid) was the partition of Austria, following the German development. And this was clearly not in the Soviet interest.

8 Richard Saage, *Der erste Präsident. Karl Renner – eine politische Biografie* (Vienna: Zsolnay, 2016).
9 *Ibid.*, 304-313.

After having established the link with the USSR, Renner was looking for partners he needed to form a cabinet. He was looking for (former) Christian Socials, following the recipe of 1918. The republic must be founded on a common understanding between the Socialist and the Catholic Conservative "camp". Renner found his partner in Leopold Kunschak, who, despite being an outspoken and even vulgar anti-Semite, had the advantage of not being too involved in the Dollfuß-Schuschnigg dictatorship. Kunschak, soon to be replaced by Leopold Figl, a survivor of Nazi concentration camps, as the main representative of the newly founded Austrian People's Party (ÖVP), accepted the necessity of a power-sharing arrangement.

The third "camp", which played a significant role in 1918 and the following years, was the Pan-German "camp", which was discredited because almost all of its representatives had been members of the NSDAP. The role of a third partner fell to the Communists whose importance was based on their political alliance with the USSR. In spring and summer 1945, the great "unknown" of Austrian politics was the strength of KPÖ—their strength due to possible direct intervention by the USSR and their strength as a result of the elections.

Due to his behaviour in April, Renner had given the impression of being Stalin's man. The coalition Renner was able to form seemed to fit perfectly into the strategy the USSR followed all over Central and Eastern Europe: to back broad coalition governments and make them, step by step, dependent on the USSR. But as Renner was able to make a deal with the centre-right ÖVP, a deal that included the KPÖ, he also was able to start overcoming the scepticism of the Western Allies. The decisive point was the November elections, the defeat of the KPÖ, and the ability of SPÖ and ÖVP to implement far-reaching power sharing agreements, which de facto excluded the Communists. Renner may have been a pragmatist and an opportunist, but he was never "Stalin's man". He was a man who came from the past who had learned his lessons from the past.

In the summer of 1945, Renner still had problems winning over the Western Allies. The US, France, and the UK had to be convinced that Renner and his government were not following Soviet directions, despite the fact that the "Provisional Government" was established in April 1945 within the Soviet zone. The Western powers increasingly got the impression that Renner was not Stalin's stooge. Renner used his political experience and charm to win over the Western Allies. And by fulfilling the Western de facto condition for his government's recognition by the West—free elections at the first possible date—he was instrumental in the weakening of the KPÖ and, indirectly, of the impact the USSR has on the future of Austria's democracy.[10]

Renner's behavior in the spring, summer, and autumn of 1945 combined the external factors with the internal ones. His strategy was to establish trust between his provisional government and the Allies and trust between the two decisive internal actors. Trust on both fronts enabled Austria's democracy to restart.

The Elections of November 1945

The November elections were the first important indicator that Austrian democracy was on the road to stability. The elections were considered legitimate by all Austrian parties and by the Allies, and the results were respected by everybody. From November 1945 on, Austrian democracy was based on a normal political procedure. And differently from the "First Republic", the 1945 elections were used to deepen the political culture of power sharing, which was missing in the years after 1920. Austria became a "consociational democracy" in the form Gerhard Lehmbruch and Arend Lijphart soon were able to describe and analyze.[11]

Elections to the National Council, November 25, 1945[12]

Number of persons, entitled to vote: 3,449.606 *
Electoral Turnout: 94.3 %

	Percentage of Votes	Seats in Parliament
Austrian People's Party (ÖVP)	49.50	85
Socialist Party of Austria (SPÖ)	44.60	76
Communist Party of Austria (KPÖ)	5.42	4
Others**	.18	0

* Former members of the NSDAP (more than half a million) were excluded
** Democratic Party of Austria (competing in Carinthia only)

10 Günter Bischof, *Austria in the First Cold War, 1945-55: The Leverage of the Weak* (Houndmills-New York: Macmillan-St. Martin's, 1999), 43-51, 69-70.

11 Gerhard Lehmbruch, *Proporzdemokratie. Politisches System und Politische Kultur in der Schweiz und in Österreich.* (Tübingen: J.C.B.Mohr, 1967); Arend Lijphart, *Patterns of Democracy: Government Forms and Performance in Thirty-Six Countries* (New Haven: Yale University Press, 1999).

12 Andreas Kohl et al., eds., *Österreichisches Jahrbuch für Politik 2006.* (Vienna: Verlag für Geschichte und Politik – Oldenbourg, 2007), 715.

That the elections were already organized in 1945 was part of a strategic calculation, especially from the side of the US. The expectation was that the KPÖ, who controlled about one third of the administration within the "Provisional Government", would be diminished. This was exactly what happened but to an extent that surprised everybody (Renner 1952, 238). The results underlined the survival of the two major ideological political "camps". After more than a decade of non-democratic rule, the two major pillars of the Austrian party system were confirmed in their old strength. The KPÖ was defeated beyond the expectations of the Western Allies and beyond the expectations of the other parties. The visibility of the "Red Army", the dominant force in about one third of Austria, may have had an even counterproductive influence. The behavior of the Soviet armed forces was seen in an unfavourable light when compared with the Western Allies.[13]

In March 1938, practically nobody thought of the possibility that, seven years after being extinguished as an independent state, Austria would come into existence again within the borders of 1937 and based on the republican constitution of 1920, thus reviving the democratic consensus that had died during the polarizing years before 1934. But Austria not only regained its independence as a democratic republic; Austria redefined Austrian democracy. The elections of November 1945 demonstrated an Austrian version of competitive liberal democracy beyond the framework of a Westminster-style democracy. The Second Republic developed a democratic political culture different from what Arend Lijphart sees as the very essence of Westminster democracy: the clear distinction between government and opposition, of majority and minority. The Second Republic became, in Lijphart's terminology, a consensus-oriented democracy, blurring the difference between majority and minority by inviting all major political actors to play a role in a maximum coalition and/or in the networks of social partnership.[14]

The results of the November elections were also used to legitimize the administration of the nine states ("*Bundesländer*"). The states resembled, in their power-sharing procedures, very much what had been established on the national level. Republic and democracy were restored—on the national, as well as on the regional, level.

---

13 Josef Leidenfrost, "Die Nationalratswahlen 1945 uns 1949: Innenpolitik zwischen den Besatzungsmächten," in *Die bevormundete Nation: Österreich und die Alliierten 1945-1949*, ed. Günter Bischof and Josef Leidenfrost (Innsbruck: Haymon Verlag, 1988), 127-154 (here 127-137).

14 Arend Lijphart, *Patterns of Democracy. Government Forms and Performance in Thirty-Six Countries.* New Haven (Yale University Press).

The elections of 1945 were free and fair, the results accepted by all parties and all the Allies: by the Western powers, whom could see in the defeat of the KPÖ a particular positive result, and by the USSR, whom had been disappointed. But there was one important argument why the November elections were not just a long-lasting, permanent success of Austrian democracy: the exclusion of the (former) members of the NSDAP was the exclusion of a significant minority from the political process. Something must be done to end the political exclusion of about ten percent of the electorate. Soon, the coalition government found a way to deal with this problem, which, on the long run, must have become a grave democratic deficit. For the next general elections of 1949, most of the former NSDAP-members were allowed to re-enter the political process—with the exception of the minority of "major incriminated" former Nazis, high-ranking functionaries of Hitler's regime, as well as activists who had undermined Austria's independence illegally before the days of March 1938.

What ever can be and must be said critically concerning the ambiguities of the "Second Republic's" dealing with the "Nazi Question"; what ever can be observed about the "amnesia" in Austria concerning the Austrian involvement in the criminal regime which ruled over Austria between 1938 and 1945.[15] Despite all the short-comings, which were the product of political opportunism all parties were responsible for, Austrian democracy became a model of democratic stabilization: stability, compared with the fate of the "First Republic", and stability, compared with the development in the other post-Habsburg successor states.

Conclusion

The Republic of Austria had failed in its first attempt to stabilize democracy—democracy as enshrined in the constitution of 1920. The reason for this failure has been manifold. But of particular importance was that the founders of the republic and its constitution were unable, or even unwilling, to develop a common ground for democracy. Democracy was understood either as a simplistic "the winner takes all"; or as an imported, foreign system, standing in the way of "true democracy", enforced upon Austria by ("Western") traditions alien to Austria; or just as a stepping stone on the way to "socialism".[16]

15 Meinrad Ziegler and Waltraud Kannonier-Finster, *Österreichs Gedächtnis: Über Erinnerung und Vergessen der NS-Vergangenheit (*Innsbruck: StudienVerlag, 2016).

16 On the weak roots of democracy in post-World War I Europe, see Mark Mazower, *Dark Continent: Europe's Twentieth Century* (New York: Vintage, 2000), 3-40.

In 1945, the situation was significantly different. The victorious Allies decided to treat Austria favourable, and by defining its borders as of "1937", put an end to further speculations about the possible renaissance of the Habsburg Empire (e.g. in form of a "Danube Federation") and about a "Pan-German" solution (e.g. in the tradition of Otto Bauer's thinking). The trauma of the forbidden "Anschluss" was over, especially thanks to the reality of the "Anschluss" as experienced between 1938 and 1945.

The Allies offered Austria a new beginning. And Austria—again, like in 1918, 1919, and 1920, more or less defined by the representatives of the Socialist (Social Democratic) and of the Catholic-Conservative "camp"—was now willing and able to accept this offer as a second chance. The democracy of the "Second Republic" has been the result of the ability to learn from the political failures of the past.

That the Austrian democracy succeeded after 1945 has been the consequence of the combination of external and internal factors. Austria succeeded, and the significance of this success can be understood by looking at the fate of many of Austria's neighbours in 1945, as seen in "Year Zero"[17] . The post-World War II era signified the beginning of a very different road for Yugoslavia and Hungary and Czechoslovakia, namely the road to a Marxist-Leninist, one-party dictatorship. Not so for Austria. Austria was allowed to develop into a liberal, pluralistic, competitive democracy defined by free and fair elections. This freedom was the result of geopolitics. But, differently from 1918, Austria was able to make use of this geopolitical offer.

17 Ian Buruma, *Year Zero. A History of* 1945 (New York: Penguin, 2013).

Dealignment and the Rise of the Freedom Party and the Greens

Reinhard Heinisch

Introduction

The national elections of November 23, 1986 were a watershed in Austrian politics. Although coming within 1.8% of the Social Democratic Party's (Sozialdemokratische Partei Österreich/SPÖ)[1] share of the vote, the Christian-Conservative Austrian People's Party (Österreichische Volkspartei/ÖVP) missed a historic opportunity to regain the helm of the nation after sixteen years in opposition. It was the beginning of a dealignment and subsequent realignment in Austrian politics that would shape the two decades to come. All subsequent Austrian elections produced substantial center-right rather than center-left electoral majorities, a series of grand coalitions, and in 2000 the first conservative, right wing, populist government in Western Europe.

This chapter focuses on the rise of the Freedom Party (*Freiheitliche Partei Österreich*/FPÖ) and the Greens (*Die Grünen*) in Austria, both of which came into their own in the latter half of the 1980s. The repositioning of the FPÖ resulted in corresponding shifts by the major parties, which pursued a variety of counter strategies. Overall, however, their positions drifted to the right. Economic policies became more liberal, whereas social and sociocultural policies ended up being more conservative. This, in turn, provided new space on the liberal and environmental end of the spectrum for new parties to establish themselves, the Greens, and the Liberal Form. The stage for these developments was set in the second half of the 1980s during which the issues and themes that still dominate Austrian politics—ranging from European integration, immigration, fiscal consolidation, and de-bureaucratization to environmental protection and alternative lifestyles—entered political contestation.

This chapter first discusses the context in which these changes unfolded. It then provides an analysis of both the Freedom Party and the Greens during this period by showing their political strategies and policy positions. The conclusions draw attention to the longer-term impact of these developments for the current state of politics in Austria.

1 The SPÖ still called itself Socialist Party of Austria at that time but renamed itself soon after into Social Democratic Party.

The Political Context of Party System Change

In hindsight, it is scarcely imaginable not only how dominant SPÖ and ÖVP were in the electoral market place until the 1980s but also how quickly their support would irretrievably erode. In the first four decades following World War II, the country had de facto been a two-party system. More than 90% of the votes and seats in the legislature went either to the SPÖ or ÖVP. In 1945, these two major parties had reestablished the postwar democratic system in such a way as to minimize the political conflicts and partisan radicalization that had led to the overthrow of democracy in 1933. Central to the new consensus, democracy was a lasting, power-sharing mechanism between the Social Democrats, which the Conservatives dubbed "*Proporz*" implying the allocation of political positions in public and semipublic institutions and enterprises proportional to the parties' electoral strengths.[2] Over time, this system resulted in clientelistic insider politics leading to numerous instances of party-political influence peddling. In the 1970s, the power duopoly gave way to a decade of Social Democratic hegemony under Austria's legendary chancellor Bruno Kreisky, who achieved five successive electoral victories and three absolute majorities between 1970 and 1983.

Yet fueled by a series of major political scandals involving corruption, political nepotism, and excessively paid officials, political discontent increased markedly in the 1980s so that by the end of the decade, 43% (+10% since 1980) of the electorate had the impression that "politics is always or often failing to resolve important questions," and 68% (+31% since 1980) believed "politicians are corrupt and open to bribery."[3] As a result, 47% of Austrians at the time preferred "to see new parties in the political arena," while only 10% had favored this idea a decade earlier.[4]

The Causes of Dealignment

The Austrian Conservatives were assumed to be the natural beneficiaries of the SPÖ's dwindling popularity. As a result, the SPÖ sought

2 Emmerich Talos, "Entwicklung, Kontinuität und Wandel der Sozialpartnerschaft," in *Sozialpartnerschaft: Kontinuität und Wandel eines Modells*, ed. Emmerich Talos (Vienna: Verlag für Gesellschaftskritik, 1993), 11-34;

Randall W. Kindley, "The Evolution of Austria's Neo-Corporatist Institutions," in *Austro Corporatism; Past-Present-Future*, ed. Günther Bischof and Anton Pelinka (New Brunswick: Transaction Publishers, 1996).

3 Peter Ulram, "Political Culture and the Party System in the Kreisky Era," in *The Kreisky Era inAustria*, ed. Günter Bischof and Anton Pelinka, (New Brunswick NJ: Transaction Publishers, 1994), 79-95 (here 93).

4 Ibid.

to overcome this problem by forging a coalition with the pre-Haider Freedom Party in 1983, which would allow the Social Democrats to maintain the chancellorship while keeping the ÖVP away from government. However, the SPÖ's coalition with a coalition partner, such as the FPÖ of which was inexperienced at government and internally divided, proved to be something of a political albatross. However, the reasons for the dealignment between the SPÖ and its "social-liberal" electoral coalition went beyond causes such as the poor policy performance of their new partner FPÖ, which was being led by someone unable to fill Kreisky's large shoes and facing many new political issues.[5] More fundamentally, throughout the 1970s, the percentage of white collar workers rose steadily, reaching 42% in 1980. This social trend went hand in hand with a pervasive change in lifestyle and cultural values, which was not only undermining the traditional Christian-Conservative milieu and as such the base of the ÖVP, but it was also beginning to shake up the Social Democratic voter groups. While some had advanced to the new middle class, others found themselves as the losers in Austria's on-going economic modernization. Even middle class support for the SPÖ was waning as incomes stagnated or declined relative to expectations. Simultaneously, the sociocultural changes underway in Austria prepared the path for new political groupings and new political issues outside the fold of traditional Austrian party politics.

The Green Alternative and the environmental movement were the main beneficiaries. Only its initial lack of professional organization prevented the Greens from playing a more substantial role in national politics in the early 1980s. The Social Democrats were slow to embrace "the environment" as an important political concern, although it was fast becoming one of the hottest political issues at the time. From 1980 to 1985, the percentage of the electorate viewing the protection of the environment as a "very important" issue jumped from 55% to 76%.[6] The SPÖ's political program and policy stance owed much to the input of labor unions. These, however, regarded substantial parts of the Green agenda, such as the rejection of nuclear energy and the construction of new power plants as well as the opposition to expanding Austria's *Autobahn* system, as incompatible with economic growth and job creation.

As a result, the congruence in the political agenda between the SPÖ and the electorate began to decline at the end of the 1970s. Surveys clearly indicate a growing alienation between the ruling Social Democrats and the

5 Ulram, "Political Culture and the Party System in the Kreisky Era", 79.
6 Ibid., 94.

key constituent groups. From 1976 to 1985, the percentage of people feeling that the SPÖ represented "people like me" declined from 57% to 42%.[7] This sentiment was shared in several crucial population segments such as "middle class voters" (-16%), "white collar workers" (-7%), "families with children" (-13%), "employed women" (-11%), "housewives" (-14%), "pensioners" (-12%), and even "blue collar workers" (-6%). There was also growing doubt about the "issue competence" of the Social Democrats. The percentage of the electorate that considered the SPÖ most competent to handle issues such as "job security" (-18%), the "creation of new jobs" (-17%), and "the protection of the environment" (-11%) declined substantially.[8]

The growing dealignment in the SPÖ electorate between the mid-1970s and mid-1980s is evident also in the declining party identification among both blue collar workers (-18%) and people from Social Democratic milieus (-31%). Moreover, voters living in a traditional social democratic milieu were increasingly less likely (-31%) to identify themselves with the Social Democrats.[9] Moreover, the expansion of the welfare state coupled with recessionary pressures in the 1970s led to a rise in public debt and substantial tax increases for which the Social Democrats were blamed given that they had dominated national politics for over a decade.

The ÖVPs stood to gain from the Social Democrats' problems as middle-class voters were defecting from the Social Democrats and as the Conservative's neoliberal economic reforms and push for European integration were more in line with general political trends in Western democracies at the time. Yet the Christian-Conservatives failed in their attempts in 1983 and 1986 to bypass the Social Democrats. The SPÖ had in time replaced the ungainly previous party leader and chancellor, Fred Sinowatz, with the smart-looking former banker Franz Vranitzky, who projected leadership qualities and expertise in the economy.

Adding insult to injury, ÖVP leader Alois Mock, who had campaigned to the point of complete exhaustion, suffered a physical breakdown in front of a nationwide television audience on election eve. Having denied Austria's Kreisky a fourth absolute majority in 1983, Mock had been the ÖVP's most promising leader since the late 1960s. Under his direction, the party was not only poised to take the reins from the Social Democrats but was successful

7 Ulram, "Political Culture and the Party System in the Kreisky Era", 94.
8 Ibid., 95.
9 Ulram, "Political Culture and the Party System in the Kreisky Era", 93.

in reorienting national politics toward fiscal consolidation, economic liberalization, and European integration.[10]

Yet Mock and the ÖVP suddenly found themselves confronted with a new competitor on the right. Representing the nationalist FPÖ base, Jörg Haider, this charismatic regional leader of the party toppled the liberal party leadership in 1986. In response, the Social Democrats under Vranitzky ended the coalition and called for new elections. By repositioning the FPÖ as a middle class protest party, he induced 7% of former ÖVP voters to switch to the Freedom Party. A further 2% of conservative partisans shifted their support to the Greens.[11] Although drawing more voters away from the Social Democrats than losing to them, the Conservatives exhibited for the first time a problem that would plague them for the following fourteen years: their declining capacity to retain voters. Whereas in 1983, 94% of previous ÖVP voters had remained loyal, this percentage declined to 86% in 1986 and was to drop further into the 70+% range in the 1990s.[12] Thus, the ÖVP was shedding voters on both sides of its spectrum and facing a dealignment process of its own. The SPÖ had a similar problem but could count, for the time being, on the loyalty of older voters.

Nineteen eighty-six was also the year in which former UN Secretary General Kurt Waldheim, a candidate nominated by the ÖVP, was elected Federal President of Austria. Stung by the international criticism of the election of Waldheim—he stood accused of having been a closeted member of the Nazi party and a wartime intelligence officer in areas of mass deportations and massacres among civilians—many Austrians rallied around the embattled president. They had regarded the Nazis and the Holocaust essentially a German problem and perceived the foreign reactions as an attack on Austria's honor and sovereignty. In turn, this allowed Haider to criticize the Social Democrats for allegedly having leaked this information to the international media. Compared to the ÖVP, the FPÖ had fewer qualms about appearing anti-Semitic and soft on Nazism and was thus eager to rouse Austrian nationalist sentiments.[13]

---

10 Paul Luif, *On The Road to Brussels -- The Political Dimension of Austria's, Finland's, and Sweden's Accession to the European Union,* (Vienna: Braunmüller, 1995); Helmut Kramer, "History and International Context," in *Contemporary Austrian Politics*, ed. Volkmar Lauber (Boulder CO: Westview Press, 1996).

11 Christoph Hofinger, Jenny Marcelo, and Günther Ogris, "Steter Tropfen höhlt den Stein. Wählerströme und Wählerwanderungen 1999 im Kontext der 80er und 90er Jahre," in *Das österreichische Wahlverhalten,* ed. Fritz Plasser, Peter Ulram, Franz Sommer, (Vienna: Signum Verlag, 2000), 117-140.

12 Christoph Hofinger, Jenny Marcelo, and Günther Ogris, "Steter Tropfen höhlt den Stein. Wählerströme und Wählerwanderungen 1999 im Kontext der 80er und 90er Jahre."

13 Susan Howell and Anton Pelinka, "Duke and Haider: Right Wing Politics in Comparison," in *The Kreisky Era in Austria,* ed. Günter Bischof and Anton Pelinka, (New Brunswick NJ: Transaction Publishers, 1994).

This was the context in which the rise of the Freedom Party and also of the Greens occurred. Both parties were at opposite ends of a newly emerging political spectrum: liberal, environmental, and cosmopolitan on one end and traditional, authoritarian, and protectionist on the other. They would continue to cut into the dominant electoral positions of Austria's two major parties. The latter's decline in voter support and party membership, as well as their various strategies to respond to these new pressures, were the defining developments of the Austrian political system from the mid-1980s forward.

Table 1: National Election Results and Government Participation

		Political Parties					
Year of Election	Greens	Social Democrats (SPÖ)	People's Party (ÖVP)	Freedom Party (FPÖ)	Alliance (BZÖ)	Team Stronach	Liberals/ NEOS
1983		47.7	43.2	5.0	-	-	-
1986	4.8	43.1	41.3	9.7	-	-	-
1990	4.8	42.8	32.1	16.1	-	-	-
1994	7.3	34.9	27.7	22.5	-	-	6.0
1995	4.8	38.1	28.3	21.9	-	-	5.5
1999	7.4	33.2	26.9	26.9	-	-	-
2002	9.5	36.5	42.3	10.0	-	-	-
2006	11.1	35.3	34.3	11.0	4.1	-	-
2008	10.4	29.3	26.0	17.5	10.7		-
2013	12.4	26.8	24.0	20.5	-	5.7	5.0
2017	3.8	26.8	31.4	25.9	-	-	5.3

Source: Compiled from official election data/Ministry of the Interior
https://www.bmi.gv.at/412/Nationalratswahlen/Nationalratswahl_2017/start.aspx

Vote shares in % in national elections
Areas marked in grey denote participation in government

The FPÖ's Transformation into a Radical Right Populist Party

Founded in large part by former Nazi-sympathizers and war veterans in 1956, the FPÖ initially represented a German-nationalist but also libertarian and anti-clerical tradition dating back to the 19th century. It opposed Austria's post-war *partitocrazia* established by ÖVP and SPÖ. However, the FPÖ's radical right character locked the party into a political ghetto,[14] preventing it from forming effective organizational linkages to mainstream institutions such as labor unions and employer organizations. Polling around 5% in national elections, the FPÖ slowly gained political acceptance in the 1960s and 1970s but remained a marginal force overall.

In 1970, it supported a Social Democratic minority government in exchange for a favorable electoral reform, and in 1983 it formed a coalition with the SPÖ. However, government participation exposed irreconcilable differences between nationalists and liberals, allowing the young and charismatic Haider, leader of the regional Carinthian party branch, to take over the chairmanship in 1986. Subsequently, he transformed the FPÖ into a radical, right wing, populist party by adopting a relentless voter-seeking strategy.[15] The breakthrough elections came in 1986 when the FPÖ nearly doubled its vote share with 9.7% (see Table 1).

Authoritarian Leadership and Permanent Revolution

The FPÖ's move to the right went hand in hand with changes in the party's senior leadership, style, and political discourse. Haider's ascent to power in the FPÖ forced many exponents of liberalism and political moderation to "convert"[16] or leave the party. The transformation of the FPÖ into a tightly controlled "*Führerpartei*"[17] was so striking because the Freedom Party had previously existed as a comparatively loosely organized formation. This development was achieved not so much through major changes in

14 Luther Kurt Richard. "Die Freiheitliche Partei Österreichs," in *Handbuch des Politischen System Österreichs*, eds. Dachs, Herbert, Gerlich, Peter, Gottweis, Herbert, Horner, Franz, Kramer, Helmut, Lauber, Volker, Müller, Wolfgang C., Tálos, Emmerich (Vienna: Manz Verlag, 1995), 247-62.
15 Kurt Richard Luther, 2003, "The self-destruction of a right-wing populist party? The Austrian Parliamentary Election of 2002," *West European Politics*, vol. 26, no. 2, pp. 136-152.
16 Some former FPÖ liberals like Hilmar Kabas and Helene Partik-Pablé became loyal supporters of Haider's political direction and were politically rewarded.
17 Max Riedlsperger, "The Freedom Party of Austria: From Protest to radical Right Populism,"in *The New Politics of the Right: Neo-Populist Parties and Movements in Established Democracies*, ed. Hans-Georg Betz and Stefan Immerfall (New York: St. Martin's, 1998), 27-44 (here 30).

the party's organization but by making subtle adjustments in party statutes and by enforcing the political line proclaimed by the FPÖ leader through strategic alliances, as well as a system of deputies devoted to Haider personally. Party tribunals, loyalty pledges, gag orders, and the party leader's power of sanction over all members led to a concentration of political control in the hands of the top leadership of the party beyond what would have been acceptable in Austrian parties.

Under Haider, the role of the leader was redefined in the sense that the party became more and more of an instrument of executing the political direction announced by its chairman. Initially, Haider still depended on internal allies to consolidate his position. When this phase of relative toleration of dissent within the FPÖ came to an end, a mass exodus of FPÖ functionaries and former officials began. In 1992 alone, the Freedom Party shed two federal deputy party leaders, one federal party executive, five regional party leaders, and a large number of candidates and functionaries at the regional and local levels. In the same year, two of its previous national chairmen, along with two of its most important architects of liberal economic policy, quit the FPÖ. The departure of former FPÖ officials from both the liberal and the far right nationalist wing consolidated Haider's hold over the party.

Haider also took advantage of his access to the media and pursued a strategy of "jumping the gun" in terms of announcing policy positions and personnel promotions through the media, thus prejudicing decisions before they were internally debated and taken by the party. Because of his charisma, ideological flexibility, and election victories, Haider was able to count on the party's base, especially in the most important regional organizations of Carinthia, Upper Austria, Styria, and Salzburg. Thus, he was able to influence the selection of candidates and their ranking, often replacing internal critics with loyal supporters.[18] Frequent rotations of officials and periodic shake-ups of the composition of decision-making bodies added a dimension of "permanent revolution"[19] to Haider's FPÖ.

Strategy and Programmatic Positions

In the early stages of the FPÖ's drive for political power after 1986, the party was faced with several tasks. First, it needed to mobilize voters quickly and solidify the tentative support it already had. In response, Haider

18 Kurt Richard Luther, "Die Freiheitlichen," in *Handbuch des Politischen Systems Österreichs – Die Zweite Pepublik*, ed. Herbert Dachs, Peter Gerlich, Herbert Gottweis et al. (Vienna: Manz, 1997), 286-304 (here 290).

19 Luther, "Die Freiheitlichen," 290.

moved the FPÖ to the right to win back the support of its traditional, right wing clientele and take advantage of the ongoing Waldheim debate in 1986. Thematically, the FPÖ focused on public corruption and political influence peddling inherent in the *Proporz* system while defending the "war generation" and even praising SS men as honorable. Yet Haider had recognized that the hardcore nationalist fringe, numbering most likely fewer than 10% nationally, offered no long-term growth perspective but did play an important role in regions like Carinthia where the party was comparatively strong. As a result, the FPÖ did not want to abandon these interests and carry out a voter swap.

The resuscitation of the old Grand Coalition between SPÖ-ÖVP in 1986 provided the opportunity for Haider to attack the major parties by accusing them of moral bankruptcy and misusing tax money. This strategy meant that, for the foreseeable future, the FPÖ would have no opportunity to coalesce with either SPÖ or ÖVP. Thus, tactical circumspection was not warranted when attacking political opponents.

Verbal aggressiveness, gross exaggeration, and blatant disinformation became the chief weapons in the FPÖ's strategy. Their aim was the mobilization of voters by appealing to raw emotions and potent symbols. Haider understood that if it were possible to shape the affective dimensions of political discourse, neither rational arguments nor empirical evidence would easily undo the public perception of an issue. Meanwhile, the political rivals remained bogged down in the complex and dreary realm of *Sachpolitik* (factual politics), where torturous compromise, internal trade-offs, and the appeasement to powerful factions were unavoidable by-products.

A further element in the FPÖ's embrace of populism was the designation of "enemy groups" and "scapegoats." The key to this approach was to propagate notions of a sharply dichotomous society consisting of "us" versus "them." The former always referred to a "naturally evolved," organic community that was somehow threatened by the presence of the latter (the enemy group). Depending on the political circumstances, "the collective" could be defined at will as "Austrians," "Carinthians," "Viennese," or "decent folks," etc. Meanwhile, the enemy groups were either involved in conspiratorial activities against "the people" or advocated ideas that were outside that which the community considered "healthy," "normal," or "acceptable."

These multiple mobilization strategies were immediately successful so that, in the first election campaign the FPÖ fought under Haider's leadership, the party nearly doubled its voters (from 4.9% to 9.3%). Analyses show also that Haider was effective not only in attracting new voters but in retaining a relatively larger share of former FPÖ voters (1986: 65%; 1990: 77%) than the previous leadership under Steger (1983: 61%)[20].

The Freedom Party's effort to present itself as a new and different political force in Austria was underscored by a political marketing campaign that featured the FPÖ leader and his new team in the party leadership as vigorous and energetic. Physical and, in Haider's case, even sexual attributes became key elements in creating what one could call the political "brand" of Jörg Haider. Posing in jeans and with a naked torso in a sensual photo shot,[21] as well as in numerous depictions as an athlete, mountaineer, parachutist, bungee jumper, hockey player, and runner with the requisite sports paraphernalia, Haider fostered the image of a youthful and ever dynamic anti-politician. The FPÖ was particularly effective in reaching young and male voters. In the 1986 and 1990 elections, the FPÖ attracted nearly twice as many male voters as females.[22] Moreover, in both elections, the party performed best among the age groups of nineteen to twenty-nine-year olds.[23]

During this period, which we may dub the (middle class) protest phase in party evolution, the FPÖ attracted especially the better educated strata, for these were also politically the most independent voters with the fewest attachments to the traditional ideological camps.[24] By contrast, in later years, support for the Freedom Party among Austrians with advanced secondary and university educations stagnated while the FPÖ managed to attract more voters with lower levels of educational attainment. In fact, a comparison between the first (1986) and the last (1999) general elections fought by the FPÖ under Haider demonstrates the astonishing change in the demographic makeup of the party's electorate. Whereas only 15% of FPÖ voters in 1986 were blue collar workers, their percentage increased almost fivefold (47%) by 1999. White collar support, by contrast, peaked more or less in 1990.[25]

In the wake of European integration and globalization, the Freedom Party began modifying its political priorities. In doing so, it was careful to

20 Fritz Plasser and Peter Ulram, "Rechtspopulistische Resonanzen: Die Wählerschaft der FPÖ" in *Das österreichische Wahlverhalten,* eds Fritz Plasser, Peter Ulram, and Sommer Franz, Vienna: Signum Verlag, 2000), 225–41. See esp. Table 10 on p. 130.
21 Klaus Ottomeyer, *Die Haider-Show: Zur Psychopolitik der FPÖ*, (Klagenfurt, Austria: Drava Verlag, 2000), here 40.
22 Reinhard Heinisch, *Populism, Proporz and Pariah – Austria Turns Right: Austrian Political Change, Its Causes and Repercussion,* (Huntington NY: Nova Science Publishing, 2002), 118.
23 Ibid.
24 Plasser and Ulram, "Rechtspopulistische Resonanzen: Die Wählerschaft der FPÖ", 128-33.
25 Fritz Plasser and Peter A. Ulram, "Rechtspopulistische Resonanzen – Die Wählerschaft der FPÖ," in *Das Österreichische Wahlverhalten*, ed. Fritz Plasser, Peter A. Ulram and Franz Sommer, (Vienna: Signum Verlag, 2000), 222-243 (here 232).

maintain a degree of continuity to earlier phases. The enemies in the post-Cold War were no longer "Slavic barbarians"[26] but asylum seekers and labor migrants. Already in 1987, Haider had raised the issue of foreign workers in a series of newspaper interviews. This new direction first took hold in the east of the country given that Austria's eastern provinces were most directly affected by the dismantling of the Iron Curtain. The Freedom Party relentlessly emphasized that the waves of asylum seekers and immigrants put pressure on the housing sector and drove Austrians from their jobs. The FPÖ also claimed that German-speaking children were reduced to 20% minorities in some Viennese districts. This tactic proved so successful that in the 1991 elections to the Vienna City Council (*de facto* a state legislature), the FPÖ gained some 162,000 votes (22.5%; up from 9.7% in 1987), trouncing the Conservatives (18%; down from 28% in 1987). This was the first time that the Freedom Party had pulled ahead of the ÖVP in a statewide election outside Haider's home province. In Carinthia, the FPÖ had surpassed the Conservatives already in 1989, and Haider subsequently became (albeit briefly) state governor. For Haider, it was also a personal triumph in light of the fact that in previous elections, the FPÖ had gained barely more than 5% in traditionally "Red Vienna." Haider and his party could no longer be dismissed as peddlers of an antiquated, right wing ideology that resonated only in Alpine backwaters. The success of his aggressive strategy and the new programmatic focus vindicated Haider's change in direction, silencing critics within the party.

Increasingly, the FPÖ began breaking into the SPÖ's core constituencies in the industrial regions of Styria and Upper Austria by combining the themes of "going after welfare cheats" with the "dangers posed by foreigners."[27] In the fall of 1992, the Freedom Party launched its "Austria First" initiative, a part of which proposed a constitutional amendment declaring that Austria was not a classic country of immigration. The initiative advocated a catalogue of measures against foreigners, covering everything from education, health, public welfare, housing, and crime.

When examining the ideological positions of the FPÖ and its electorate, it would be difficult to distinguish clearly between a far-right core and a populist mainstream. In reality, there was a continuum between the extremist and anti-democratic fringe and those parts of the party that had activists and voters with mainstream, right wing positions. This has enabled the FPÖ to appeal to a large section of the political spectrum by subtly adjusting and broadening its political message. Data from studies

---

26 Riedlsperger, "The Freedom Party of Austria: From Protest to radical Right Populism," 31.
27 Riedlsperger, "The Freedom Party of Austria: From Protest to radical Right Populism," 36.

carried out in the early 1990s does suggest, however, that of all the parties, the authoritarian potential was greatest (70%) among FPÖ voters when compared with those of all other parties (SPÖ: 41%, ÖVP: 40%, Greens: 22%).[28] Likewise, Freedom Party sympathizers were far less likely to reject Nazism unequivocally (32%) when contrasted with other voters (SPÖ: 55%, ÖVP: 61%, Greens: 84%). In a survey conducted by the American Jewish Committee,[29] 41% of FPÖ supporters felt that Jews had wielded too much influence in world affairs (Austrian average: 27%), 36% preferred not to live next a Jewish neighbor (Austrian average: 24%), and 28% saw Jews as having too much influence in Austria (Austrian average: 17%).

By broadening the FPÖ's appeal, especially to blue collar workers feeling the effects of wage stagnation and welfare retrenchment, the party managed to craft a broadly appealing, winning formula combining welfare chauvinism, identity politics, Euroscepticism, and aspects of Austrian traditionalism to reach sizeable segments of both Social Democratic and conservative voters. By transforming the FPÖ, Haider created one of Europe's first radical, right wing, populist parties. Its main characteristics, like that of many similar parties that have since emerged across Europe, were nativism and xenophobia coupled with claims about an antagonistic relationship between a homogenous, virtuous people and corrupt elites. Ideologically, the party was voter seeking and thus undogmatic and flexible while it used unconventional stylistic and rhetorical modes of engaging with voters.

The Emergence of Green Party in the 1980s

The cultural changes under way in Austria made new and, by Austrian standards, unconventional forms of political participation more acceptable. From the beginning, the environmental agenda attracted a larger proportion of liberal and conservative voters in Austria, making the movement more centrist compared with their anti-establishment-oriented German counterpart. The Green Party came to benefit from this development. Although its overall party political impact was much less than that of the FPÖ— the Greens even lost parliamentary representation in 2017— they shaped Austria's environmental and leftist, liberal politics like no other party.

28 Fritz Plasser and Ulram, Peter. "Ausländerangst als parteien- und medienpolitisches Problem". *Ein Forschungsbericht des Fessel & GFK-Instituts und des Zentrums für angewandte Politikforschung*, (Vienna: Fessel & GfK, 1992), 46.

29 Gallup-Institute, *Einstellungen der Österreicher zu Juden und dem Holocaust*, (Vienna: Dr. Karmasin Marktsforschung, 1995).

A Green Camp Divided

In comparison to other West European countries, Austria had lacked a significant student protest movement that could have served as a catalyst for the kind of radical, new social movements that surfaced elsewhere. During the 1970s, there emerged a Citizen Initiative and a New Ecology Movement (*Neue Bügerinitiativ- und Ökologiebewegung*). It was concerned primarily with preserving scenic beauty and participating in urban planning but remained politically fairly moderate.[30] More fundamentally, the emergence of environmental concerns in the 1970s, especially in conservative circles, tapped into latent, deeply traditionalist sentiments dating back to 19th century romanticism.[31] The first massive manifestation of "green ideas" was the anti-nuclear power movement, which counted some 500,000 supporters during its peak and forced the government to hold a referendum on the future of Austria's only nuclear power plant.

It is therefore not surprising that, initially, leading members of the emerging *bürgerliche Grüne* (bourgeois Greens) were found to hold rather conservative and even profoundly reactionary political views. The idolized figurehead of the conservative Greens was the Austrian Nobel Prize winner Konrad Lorenz, whose earlier writings in the 1940s had shown a certain affinity to the Nazi ideology. Thus, a more leftist Green movement emerged exclusively in major cities such as Graz and Vienna with their larger, counter-cultural milieus.

Calling itself the "Green-Alternative List," it was mainly rooted in autonomous urban youth movements, student circles, and neighborhood initiatives pursuing alternative lifestyles and seeking to influence communal politics.[32] The early 1980s saw the rise of a genuinely alternative Austrian mass movement in the form of the "Peace Movement" and the "Third World Movement." The deployment of NATO missiles in Europe, as well as Austrian arms exports to Chile and other authoritarian regimes, led to a broad public debate about international solidarity, which raised people's sensitivity about foreign policy. Many of the political concepts developed in this context influenced the Green Party platform.

In terms of actual party-political organization, the first formal step from citizen initiative and issue advocacy to political contestation was undertaken in the city of Salzburg by the so-called *Bürgerliste* (Citizen's

30 Herbert Gottweis, "Neue Soziale Bewegungen," in *Handbuch des Politischen Systems Österreichs – Die Zweite Republik*, ed. Herbert Dachs, Peter Gerlich, Herbert Gottweis et al. (Vienna: Manz, 1997), 342-359.

31 Koppel S. Pinson, *Modern Germany*, (New York: Macmillan, 1966), 44-47.

32 Gottweis, "Neue Soziale Bewegungen,".

List). It gained 5.6% of the votes in the local elections in 1977, achieving representation on the city council.

The Austrian Greens adapted to the political context by linking general environmental issues (acid rain, nuclear power, clean air) with specific Austrian topics such as campaigning against the power and privileges of political elites and by attacking the excesses of the *Proporz* system. The first national Green Party, the so-called *Vereinte Grüne Österreichs* (United Greens of Austria/VGÖ), was a more conservative, middle class formation that developed from the anti-nuclear power movement of the 1970s. Both the *Bürgerliste* in Salzburg and the VGÖ rejected a far-reaching societal agenda and focused instead on limited reforms and policy issues within the established political framework. They were mainly opposed to the technocratic policies and progressivism of the Social Democrats, who regarded infrastructure investments in the transportation and energy sector as well as industrial development as important for job creation.

By contrast, the so-called *Alternative Liste Österreichs* (Alternative List of Austria/ ALÖ), which had formed in 1982 out of various local initiatives, particularly in Graz and Vienna, embraced more utopian goals and much further-going reforms of the state and society. Its tenets (ecology, grassroots democracy, pacifism, and social solidarity) were similar to that of the German Greens, giving the movement a more leftist profile. The bitter rivalry between VGÖ and ALÖ meant that both new parties failed to enter Parliament in the 1983 elections as each group obtained fewer than 2% of the votes. The ALÖ was itself split between the more Marxist-oriented, Vienna organization, championing the causes of marginalized societal groupings, especially minorities and immigrants, while the Graz branch emphasized ecological themes and grassroots communal policies.

The Breakthrough Years

The disappointing 1983 elections resulted in a period of reflection and reorientation in the Green camp. Subsequently, regional alliances between the two different Green movements proved successful so that in the province of Vorarlberg, a joint Green platform achieved even 15% in the state election of 1984. What followed was a period of public mobilization and consciousness raising. In this, the Greens received unintentional help by the SPÖ-FPÖ coalition government. The announcement to construct a large, hydro-electric power plant in the last pristine Danube marshlands east of Vienna near the town of Hainburg galvanized the environmental camp. Heavily supported by Austria's mass media, Hainburg became a *cause célèbre*, which not only united the different currents of Green activism but also reached far into mainstream society. When dramatic television images showed riot police and construction workers going after young protesters that were essentially defending trees during the Christmas holiday season, the Sinowatz government had lost the public relations war. Eventually, the SPÖ-FPÖ government cancelled the project.

Regardless of the merits of this case, Hainburg became a metaphor for the arrogance of political elites and in particular of Social Democratic policymaking. Aside from its political symbolism, Hainburg also united the two Green camps. The area along the Danube had once been the stomping ground of Konrad Lorenz, who now lent his name to a well-publicized petition drive for a referendum (*Konrad-Lorenz-Volksbegehren*) about the future of the Danube marshes. In the referendum campaign, a group of personalities emerged that managed to integrate many of the disparate elements of the Green spectrum. The subsequent candidacy of Freda Meissner-Blau, one of the figureheads of the Hainburg campaign for the 1986 presidential elections, ensured that Green issues and personalities retained their presence in the media after Hainburg.

The Green cause also received a boost following the Chernobyl disaster in the spring of that year in which, especially, Eastern Austria was directly affected by radioactive fallout. Nonetheless, the disparate groups and organizations found it at first difficult to unite in a single party. Thus, leading personalities from different corners of the environmental camp formed an initiative called *Bürgerinitiative Parliament* (Citizen's Initiative for Parliament/ BIP) aiming to enter parliament in the 1986 national elections. This project eventually resulted in a party-like organization bearing the name "*Grün-Alternative Liste/Freda Meissner-Blau* (Green-Alternative List/Freda Meissner-Blau), which received 4.8% of the vote in 1986, thus gaining eight seats in the legislature. For the first time since 1959, a fourth party achieved parliamentary representation in Austria.

Calling itself officially the Green-Alternatives (GA) after the party's foundational meeting in 1987, the Greens established themselves in Austrian politics. They represented a consensus of sorts between the various currents of the Austrian environmental movement. Nonetheless, the conservative VGÖ, once the biggest of the Green groups, was the major loser of this consolidation process. Their merger with the GA produced a split in the process of which leading members of the VGÖ even offered themselves to the Freedom Party to become the FPÖ's "ecological wing."[33] Despite constant internal squabbling and fractiousness, sometimes bordering on outright chaos, the Green-Alternatives managed to transform themselves into an important force in Austrian politics by attracting a steady following among urban liberals and young voters. In most elections, the Greens drew voters about equally from the SPÖ and the ÖVP.[34] Besides their modest electoral achievements, the Green's most important contribution was their influence on the national political agenda. Green topics have become such mainstream concerns in Austria that they were incorporated into the programs of all other parties.

Programmatic Orientation

While issues such as the privileges of politicians, as well as influence peddling and corruption in Austria's *Proporz* system, formed a cornerstone in the early Green campaigns, the appropriation of these topics by the Freedom Party saw a shift in the Green agenda towards social causes and the situation of foreigners and minorities in Austria. Despite the fact that both the Greens and the FPÖ rejected Austria's membership into the European Union, the mutual hostility between the Haider party and the GA, as well as the latter's emphasis on social concerns in the wake of economic liberalization, resulted in a political convergence between the Greens and the Social Democrats.[35]

Regardless of the relatively close political relationship between Social Democrats and Greens, the fact remains that the latter contributed to SPÖ-dealignment. As the Social Democrats were increasingly pulled to the right by their coalition with the Conservatives, political space opened up on the left, which the GA was eager to fill. Left-leaning liberals and younger, well-educated voter groups, who, in the 1970s, would have been likely Kreisky voters, were largely lost to the SPÖ by becoming regular Green supporters in the 1980s and 1990s. Despite its modest size, the Green Party has played a defining role in Austrian politics, both in terms of issue advocacy and grassroots mobilization.

33 Herbert Dachs, "Grünalternative Parteien," in *Handbuch des Politischen Systems Österreichs – Die Zweite Pepublik*, ed. Herbert Dachs, Peter Gerlich, Herbert Gottweis et al. (Vienna: Manz, 1997), 304-314 (here 309).

34 John Fitzmaurice, *Austrian Politics and Society Today – In Defense of Austria* (Basingstoke.: MacMillan, 1991), 110.

35 Wolfgang C. Müller and Franz Fallend, "Changing Patterns of Party Competition in Austria: From Multipolar to Bipolar System," *West European Politics 27*, no. 5 (2004): 801–35.

Conclusions

The 1980s were a period of massive societal change. Nineteen eighty-six was especially significant in that it saw the convergence and culmination of several developments. This includes the beginning of the transformation of the Freedom Party under Haider, the unification and entry into parliament by the Greens, and the formation of the grand coalition that embarked on structural economic reforms and Austria's integration into the European Union. Both Freedom Party and Green Austrians contributed significantly to the transformation of the political system. By projecting the different images of anti-party or anti-establishment parties, they were able to tap into the growing middle class protest culture. As a new political phenomenon, they managed to draw voters away from both traditional parties by appealing to former SPÖ and ÖVP supporters.

Although the trend lines in drawing support away from the major parties are astonishingly similar between FPÖ and Greens, the former have had by far the biggest and most lasting impact.[36] By the early 1990s, the contours of the FPÖ realignment were beginning to take shape. There was first a clear gender and generational realignment, in which younger male voters opted predominantly for the Freedom Party. Meanwhile, young women were realigning themselves more strongly with the Greens. A second realignment was that of the blue-collar working class, which supported the Haider party in ever larger numbers. A third such development came in the form of a growing cleavage between the exposed and the protected sectors of the economy. Whereas the latter remained loyal to the Social Democrats, the former voted increasingly for the Freedom Party.

Lastly, there was new value cleavage between increasingly libertarian and authoritarian voter orientations.[37] While the Social Democrats were forced to compete with the Greens, the Liberals, and centrist Conservatives for the former, the FPÖ had less competition in appealing to Austrians with authoritarian orientations.

36 Heinisch, *Populism, Proporz and Pariah,* 119.

37 Fritz Plasser, Gilg Seeber and Peter A. Ulram, "Breaking the Mold: Politische Wettbewerbsräume und Wahlverhalten Ende der neunziger Jahre," in *Das Österreichische Wahlverhalten*, ed. Fritz Plasser, Peter A. Ulram and Franz Sommer, (Vienna: Signum Verlag, 2000), 55-116 (here 99).

III. Democratic Diversity in Post-Cold War Austria (1990-2018)

Democracy in Austria in Comparative Perspective

David M. Wineroither

1. Pillars of Post-WWII Democratic Practice

Both Austria's First and Second Republic originated from lost wars. The country participated in two "waves of democratization" (Samuel P. Huntington). The second trial with democracy following WWII would take the shape of a fully-fledged power-sharing polity. What accounted for this intriguing switch away from centrifugal developments that had characterized, and eventually brought down, its predecessor during the interwar period?

Austria, like a bunch of other continental European countries, was a fragmented society along three major cleavages. The corresponding three major political camps (Christian-conservative, Social democratic/socialist, and German-national) operated along antagonist stances created by the "social question", the "German question", and the secular-religious demarcation line.[1] Unlike the First Republic, democracy prevailed over the storms of those times in the Netherlands, Belgium, and Switzerland. All three were characterized by consociationalism, which rests on four pillars of non-majoritarian practice among relevant political camps: (oversized) grand coalition government, mutual veto rights, proportionality in appointments, and segmental autonomy in running affairs within each strata/camp of society.[2]

In the Austrian case, the turn towards power-sharing was consequential of a basket of behavioral changes that themselves were based on rational considerations.[3] First, the disaster of the First Republic resulting in two dictatorships, more so than the concrete example of other consociational countries, paved the way for collective learning processes. Second, internal unity helped the Austrian position in dealing with Allied powers during the period of

1 Adam Wandruszka, „Österreichs politische Struktur: Die Entwicklung der Parteien und politischen Bewegungen," in *Geschichte der Republik Österreich*, ed. Heinrich Benedikt (Munich: Oldenbourg, 1954), 289-485.

2 Arend Lijphart, *Democracy in Plural Societies: A Comparative Exploration (*New Haven: Yale University Press, 1977), 25.

3 David M. Wineroither, „Vom Konflikt zum Konsens: Die Evolution des Konzepts der Konkordanz," in *Geschichte und politischer Konsens: Übergänge der Nachkriegszeit (1945-1955)*, ed. Maurizio Cau, Günther Pallaver (Berlin: Duncker und Humblot, 2010), 106-140.

occupation (until 1955).[4] This was accompanied by an instrumentalization of political taboos and cemented the myth of Austria as having been Hitler-Germany's first victim. Third, given largely frozen party competition thanks to the vast majority of party identifiers among voters, both remaining major camps, conservative and socialist, had to anticipate and fear that slight societal changes would lock in their minority status. With the stakes being that high, institutionalized power-sharing with somewhat guaranteed representation in government and veto rights promised valuable relief from political dangers.

That said, some of the foundations of the Second Republic's power-sharing polity and mentality are linked to more distant roots. Austria from the 1950s to the mid-1980s formed part in what, retrospectively, can be summarized as the golden era of welfare state expansion in Western Europe. The configuration of the continental welfare state type is based on cross-class compromise, essentially promoted by social partnership. This Austrian version of neo-corporatism can itself be linked to historical precursors in the region of Western Central Europe, as has been pointed out by Gerhard Lehmbruch.[5] At this crossroad, organizational traditions (guild structure) are met with consociational practice in the multi-ethnic Habsburg monarchy and traditions of state-interventionism.

Rationality, mentality, and tradition forcefully combined to create a comprehensive party state in a federal polity engaged in power-sharing. On the downside, these pillars of governing gave way to extensive clientelism and patronage. On the upside, they supplied and secured political stability, lasting economic growth, and a balance between fighting employment and inflation. Still, in the early 1980s, the word spread of Austria's *Insel der Seligen* (Pope Paul VI. paraphrased by chancellor Bruno Kreisky).

2. De-Austrification and Grand Coalition Governing 1987-2000

Power-sharing practice certainly had peaked during the 1960s and remained at high levels throughout the 1970s. By the late '70s and early '80s, it became apparent that continued large-scale consociationalism started to meet increasingly forceful structural challenges. Many of these challenges

4 Oliver Rathkolb, "Demokratiegeschichte Österreichs im europäischen Kontext," in *Die österreichische Demokratie im Vergleich*, ed. Ludger Helms, David M. Wineroither, 2nd edition (Baden-Baden: Nomos, 2017), 71-103 (here 81-85).

5 Gerhard Lehmbruch, „Die korporative Verhandlungsdemokratie in Westmitteleuropa," Swiss Political Science Review 2 (1996): 19-44. See also Herbert Obinger, „Das Staatstätigkeitsprofil der Zweiten Republik im internationalen Vergleich," in *Die österreichische Demokratie im Vergleich*, ed. Ludger Helms, David M. Wineroither, 2nd edition (Baden-Baden: Nomos, 2017), 395-420.

found a visible expression in the "critical" parliamentary election of 1986. In that election, the party system previously characterized by hyperstability got shaken up by the successes of two movement-type parties: left-libertarian Greens and right-wing, populist Freedom Party. The latter had quickly transformed itself away from an old-style, honorary party, representing the remnants of the old German-national camp, under new leadership.

More specifically, the formation of environmentalist groups pointed to the growing dissatisfaction with top-down, decision-making processes. Neo-corporatist policy concertation, a building block of consociational rule, proved largely unable to adapt to new salient issues arising from shifting or not-known-before cleavages. The "populist anti-statist right", on the other hand, capitalized on voters' discontent over political clientelism, patronage, and corruption.[6] Its young and charismatic chairman gave the party a competitive edge as the country was heading towards a personalized era of political communications and voter reasoning.[7] Speaking of the power of commemoration, Haider vividly engaged in the breaking of political taboos, including references to Austria's Nazi-past and German-Austrian relations.

How deep into the flesh of consociationalism and power-sharing did these structural changes cut? It should be noted that at the time consociationalism peaked, and the very concept started to resonate within academia, it had already lost its *raison d'être*; *Lagerkultur* and political hostility had been stomped "not, it is worth emphasizing, as a result of the failure of consociation democracy, but because consociationalism by its very success has begun to make itself superfluous"[8]. In contrast to consensus democracy, which seeks to protect (potential) minorities defined around societal cleavages, consociationalism targets the roots of societal segmentation through integration, compromise, and fair representation.

In this vein, the generations-old tight agency relations and affectual bonds between political parties and certain groups of society weakened considerably since the late 1960s. Continued consensus at the elite level, as noted above, resulted in depoliticization to some degree. More importantly, however, are processes of electoral dealignment and realignment throughout the 1980s and 1990s. Dealignment processes among core constituency hurt SPÖ and ÖVP, which were gradually turning into "public sector"-establishment vehicles of interest.

6 Herbert Kitschelt, Anthony J. McGann, "The Radical Right in the Alps: Evolution of Support for the Swiss SVP and Austrian FPÖ", *Party Politics* 11 (2005): 147-172.

7 Wolfgang C. Müller, Fritz Plasser, Peter A. Ulram, "Party Responses to the Erosion of Voter Loyalties in Austria: Weakness as an Advantage and Strength as a Handicap," in *Political Parties and Electoral Change*, ed. Peter Mair, Wolfgang C. Müller, Fritz Plasser (London: Sage, 2004), 145-178.

8 Arend Lijphart, "Unequal Participation: Democracy's Unresolved Dilemma", American Political Science Review 91 (1997): 1-14 (here 1-2).

Both parties had quickly transformed into catch-all parties (i.e. the ÖVP abandoning political Catholicism in the Mariazeller Manifesto) following WWII.[9]

On the realignment end of reconfigured party-voter alliances, the FPÖ became the champion of the blue-collar vote in the 1999 federal election.[10] After its initial shift to populist (personalist) anti-statism, the party had continued adjustments. Throughout little more than a decade, it replaced German-national ideology with Austrian patriotism and abandoned its relatively pro-European, integrationist stance in favor of Euroscepticism. Even more, the German-national camps' traditional anti-clerical positions disappeared in favor of "militant Christianity". Radical critics of key institutions of representative democracy, the party completed its adaptation of the preliminary, electoral-winning formula by forcefully addressing the arising pivotal issue of migration policy and identity politics in general. In the socioeconomic dimension, the Haider-FPÖ would partially (incoherently) move to the left, not least for welfare, chauvinist policy proposals. This basket cemented relations with large portions of blue-collar voters paving the road to realignment.

By the end of the 1990s, Austria's polity still represented a rather clear example of power-sharing politics despite pressure from below, outside (post-Cold War neutrality partially undermined by the EUs Common Security and Defence Policy, CSDP), and within the consociational core. In international perspective, it had preserved its status as "the country of corporatism"[11] despite some retreat. Mainstream left and right parties governed together, holding a shrinking but comfortable majority over opposition parties since 1987, a coalition-making pattern only to be found here.[12] Membership in trade unions and parties alike stayed among the highest in the entire Western democratic hemisphere. Key policies kept dealt with in a rather consensual fashion that secured low electoral saliency, including

9 Maximilian Liebmann, „Die ÖVP im Spiegel der Bischofskonferenzakten von 1945 bis zur staatlichen Anerkennung des Konkordates," in *Volkspartei – Anspruch und Realität. Zur Geschichte der ÖVP seit 1945*, ed. Robert Kriechbaumer, Franz Schausberger (Vienna: Böhlau, 1995), 253-280.

10 GfK Austria, *Repräsentative Wahltagsbefragungen (Exit Polls) zu den Nationalratswahlen 1986-2006*; GfK Austria, Repräsentative Wahltagsbefragung 2008. http://members.chello.at/zap-forschung/download/Analyse_NRW_2008_Plasser_Ulram.pdf (accessed 02.03.2012).

11 Franz Traxler, "Austria – Still the Country of Corporatism," in *Changing Industrial Relations in Europe*, ed. Anthony Ferner, Richard Hyman (Oxford: Blackwell, 1998), 239-261; see also Alan Siaroff, Corporatism in 24 Industrial Democracies: Meaning and Measurement, *European Journal of Political Research 36* (1999): 175–205.

12 Wolfgang C. Müller, Kaare Strøm, „Coalition Governments in Western Europe – an Introduction," in *Coalition Governments in Western Europe*, ed. Wolfgang C. Müller, Kaare Strøm (Oxford: Oxford University Press, 2000), 1–31; Ludger Helms, David M. Wineroither, „Demokratischer Prozess und Koalitionsbildung in der Zweiten Republik Österreich," in *Die deutsche Koalitionsdemokratie vor der Bundestagswahl 2013* (Baden-Baden: Nomos, 2013), 561-76.

the *Fristenlösung* of the 1970s that legalized abortion under certain conditions and an effective ban of nuclear energy. Welfare state retrenchment did not dismantle the consensual core of socio-economic policy-making—the Austrian, continental-type system, introduced as a cross-class compromise, is based on the insurance principle and engaged in moderate redistribution cross-class compromise on social and economic policies. A similar ambivalence characterizes the emerging late-consociational political culture in the wider public with a seminal international study resuming Austrians seeing "their government as having low responsiveness and their individual potential for influence as low in both an absolute and relative sense, this did not appear to lead to a serious feeling of dissatisfaction with the policy performance of the government."[13] Correspondingly, the Freedom Party, while advocating full-scale, direct democracy and experimenting with stripped-down party organization, succeeded as a rather conventional party outlet.

3. Majoritarian Rule? The Wende, 2000-2007

Following the inauguration of a black-blue coalition in February 2000, the new power relations demonstrated that substantial portions of power-sharing rule hinged upon consensus-seeking strategies employed by Social democrats and Christian conservatives, whether formalized in grand coalition government or engraved by other means to restrain majoritarianism. In contrast to the setting in her peer group—in Western Europe: Belgium, the Netherlands, and Switzerland—the Second Republic exhibits a staged body of power division with consociationalism at its regulatory center (as opposed to counter-majoritarian institutions provided for by the constitution).

Why is that? The argument runs from the number of underlying cleavages to party system format to constitutional framework. As Lijphart et al., have summarized, division of power may be organized in a different fashion, all of them coming with alternate consequences for system stability.[14] In Austria, institutionalized veto structures largely depended upon the will of the two dominating parties of grand coalition government. From this we can point to some sort of pyramidic relations between what elsewhere has been described as equal-righted pillars of consensus democracy in the observation, as well as preservation and re-establishment, of political power-sharing.

13 Samuel H. Barnes, Max Kaase, Klaus R. Allerbeck et al., *Political Action: Mass Participation in Five Western Democracies* (Beverly Hills: Sage, 1979), 490.

14 Arend Lijphart, Ronald Rogowski, R. Kent Weaver, „Separation of Powers and Cleavage Management," in *Do Institutions Matter? Government Capabilities in the United States and Abroad*, ed. R. Kent Weaver, Bert A. Rockman (Washington, DC: Brookings Institution), 302-344.

In Austria alone, consociationalism in the executive arena has a gatekeeping function for power-sharing decline, rejuvenation, and relaunch (if applicable).

Unlike in Belgium, the Netherlands, and Switzerland, not to speak of the cases of Lebanon, Northern Ireland, and contemporary Iraq, the number of societal cleavages to be politically embraced was low in the absence of vast ethnic, language-based, or religious minorities. This is reflected in the dominance of three ideological camps from the late 19th century until the late 1920s, when political antagonism characterized the scene with Social democrats/socialists battling the so-called *Bürgerblock*. This polarization aligned traditional cleavages such as labor versus capital, center versus periphery, and aspects of religious freedoms. Since the largely discredited German-national camp had shrunk considerably after 1945, the Austrian party system until the 1986 GE operated as a two- and two-and-a-half party system despite a proportional electoral formula.[15] This shares resemblance with the situation in Western Germany but contrasts patterns of party competition in consociational democracies.[16]

The majoritarian turn in 2000 quickly started to affect all three dimensions of consensual democracy: party-behavioral consociationalism, neo-corporatist tripartite interest mediation, and counter-majoritarian veto structures.[17] In the legislative arena, "speed kills" (famously paraphrased by ÖVP party whip Andreas Khol) became the blueprint of a new, conflictual style of governing that acted largely unconstrained by social partnership and other veto players in the political system's power structure. That said, in contrast to assertions made in many case studies of Austrian politics during the years of 2000 and 2006-07, assessment of this period based on Lijphart's framework signals a further move towards consensualism on both dimensions. The first dimension ("executive-parties") represents consociational features, including neo-corporatism. The second dimension ("federal-unitary") consists of the role played by counter-majoritarian institutions. This primarily points to the preservation of consensus and status quo as a windfall of missing coherence on behalf of collective political actors willing to fully implement majoritarian reforms. It does, however, also reflect upon limitations set by political opponents and aversion of much of the public to adversarial-style politics.

15 David M. Wineroither, Herbert Kitschelt, „Die Entwicklung des Parteienwettbewerbs in Österreich im internationalen Vergleich," in *Die österreichische Demokratie im Vergleich*, ed. Ludger Helms, David M. Wineroither (Baden-Baden: Nomos, 2012), 193-221 (here 209-210).

16 Alan Siaroff, „Two-and-a-Half-Party Systems and the Comparative Role of the Half," *Party Politics* 9 (2003): 267-290 (here 287).

17 See the summative accounts in Anton Pelinka, "Legacies of the Schüssel Years," in *The Schüssel Era in Austria*, ed. Günter Bischof, Fritz Plasser (New Orleans/Innsbruck: UNO Press & UIP, 2010), 320-338; David M. Wineroither, „Windstille oder Fahrtwind? Wandel und Zukunftsfaehigkeit österreichischer Konkordanz," in *Konkordanzdemokratie. Ein Demokratietyp der Vergangenheit?*, ed. Stefan Köppl, Uwe Kranenpohl (Baden-Baden: Nomos, 2012), 73-98.

The evolution of Austria's location in Lijphart's two-dimensional mapping of liberal democracies

Variable	1945-1996 (t1)	1971-1996 (t2)	2000-2007 (t3)	Tendency cabinets Schüssel I/II) t3/ t2
Effective number of parliamentary parties	2.48	2.27	3.14	consensual
Minimum winning/ one party cabinets (percentage)	41.4	65,1	50.0	consensual
Index of executive dominance	5.47	5.52	5.20	consensual
Index of proportionality	2.47	1.34	1.42	consensual
Index of interest group pluralism	0.62	0.62	0.75	
DIM I: Executive Parties	**0.33**	**0.26**	**0.46/0.481**	**Power-sharing**
Index of federalism	4.5	4.5	4.5	no change
Index of bicameralism	2.0	2.0	2.0	no change
Index of constitutional rigidity	3.0	3.0	3.0	no change
Index of judicial review	3.0	3.0	3.0	no change
Index of central bank independence	0.55	0.53	0.9165	consensual
DIM II: Federal Unitary	**1.12**	**1.08**	**1.99/2.00**	**Power-sharing**

Source: Arend Lijphart, *Patterns of Democracy. Government Forms and Performance in Thirty-Six Countries*, 2nd edition (New Haven: Yale University Press, 2012) for t1+t2; Gilg Seeber, David M. Wineroither, *Die Ősterreichische Demokratie und die vergleichende Politikwissenschaft*, Innsbruck 2012 (unpublished manuscript) for t3.

Note: One might object that the missing of updates for other countries in the sample distorts the dimensional scoring in the case under investigation. We acknowledge this possibility but neglect differences of sigma and delta convergence as effects on scoring are minimal. The first score revealed is based on Lijphart's (1999/2012) country values for period t1, the second refers to period t2.

It is important to recall that this majoritarian turn did not prevail for long in some crucial arenas and domains of policy making. The government during Wolfgang Schüssel's second term faced much stronger opposition as the SPÖ had accepted its role as leading parliamentary opponent. The chancellor himself preferred a coalition agreement with the left-libertarian Greens following his convincing reelection in 2002 but ended up in a remake with a much weaker FPÖ in order to preserve his reform agenda. Interparty relations and majority building in parliament clearly broke with consensus patterns from the past. But this change did reflect little more than the switch in coalition composition. For most policy areas, authors have resumed predominance of business as usual, albeit less so for key portfolios of fiscal, economic, and social policies, and reforms in the health care sector. [18]

Even more, the initially bypassed corporatist actors celebrated a partial comeback. In particular, the SP-dominated trade union demonstrated mobilization strength and organizational capacity in rallying against pension reform in 2003. Long before that, the government had started to shift away from its "speed kills" and balanced budget paradigm, now more and more closely following the electoral cycles. In other instances, the ability of the federal government to push through large scale reforms proved to be simply inexistent from the very beginning. Political and public resistance and organizational inertia could not be overcome in dealing with constitutional and armed forces reform. Federalism in a party state stroke back.

4. The Pendulum Swings Back: Grand Coalition Governing, 2007-2017

Social democrats restored their position as the largest party in 2006. Seven years of center-right government would now be followed by ten (more) years of grand coalition government against all odds. There are two main reasons for such a comeback. First, arithmetic weighed in, as in this pluralistic party system, only the cooperation of SPÖ and ÖVP at that time secured a stable majority of seats in a coalition of two parties. We have seen similar things happening in Germany since 2005. For the ÖVP, representation in government granted her a veto player position to lock in key reforms developed and implemented during the Schüssel chancellory. This policy heritage would only slowly fade with a first blow in 2008.

18 David M. Wineroither, "The Schüssel Era Today," in *Austrian Studies Today*, ed. Günter Bischof, Ferdinand Karlhofer (New Orleans, Innsbruck: UNO Press and Innsbruck University Press, 2016), 195-203.

More importantly, the outbreak of the international financial and economic crisis that started to hit most countries in the aftermath of the Lehman Brothers collapse in September 2008 activated long-standing, etatist patterns.[19] Crisis management through state intervention, deficit spending, and policy mixes rejuvenated social partnership. The wider public approved of these measures. It is not by coincidence that the tandem of social (Rudolf Hundstorfer, SP) and economic (Reinhold Mitterlehner, VP) affairs ministers became the focus of attention. Enjoying high levels of support, these two politicians, both latecomers in top-tier positions, now shaped as frontrunners for the highest offices: Hundstorfer in pole-position for the 2016 presidential election and Mitterlehner as vice-chancellor and party chairman challenging chancellor Werner Faymann.

Finally, the cabinets of chancellors Gusenbauer and Faymann did show appreciation of consociational history by symbolic acts as well. The SPÖ had been irritated by the ahistorical allocation of government portfolios during the Schüssel years. Specifically, the then-opposition party had criticized the fusion of labor and economic affairs (Schüssel I) and the Ministries of Interior and Defense being held by the same party (ÖVP, Schüssel II).

Pendulum swings and rupture were not characterizing all key policy areas. The immigration topic stayed controversial at both the elite and mass level throughout the last thirty years. Remarkably, the legislative output since the mid-1990s shows continuity instead of rupture. In fact, years ago Haider made the same claim, announcing the agenda of his notorious 1993 "Austria First" initiative, which had been cleared primarily during the years of grand coalition government before the birth of the "Wende." In other words, the SPÖ during the 1990s already had to pay tribute to the structural majority of the political right.[20]

In sum, political culture and the country's institutional landscape identified Austrian democracy as predominantly geared towards consensus-seeking past the Schüssel-Haider years. And again, on a number of issues that are highly salient, and that in fact are structuring party competition elsewhere, parliamentary parties are not campaigning seriously. This applies to the handling of nuclear energy, a whole bunch of sensitive governance of life topics, and, to a somewhat lesser degree, the legislative status quo on "pro-choice" versus "pro-life".[21] The evergreen of everlasting neutrality became salient in

19 For past instances see Fritz W. Scharpf, *Sozialdemokratische Krisenpolitik in Europa* (Frankfurt/New York: Campus, 1987).

20 Wineroither, *The Schüssel Era Today*, 198-200.

21 Simon Fink, „An den Grenzen der Konkordanz? Die Bilanz von Konkordanzdemokratien in der Biopolitik," in *Konkordanzdemokratie – ein Demokratietyp der Vergangenheit?, ed. Stefan Köppl, Uwe Kranenpohl* (Baden-Baden: Nomos, 2012), 317-334; Ulrich H.J. Körtner, *Wider die Tabuisierung der Hirntod-Debatte*, in Der Standard, November 15, 2012.

the EP election of 1999, as both ÖVP and FPÖ supported joining NATO. Both parties have changed their position ever since, with the ÖVP deeming the question "irrelevant", while the FPÖ, under new leader Strache , started to enthusiastically advocate the status quo.

That said, regardless of parties' repeated moves in building electoral alliances, constituents refused to reenact consociational routine politics. Voter-party interactions continued to weaken (dealignment) and eradicate (realignment) historical bonds between parties and voters. In the 2006 FE, strikingly, SPÖ and ÖVP underperformed among societal groups that had formed an integral part of their respective political camp throughout many generations. Low-skilled and manual routine workers abandoned the SPÖ, and free lancers and the petit bourgeoise turned their backs on the ÖVP.[22] Mainstream establishment parties became the natural habitat for voters sheltered to varying degree from (free) market dynamics: civil servants, pensioners, and farmers.

While the early 2000s unveiled the regulatory power of governmental composition, external shocks have accounted for the ups and downs of consensus-seeking politics more recently. In response to the outbreak of the international finance crisis in September 2009, citizens and political elites alike enjoyed a honeymoon of old-style, corporatist policy-concertation. Tides turned with the ebb of the crisis accompanied by the flow of migrant influx in 2015. It prompted the rise of the FPÖ in opinion polls but got reinforced by the grand coalition being increasingly unable, and unwilling, to identify and tackle lowest common denominators.

5. Completing the Wende? The Triumph of Sebastian Kurz

Parallel to reestablished grand coalition government (since 2007), both mainstream-establishment parties continued to lose ground in federal elections. The ascend of the migration topic removed the state of the economic as primary concern for many citizens. Heading into the election year of 2017, the FPÖ outpolled the SPÖ by several points with the ÖVP trailing in double-digits. In addition to the shift in issue saliency, SPÖ and ÖVP suffered from their establishment status. While conventional parties still prove competitive in dealing with movement-type competitors, it is a combination of mainstream positioning, catch-all approach, and an extensive record of government representation that blurs their fortunes at the polls.

22 David M. Wineroither, Gilg Seeber, *Right-Wing Populists in Austria on the Rise Again: The Winning Formula of Portfolio Diversification*. Paper presented at ASN World Conference, Columbia University, NYC, May 5, 2018.

While both acknowledged the task to transform their parties, it was only the ÖVP that managed to do so in a comprehensive manner. Discontent in the People's Party had been widespread, fueled by the gradual facing of the Wende-legacy. Unlike in the SPÖ, the party would almost unanimously rally behind Minister of Foreign Affairs Sebastian Kurtz, who assumed party leadership and a mandate to reform intra-party candidate selection.[23] He was then 30 years of age, having spent no fewer than six years in cabinet positions.

In order to enhance competitiveness, the party tried to combine the best of two worlds, thereby creating a hybrid of "party machine" and movement-type features. Mobilization in party-internal contests continued to occur through traditional party branches that operated without any restraint and largely decided over the fate of those running. Paradoxically, but unsurprisingly, primaries partly overrode the new formula of gender-balance the Kurz-ÖVP had applied to candidate nomination. Nevertheless, the ÖVP under Kurz's leadership enjoyed a fresh start getting rid of the blame that typically hurts governmental parties at the ballots. In other words, this transformation has been remarkable for successfully crossing (or rather blurring) the lines between a party's challenger and establishment profile of representation and accountability, combining the "best of two worlds" in terms of enhancing electoral competitiveness by augmenting "party machine" features with populist-personalist elements.[24]

Whether these changes amount to a significant populist swing is a matter to be disputed, though. The "ÖVP new" fails to engage in ad hoc style and cycling policy drafting. But party and leadership embrace anti-establishment sentiment: For one, Kurz, as party chairman and designated frontrunner in his election bid, refused to take over the position as vice-chancellor in the outgoing cabinet of Christian Kern; the party now would also push a tougher stance in certain areas of fighting crime, framed around widespread public disgust for sexual offenders. Here, as in several other drafts and pieces of legislation passed by the ÖVP-FPÖ-coalition government, proposals would meet strong resistance from constitutional lawyers and other experts. Most significantly, Kurz, in his attempt to distance himself from establishment and make a bid for leadership, circumvented Brussels' super-establishment of supranational coordination through bilateral and multilateral action on closing the "Balkan route" for migrants.

23 Quite a few elements of the party reforms demanded by Kurz had actually been initiated or prepared for during the previous two to three years.

24 For the depth of the establishment-challenger demarcation line across Europe see David M. Wineroither, Gilg U.H. Seeber, "Three Worlds of Representation: A Linkage-Based Typology of Parties in Western and Eastern Europe," East European Politics and Societies 32 (2018): 493-517.

Intriguingly, in the policy domain, the party reinvigorated the populist, anti-statist formula introduced by Haider precisely thirty years ago: strikingly liberal on socioeconomic policies (greed), tough on migration (group), moderately but consistently conservative on issues of socio-political governance (grid), and increasingly critical over any deepening of European integration. This package closely resembles the electoral-winning formula embraced by Western European right-wing populist leaders during the mid and late 1980s.[25]

What are the midterm consequences of the successful transformation of the ÖVP? First, it puts more pressure on the SPÖ. Second, its example might set a trend for other mainstream-conservative parties battling the Eurosceptic, nativist far-right. The idea of division of labor along party lines—one for the establishment, one for the challenger part—as exemplified in the current struggle of CDU and CSU and the quest for CDU-leadership, proved ill-defined, however. Arguably, the leadership element proved key in managing this transformation but was itself conditional upon certain prerequisites.

Third, the reembodied black-blue government enjoys a solid majority, the clearest in history, with the political right outnumbering the political left by almost two to one. It remains unclear where social partnership, the Austrian version of neo-corporatism, is heading to under similar pressure than during the early 2000s, less able to defend itself against a government better equipped than its black-blue predecessor.

6. Conclusion: A Case of Democratic Convergence?

Democratic convergence represents a key political development in the age of supranational integration and globalization. As such, it has been addressed in many diverse areas of vibrant research, stretching from policy diffusion over Europeanized party competition all the way to probation into the comparative quality of democracy. Surprisingly few studies, however, explicitly deal with converging democratic practice in a comprehensive manner.

Austrian democracy represents a pivotal case. As a (former) outlier of late-coming democratization and neutralization during the Cold War, it has come a long way in terms of convergence—denoted by the label of de-Austrification.[26] Mostly, convergence in the Austrian case took the shape of growing similarity towards all-European average profiles, for example, with regard to party state-related features and the ideological composition of

25 Herbert Kitschelt, Anthony McGann, *The Radical Right in the Alps*.
26 Anton Pelinka, „Die Entaustrifizierung Österreichs. Zum Wandel des politischen Systems 1945-1995," Österreichische Zeitschrift für Politikwissenschaft 24 (1995): 5-16.

the party system. In a few notable instances, the latecomer has advanced to become a trendsetter. This includes a voting age of 16, right-wing populist representation in government (hinting at "pathological normalcy"[27]), and possibly the transformational patterns of mainstream-establishment parties.

The shifts and drifts in democratic practice in Austria potentially form a role-model that mitigates in crucial ways against any equation of European democratic average with a notion of democracy without adjectives. Since the late 1980s, the Second Republic has become more similar to democratic practice in the bulk of European countries on crucial aspects of democracy in procedural terms and by looking at generated output. It has not, however, lost all of its traditional peculiarities; Austria has not approached European average by losing its adjectives of party democracy and neo-corporatism. In other words, on a range of issues, various sets of countries (peers) have themselves moved towards Austrian practice (i.e. due to rising party membership in newer democracies in Eastern Europe, grand coalitions in Germany and coalition government in the UK).

Austrian politics over the past three decades has been uniquely characterized by pendulum swings between predominantly majoritarian and consensus-based handling of political power. Arguably, this ability of adaptation has secured high levels of democratic quality, social peace, and economic prosperity in challenging times. In doing so, it contrasts developments in immobile, power-sharing polities (the case of Belgium) while also outperforming countries governed in Westminster style and the EU locked-in hybrid of compound polity and QMV. Time will show whether this pattern of alternation has a future. The Austrian polity might have sailed for a more asymmetric (imbalanced) configuration. It may, however, also extend into its hybrid status.

David M. Wineroither,
Senior Research Advisor at National University for Public Service, Budapest,
and Senior Research Fellow, Hungarian Academy of Sciences.

27 Cas Mudde, "The Populist Radical Right: a Pathological Normalcy," *Brandt Series of Working Papers in International Migration and Ethnic Relations*, March 2007, Malmö. https://muep.mau.se/bitstream/handle/2043/6127/WB%203_07%20MUEP.pdf (accessed December 5, 2018).

From Party State to Movement Society? Conventional and Unconventional Democratic Practices in Austria, 1974–2018

Martin Dolezal

Introduction[1]

Austria has long been considered as the archetype of a party state, thus of a democratic political system dominated by political parties. Such a political system is also characterized by party-based, conventional forms of political participation. In a party state, parties not only dominate the electoral arena, but they also tend to monopolize all channels of interest articulation and therefore minimize the role of civil society actors. Is this traditional feature of Austrian politics, which has also been stressed by several classics of comparative research, still alive, or has the process of "De-Austrification"[2] also transformed the prevalent patterns of participation? Drawing from the literature on social movements and protest politics, this chapter analyzes the development of conventional and unconventional democratic practices since the 1970s and explores whether Austria has changed from a party state into what scholars of protest politics have called a "movement society."[3]

Classic studies of Austrian politics have typically stressed the powerful role of parties and their affiliated interest groups.[4] Historians too have pointed at the dominant role of political elites or the state as agents of political change and underlined the passive role of civil society.[5] This particular constellation was often explained as direct consequence of the

---

1 An earlier version of this chapter was presented at the *Tag der Politikwissenschaft 2018* in Innsbruck. I would like to thank the discussant, Julian Aichholzer, and other participants for their helpful comments.

2 Anton Pelinka, "Die Entaustrifizierung Österreichs. Zum Wandel des politischen Systems 1945–1995," *Österreichische Zeitschrift für Politikwissenschaft* 24, no. 1 (1995): 5–16.

3 David S. Meyer and Sidney Tarrow, eds., *The Social Movement Society. Contentious Politics for a New Century* (Lanham: Rowman & Littlefield Publishers, 1998); David S. Meyer, "Movement Society," in *The Wiley-Blackwell Encyclopedia of Social and Political Movements*, ed. David A. Snow, et al. (Chichester: John Wiley & Sons, 2013), 783–785.

4 Kurt Steiner, *Politics in Austria* (Boston: Little, Brown and Company, 1972).

5 Ernst Hanisch, *Der lange Schatten des Staates. Österreichische Gesellschaftsgeschichte im 20. Jahrhundert* (Vienna: Ueberreuter, 1994).

turbulent development of the First Republic (1918–1933/34). While this period was characterized by open political conflict, including violent mobilization,[6] and even a short civil war between the Social Democrats and the authoritarian government in 1934, a peculiar system of consociational and corporatist patterns was developed after 1945.[7] These patterns reduced the political involvement of citizens mostly to taking part in elections, but until the 1980s, the system was characterized by a high level of output legitimacy. Comparative analyses pointed at genuine trust in political elites[8] and extremely high rates of turnout and party membership. The latter, however, was typically accompanied by low levels of active involvement[9] because instrumental reasons for party membership, namely patronage, prevailed.[10]

Since the 1980s, many traditional features of the post-war system have come under pressure. The electoral arena especially has dramatically changed as new actors, such as the Greens and, above all, the populist radical right, *Freiheitliche Partei Österreichs* (FPÖ), have successfully challenged the longtime dominance of the Social Democrats (SPÖ) and the Christian Democrats (ÖVP). Summing up the development with a focus on political culture, Pelinka observed a change from a "subject" to a "participant orientation."[11] Given this broad development, the following analyses explore how conventional and unconventional modes of political participation have changed over time.

The chapter proceeds as follows: After a short review of the movement society thesis, which serves as yardstick, I develop some hypotheses on changing patterns of participation in Austria. Then I introduce the data used for the subsequent analyses and present my empirical findings. The focus will be on the temporal change, but to complement these findings and to facilitate their interpretation, the Austrian case will be compared with a

6 Gerhard Botz, *Gewalt in der Politik. Attentate, Zusammenstöße, Putschversuche, Unruhen in Österreich 1918 bis 1934* (Munich: Wilhelm Fink Verlag, 1976).
7 Gerhard Lehmbruch, *Proporzdemokratie. Politisches System und politische Kultur in der Schweiz und in Österreich* (Tübingen: J. C. B. Mohr, 1967).
8 Samuel H. Barnes and Max Kaase, *Political Action. Mass Participation in Five Western Democracies* (Beverly Hills: Sage Publications, 1979).
9 Sidney Verba, Norman H. Nie, and Jae-On Kim, *Participation and Political Equality. A Seven-Nation Comparison* (Cambridge: Cambridge University Press, 1978), 58–60.
10 Wolfgang C. Müller, "The Development of Austrian Party Organizations in the Post-War Period," in *How Parties Organize. Change and Adaptation in Party Organizations in Western Democracies*, ed. Richard S. Katz and Peter Mair (London: SAGE, 1994), 51–79 (here 65).
11 Anton Pelinka, "Austrian Political Culture: From Subject to Participant Orientation," in *Austria 1945–95. Fifty Years of the Second Republic*, ed. Kurt Richard Luther and Peter Pulzer (Aldershot: Ashgate, 1998), 109–119.

small group of countries for which comparable survey data covering five decades since the 1970s are available. These are the eight countries included in the seminal *Political Action* study.[12]

Re-Visiting the Movement Society Thesis

Since about the turn of the millennium, research into political protest and social movements, the type of actor typically associated with "unconventional" modes of political participation, has been influenced by the movement society thesis.[13] This thesis, as well as similar concepts,[14] are reactions to the changing nature of political protest in established democracies. Contemporary protests, it is argued, are characterized by an increasing frequency of mobilization as well as by a growing diversity of actors involved and issues addressed. While contentious acts are still more often done by younger cohorts, men, and those with progressive or left-leaning attitudes, these differences tend to diminish: "[...] the last thirty years have seen a generalization of the repertoire of contention across age groups, from men to women, from left to right, and from workers and students to other social groupings."[15] This generalization has also been interpreted as a "normalization"[16] of protesters and protest behavior respectively. Other observed changes in the protest arena refer to the rise of non-state actors, including the general public, as targets of protests as well as to increasingly routinized relations between the state, often represented by police forces, and protesters who rather use moderate or at least non-violent repertoires. Finally, it is assumed that in Western countries, the acceptance of unconventional participation has significantly increased in recent decades. In an authoritative overview of contemporary research, Rucht interpreted this ongoing development similarly and wrote about a "multidimensional spread" of protest politics.[17] This "spread" refers to the already mentioned

12 Barnes and Kaase, *Political Action*. These countries are Austria (A), Finland (FIN), Germany (D), Italy (I), the Netherlands (NL), Switzerland (CH), the United Kingdom (UK), and the United States (USA).

13 Meyer and Tarrow, *The Social Movement Society*; Meyer, "Movement Society".

14 Friedhelm Neidhardt and Dieter Rucht, "Auf dem Weg in die "Bewegungsgesellschaft"? Über die Stabilisierbarkeit sozialer Bewegungen," *Soziale Welt* XXXXIV (1993), 305–326.

15 Meyer and Tarrow, *The Social Movement Society*, 11.

16 Peter van Aelst and Stefaan Walgrave, "Who is that (wo)man in the Street? From the normalisation of protest to the normalisation of the protester," *European Journal of Political Research* 39, no. 4 (2001): 461–486.

17 Dieter Rucht, "The Spread of Protest Politics," in *The Oxford Handbook of Political Behavior*, ed. Russell J. Dalton and Hans-Dieter Klingemann (Oxford: Oxford University Press, 2007), 708–723 (here 713–717).

increasing diversity of actors and issues but also to the growing relevance of transnational forms of mobilization, which he defines as an additional new feature of protest politics in the twenty-first century.

Such far reaching propositions on the salience and especially the specific features of political protest have naturally led to critical reactions in the literature. Researchers using survey data to assess protesters' characteristics, as well as the overall level of involvement, have argued that activism is still restricted to specific strata of the population. In the United States, for example, Caren et al. did not find a general increase of protest participation.[18] They rather pointed at the strong impact of a "social movement generation" built by those who were socialized in the heydays of the civil rights movement and protests against the Vietnam War. McCarthy et al. could also not find much support for the movement society thesis, but they highlighted a "stark contrast with trends in many Western European nations."[19] However, using cross-national data, Dodson did not find clear trends but rather reported mixed findings.[20] Other researchers have indeed found patterns of change, such as reduced gender differences between activists and non-activists, but they also stressed patterns of stability, such as stratification based on education.[21] With respect to ideology, Van der Meer et al. found activism in the protest arena to be still associated with left-wing attitudes, irrespective of contextual factors.[22]

Studies on the number and characteristics of protest events, the other major research tradition in this field, also point at some deviant patterns. Starting again with the United States, Soule and Earl stressed that the movement society thesis is correct as it regards, for example, an increase

---

18 Neal Caren, Raj Andrew Ghoshal, and Vanesa Ribas, "A Social Movement Generation: Cohort and Period Trends in Protest Attendance and Petition Signing," *American Sociological Review* 76, no. 1 (2011): 125–151.

19 John D. McCarthy, Patrick Rafail, and Ashley Gromis, "Recent Trends in Public Protest in the United States: The Social Movement Society Thesis Revisited," in *The Future of Social Movement Research. Dynamics, Mechanisms, and Processes*, ed. Jacquelien Stekelenburg, Conny Roggeband, and Bert Klandermans (Minneapolis: University of Minnesota Press, 2013), 369–396 (here 369).

20 Kyle Dodson, "The Movement Society in Comparative Perspective," *Mobilization* 16, no. 4 (2011): 475–494.

21 Dietlind Stolle and Marc Hooghe, "Shifting Inequalities. Patterns of Exclusion and Inclusion in Emerging Forms of Political Participation," *European Societies* 13, no. 1 (2011): 119–142; Sofie Marien, Marc Hooghe, and Ellen Quintelier, "Inequalities in Non-Institutionalised Forms of Political Participation: A Multi-Level Analysis of 25 Countries," *Political Studies* 58, no. 2 (2010): 187–213.

22 Tom W. G. van der Meer, Jan van Deth, and Peer L. H. Scheepers, "The Politicized Participant. Ideology and Political Action in 20 Democracies," *Comparative Political Studies* 42, no. 11 (2009): 1426–1457.

in the claims expressed.[23] Other components of the thesis, such as a rising number of protests, they could not validate. For France, by contrast, Mayer reported rising levels of mobilization.[24] But with respect to the characteristics of these protests, her findings did not support the thesis (which she did not mention) because class-based protests prevailed, and protest events were mainly organized within the boundaries of the nation state. The dominant role of traditional, class-based issues and organizations was also emphasized when analyzing protests against austerity measures in Southern Europe after the great recession.[25] However, in a recent overview of the general development of protests in Germany since the 1980s, Rucht and Teune observed more diversity of actors and issues.[26]

The Austrian case has so far not been explored with respect to the movement society thesis or related concepts of a "normalization" of protest. In general, this country has not featured prominently in studies on protest politics or social movements and was, for example, not included in a recent overview of research in Europe.[27] Extant research on protest politics in Austria has most often focused on specific issues and actors and less on the general development. In recent years, scholars have above all explored protests associated with the migration issue and students' protests against reforms at universities.[28] Earlier studies had often dealt with various branches of the environmental movement and their

23 Sarah A. Soule and Jennifer Earl, "A Movement Society Evaluated: Collective Protest in the United States, 1960–1986," *Mobilization* 10, no. 3 (2005): 345–364.

24 Nonna Mayer, "The 'Contentious French' Revisited," in *The Future of Social Movement Research. Dynamics, Mechanisms, and Processes*, ed. Jacquelien Stekelenburg, Conny Roggeband, and Bert Klandermans (Minneapolis: University of Minnesota Press, 2013), 397–418.

25 Guya Accornero and Pedro Ramos Pinto, "'Mild Mannered'? Protest and Mobilisation in Portugal under Austerity, 2010–2013," *West European Politics* 38, no. 3 (2015): 491–515.

26 Dieter Rucht and Simon Teune, "Einleitung: Das Protestgeschehen in der Bundesrepublik seit den 1980er Jahren zwischen Kontinuität und Wandel," in *Protest in Bewegung? Zum Wandel von Bedingungen, Formen und Effekten politischen Protests* (= Leviathan Sonderband 33/2017), ed. Priska Daphi, et al. (Baden-Baden: Nomos, 2017), 9–33.

27 Olivier Fillieule and Guya Accornero, eds., *Social Movement Studies in Europe. The State of the Art* (New York: Berghahn, 2016). Almost 30 years ago, by contrast, Austria was included in a similar volume; see Anton Pelinka, "The Study of Social Movements in Austria," in *Research on Social Movements. The State of the Art in Western Europe and the USA*, ed. Dieter Rucht (Frankfurt: Campus Verlag, 1991), 230–246.

28 Miriam Haselbacher and Sieglinde Rosenberger, "Protests against the Reception of Asylum Seekers in Austria," in *Protest Movements in Asylum and Deportation*, ed. Sieglinde Rosenberger, Verena Stern, and Nina Merhaut (Cham: Springer Open, 2018), 247–269; Axel Maireder and Christian Schwarzenegger, "A Movement of Connected Individuals. Social Media in the Austrian Student Protests 2009," *Information, Communication & Society* 15, no. 2 (2012): 171–195.

successful opposition to nuclear power or the use of genetically modified organisms (GMOs) in agriculture.[29] Apart from some publications by movement activists,[30] Dolezal and Hutter's study of the Austrian protest arena covering the development from 1975 to 2005 has remained the sole exception.[31]

Hypotheses

The presumed change towards a movement society is related to various features of political participation and the nature of the protest arena respectively. For reasons of space, the present analysis focuses on three features: 1) the relative importance of unconventional participation, 2) the socio-structural and ideological characteristics of protesters, and 3) the variety of issues addressed in the protest arena.

Starting with the most general and perhaps most important development associated with the establishment of a movement society, Hypotheses 1 (H1) and 2 (H2) refer to the amount of political participation. Here, the movement society thesis is mainly interested in the unconventional part so that a stable, or even rising, development of conventional participation is theoretically possible. Given that resources of time and energy are limited, a zero-sum relationship between conventional and unconventional forms might be a realistic interpretation. However, we know that, at least on the individual level, protest activism typically supplements and does not replace conventional modes, such as voting and involvement in political parties. I nevertheless expect that conventional or institutionalized forms of participation have decreased (H1) and that unconventional or non-institutionalized forms of participation have increased over time (H2).

According to the movement society thesis and related concepts, the profile of activists has become more similar to the general population. This refers, first, to the socio-structural characteristics of activists: Former differences based on age, gender, and education should decrease (H3). In addition

29 Max Preglau, "The State and the Anti-Nuclear Power Movement in Austria," in *States and Anti-Nuclear Movements*, ed. Helena Flam (Edinburgh: Edinburgh University Press, 1994), 37–69; Franz Seifert, "Consensual NIMBYs, Contentious NIABYs: Explaining Contrasting Forms of Farmers' GMO Opposition in Austria and France," *Sociologia Ruralis* 49, no. 1 (2009): 20–40.

30 Robert Foltin, *Und wir bewegen uns doch. Soziale Bewegungen in Österreich* (Vienna: edition grundrisse, 2004); id., *Und wir bewegen uns noch. Zur jüngeren Geschichte sozialer Bewegungen in Österreich* (Vienna: Mandelbaum, 2011).

31 Martin Dolezal and Swen Hutter, "Konsensdemokratie unter Druck? Politischer Protest in Österreich, 1975–2005," *Österreichische Zeitschrift für Politikwissenschaft* 36, no. 3 (2007): 338–352.

to these features, ideological differences between activists and non-activists should also decline over time (H4).

The third proposition of the movement society thesis explored in this study is concerned with the issues addressed in the protest arena. As explained above, the thesis expects more diversity, thus a declining concentration of topics typically associated with protests, such as environmental concerns or women's rights. I therefore expect the issues addressed to become more heterogeneous over time and to cover now (almost) all policy fields (H5).

Data

The following analyses are based on two types of data used by scholars of protest politics: mass surveys and protest event data. Both have their merits—but also their limits.

Survey data are the main source to compare the amount of participation over time and space and even more so to explore the socio-structural and ideological profile of activists. Since the 1970s, data on unconventional participation have been collected in numerous national and several international studies. A comparatively small but nevertheless important change in the typical question format used hinders temporal and spatial comparisons, unfortunately: Earlier studies have asked whether someone has *ever* taken part in a particular type of unconventional mobilization (e.g. a demonstration). Recent studies, by contrast, typically ask whether someone has participated during the last twelve or so months. The major disadvantage of the survey method, however, is the lack of contextual information. We do not know in what kind of protest event people took part and which concern they addressed. Core elements of the movement society thesis are therefore difficult to explore.

Protest event data do provide information on the issues addressed as well as on the organizers of protests and other contextual information, such as reactions by the state, but they cannot explore the characteristics of individual participants.[32] To collect these data, researchers have used various sources that can be grouped into two broad categories: mass media (most often quality newspapers) and police data. Naturally, no source covers all protests that happen in a country or other territorial unit. The problem of selection bias, i.e. the specific chance that an event is reported by media

32 Ruud Koopmans and Dieter Rucht, "Protest Event Analysis," in *Methods of Social Movement Research*, ed. Bert Klandermans and Suzanne Staggenborg (Minneapolis: University of Minnesota Press, 2002), 231–259.

(or noticed by the police) and thus becomes known to the researcher, is therefore a major issue.[33]

To capture the amount of protest and the profile of activists based on survey data, I focus on three forms of unconventional participation: signing petitions, taking part in demonstrations, and boycotting products. In recent years, many researchers have vehemently argued for also including political consumerism into participation studies, not least to account for gender-specific differences.[34] In addition to boycotts, the classic negative form of political consumerism, "buycotts" have also been included in current surveys, typically by reformulating the original item so that these two types are no longer distinguishable. Buying articles for various political or ethical reasons has certainly become a widespread phenomenon in Western societies. However, this tends to inflate any measurement of unconventional political participation. All survey data on political consumerism included in the following analyses are therefore related to boycotts only. Moreover, all survey data on activism are based on the traditional "ever done" question format, which was the only format used until the 1990s. The surveys chosen for the present chapter are, above all, the *Political Action* data set and four waves of the EVS (*European Values Study*), including the pre-release of the EVS 2017 as published in December 2018.[35] Additional individual-level data are taken from the WVS (*World Values Survey*) and the SSÖ (*Sozialer Survey Österreich*) as well as from the literature.

The protest event data combine results from a comparative project[36] with first results from an ongoing project on political protest in Austria by the author.[37] Two methodological differences must be considered: The older project used quality newspapers (Austria: *Die Presse*) as source and sampled Monday issues only. This was a typical procedure in the pre-online or pre-digital period when the selection of articles had to be done manually by flicking through thousands of pages. The current project, by contrast, does not apply sample days, as it makes use of electronic full-text-search. As source, it does not employ newspaper articles but reports by the Austrian news agency, APA.

33 Jennifer Earl et al., "The Use of Newspaper Data in the Study of Collective Action," *Annual Review of Sociology* 30 (2004): 65–80.
34 Dietlind Stolle, Marc Hooghe, and Michele Micheletti, "Politics in the Supermarket: Political Consumerism as a Form of Political Participation," *International Political Science Review* 26, no. 3 (2005): 245–269.
35 This pre-release, unfortunately, does not yet include weighting variables.
36 Hanspeter Kriesi et al., *Political Conflict in Western Europe* (Cambridge: Cambridge University Press, 2012); Dolezal and Hutter, "Konsensdemokratie unter Druck?".
37 *The Austrian Protest Arena in the 21st Century: Issues, Actors, Targets, and Repertoires;* Austrian Science Fund FWF (Project 28180).

Data on conventional participation include official results of turnout in national elections provided by IDEA, the *International Institute for Democracy and Electoral Assistance*,[38] and survey figures on party membership quoted in the literature or taken from additional surveys such as the ESS (*European Social Survey*) and the ISSP (*International Social Survey Programme*). Naturally, membership differs from active participation in parties, but the latter is rarely asked in (international) surveys. To assess the level of party membership, scholars have also used figures provided by the parties.[39] However, these figures are not always reliable since parties use different definitions of membership and tend to over-report.[40]

Figure 1: Conventional Participation: Turnout in National Elections and Rates of Party Membership, 1945–2018 (percent)

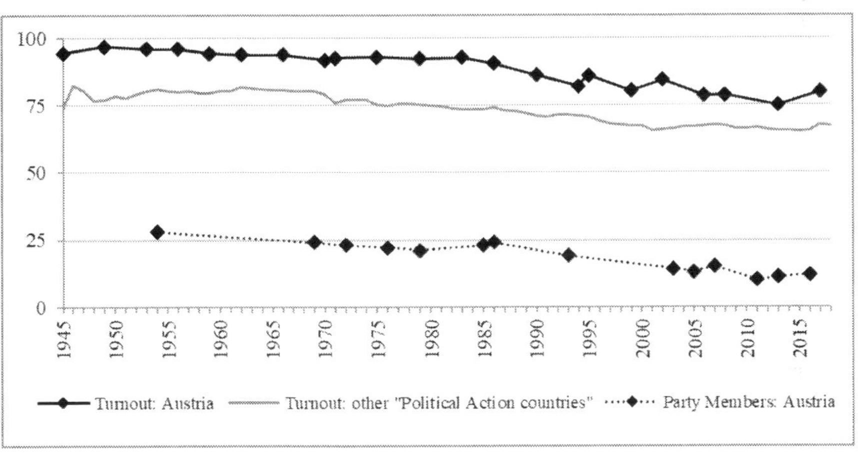

Sources: IDEA Voter Turnout Database. Party members: 1954 Peter A. Ulram, "Politische Kultur der Bevölkerung," in *Politik in Österreich*, ed. Herbert Dachs et al. (Vienna: Manz, 2006), 512–524 (here 514); 1969–1985 Fritz Plasser, *Parteien unter Streß* (Vienna: Böhlau, 1987), 119; 1986 and 1993 SSÖ; 2003–2013 ESS; 2016 ISSP.

38 www.idea.int/data-tools/data/voter-turnout, accessed Dec. 24, 2018,
39 Ingrid van Biezen, Peter Mair, and Thomas Poguntke, "Going, Going, ...Gone? The Decline of Party Membership in Contemporary Europe," *European Journal of Political Research* 51, no. 1 (2012): 24–56.
40 Knut Heidar, "Party Membership and Participation," in *Handbook of Party Politics*, ed. Richard S. Katz and William Crotty (London: Sage Publications, 2006), 301–315.

Results: Towards a Movement Society?

Starting with the development of conventional participation, Figure 1 shows turnout in national parliamentary elections as well as the share of party members in the electorate since the beginning of the Second Republic in 1945. To put the Austrian data into context, the figure also displays the average turnout in the seven other countries included in the *Political Action* study.

Since the early years of the Second Republic, turnout in Austria has significantly decreased by about 20 percentage points. However, in a comparative perspective, the rates are still high, and there were also some reverse developments when programmatic differences, especially between the major parties, were stressed in the campaign. In the most recent election of 2017, for example, turnout increased by more than five percentage points to eighty percent. Average turnout in the other countries covered by the *Political Action* study has been clearly lower: on average by about 15 percentage points, even though countries with compulsory voting (Italy until 1993; Netherlands until 1967)[41] are included in this group. Survey data on party membership in Austria are less often available, and a long-term comparison with the other countries is not possible. Until the 1980s, about a quarter of adult Austrians were party members. Since then, the parties have lost about half of them. Compared to turnout, the decline of party membership is by far stronger.

Figure 2 compares the present situation of conventional participation in Austria with the seven other countries. It shows the average turnout in all parliamentary (USA: presidential) elections since 2000 as well as the latest available comparable data on party membership. To account for some idiosyncrasies of American politics, both measures had to be adapted for this country (as explained below the figure).

41 www.idea.int/data-tools/data/voter-turnout/compulsory-voting, accessed Jan. 1, 2019.

Figure 2: Conventional Participation: Turnout in National Elections and Current Rates of Party Membership in the "Political Action Countries" (percent)

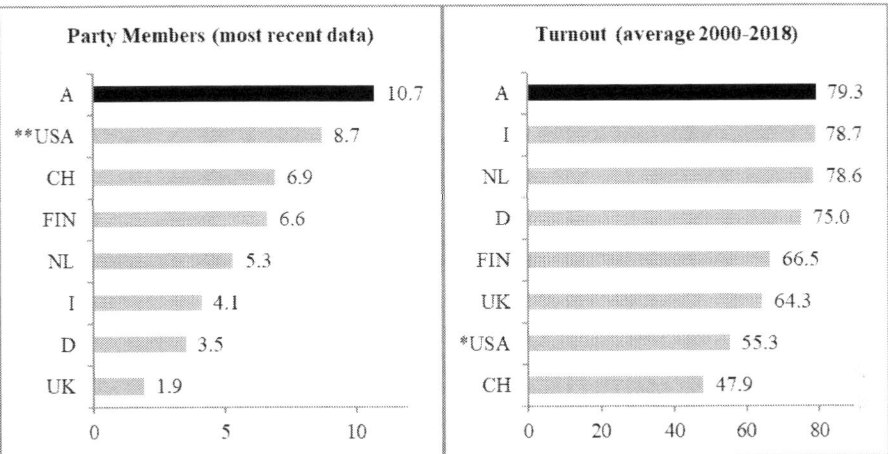

Sources: IDEA Voter Turnout Database; Party Members: ESS 2010 (Italy: ESS 2004; USA: ISSP 2014).

Notes: *Refers to voting age population, not to registered voters; **Refers to respondents who belong to a party and actively participate (because formal membership is hardly known).

The two bar graphs indicate that Austria still differs from comparable countries when it comes to the amount of conventional participation. With respect to the rates of turnout in the new millennium, Austria narrowly leads the field, followed by Italy and the Netherlands. What is more, the share of party members in Austria is still far bigger than in the other countries.

Switching now to unconventional forms of political participation, the movement society thesis expects a clear increase over time. Otherwise, any debate on its establishment would be pointless. Figure 3 shows the shares of Austrians who report to have ever taken part in three moderate forms of protests: petitions, demonstrations, and boycotts. It covers the longest possible period for which (comparable) data are available, thus the period from 1974 to 2018.

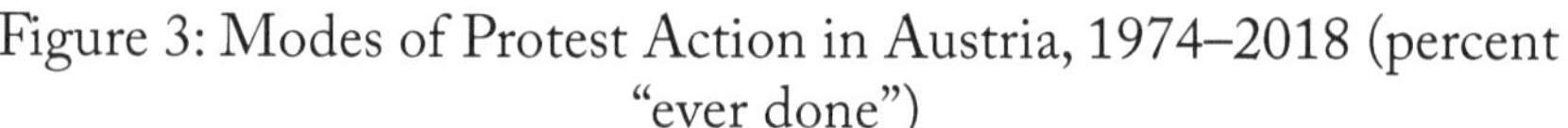

Figure 3: Modes of Protest Action in Austria, 1974–2018 (percent "ever done")

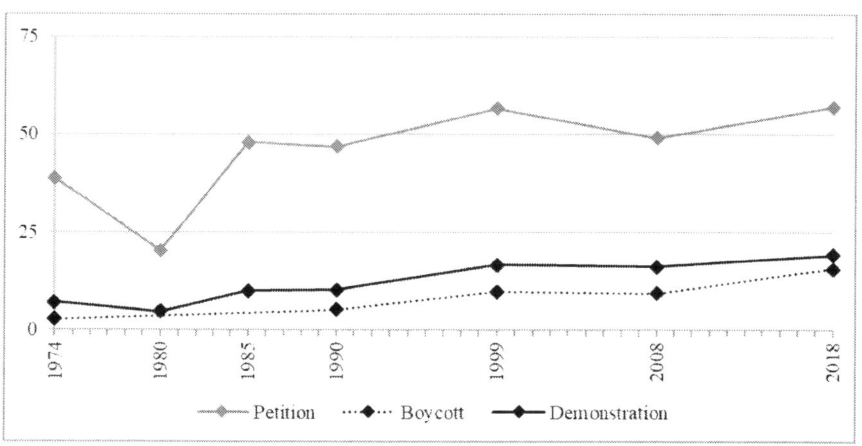

Sources: 1974 Political Action; 1980 Roland Deiser and Norbert Winkler, *Das politische Handeln der Österreicher* (Vienna: Verlag für Gesellschaftskritik, 1982), 248 and 253; 1985 Peter A. Ulram, *Hegemonie und Erosion* (Vienna: Böhlau, 1990), 156; 1990–2018 EVS.

In general, all three kinds of moderate protest action have been used by an increasing number of Austrians since the 1970s. Similar to other countries, signing petitions is by far the most widespread form of non-institutionalized participation. In the most recent survey, about fifty-seven percent of the respondents claim to have used this repertoire at least once. Taking part in demonstrations is a by far less widespread phenomenon, but compared to the early 1970s, it has nevertheless significantly increased from about seven to about nineteen percent. Boycotts, finally, are still a quite rare phenomenon, though in the last survey, about sixteen percent of the respondents reported to have taken part. However, there is a huge difference between this "negative" form of political consumerism displayed in Figure 3 and its already mentioned "positive" twin: In the ISSP 2014 survey, for example, no less than fifty-five percent of the Austrians claim to have "boycotted, or deliberately bought, certain products for political, ethical or environmental reasons."[42] The trends displayed in Figure 3 thus support the above formulated expectation (H2). To put the Austrian development again into perspective, Figure 4 compares the eight countries of the *Political Action* study using a dichotomous measure of protest participation, i.e. of

42 ISSP 2014 – Citizenship II, Q14.

participation in at least one of the three modes. The two bar diagrams are based on the oldest (*Political Action*)[43] and most recent comparable surveys (EVS and WVS).

Figure 4: Protest Action 1974 & 2017/2018: Austria in Comparative Perspective (percent "ever done")

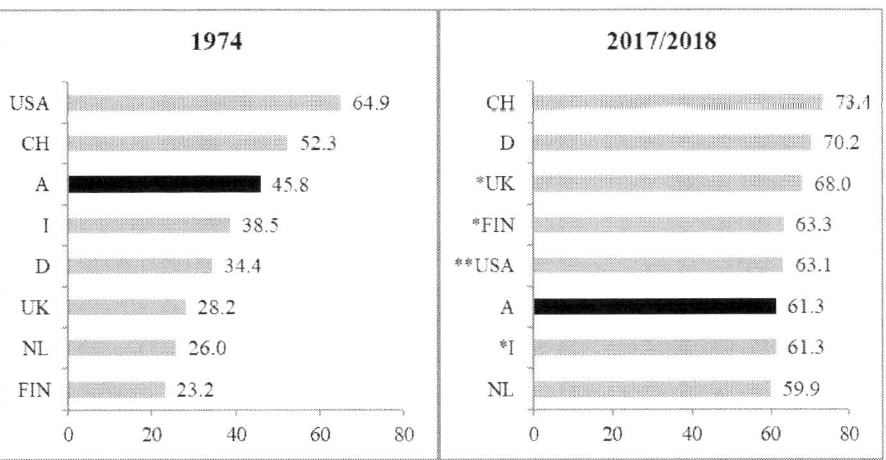

Sources: 1974 Political Action; 2017/2018 EVS 2017 (A 2018; CH, D, NL 2017).

Note: *EVS 2008; **WVS 6 (2011).

Note: The bars represent the shares of respondents who have ever taken part in at least one of the three types of protest shown in Figure 3: petitions, boycotts, and demonstrations.

The figures highlight that once-relevant differences between the eight countries have become significantly smaller. In 2017/2018, between sixty (Netherlands) and seventy-three percent (Switzerland) of the respondents report to have participated in at least one of the three modes. Like in 1974, Austria takes in a middle position, though the differences between the five countries below the Top 3 are hardly relevant. A declining but, compared to other countries, still high level of conventional participation is thus combined with a medium level of participation in moderate forms of protest. These findings contradict traditional assessments of Austria as a country

43 The survey includes a "do not recognize" response category that is defined as missing value. I follow this definition but when interpreting this category as "not done", the share especially of protesters in Italy drops from 38.5 to 24.1 percent. Austria (45.8 vs. 39.5) as well as Switzerland (52.3 vs. 47.0) are affected, too. In the other countries the differences are between 0 (Finland) and 2.5 (USA) percentage points.

with low levels of unconventional participation that have been reproduced numerous times.[44]

Turning now to the characteristics of protest participants, and focusing from now on only on Austria, the movement society thesis expects a significant *decrease* in differences between active and non-active citizens, thus a less distinctive profile of activists with respect to socio-demographic (H3) and ideological characteristics (H4). Table 1 reports results of logistic regressions that examine the impact of these factors for all years with comparable and comprehensive survey data. Demographic factors include age, gender, and three levels of education (primary, secondary, and tertiary). The reference category for gender is women so that positive coefficients indicate higher participation rates of men. With respect to education, the regressions show the impact of secondary and tertiary levels compared to primary education. To analyze the ideological background, the regressions include a left-right scale (with high figures referring to right-wing attitudes) and a measure of extremism, which is calculated as absolute distance from the left-right-scale's center. As dependent variable, the regressions capture participation based on the dichotomous measure summarizing all three kinds of protest activity that was already used in Figure 4. In order to distinguish the influence of socio-structural and ideological characteristics, the regressions were conducted in two steps: first without, then with the two ideological variables. The regression coefficients displayed in the table, however, only report the second step when all variables were included.

Results indicate that the combined explanatory power of the three socio-structural variables has rather decreased in recent years, which supports the movement society thesis. The first of the two Pseudo R^2 statistics shows lower values after the 1990s. A closer look at the three factors indicates important differences as education has remained a significant factor, while former differences based on gender have disappeared. Age, too, has remained a significant factor even though the question format used certainly influences the impact of this variable because younger people simply have had fewer opportunities to have ever taken part in protests. This disadvantage of the question format might explain the surprising reversion of the sign from negative (younger people are more likely to protest) to positive (older people are more likely to protest) in the most recent survey. Ideological differences, by contrast, hardly contribute to the explanatory power of these models. But in the last three surveys, protest participants expressed left-wing attitudes, and in the most recent survey, extremism is also a significant factor.

44 Fritz Plasser and Gilg Seeber, "Politische Kultur und Demokratiebewusstsein in der Zweiten Republik im internationalen Vergleich," in *Die Österreichische Demokratie im Vergleich*, ed. Ludger Helms and David Wineroither, 2nd ed. (Baden-Baden: Nomos, 2017), 337–364.

Table 1: Socio-structural and Ideological Characteristics of Protest Participants, 1974–2018 (Logistic Regressions)

	1974	1990	1999	2008	2018
Age	-0.00	-0.01**	-0.01**	-0.01	0.01**
	(0.00)	(0.00)	(0.00)	(0.00)	(0.00)
Gender Reference: women	0.39**	-0.13	-0.04	0.04	-0.02
	(0.13)	(0.12)	(0.13)	(0.12)	(0.11)
Education Reference: primary level (I)					
secondary level (II)	0.82***	0.84***	0.54***	0.62***	0.92***
	(0.14)	(0.13)	(0.13)	(0.17)	(0.17)
tertiary level (III)	1.00**	1.61***	1.36***	1.62***	1.93***
	(0.38)	(0.23)	(0.22)	(0.26)	(0.23)
Left-Right: linear	0.04	-0.05	-0.12**	-0.08*	-0.10**
	(0.03)	(0.04)	(0.04)	(0.03)	(0.03)
Left-Right: distance from center	-0.06	0.03	0.10	0.07	0.10*
	(0.05)	(0.06)	(0.06)	(0.05)	(0.05)
Pseudo R^2 (Cragg-Uhler/ Nagelkerke) variables: age, gender, education	0.05	0.11	0.11	0.06	0.08
Pseudo R^2 (Cragg-Uhler/ Nagelkerke) all variables	0.07	0.11	0.09	0.07	0.10
(n)	(984)	(1177)	(1202)	(1198)	(1456)
Predicted probabilities of participation in protests (all other factors are set at mean or mode value)					
Men	47%	40%	55%	56%	62%
Women	37%	43%	56%	55%	62%
Education: primary level (I)	37%	43%	56%	40%	40%
Education: secondary level (II)	57%	64%	68%	55%	62%
Education: tertiary level (III)	62%	79%	83%	77%	82%

* p<0.05; ** p<0.01; *** p<0.001

Figures are regression coefficients with standard errors in parentheses.

Sources: 1974 Political Action; 1990–2018 EVS. Levels of education (variables: recoding of categories): Political Action (v384: "1 basic level" & "2 lower level" = I; "3 extended lower level" & "4 middle level" = II; "5 higher level" = III), EVS 1990 (x023 "What age did you complete your education": <17 = I; 17–20 = II; >20 = III), EVS 1999 and 2008 (x025r); EVS 2017 (v243_r).

The important differences in protest activity caused by the educational divide and the disappearance of the gender-gap are best illustrated when directly comparing the probability that respondents have taken part in protests. The percentages at the bottom of Table 1 indicate for men and women, as well as for all three levels of education, the chance, which is displayed in percent, that individuals belonging to these groups have been active. To extract the specific impact of gender and education, all other influencing factors are set to their average (age, both left-right measures) or mode (gender, education). Relevant differences between men and women are only visible in the 1970s. In those days, men were about ten percentage points more likely to take part in protest events than women. The educational divide, by contrast, has remained a stable factor. Throughout the period of observation, the gap between respondents with primary and tertiary education was about thirty percentage points. In the most recent survey, this gap even broadened to forty-two points.

The summary variable of protest participation naturally tends to blur differences between activism in public protests, such as demonstrations, and rather weak forms of political engagement, like signing petitions or taking part in boycotts. Results of logistic regressions that differentiate between these three specific forms, which are not shown due to limited space, indicate that the profile of petitioners and participants in boycotts has been less distinctive than the profile of demonstrators. With respect to the social-structural variables, gender-differences disappeared in the two moderate forms after the 1970s, but they are still observable in demonstrations where men are more active. The surprising positive impact of age in the most recent survey is driven by participation in petitions as well as boycotts that have become a relevant repertoire for older generations. Middle and especially higher education, by contrast, remains a stable and relevant factor explaining participation in all three forms. Ideological differences are observable in all three forms too, but the impact of left-wing attitudes (and extremism) is much stronger for taking part in demonstrations than in boycotts and petitions.

Hypothesis 5, finally, refers to the characteristics of protests for which the movement society thesis expects, amongst other features, a rising variety of issues addressed. As explained above, survey data do not provide this information, which is why this hypothesis will be tested using protest event data. Figure 5 shows the variety, or dispersion, of issues based on a system of twelve aggregated categories: cultural liberalism, culture, economy, education, environment, Europe, institutional reform, international conflicts (e.g. wars), migration, parties & coalitions (which includes above all protests against the ÖVP-FPÖ government in 2000ff.), security, and welfare. These categories always encompass different political demands as the focus of the present analysis is on the issue areas only. "Cultural liberalism", for example, includes protests supporting women's rights but also protests opposing equal rights for gays and lesbians, which were always systematically differentiated when the protest data were coded. As the number of events in the older project is low for some years (not least due to the sampling method mentioned above), the data are aggregated into periods of five years. The two lines are based on an inverted, normalized coefficient of variation running from 0 (only one issue is addressed in protests) to 100 (all twelve issues are equally important). Higher figures thus represent higher levels of issue variation.

Figure 5: Protest Events in Austria, 1975–2016: Variety of Issues

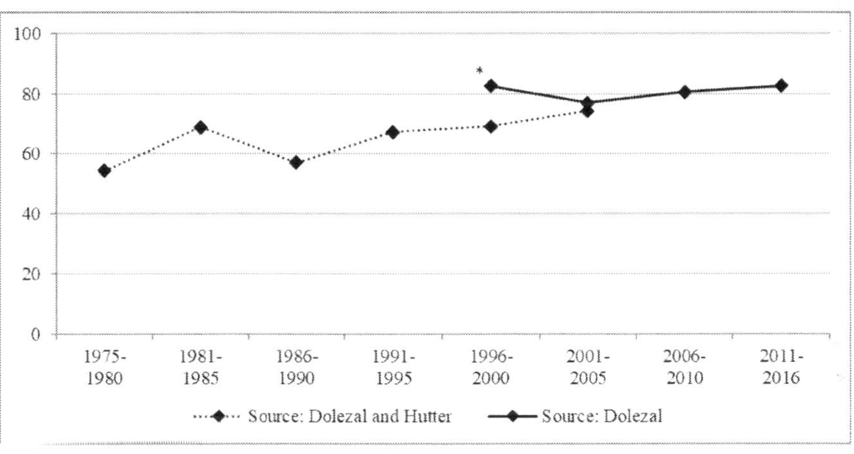

Sources: Dolezal and Hutter, "Konsensdemokratie unter Druck?"; Dolezal (ongoing project, see FN 37).

The scale is based on an inverted normalized coefficient of variation summarizing the distribution of twelve issue categories. It runs from 0 (all protests mention the same issue) to 100 (all issues are equally important).

Note: The issues of the older data set were re-coded for the present analysis.

*The oldest period captured by the new data set starts in 1998 (not in 1996).

The results of the two protest event analyses support the expectation of a rising variety of concerns addressed. The two lines indicate that the dominance of certain issues in the protest arena has declined. For example, in the second half of the 1970s, aspects related to cultural liberalism dominated the protest arena (47%); in the second half of the 1980s, no less than forty-three percent of the protest events identified addressed environmental concerns. These two periods therefore feature the lowest scores of issue variation (54 and 57 points, respectively). In the last period shown (2011–2016), migration was the dominant issue, but the share of related protests was by far smaller (23%) than in the two older periods, which is why the overall variation of issues is by far larger (83 points).

Conclusion

Classic studies of Austrian politics have typically stressed the dominance of party-based, institutionalized, or conventional forms of political participation and the relative weakness of unconventional, non-institutionalized repertoires. When evaluating the movement society thesis, which served as yardstick for the present analysis, a study of Austria might therefore be interpreted as an "extreme case". Many scholars would regard this country as a least likely example of an emerging movement society. Based on two types of data, survey data and protest event data, the present chapter nevertheless explored the development of political participation in Austria since the 1970s and asked whether aspects of a movement society are observable.

Data on conventional forms of participation, i.e. voting in national elections and membership in political parties, indicate declining trends. Nevertheless, compared to other Western countries, the level of conventional participation in Austria has remained high. This well-known feature of Austrian politics is accompanied by an increasing share of people who are active in the protest arena. This latter aspect has not always been recognized by extant research. A comparison of the Austrian development with a (small) group of countries for which data are available since the mid-1970s demonstrates that this country is not an outlier but rather representative of the general development in Western Europe.

The increasing relevance of unconventional participation provided the basis for an evaluation of the movement society thesis. All in all, the results are mixed as the analyses indicated aspects of change as well as stability: The most important change is the disappearance of the once-strong gender gap in protest participation. Medium and high education, by contrast, and left-wing attitudes–the latter especially in less moderate forms of contention, such as demonstrations–have remained a stable factor in distinguishing activists from non-participating people. These results resemble the situation in other countries and highlight the importance of differentiating between various forms of protests. With respect to the variety of issues addressed in the protest arena, the movement society thesis is correct. A combined analysis of two major protest event data sets showed a rising diversity of topics since the mid-1970s. Any assessment of the movement society thesis should thus be based on survey as well as protest event data.

Millennials and Austrian Democracy

Hannes R. Richter

Introduction

Austria garnered some international media attention in 2017 when voters elected the first millennial to the top of the Austrian federal government: Federal Chancellor Sebastian Kurz, who is currently the youngest head of government serving in the world.[1,2,3] However, most millennials do not run countries (yet), and over the past few years, millennials as a demographic group have been receiving scholarly attention ranging from their consumption patterns and their social media use to their political preferences and behavior, and beyond. This paper focuses on one particular aspect that recently has gained wider exposure and has caused some concern among political scientists and observers: the ongoing decline in support for liberal democracy among millennials.[4] These concerns have been going hand in hand with the recent successes of populist parties and candidates in the United States and in several EU member states. While millennial vote choices are not the subject of this work, per se, their support for the institutions and mechanics of liberal democracy in Austria is. Thus, I will investigate Austrian millennials' support for democracy in general, their support for specific aspects of democracy and Austrian government institutions, and if they, in fact, differ from their older cohorts, also when controlling for standard predictors.

This paper is structured in five sections: (1) a brief discussion of the relevant literature regarding millennials and their support for liberal democracy, (2) a review of existing findings of millennials' political preferences in

1 Simon Shuster, "Austria's Millennial Chancellor Is Unafraid to Defy the E.U.," *time.com* (October 16, 2018), accessed October 4, 2018, http://time.com/collection-post/4983868/sebastian-kurz-chancellor-austria-europe-next-generation-leaders/

2 George Jahn, "Austrian poised to become Europe's first millennial leader", *chicagotribune.com* (October 16, 2017), accessed October 4, 2018, https://www.chicagotribune.com/news/nationworld/ct-sebastian-kurz-austria-leader-20171016-story.html

3 Ofer Aderet, "Sebastian Kurz, an Anti-immigration Millennial, Elected Austria's Next Chancellor," *haaretz.com* (October 15, 2017), accessed October 4, 2018, https://www.haaretz.com/world-news/europe/sebastian-kurz-elected-austria-s-next-chancellor-1.5457846

4 See e.g. Keith Breene, "Millennials are rapidly losing interest in democracy" *weforum.org*, (June 8, 2017), accessed October 16, 2018, https://www.weforum.org/agenda/2017/06/millennials-are-rapidly-losing-interest-in-democracy

Austria, (3) a description of the data and methodology used in this research, (4) a presentation and discussion of the results of the statistical analyses, and (5) concluding remarks.

Background

In 2017, shortly after the Austrian parliamentary elections that propelled millennial Sebastian Kurz to power as the world's youngest head of government, Neil Howe asked in *Forbes* if millennials are giving up on democracy, citing a "global youth insurgency that boosted parties and candidates at the political extremes."[5] Likewise, in a widely cited paper, Yascha Mounk and Roberto Stefan Foa, too, lamented the end of the democratic century and the global rise of autocratic tendencies, arguing that two-thirds of Americans aged over sixty-five say it is absolutely important for them to live in a democracy, while less than one-third of millennials (under the age of thirty-five) feel the same way.[6] The authors illustrate the general trend in a figure that is reproduced here as Figure 1, as it makes clear at a glance why this is cause for concern: It shows the overall trend of the declining number of citizens in Europe and the United States who state that it is essential to live in a democracy by age group. In the United States, seventy-two percent of those born in the 1930s state that they deem it essential to live in a country that is governed democratically. However, only some thirty percent of those born in the 1980s make the same statement. A similar (yet slightly different) picture presents itself when inspecting the trend in the European Union. Among the youngest Europeans included in the data, less than forty-five percent state that living in a democracy is essential. It is noteworthy to point out that in Europe this sentiment has at no point in time reached sixty percent, with its highest value recorded in the aftermath of World War II. Foa and Mounk find their results "deeply concerning"[7] and identify a significant "generational reversal"[8] in the support for democracy and a withdrawal from democratic institutions, a reversal that is most pronounced among millennials.

---

5 Neil Howe, "Are Millennials Giving Up on Democracy?," *Forbes.com* (October 31, 2017), accessed November 3, 2018, https://www.forbes.com/sites/neilhowe/2017/10/31/are-millennials-giving-up-on-democracy

6 Yascha Mounk and Roberto Stefan Foa, "The End of the Democratic Century," *Foreign Affairs* 97, no. 3 (2018): 29-36.

7 Ibid., p.8

8 Ibid., p.8

Figure 1. Essential to Live in a Country that is Governed Democratically, by Age Cohort (Decade of Birth)

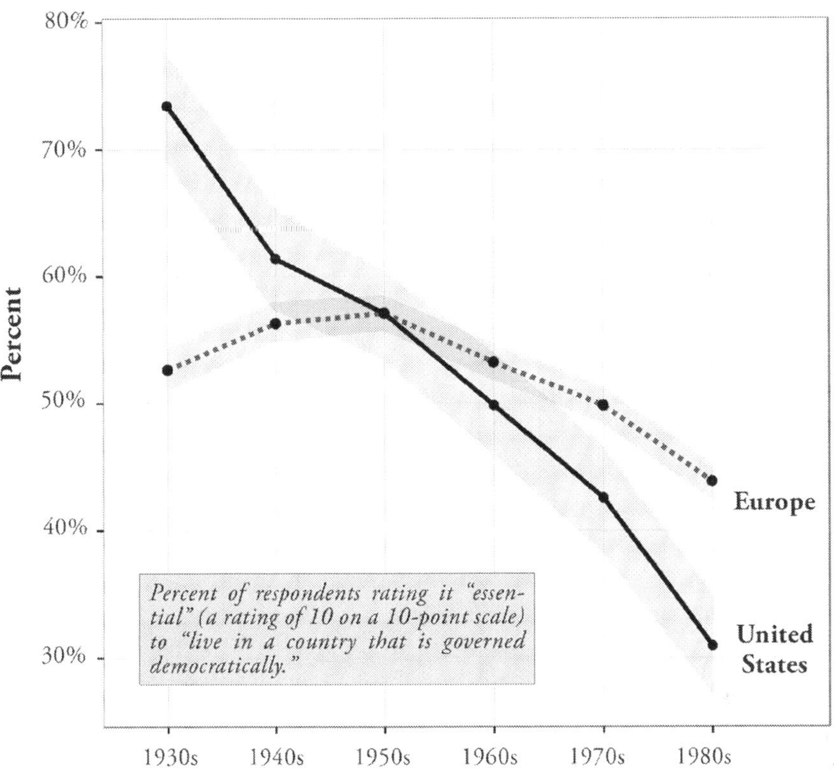

Source: Roberto Stefan Foa and Yascha Mounk, "The Democratic Disconnect," *Journal of Dcmocracy* 27, no. 3 (2016): p. 7.

Data has been pooled from the *World Values Surveys* (2005-2014), Waves five and six. The 95% confidence interval is shown in grey.

However, while the focus here is on millennials, Figure 1 also underlines the fact that the decline in support for democracy is by no means unique to the millennial generation. On the contrary, the downward trend began with those born in the 1940s in the United States, while the decline in Europe commenced with the generation born in the 1950s, generations that both predate today's millennials. Those generations have one thing in common: They did not experience World War II and its effects, nor did they experience the totalitarian governments at the time, most notably Hitlerite Germany. Based on this, one could also theorize that this decline is also a matter of temporal distance. Those in the West who have not experienced non-democratic government and totalitarianism over time are less likely to put a premium on living in a liberal democracy the farther they are chronologically removed from experiencing the alternatives. The advantages of democracy, in turn, become less apparent, while frustrations with aspects of the democratic process continue to mount.

Regardless, additional empirical evidence on the millennial matter is available. Corbet and Gurdgiev, too, support the claim of decreasing support for liberal democracy among millennials in Western nations. They present evidence showing that the recent decline in support for liberal democracy's values and its institutions is "more pronounced within the younger cohort of voters, especially the Millennials."[9] These findings are indeed cause for concern, as the broad and often universal support for liberal democracy has been eroding. In the aftermath of the Cold War, an optimistic worldview prevailed and democracy had emerged victoriously from the struggle against communism, with democracy being seen as the logical and best choice for governance.[10] However, a much bleaker picture presents itself today, as more people seem to be falling out of love with democracy. And millennials are currently at the center of this debate.

This debate has also been linked with technological developments that accompanied millennials coming of age, such as the Internet and many of its popular, contemporary applications, most notably social media and how it affects information-gathering habits. In 2018, the Pew Research Center found that while a majority of Americans today use Facebook (sixty-eight percent), some platforms are particularly prominent among the younger generation. Specifically, the Center reported that Snapchat, Instagram, and Twitter in particular appeal to the younger generation.[11] While the proliferation of these new tools progresses further, their effects on receiving political information in particular continue to be studied.[12] These tools have become synonymic with millennials, and their use likely plays a role in how

9 Corbet, Shaen and Gurdgiev, Constantin, "Millennials' Support for Liberal Democracy Is Failing: A Deep Uncertainty Perspective" (September 11, 2017), accessed November 9, 2018: https://ssrn.com/abstract=3033949

10 See e.g. Francis Fukuyama, *The End of History and the Last Man*, (New York: Avon Books, 1992).

11 Aaron Smith and Monica Anderson, "Social Media Use in 2018," *Pew Research Center* (March 1, 2018), accessed October 12, 2018, http://www.pewinternet.org/2018/03/01/social-media-use-in-2018

12 Cacciatore, Michael A., Sara K. Yeo, Dietram A. Scheufele, Michael A. Xenos, Dominique Brossard, and Elizabeth A. Corley. "Is Facebook Making Us Dumber? Exploring Social Media Use as a Predictor of Political Knowledge." *Journalism & Mass Communication Quarterly* 95, no. 2 (June 2018): 404–24.

their political views are shaped by the information they receive (or do not receive) in this manner. In addition, these new tools have also brought about changes in political participation and collective action, often in a departure from the norms of "traditional" political participation.[13] Despite the gloomy outlook, research has shown that while millennials have become increasingly detached from traditional party politics, they do care about issues and exhibit other less traditional types of political participation. And while these complex interactions in the new communications environment are very important, they must not distract from the focus of this work: millennials' support for democracy in Austria. In order to shed more light on their characteristics, I will review the main findings of two recent studies on millennials in Austria in order to set the stage for the subsequent quantitative analysis.

Setting the Stage: Millennials in Austria

In this section, I review relevant results from two recent reports on millennials in Austria in order to describe key characteristics of this demographic and to set the stage for the subsequent analysis.

The *Austrian Millennial Report 2018* is based on 2,500 online interviews and included individuals aged fifteen to forty-nine. It is noteworthy that this study employs a narrower definition of the term millennial: individuals aged fifteen to twenty-five. I discuss competing definitions of millennials in the methodology section below and will refer to the demographic in this report as "young millennials" in order to underline the fact that the age bracket here is defined quite differently compared to other studies. The focus of this report is not on political preferences but on millennials' preferences in technology, worldviews, and their career ambitions. It does not find differences between millennials and older Austrians in many issue areas. For example, in terms of support for gender quality, no substantial differences in opinions were recorded.[14] In contrast, according to these data, young millennials differ from their older peers regarding the biggest global challenges. Thirty-two percent cite immigration and refugees as the biggest problem, while forty-six percent of their older peers made that choice.[15]

13 See e.g. Ekström, Mats, and Adam Shehata, "Social Media, Porous Boundaries, and the Development of Online Political Engagement among Young Citizens," *New Media & Society* 20, no. 2 (February 2018): 740–59.
14 (KTHE). 2018. *Ready for Change, Austrian Millennial Report (September 2018)*, accessed November 3, 2018, https://www.kthe.at/wordpress/wp-content/uploads/2018/09/Austrian_Millennial_Report_2018.pdf
15 Ibid.

In terms of media consumption and technology use, the report confirms that young millennials in Austria do not differ in their behaviors from their peers in other countries. Only sixteen percent reported that they would give up their mobile phone for a week, and only thirteen percent believe they could go that long without Internet.[16] Also, seventy-two percent of young millennials said that checking their mobile phone is the first thing they do after waking up in the morning, while only forty-seven percent of older Austrians exhibit this behavior.[17] In addition, there exist substantial differences in media consumption patterns. For example, forty-five percent of young millennials in Austria said they use YouTube on an almost daily basis, while only eleven percent of Austrians aged forty or older do so.[18] Also, the data show substantial differences in social media use. Facebook, for example, is no longer among the top three social media applications used by young millennials in Austria in terms of popularity. Rather, WhatsApp, Instagram, YouTube, and Snapchat are on top of the list among this age group today.[19] Overall, the findings of this report confirm existing perceptions of millennials and some of their preferences in life. However, they do not tell us much about their political views or their support for democracy in Austria.

The Millennial Dialogue Report [20] for Austria bases its findings on an online survey of initially 1,105 Austrians age fifteen to thirty-four, as well as a week-long, moderated follow-up dialogue with forty Austrians that were segmented into three groups: the politically engaged, the mainstream, and the politically disaffected. This survey particularly focuses on millennials' expectations of government, their political interest and involvement, as well as their trust (or lack thereof) in government institutions, parties, and politicians. Its results will therefore provide a welcome departure point for the subsequent analysis. However, since only the millennial age bracket was included in the survey, no comparisons to other age groups are possible.

The findings, summarized in Table 1, show that, in general terms, millennials in Austria are happy with their lives and optimistic about their future; they list music, film, and using social media as their top interests.[21] At the same time, however, their political interest is low. Only eighteen percent indicated that they were "very interested" in politics, and a majority fifty-six percent said that compared to their parents and grandparents,

16 Ibid.
17 Ibid., 39.
18 Ibid., 12.
19 Ibid., 54
20 Foundation for European Progressive Studies et al. *The Millennial Dialogue Report (Austria)*, accessed November 3, 2018, https://www.millennialdialogue.com/media/1233/millennial-dialogue-austria-v5.pdf
21 Ibid., 6

their generation is less interested in politics, while only eighteen percent expressed the opposite sentiment.[22] The primary reasons cited for this apparent disinterest can be summarized as a feeling that millennial engagement in politics would not change anything, a perception that politicians do not keep their promises, and that political parties do not relate to young people. In addition, outdated structures of the political system were also cited as a reason for the prevailing disinterest.[23]

Table 1. Austrian Millennials and Politics, Select Findings

Millennials in Austria...	
are generally happy with their lives	92%
are optimistic about the future	81%
are very/ fairly interested in music	89%
are very/ fairly interested in film	88%
are very/ fairly interested in using social media	77%
are very/ fairly interested in politics	54%
are fairly/ very interested in religion	21%
Feel that their generation is less interested in politics than their parents' or grandparent's generation	56%
have attended a political meeting	7%
have taken part in protest/ demonstration	19%
have attended religious services/ meetings/ events	12%
felt confident that they and their peers could make themselves heard	12%
think very few, if any, politicians encourage young people to get involved in politics	65%
The views of young people are largely ignored by most politicians	64%
The views of young people are greatly valued by most politicians	16%

Source: The Millenial Dialogue Report – Austria.
n = 1,105 Austrians residents aged 15-34

22 Ibid., 5
23 Ibid., 8, 9.

An apparent discontent with the current political system can also be found in the fact that only a mere twelve percent of respondents said they "felt confident that they and their peers could make themselves heard,"[24] also contending that views of young people are ignored by politicians (sixty-four percent).[25] These findings already point to underlying frustrations with the current political system. A large majority of millennials believe that their concerns are not being heard, that their opinions are not important to the political establishment, and, more generally, that their involvement will not produce anything meaningful to them. Before investigating these notions in greater detail, I will describe the data and methodology used for the following bi- and multivariate analyses.

Data and Methodology

Before describing the data and methodology employed in this work, a definition of what a millennial actually is seems to be in order, particularly since there are competing definitions being used. The term "millennial" was likely coined by Neil Howe and William Strauss, noting that millennials are born "in or after 1982."[26] The Merriam-Webster's dictionary defines a millennial as "a person born in the 1980s or 1990s,"[27] while the *Pew Research Center* discussed these definitions in more detail and determined a cutoff point between millennials and the generation following behind it (Generation Z), defining 1996 as the last birth year for millennials, with the first being 1981. In other words, according to this definition, anyone between the ages of twenty-two and thirty-seven in 2018 will be considered a millennial. However, the recently commissioned survey by Vienna-based creative agency Kobza and the Hungry Eyes (discussed above), in contrast to the above definitions, defines millennials as fifteen to twenty-five year olds.[28] At the same time, the previously mentioned *Millennial Dialogue on Europe* defines millennials as aged eighteen to thirty-five.[29] For the purpose of this

24 Ibid., 13.
25 Ibid., 13.
26 Neil Howe and William Strauss, *Millennials Rising: The Next Great Generation*, (New York: Vintage Books, 2000), 4.
27 "millennial." Merriam-Webster.com (2018), accessed November 13, 2018, https://www.merriam-webster.com/dictionary/millennial
28 (KTHE). 2018. *Ready for Change, Austrian Millennial Report (September 2018)*, accessed November 3, 2018, https://www.kthe.at/wordpress/wp-content/uploads/2018/09/Austrian_Millennial_Report_2018.pdf, 84.
29 Foundation for European Progressive Studies et al. *The Millennial Dialogue Report (Austria)*. Available: https://www.millennialdialogue.com/media/1233/millennial-dialogue-austria-v5.pdf, 2.

study, I will resort to a definition that allows me to include the youngest voters in Austria at age sixteen and voters up to age thirty-four in the analyses.

I will employ data from the Austrian National Election Studies (AUTNES) Multi-Mode Panel Study 2017[30] first to conduct a series of bivariate regression models to determine if millennials significantly differ from older Austrians in their opinions on a number of issues pertaining to the political system and Austrian democracy. In a second step, I will test the hypothesis that millennials have less regard for Austrian democracy than their older peers, employing two multivariate models controlling for standard predictors. These two models are now described in more detail:

The Satisfaction Model

To go beyond the bivariate tests of hypotheses, I employ the AUTNES data to test for millennials' satisfaction with Austrian democracy in a multivariate environment. In this model, the dependent variable—satisfaction with democracy in Austria—is measured by asking respondents, "On the whole, are you very satisfied, fairly satisfied, fairly dissatisfied, or very dissatisfied with the way democracy works in Austria?" The variable is coded 1=satisfied, 2=fairly satisfied, 3=fairly dissatisfied, and 4=very dissatisfied. The independent variable—millennials—is a dummy variable coded 0=millennial and 1=respondents aged thirty-five and older. Therefore, millennials are coded to include respondents aged sixteen to thirty-four. Control variables include gender (coded 1=male, 2=female), ideology (self-placement on a ten-point scale from left to right), education (highest level achieved, coded from 1=did not attend school to 15=doctorate/ PhD), monthly net household income (includes state transfers and is coded in brackets from 1=below €450 to 20=€3,900 and more), and union membership (where 1= yes and 2=no), as well as political interest, which is measured by asking respondents, "Generally speaking, are you very, fairly, a little, or not at all interested in politics?" (coded 1=very interested, 2=fairly interested, 3=a little interested, 4=not at all interested). In addition, I also include a basic political knowledge variable, which in this instance is simply measured by asking respondents what percentage of votes a political party in Austria needs in order to enter into the National Council; it is coded 0=incorrect answer or don't know and 1=correct answer (four percent). Some twenty-seven percent of Austrians were able to provide the correct answer to that question.

30 Kritzinger, Sylvia; et al., 2018, "AUTNES Multi-Mode Panel Study 2017 (SUF edition)," doi:10.11587/NXDDPE, AUSSDA Dataverse, V2.

The Strong Leader Model

The Strong Leader Model replicates the above Satisfaction Model using the identical dataset but includes a different operationalization of the dependent variable in order to add robustness to the findings. Instead of measuring satisfaction with Austrian democracy, this model employs a variable that captures respondents' agreement to the statement, "It is good for Austria to have a strong leadership personality in government, who decides things on their own" (similarly coded from 1=completely agree to 5=completely disagree). This second model is designed to re-test the results of the Satisfaction Model with this modified operationalization of an individual's support for democracy. While exhibiting dissatisfaction with Austrian democracy can be interpreted as a lack of support for certain aspects of the political system rooted in disappointment, it still allows for the possibility that overall support for liberal democracy is still solid. Changing the dependent variable—now testing for authoritarian tendencies—offers an alternative measure of support for liberal democracy. In this case, support for democracy while also supporting a sole, strong leader at the top is considerably more difficult to argue, particularly if viewed in tandem with the Satisfaction Model. The independent and control variables in this model are identical to the above Satisfaction Model.

Results

Bivariate Regressions

Table 2 summarizes the results for the bivariate regressions to test if millennials have significantly differing opinions than their older peers, net of other factors. Overall, these results confirm previous findings suggesting that generational differences in Austria, too, are real and substantial. With few exceptions, Austrian millennials differ from their older peers in their opinions on political institutions, their trust in these institutions and actors, as well as on a wide number of policies.

Specifically, on the key question regarding this inquiry, the results show millennials are significantly less satisfied with democracy in Austria than their older cohorts. In addition, the data also show negative trends for millennials on a number of variables pertaining to the support of the current political system. Compared to older generations, millennials in Austria are less trusting of the National Council and the Constitutional Court. At the same time, no significant differences could be detected in their trust of the media and political parties. However, millennials are more likely than older Austrians to agree that political parties are the main problem in politics. Even more concerning is the finding that millennials, in this bivariate scenario, are significantly more likely to support a strong leader in government who decides alone and are more likely to agree with the statement that politicians only care about the rich and powerful. What is more, they also prefer independent citizens instead of party members and are more likely to believe that corporations, and not the government, decide over politics. It seems that compared to older citizens, millennials have a deeply rooted distrust against many government organizations and politicians as well, echoing some previous findings discussed above. One variable, however, seems to withstand the trend. While millennials in general exhibit more negative views towards government and the performance of Austrian democracy, they are more likely than older Austrians to agree that most politicians are trustworthy. This particular finding seems counterintuitive, and after double-checking the variable's coding, it can be confirmed nonetheless.

In addition, millennial differences also become apparent in a number of policy positions. For instance, they tend to agree that today's youth will have a better life than their parents. In that respect, this generation in Austria is more optimistic about their own future than older Austrians see it. Other issues affected by generational differences include the notion that politics should fight social inequality (millennials are more likely to agree), that women with equal qualifications should be favored at job applications, or that the environment needs to be protected even if life becomes more expensive. Yet these liberal policy positions stand in contrast with millennial preferences in other policy areas, most notably immigration and law and order. This same age group also is more likely to agree that immigration into Austria should only be possible in exceptional cases and that police authorities should be extended. In other words, while millennials exhibit liberal policy preferences (per the American sense of the term) in social issue areas, they do at the same time support more restrictive policies in the realm of immigration and law and order, always in comparison with their older cohorts.

Overall, these bivariate comparisons offer a rather pessimistic picture regarding the millennial support for Austrian democracy today, as it seems that these notions are indeed founded in empirical fact. In order to further sharpen our focus on this specific aspect, I will now present the results of the two multivariate models to test the central hypothesis that millennials show less support for Austrian democracy than their older peers.

Table 2. Bivariate Regression Results: Millennials vs. Austrians 35+

Issue	Millennial Direction on Issue	t	P>|t|
Overall satisfaction with political system			
*Satisfaction with Democracy: Austria****	Negative	-6.54	0.000
Trust in political institutions:			
*Trust in National Council****	Negative	5.02	0.000
Trust in Political Parties	Not significant	1.21	0.227
Trust in the Media	Not significant	1.51	0.131
*Trust in the Constitutional Court****	Negative	7.80	0.000
Opinion regarding politics			
*Parties are the main problem in Austria****	Agree	-3.67	0.000
*Have a strong leader in government who decides alone****	Agree	-6.24	0.000
*The people should take most important decisions, not politicians****	Agree	-5.16	0.000
*Politicians only care about the rich and powerful****	Agree	-5.87	0.000
*Most politicians are trustworthy****	Agree	-5.87	0.000
*The people should take most important decisions, not politicians****	Agree	-5.16	0.000
*"Compromises" in politics means betraying one's principles****	Agree	-7.28	0.000
*Corporations and not the government decide over politics****	Agree	-5.97	0.000
*Prefer independent citizen instead of a party member****	Agree	-5.73	0.000
Political interest**	less	-6.10	0.000

Issue Preferences/ Opinion			
*Today's youth will have a better life than their parents***	Agree	-2.32	0.020
*Politics should fight social inequality****	Agree	-3.53	0.000
*Favor women with equal qualification at job application****	Agree	-4.38	0.000
*Immigration to Austria only in exceptional cases***	Agree	-3.00	0.003
*Police authorities should be extended****	Agree	-4.18	0.000
*Protect the environment, even if life becomes more expensive****	Agree	-5.03	0.000

Note: *** p < .001, ** p< .05

Data Source: Austrian National Elections Studies Multi-Mode Panel Study 2017

Democracy Satisfaction Model OLS Regression Results

The results from the multivariate Democracy Satisfaction Model are presented in Table 3. The millennial dummy variable in this model is highly significant also when controlling for standard predictors. Millennials in this model exhibit lower levels of satisfaction with democracy in Austria than older generations. In addition, several control variables also show a significant relationship with the dependent variable: Education is positively correlated with the satisfaction variable, and the higher a person's level of formal schooling, the higher their satisfaction with democracy in Austria. Being a member of a union, too, is a highly significant, positive predictor, for union membership in Austria increases satisfaction with democracy. I also find a highly significant effect of the ideological self-placement variable; those who identify with the right of the political spectrum are less satisfied with democracy than those who identify as being leftist. Political interest, too, is significantly related to the dependent variable; the higher a person's general interest in politics, the higher their levels of satisfaction with democracy are. Finally, political knowledge exhibits a positive relationship with the dependent variable, albeit at a lower level of significance. Unsurprisingly, the more politically knowledgeable are more satisfied with democracy. Gender and household income, on the other hand, did not exhibit any significance in this model. However, despite the significant impact of most of the control variables, being a millennial in Austria is, in itself, significantly connected to lower levels of satisfaction with democracy. The generational effect is not wiped out by the influence of other predictors. Next, I will present results from the second multivariate model, which is identical but employs a different operationalization of the dependent variable. Instead of support for democracy, it measures support for the idea of a strong leader who decides alone.

Table 3. Democracy Satisfaction Model – OLS Regression Results

Dependent Variable	**Coefficient**	t	**P>|t|**
Satisfaction with Democracy - Austria			
Independent Variable			
*Millennial****	-1.599307	-4.37	0.000
Control Variables			
Gender	.0143907	0.50	0.616
*Education****	.0548155	5.78	0.000
*Ideology****	.0569931	8.08	0.000
*Union membership****	.0521813	4.33	0.000
Income	-.0076505	-1.48	0.140
*Better life than parents****	.1233781	10.66	0.000
*Political Interest****	.3603521	12.83	0.000
*Political Knowledge***	-.8092654	-2.16	0.031

Note: *** p < .001, ** p< .05
n =3,845
Prob > F = 0.000
R2 = 0.1305

Data Source: Austrian National Elections Studies Multi-Mode Panel Study 2017

Strong Leader Model OLS Regression Results

The Strong Leader Model tests for an independent effect of being a millennial on supporting the idea of a strong leader who decides alone. It offers a different operationalization of the dependent variable, support for democracy. Otherwise the two models are identical. The results here are very similar to those of the Democracy Satisfaction Model and are summarized in Table 4. Just as in the previous model, being a millennial in Austria is a strong predictor of a reduced level of support for democracy, in this case support for a strong leader who decides alone, which essentially can be interpreted as support for authoritarianism. The millennial variable is again highly significant, where millennials are more likely than their peers to support this statement. Education in this model is a negative predictor of the dependent variable; higher levels of formal schooling decrease support for the idea of a strong leader. And ideology, too, follows the pattern of the previous model; the variable is highly significant, where respondents who consider themselves to be to the political right exhibit more support for the idea of a strong leader than those to the left. Being a member of a union is also significant and reduces a person's support for this statement. Political interest is again highly significant, where higher interest in politics is connected with rejection of the strong leader paradigm. Interestingly, those who strongly believe that today's young people will have a better life than their parents tend to support the idea of a strong leader, while those who expect today's youth to be worse off than their parents' generation are more likely to reject it. And as in the previous model, both gender and household income do not show any significant effect. Political knowledge, finally, is not significant in this model. Thus, the main findings of the Satisfaction Model are confirmed by the Strong Leader Model: Millennials show less support for democracy than older Austrians.

Table 4. Strong Leader Model – OLS Regression Results			
Dependent Variable	**Coefficient**	t	P>|t|
(Agree) Have a strong leader who decides alone			
Independent Variable			
*Millennial****	-2.077165	-4.19	0.000
Control Variables			
Gender	.0427483	1.10	0.271
*Education****	.1538297	4.85	0.000
*Ideology****	.0823847	8.98	0.000
*Union membership****	.1011226	6.20	0.000
Income	.0031382	0.45	0.655
*Better life than parents****	.1708496	10.91	0.000
*Political Interest****	.1576143	4.15	0.000
Political Knowledge	-.9341636	-1.84	0.066

Note: *** $p < .001$, ** $p < .05$
n =3,845
Prob > F = 0.000
R2 = 0.0949

Data Source: Austrian National Elections Studies Multi-Mode Panel Study 2017

Conclusion

The results presented here confirm the observations previously made elsewhere: Millennials in Austria, too, show less support for liberal democracy than previous generations. This finding manifests itself in several characteristics. For one, lower levels of support for democracy and trust in democratic institutions go hand in hand with beliefs that millennial voices are not heard or taken into account by politics. There exist sentiments of a disconnect between this generation and the current political establishment. Political parties in particular seem to be seen as symbols of "old" politics; they are regarded as one of the biggest problems in politics by this generation today. At the same time, we should take into account that the sentiments voiced in the survey used here were still also reflections on the outgoing government: the *Grand Coalition* of the Social Democrats and the Austrian People's Party. It would not be too far-fetched to assume that millennials' attitudes towards the current government—with a millennial at its helm—might yield slightly different results. And while millennials' frustrations with politics seem to be manifold, a vast majority—over ninety percent—indicated that they are generally happy with their lives, and eighty-one percent stated that they are optimistic about their future.

Of course, substantial questions remain unanswered. To better understand the mechanics that contribute to the millennial decline in support for democracy, further research far beyond the scope of this work is needed. Among other inquiries, future work will have to investigate the role of social media as the primary tool used to collect political information, it will have to develop theories regarding millennials' vote choices in Austria, and it will also have to investigate different forms of political participation unique to the social media generation.

At the same time, one should not forget that age in general has always been an important variable in explaining political behavior and preferences, which at the end of the day begs the question: Do millennials really differ that much from other previous "young" generations? The only answer we can give here is that, with respect to appreciation of liberal democracy, the answer is yes.

IV. Challenges and Opportunities (Post-2018)

The Use of Social Media in the 2016 Presidential Election Campaign: Reframing the "Homeland"-Story as an Inclusive Concept

Karin Liebhart
Petra Bernhardt

Preface

When Austrian voters rejected the FPÖ candidate Norbert G. Hofer in the repeated run-off vote of the federal presidential election on December 4, 2016, *Reuters UK* stated that Austria had "at least temporarily" halted "the wave of populism sweeping Western democracies."[1] The international news organization called the election of the independent but Green-backed Alexander Van der Bellen as head of the state "[a] red, white and red signal of hope and of positive change ... beamed from Vienna through Europe."[2] Numerous other news agencies and media outlets throughout Europe and abroad responded similarily to the result of the rerun of the second round. The result of the first run-off election had been annulled by the Constitutional Court of Austria due to irregularities such as the mishandling of postal votes. Eventually, evidence of deliberate manipulation was not found by the Constitutional Court.[3] The date for the second run-off election had been postponed from October 2nd to the ultimate date because the glue on the envelopes for some postal ballots did not stick properly.

The clear victory of Alexander Van der Bellen, who eventually gained 53.8 percent of the vote,[4] was widely termed "a sigh of relief for Europe"

---

1 "Austrians roundly reject far right in presidential election," *Reuters UK* (Dec. 4, 2016), accessed Dec. 14, 2018, https://uk.reuters.com/article/uk-austria-election-idUKKBN13T00Z. Cf. also Francois Murphy, Kirsti Knolle, Philip Oltermann,"Austrians roundly reject far right in presidential election", *The Guardian*, Dec. 4, 2016.

2 "Austrians roundly reject far right in presidential election", *Reuters UK* (Dec. 4, 2016), accessed Dec. 14, 2018, https://uk.reuters.com/article/uk-austria-election-idUKKBN13T00Z.

3 https://www.vol.at/verfassungsgerichtshof-hat-bp-stichwahl-aufgehoben/4771127, accessed April 13, 2018. For detailed information concerning the organization of the presidential election 2016 see https://www.sora.at/fileadmin/downloads/wahlen/2016_BP-Wiederholung_Wahlanalyse.pdf, accessed May 8, 2017.

4 David F.-J. Campbell, Matthias Keppel, "Eine Analyse des österreichischen Nationalratswahlkampfs und der Nationalratswahl 2017: eine kurze vergleichende Betrachtung der Nationalratswahl 2017 und der österreichischen Bundespräsidentschaftswahl 2016", *Sozialwissenschaftliche Rundschau* 58, no.3 (2018): 275-298 (here 291).

after "the twin traumas of Trump and Brexit" and described as an indicator that "the advancing forces of nativist populism" had been stopped for the moment.[5] The majority of European political leaders also reacted enthusiastically to the election outcome and were pleased that a pro-EU politician had become "the face of Austria."[6] Hence, the vote was widely seen as a sign of openess and as a promise for Europe.[7]

But 46.2 percent of Austrian voters finally supported Norbert G. Hofer, who in December 2016 achieved the FPÖ's biggest victory to date. Hofer, the Transport and Infrastructure Minister in the ÖVP-FPÖ coalition government, had won the first round by a wide margin with 31.1 percent and even achieved 49.7 percent in the first run-off election. Accordingly, it quickly became clear that the positive assessment of Austrian voters' openess to the world, expressed in most political and media commentaries on Van der Bellens's victory, was somewhat too optimistic in view of the results of the next legislative election. These snap elections took place about a year later in December 2017 and eventually resulted in the formation of an overall right-wing populist coalition government. The leader of the center-right conservative Kurz List–The New People's Party (31.5 percent) chose the far-right Freedom Party (26 percent)[8] as a junior partner. Both parties had focused their election campaigns primarily on anti-immigration policy and corresponding rhetoric—in stark contrast to Alexander Van der Bellen's inlcusive, and almost exclusively positive, campaign strategy.

Characteristics of the 2016 Presidential Election

With the exception of the 1986 "Waldheim affair," which emerged during the election campaign of the then candidate of the Austrian People's Party and former Secretary General of the United Nations Kurt Waldheim

---

5 Simon Tisdall, "Victory for Van der Bellen and the left is a sigh of relief for Europe", *The Guardian*, Dec. 4, 2016.

6 https://uk.reuters.com/...austria...vanderbellen/pro-eu-van-der-bellen-becomes-the-fac..., accessed Dec. 16, 2018.

7 Cf. http://www.dw.com/en/eu-leaders-rejoice-at-alexander-van-der-bellen-in-austrian-election/a-36651022, accessed April 13, 2017. Julia Ebner, "Austria defeated the far-right Norbert Hofer – finally, some hope for Europe", *The Guardian*, Dec. 7, 2016.

8 David F.-J. Campbell, Matthias Keppel, "Eine Analyse des österreichischen Nationalratswahlkampfs und der Nationalratswahl 2017: eine kurze vergleichende Betrachtung der Nationalratswahl 2017 und der österreichischen Bundespräsidentschaftswahl 2016", *Sozialwissenschaftliche Rundschau* 58, no.3 (2018): 275-298 (here 286).

and reveiled the embedding of antisemitic views in Austrian society,[9] none of the other Austrian presidential elections after 1945 had ever attracted such broad national and international attention and entailed such huge media coverage. Usually presidential elections in Austria are not considered prime political events. Even though presidential elections are the only *ad personam* elections in Austria, which means that the Federal President is the only political representative directly elected by the citizens of the Republic, the office is not considered particularly powerful. Although the 1929 constitutional amendment gave the Federal President more power than the 1920 Constitution, the presidential office is mostly a ceremonial post. Accordingly, all of the presidents of the Second Republic have acted mainly as figureheads.[10]

However, there are many good reasons for the remarkable international interest in the 2016 Austrian presidential election:

- First, notwithstanding that all former federal presidents of the Second Republic of Austria had been supported either by the Social Democrats or the People's Party, none of the candidates of these two parties—which had dominated Austrian politics for decades and also ruled the country in coalition in 2016—managed to reach the run-off election. Neither Rudolf Hundstorfer (SPÖ) nor Andreas Khol (ÖVP) earned enough votes to enter the second round. In 2016, the field of candidates was diverse as never before. During the first round, six candidates stood for election. Besides Rudolf Hundstorfer and Andreas Khol, four other candidates canvassed: Norbert G. Hofer for the Freedom Party, Alexander Van der Bellen as an independent candidate supported by the Greens, Irmgard Griss as an independent candidate, and entrepreneur Richard Lugner as an independent candidate. In the first ballot (April 24, 2016), the far-right candidate Norbert G. Hofer received the lion's share of the vote (35.1 percent). Alexander Van der

9 Ruth Wodak, "The Waldheim affair and antisemitic prejudice in Austrian public discourse', *Patterns of Prejudice*, Volume 24, Issue 2-4/ 1990: 18-33, https://doi.org/10.1080/0031322X.1990.9970049. For details concerning the "Waldheim affair" cf. also Richard Mitten, *The Politics of Antisemitism, The Waldheim Phenomenon in Austria* (Colorado: Boulder, 1990).

10 https://www.austria.org/presidential-elections, accessed Dec. 16, 2017. For further information please see Manfried Welan, Bernhard Moser, "Das österreichische Staatsoberhaupt in Diskussion", in *Jahrbuch für Politik 2010,* ed. Andreas Khol et al., (Vienna, 2011): 195-208, and Manfried Welan, *Der Bundespräsident – Kein Kaiser in der Republik* (Vienna-Cologne-Graz: Böhlau, 1992).

Bellen, former chairman of the Austrian Greens who ran as an independent candidate, achieved second place (21.3 percent), followed by the equally independent Irmgard Griss (18.9 percent). The candidate of the Social Democratic Party took fourth place (11.3 percent), the candidate of the Austrian People's Party fifth place (11.1 percent), and Richard Lugner sixth place, far behind the other candidates (2.3 percent).[11] For the first time since 1945, either a far-right candidate or a Green-backed, liberal candidate would become the President of Austria. Thus, the run-off election was also perceived in a sharpened form as a competition between two antagonistic political worldviews: a far-right, nationalist, anti-immigration, anti-EU one, on the one hand, and a liberal, slightly leftist but certainly open-minded, EU-friendly, and above all humanitarian one, on the other. Against the background of the European-wide upswing of right-wing populist and right-wing extremist parties and movements, the Austrian presidential election of 2016 was given additional significance.

• Second, Alexander Van der Bellen's inauguration as Austria's ninth Federal President on January 26, 2017 was preceded by an exceptionally long and hard-fought election campaign. The campaign started in January 2016 and lasted almost twelve months. The key dates were as follows: April 24th (first round of the election), May 26th (first run-off vote), July 1st (annulment of the result of the first run-off by the Austrian Constitutional Court because of irregularities in connection with the electoral procedure), and December 4th (second run-off vote). Both the Brexit vote and the election of Donald Trump as President of the United States took place between the first and the second run-off. While it is not fully clear what effect the Brexit and the election of Donald Trump had on the Austrian presidential election, survey data of the Austrian institute SORA suggest that Van der Bellen's explicitly pro-European campaign had convinced a remarkable number of voters. Supporters of the now incumbent president mentioned it as the second strongest reason (65 percent) for casting their vote for him, the strongest inducement being the assumption that Van der Bellen would best represent the country abroad (67 percent). Hence, the

11 https://www.vienna.at/specials/bundespraesidentenwahl, accessed Dec. 16, 2018.

election was also seen as an indicator for the country's future development, especially in terms of the importance of democratic political values such as societal pluralism, openess, diversity, and tolerance. 54 percent of those who supported Alexander Van der Bellen and 45 percent of those who voted in favor of Norbert G. Hofer considered their choice a clear decision on the direction.[12]

• Third, all candidates standing for the 2016 presidential election used social media as messaging tools. Each candidate ran a campaign via different channels. Overall, the campaigns for the Austrian presidential election of 2016 can be characterized by a diversification of campaign media and the systematic use of hybrid strategies, linking different types of traditional and social media.[13] While political posters have retained their importance as a well-established medium for campaign communication, the two campaign cycles—and the second one in particular—have experienced the growing importance of online campaigns, with a focus on the increased use of social media platforms. Each candidate who ran in the first round had a campaign website and a Facebook account, five candidates used the micro-blogging platform Twitter, five candidates distributed videos on YouTube, and three candidates shared photos from the campaign trail on platforms such as Instagram and Flickr. One candidate even ran an online fan shop for fundraising purposes. Especially the campaigns of the two run-off candidates, Alexander Van der Bellen and Norbert G. Hofer, were characterized by a clear modernization and professionalization of communication strategies and target group-tailored messages. Messaging activities and channels included both traditional means (such as a media presence, campaign posters, leaflets, give aways, rallies, and personal contact with the candidate) and more innovative ones (such as photos of campaign-related events, selfies with supporters and fans, semi-private photos, throwback photos, and image videos distributed via social media). In addition, the increased diversification of campaign communication was accompanied

12 https://www.sora.at/fileadmin/downloads/wahlen/2016_BP-Wiederholung_Wahlanalyse.pdf: 1-3 (here 6f.), accessed May 8, 2017.
13 Andrew Chadwick, *The Hybrid Media System: Politics and Power* (New York, NY: Oxford University Press, 2013).

by an increased visualization of campaign media and content. The presidential campaigns presented several poster waves, produced kick-off and image videos, or shared campaign photos. Online campaigns in particular were heavily dependent on the use of various visuals such as photos, short videos, GIFs, or graphics. In summary, it can be said that the campaign teams of the two candidates who eventually competed for the office of Federal President used various campaign tools but above all social media platforms such as Facebook, Twitter, or Instagram.[14] The special emphasis on social media made it possible to address target groups more directly and to influence the agenda for traditional media coverage while at the same time circumventing the gatekeeper function of journalists, a strategy that can be qualified as a new step in Austrian political communication. Even though the former Austrian Federal President Heinz Fischer had already strengthened his re-election campaign via social media in 2010,[15] the campaigns of Norbert G. Hofer and Alexander Van der Bellen were the first political campaigns in Austria to be conducted online with this intensity. However, research shows that candidates were not fully exploiting the opportunities offered by the platforms and were concentrating mainly on disseminating their messages.

Social Media and Political Storytelling Across Platforms

While there is no doubt that traditional methods of targeting, such as public appearances on television, radio advertisements, and campaigns from village to village, from city to city, and from province to province, are important tools to make a candidate better known and to disseminate campaign-related information and news, it has become common knowledge that, in particular, the use of social media channels for political campaigns opens up a variety of opportunities

14 Karin Liebhart, Petra Bernhardt, "Political Storytelling on Instagram: Key Aspects of Alexander Van der Bellen's Successful 2016 Presidential Election Campaign", *Media and Communication* 5, no. 4(2017): 15–25 (here 15).

15 Andrea Schenk, *"Bundespräsidentschaftswahlkampf 2010 von Dr. Heinz Fischer" (Diploma thesis, University of Vienna, 2011).* Heinz Fischer had already served two successive terms and was not eligible to run again in 2016.

for politicians and campaign managers. A growing number of studies[16] published in recent years testifies to the assumption that in a world of increasing interconnectedness in which the exposure of the public, and thus of the average voter, to social media is increasing, powerful political communication also results from social networks.[17] The latter are now widely used as a supplement, but also as an alternative, to the traditional media. Social media has also proven to be a powerful tool for reaching voters who are otherwise unlikely to be reached easily. Yaron Katz, for instance, recently found out how Benjamin Netanyahu, the Israeli Prime Minister, successfully used Facebook to immediately connect with potential voters, engage users in direct dialogue, and eventually achieve high participation in his 2013 and 2015 campaigns. Many other examples from throughout the globe could be added.[18] It has to be emphasized that the use of digital technologies neither means an automatic increase (or decrease) in democratic quality, nor fundamentally changes the rules of the democratic political game. Yet the tools open ample novel opportunities for direct communication and inclusion, as well as activation of hitherto less or not at all involved people (citizens and non-citizens of a relevant country). Moreover, they enable politicians to present themselves as social media savvy, innovative, and up to date.[19]

---

16 Cf. for example: Andreas Jungherr, "Twitter Use in Election Campaigns: A Systematic Literature Review", *Journal of Information Technology & Politics* 13, no. 1 (2016): 72-91, DOI: 10.1080/19331681.2015.1132401. http://dx.doi.org/10.1080/19331681.2015.1132401. Karolina Koc-Michalska, Daaren G. Lilleker, Alison Smith, Daniel Weissmann, "The normalization of online campaigning in the web 2.0. era", *European Journal of Communication* 32, no. 3: 331-350.

Melanie Magin, Nicole Podschuweit, Jörg Haßler, Uta Rußmann, "Campaigning in the fourth age of political communication. A multi-method study on the use of Facebook by German and Austrian parties in the 2013 national election campaigns", *Information, Communication & Society* 20, no. 11 (2013): 1698-1719. Karen Ross, Tobias Bürger, "Face to face(book). Social media, political campaigning and the unbearable lightness of being there", *Political Science*, Volume 66 (1) (2014): 42-62, https://doi.org/10.1177/0032318714534106. Uta Russmann, Jakob Svensson, "Interaction on Instagram? Glimpses from the 2014 Swedish Elections", *International Journal of E-Politics* 8, no.1 (2017): 50-66. Kim Strandberg, "A social media revolution or just a case of history repeating itself? The use of social media in the 2011 Finnish parliamentary elections", *New Media & Society* 15, no. 8 (2013): 1329-1347, https://doi.org/10.1177/1461444812470612.

17 Cf. http://www.pewinternet.org/2018/03/01/social-media-use-in-2018, accessed Dec. 17, 2018.

18 Yaron Katz, "Israel's Social Media Elections", *Open Journal of Political Science* 8, (2018): 525-535. https://doi.org/10.4236/ojps.2018.84032.

19 Andreas Jungherr, "Einsatz digitaler Technologie im Wahlkampf", Oct. 9, 2017, http://www.bpb.de/lernen/digitale-bildung/medienpaedagogik/medienkompetenz-schriftenreihe/257600/einsatz-digitaler-technologie-im-wahlkampf Feb. 25, 2019. Cf. also Shelley Boulianne, "Social media use and participation: A meta-analysis of current research", *Information, Communication & Society*, Volume 5 (2015): 524 – 538, Andreas Jungherr, "Four Functions of Digital Tools in Election Campaigns: The German Case", *International Journal of Press/Politics*, Volume 3 (2016): 358 – 377, and Andreas Jungherr, "Das Internet in der politischen Kommunikation: Forschungsstand und Perspektiven", *Politische Vierteljahresschrift*, Volume 2 (2017)): 285 – 316.

While scientific literature on the strategic functions of social media platforms in the field of political communication, and particularly in election campaigns, is constantly growing, the authors agree that relevant developments began in the early 2000s and were reinforced by the successful campaigns of Barack Obama in the United States in 2008 and 2012.[20] Especially Obama's 2008 grassroots campaign, which relied primarily on online services, is said to have fundamentally redefined political campaigning, especially in terms of addressing voters and digitally mobilizing supporters, as well as reaching new target groups, particularly the younger generation.

Anyway, political communication works best if a good story is told in social (and also in traditional) media.[21] Yaron Katz describes the plot as follows: "… developing and executing a social media political campaign is a complex process that requires good strategy that identifies and addresses different target audiences and creates a stable platform to highlight the candidates and their political agenda. All of these components work together to compete with the opposing parties and convince the public to make a choice and vote for a particular party or candidate."[22] Political storytelling serves as a theoretical key concept in this regard. In the context of strategic campaign communication, storytelling makes it possible to convey campaign messages in a narrative and visual form in order to instruct, entertain, and signal the candidate's personality and intentions.[23] Especially social media channels enable "long-term storytelling with few limitations on content controlled by the candidate."[24] Kevin J. Hunt considers storytelling "an inevitable part of political rhetoric," which facilitates the reference to

---

20 Nina Keim, Adrian Rosenthal, "Memes, big data und storytelling. Rückblick auf den digitalen US Wahlkampf 2012", in: *Die US Präsidentschaftswahl 2012, ed.* Christoph Bieber, Klaus Kamps (Wiesbaden: VS, 2016) 307–330. Cf. also Ognyan Seizov, Marion G. Müller, "Multimodal Campaign Strategies in the US Presidential Election 2012: A Content Analysis of the Campaign Websites of Barack Obama and Mitt Romney", *Die US Präsidentschaftswahl 2012, ed.* Christoph Bieber, Klaus Kamps (Wiesbaden: VS, 2016): 331-361.

21 Henry Jenkins, *Convergence culture: Where old and new media collide* (New York: New York University Press, 2006). Cf. also Henry Jenkins (2010), "Transmedia storytelling and entertainment: An annotated syllabus", *Continuum: Journal of Media & Cultural Studies* 24, no.6 (2010): 943–958. Leticia Bode, Emily K. Vraga, "Studying politics across media", *Political Communication* 35, no.1 (2018): 1-7, doi:10.1080/10584609.2017.1334730.

22 Yaron Katz, "Israel's Social Media Elections", *Open Journal of Political Science* 8 (2018): 525-535 (here 525). https://doi.org/10.4236/ojps.2018.84032.

23 Benjamin W. Redekop, "Embodying the story: Theodore Roosevelt's conservation leadership", *Leadership* 12 (2016): 159-185.

24 Janis T. Page, Margaret E. Duffy (2016): "What Does Credibility Look like? Tweets and Walls in U.S. Presidential Candidates' Visual Storytelling". *Journal of Political Marketing* 6, 2016, 1-29.

abstract ideas as well as to politicians who run for elections.[25] In practice, a candidate's personal and biographic story can be disseminated, the candidate can be humanized, and his/her character traits can be developed. All this can be done with the help of visuals that resonate with target audiences and specific user groups.

Transmedia storytelling is always based on a variety of strategies and allows for expanding the scope of campaign messages through synergetic use of several social and analog media, while "each piece of media" adds to the entire "story world."[26] These strategies include "references to biographically relevant settings and locations, family histories, or the use of personal photos within the context of the political campaign."[27] The quote highlights the increasing importance of personalization in political campaign communication, where the staged political personality comes to the fore.[28] Holtz-Bacha, Langer, and Merkle even determine a "shift in emphasis from the political to the personal sphere."[29] Moreover, political storytellers tend to dramatize themselves not only for entertainment purposes "but also to signal their personalities and intentions"[30] since "[p]eople … won't engage without a good story."[31]

---

25 Kevin J. Hunt, "Political storytelling and the land of make-believe", *Huffington Post*, accessed Dec. 16, 2018, http://www.huffingtonpost.co.uk/kevin-j-hunt/political-storytelling_b_6895174.html.

26 Henry Jenkins, "Voices of a new vernacular: A forum on digital storytelling. Interview with Henry Jenkins", *International Journal of Communication* 11 (2017): 1061–1068.

27 Karin Liebhart, Petra Bernhardt, "Political Storytelling on Instagram: Key Aspects of Alexander Van der Bellen's Successful 2016 Presidential Election Campaign", *Media and Communication* 5, no. 4, 2017: 15–25 (here 16).

28 Meital Balmas, Tamir Sheafer, "Personalization of politics", in: *The international encyclopedia of political communication volume II*, ed. Gainpetro Mazzoleni, Kevin G. Barnhurst, Ken'ichi Ikeda, Rousiley. C. M. Maia, Hartmut Wessler, (Hoboken, New Jersey: Wiley Blackwell, 2016): 944-952 (here 994). Diego Garzia, *Personalization of politics and electoral change (*London: Palgrave Macmillan, 2014). Lauri Karvonen, "The personalisation of politics: A study of parliamentary democracies", *Australian Journal of Political Science*, 47 no.3 (2012): DOI: 10.1080/10361146.2012.704891 September 2012. Hans-Peter Kriesi, "Personalization of national election campaigns". *Party Politics 8, no.* 6 (2012): 825-844. Peter Van Aelst, Tamir Sheafer, James Stanyer, "The personalization of mediated political communication: A review of concepts, operationalizations and key findings", *Journalism* 13, no. 2 (2011): 203–220.

29 Christina Holtz-Bacha, Ana I. Langer, Susanne Merkle, "The personalization of politics in comparative perspective: Campaign coverage in Germany and the United Kingdom", *European Journal of Communication 29, no.* 2 (2014): 153–170.

30 Benjamin W. Redekop, "Embodying the story: Theodore Roosevelt's conservation leadership", *Leadership* 12 (2016): 159-185.

31 Sarah Weber, "In a political game all about storytelling, which candidate is using narrative to get ahead?", *Quantified Communications*, accessed December 2016, 2018), www.quantifiedcommunications.com/blog/storytelling-in-politics.

Reframing "Heimat" ("Homeland")

Alexander Van der Bellen's campaign used personalized and transmedial storytelling on both the verbal and the visual level with the concept of "*Heimat*"("homeland") as the central story. Yet Van der Bellen defined "*Heimat*" in a different way than his political opponent, the candidate of the Freedom Party Norbert G. Hofer. Presenting "*Heimat*"as an inclusive and integrative concept facilitated differentiation from his far-right opponent.

The FPÖ has "owned" the issue at least since the second half of the 1980s, when Jörg Haider was elected party chairman of the FPÖ and swiftly began to reshape the party's image. This included the adoption of a new campaign focus based on anti-immigrant and later particularly anti-Muslim sentiments, on the one side, and critics of the "political establishment" as enemies of "the people," on the other. The FPÖ qualified immigration and integration issues, which previously had not been a hot topic in Austrian political discourse, as a threat to the Austrian "*Heimat*" and its culturally homogeneously constructed population. The re-positioning of the party, the corresponding radical-populist rhetoric, and an overall right-wing populist style have proved their worth in winning voters.[32] Since then, immigration and the protection of the Austrian "homeland" against the supposed danger from abroad have been the focus of the FPÖ's campaigns. Against the background of the increasing success of this topic, the FPÖ launched an initiative for a referendum on a more restrictive immigration policy in 1993, using the motto „Austria First!" In the late 1990s, the FPÖ began speaking about a threat of „Islamization" of Austria and Europe. In the wake of these developments, the Austrian Freedom Party and later the Alliance for the Future of Austria (BZÖ) as well continuously made populist, aggressive interventions into the political discourse. They portrayed Islam as a violent and extremist ideology, "alien" to Austria (and Europe). The Freedom Party, which had previously supported Austria's accession to the EU, also turned into a hard Eurosceptic attitude. This mixture of anti-immigration attitudes, anti-Muslimism, and Euroscepticism paid off well and led the party to unprecedented electoral successes on both the local and the national level. Under the leadership of the current chairman, Heinz-Christian Strache, the FPÖ has radicalized further both in its ideology and its campaign

32 Sylvia Kritzinger, Karin Liebhart, "Austria", in: *Handbook of European Elections*, ed. Donatella M. Viola (London: Routledge/Taylor and Francis, 2016): 377-395 (here 381f.). Ruth Wodak, *The Politics of Fear: What Right-Wing Populist Discourses Mean* (Los Angeles et al.: SAGE, 2016). Ruth Wodak, Anton Pelinka, *The Haider Phenomenon in Austria* (New Brunswick: Transaction Publishers, 2002).

messaging, while the main campaign topics—no matter if they related to local, regional, national, or European elections (see particularly the EP election of 2014)[33]—remained the same: anti-immigration, anti-Muslimism, and outspoken Euroscepticism. This specific combination has proven to be highly successful to the present day. In corresponding political advertisings, Austrian identity symbols, such as St. Stephen's Cathedral, the famous Viennese church bell "Pummerin," or the Clock tower in Graz, were frequently shown.[34]

The main aim of the Freedom Party was to create an image as the "Homeland-Party" and (sole) protector of the "native Austrians," their "homeland," and "Austrian identity" against migrants, as well as against the EU elites and bureaucracy. "Protect the homeland, close the borders" ("*Heimat schützen, Grenzen dicht*") was used as a slogan by the FPÖ Burgenland for the regional election of 2015.[35] The FPÖ Lower Austria launched the motto "Our country for our children. Courage for the homeland" ("*Unser Land für unsere Kinder. Mut zur Heimat*") in the regional election of 2008.[36] Similar slogans were also used at the federal level like, for example, "Homeland instead of Schüssel [former Austrian Federal Chancellor] and Brussels" ("*Heimat statt Schüssel und Brüssel*") for the 2006 parliamentary election.[37] Consistently, Norbert G. Hofer also used the "*Heimat*" concept for the first round of his pesidential election campaign in March 2016. The campaign poster showed the portrait of the candidate with the background covered by a stylized Austrian national flag. The slogan was: "Your homeland needs you now!" ("*Deine Heimat braucht dich jetzt!*")[38] Recently the FPÖ Upper Austria published a poster depicting the deputy governor of Upper Austria and member of the Freedom Party Manfred Haimbuchner in traditional costume with the background of a lake and mountains—a "typical" Austrian landscape. The

33 https://strategieanalysen.at/wp-content/uploads/bg/isa_sora_wahlanalyse_euw2014.pdf, 1-13 (here 9), accessed Feb. 25, 2019.
34 Michal Krzyzanowski, "From Anti-Immigration and Nationalist Revisionism to Islamophobia: Continuities and Shifts in Recent Discourses and Patterns of Political Communication of the Freedom Party of Austria", in: *Right-Wing Populism in Europe. Politics and Discourse.* ed. Ruth Wodak, Majid KhosraviNik, Brigitte Mral, (London-New York: Bloomsbury, 2013): 133-148.
35 https://www.dasbiber.at/blog/arbeit-fuer-unsere-leut, May 18, 2015, accessed Dec. 17, 2018.
36 http://www.wien-konkret.at/politik/wahlen/noe-landtagswahl2008/noe-wahlplakate/, accessed Dec. 17, 2018.
37 http://www.demokratiezentrum.org/de/bildstrategien/europa.html?index=10&dimension=Zeit, accessed Dec. 17, 2018.
38 https://www.fpoe.at/artikel/aufstehen-fuer-oesterreich-deine-heimat-braucht-dich-jetzt/, accessed Dec. 16, 2018.

inscription has an appealing character: "Homeland obligates. Preserve tradition. Cultivate ancient customs. Protect identity" ("*Heimat verpflichtet. Tradition bewahren. Brauchtum pflegen. Identität schützen*").[39] The corresponding statement on the FPÖ website underscores the importance of protecting and preserving tradition and ancient customs and identity, especially in times of strong immigration.[40] How the concept of "homeland" was defined by the Freedom Party is obvious: segregative and exclusionary.

In contrast, the Alexander Van der Bellen campaign used the concept of "homeland" in an integrative interpretation, and used it as core of a transmedial story. The somewhat risky strategy of appropriating a concept previously occupied by the political opponent worked very well, not least due to a well thought out social media strategy. Hence, Van der Bellen successfully challenged the issue-ownership of the FPÖ in this regard. Alexander Van der Bellen introduced the story of the "homeland" as an integrative concept and presented it as core narrative of his presidential election campaign. The "homeland"-story essentially referred to his personal childhood experiences when Van der Bellen's family found refuge in the Tyrolean Kaunertal Valley. The Kaunertal Valley became a new home for the family, a place where Van der Bellen grew up and experienced acceptance, cohesion, and solidarity. In addition, this story comprises all elements a good political story should include: appeal to both reason and emotion,[41] as well as dynamic characters and plots that evolve over time.[42]

The following analysis of Van der Bellen's transmedially communicated, highly personalized "homeland"-story focuses mainly on online storytelling strategies and the functions of visual content for hybrid political campaigns. Visuals can be seen as crucial elements in storytelling strategies:[43] "Visual images play a central role in constructing political images … they serve as arguments, have an agenda setting function, dramatize policy, aid in emotional appeals, build the candidate´s image, create identification, connect to societal symbols, transport the audience, and

39 https://www.fpoe.at/themen/parteiprogramm/heimat-identitaet-und-umwelt/, accessed Dec. 17, 2018.

40 https://www.fpoe-ooe.at/fpoe-praesentiert-heimat-verpflichtet-kampagne, accessed Dec. 17, 2018.

41 Howard E. Gardner, *Leading minds: An anatomy of leadership* (New York: Basic Books, 1995).

42 George R. Goethals, "Presidential Leadership". *Annual Review of Psychology*, Volume 56 (2005): 545-70.

43 Caroline L. Muñoz, Terri L. Towner, "The Image is the Message: Instagram Marketing and the 2016 Presidential Primary Season", *Journal of Political Marketing* 16, no. 4 (2017): 290-318, http://dx.doi.org/10.1080/15377857.2017.1334254.

add ambiguity."[44] Highlighting the important role of visual messaging in social media during the Austrian presidential election campaign from January 2016 until December 2016, it becomes clear how the so-called "visual web" particularly privileges visual forms of communication on digital platforms.

The repetition of coherent verbal and visual messaging elements in social media posts suggests which stories the campaign strategically promotes. The analysis therefore applies the method of storytracking and includes the Facebook, Twitter, and Instagram accounts of the then candidate and current Austrian President Alexander Van der Bellen throughout 2016.

The reconstructive analysis tracks direct and indirect references to the "homeland"-story in Alexander Van der Bellen's social media posts on Facebook, Twitter, and Instagram. A direct reference is made, for example, by using the word "homeland" in the visuals or texts of a social media post. An indirect reference is made by using photos of the Kaunertal Valley in the visuals of a social media post.

As part of a research project funded by the Austrian National Bank (OeNB),[45] a qualitative content and subsequent frame analysis of 1.865 social media posts between January and December 2016 were carried out in order to identify recurring narratives and recurring visual messages. A total of 91 social media posts concentrated directly or indirectly on the "homeland"-story (Instagram N=38/504, Twitter n= 32/506, Facebook n=21/855). From a purely numerical point of view, this does not seem to be a significant story. In view of the fact that it was the most popular and most discussed story of the campaign (both in traditional and social media) and that its crucial role for the success of the campaign was widely recognized by political analysts, a more detailed analysis makes sense.

The "homeland"-story was tracked over the campaign cycle of twelve months. The analysis yields the following results:

- The "homeland"-story connects the personal and biographical background of the candidate with his core political messages. The connection is established via direct and indirect references.

44 Dan Schill, "The Visual Image and the Political Image: A Review of Visual Communication Research in the Field of Political Communication," *Review of Communication* 12, no. 2 (2012): 118-142 (here 118, 122).

45 Project 17453 - *The Austrian Presidential Elections 2016: Visual Political Storytelling* (2017/02 - 2019/03).

Direct reference to the homeland story mentioning the Homeland: "HOMELAND needs cohesion"; Tweet by @vanderbellen on 21 March 2016: Poster presentation of Alexander #VanderBellen: Information about the campaign on the website vanderbellen.at/kampagne #Bpwahl16.

Indirect reference to the homeland story by showing the Kauner Valley: "Short break to gain strength and soak up the sun with my wife in the beautiful Kauner Valley, before our campaign movement kicks off for the fourth time. (vdb)"; Tweet by @vanderbellen on 27 September 2016.

• The Kaunertal Valley serves as a recurring setting for campaign visuals (e.g. posters, wallpapers, campaign giveaways, etc.) and facilitates hybrid campaign stratgies.

Tweet by @vanderbellen on 26 April 2016: Poster presentation of Alexander #VanderBellen: Information about the campaign on the website vanderbellen.at/kampagne #Bpwahl16

• The "homeland" serves as a venue for campaign activities (e.g. hiking with journalists, interviews, etc.).

Tweet by @vanderbellen on 3 August 2016 during a hiking trip with journalists in the Kaunertal: "Alpine hike #Kaunertal in fantastic weather. Let's go! #vanderbellen".

Tweet by @vanderbellen on 3 August 2016 during a hiking trip with journalists in the Kaunertal: "On a mountain hike in the 'Kaunertal: now lunch break #wanderbellen".

• The "homeland" serves as a biographical anchor of the candidate. His private story is presented with so-called throwback photos on Instagram. Several throwback photos show Van der Bellen either as a child with his parents in the Tyrolean mountains or as a young adult with his sister in an alpine landscape. These throwback photos are regarded as background stories because of their captions and the importance attached to the Tyrolean mountains, the "homeland"-story, and Van der Bellen's passion for hiking. The story of the Van der Bellen family, combined with the central campaign narrative, thus becomes a prime example of a personalized verbal and visual storytelling strategy. With the hiking photos, Van der Bellen also expresses what the (environmentally friendly) hobby means to him. At the same time, the staging of mountain landscape and him hiking make an important contribution to the "homeland"-story world.

Throwback photo, „Heute wie damals: in die Berg is er gern Instagram post by vanderbellen on 4 February 2016.

Throwback photo, „Bergluft, Familie, Natur." Instagram post by vanderbellen on 19 May 2016.

• The "homeland" serves as a carrier for campaign messages. One of Van der Bellen's core messages was that "homeland needs cohesion." He used the integrative concept of "homeland," which he introduced as a means that also enabled him to distinguish himself from his right-wing opponent. Furthermore, reframing "homeland" made it possible to separate the concept from the political categories of local/national, and respectively space/territory, and to link the local (the Tyrolean Kaunertal Valley), the national (Austria), and the supranational (Europe/EU) levels of politics. The strategy appeared to be operational. Highlighting also the emotional component of the campaign story, Molly Scott Cato (*The Guardian*) summarized, for instance, Van der Bellen's approach as follows: "[He] … ran on a ticket of unity above division; love not hate; and confidence rather than fear. … He also stood proudly and confidently as a global citizen within the family of Europe."[46]

Tweet by @vanderbellen on 17 August 2016: "Homeland needs cohesion" #VanderBellen #mehrdennje (#morethenever)

"Austria is our homeland. We all have an obligation to ensure that our homeland remains in good shape in the future. Home means to stick together, not to divide. This common ground that makes us strong must be protected."
Alexander Van der Bellen

46 Molly Scott Cato, "Austria's quiet Green victory, trading in the politics of hope not fear", *The Guardian*, Dec 7, 2016.

• The “homeland” serves as topic for further campaign-related discussions (e.g. when journalists pick up the “homeland”-story in interviews).

Retweet of Austrian news magazine @profilonline by @vanderbellen on 15 November 2015: “What does homeland mean for you, Mr. Van der Bellen?” #VanDerBellen #bpwahl16 #bpw16 @vanderbellen

- The candidate uses the "homeland"-story to explain his understanding of office and duties.

Tweet by @vanderbellen on 30 September 2016: "The Federal President should represent our homeland worthily in the world. I think it takes a personality to balance and build bridges. [...]"

Tweet by @vanderbellen on 23 October 2016: "I want to be a president for all Austrians. I will always act to the best of my knowledge and belief for the reputation of our homeland. So that Austria remains a strong country in the heart of Europe."

Alexander Van der Bellen and his campaign team have succeeded in reframing a critical political concept and thus transforming a previously completely exclusionary meaning into an integrative one. According to Robert M. Entman, frames work by elevating particular pieces of information into salience. While accentuating selected aspects of issues, they make certain interpretations more likely.[47] Connecting the notion "homeland" with the topics of migration, acceptance, and cohesion, by means of personalized storytelling on both the verbal and the visual level, suggests a particular interpretation: "Feeling home" is not bound to a place. Rather, it is a sense of longing and belonging. Hence "home"/"homeland" can be the Tyrolean Kaunertal Valley, where Alexander Van der Bellen's family found refuge during his childhood; Austria, the country of which he wanted to become president; but also Europe, respectively the European Union. The Kaunertal Valley becomes the focal point of the "homeland"-story, which extends in concentric circles from Tyrol via Austria to the European Union, a concept that perfectly fits Van der Bellen's understanding of the role of the Austrian Federal President as an integrative figure. During his campaign, Van der Bellen often repeated that he would be an "open-minded, liberal-minded and above all a pro-European president."[48] After he had actually won the second round re-vote, Van der Bellen said in a victory speech, "I will be a pro-European president of Austria open to the world."[49] Throughout the campaign, the relevant messages were communicated not only verbally but also visually via various campaign channels, most notably social media. Visual representations of (the landscape) of the Tyrolean "homeland"—especially photos of the Kaunertal Valley—obviously also relate to Austria's self-image, its external (touristic) image, and the traditional political iconography of the country. During the campaign, the "homeland"-story transformed from verbal and visual messaging elements into a political vision represented by the candidate. This visionary dimension forms an essential part of the successful political campaign. Howard E. Gardner distinguishes between three types of leaders who appear in political stories: the ordinary leader (who relates to current and traditional stories), the innovative leader (who brings a fresh twist to latent stories), and the visionary leader (who creates a new story).[50] The Van der

47 Robert M. Entman, "Framing: Toward Clarification of a Fractured Paradigm", in: *Journal of Communication* 43, no. 4 1993: 51-58 (here 51ff.).

48 Philip Oltermann, "Austrian Far-Right Party's Triumph in Presidential Poll Could Spell Turmoil", *The Guardian*, 25 April, 2016 and 4 December 2016.

49 "Austrians roundly reject far right in presidential election", Reuters UK (Dec. 4, 2016), accessed Dec. 14, 2018, https://uk.reuters.com/article/uk-austria-election-idUKKBN13T00Z.

50 Howard E. Gardner, *Leading minds: An anatomy of leadership* (New York: Basic Books, 1995).

Bellen campaign suggests that Austria's incumbent president represents an in-between the innovative and the visionary type. Positioning the candidate accordingly, by means of reframing the "homeland"-story and presenting it as an inclusive concept, Van der Bellen's campaign team has accomplished what only few political experts and analysts had considered possible after the vote count of the first round of the election in April 2016.[51] The protracted election battle that followed has divided the electorate.[52] Yet it has not questioned the fundamentals of democracy in Austria. According to a SORA report from December 2016, 83 percent of the interviewees trusted in the election procedure, the correct realization of the second run-off vote, and the vote count according to the rules. Furthermore, a huge majority of respondents (80 percent) agreed that they would accept the candidate whom they did not support as Federal President should he be elected. Such numbers indicate that Austrian voters to a very high degree support the basic rules of the democratic political game and testify to the stability of the Austrian democratic political system.[53]

---

51 https://www.vienna.at/endergebnis-der-bp-wahl-2016-hofer-bei-364-prozent-van-der-bellen-bei-204/4700510, (May 22, 2016), accessed Feb. 25, 2019.

52 Bjoern Hengst, "Bundespräsidentenwahl in Österreich. Das gespaltene Land," http://www.spiegel.de/politik/ausland/praesidentenwahl-in-oesterreich-das-gespaltene-land-a-1093556.html. accessed Feb. 25, 2019. Timo Steppat, "Der umgedrehte Trump-Effekt," https://www.faz.net/aktuell/politik/ausland/europa/wahl-in-oesterreich-2016-alexander-van-der-bellen-gewinnt-14559341.html, (Dec. 5, 2016), accessed Feb. 5, 2019.

53 https://strategieanalysen.at/wp-content/uploads/2016/12/isa_sora_wahlanalyse_bpstichwahl_2016_neu.pdf, 1-13 (here 9), accessed Feb. 25., 2019.

The Quality of Democracy in Austria in Comparative Perspective

David F.J. Campbell

1. Introduction: Research Design and Research Questions for the Comparative Analysis

This analysis focuses on quality of democracy in a comparative approach.[1] The pivotal analytical research questions are three-fold:

1. To develop, or to "proto-type," a conceptual framework of analysis for a global comparison of quality of democracy. This framework will also reference to the concept of the "Quadruple Helix innovation systems."[2] Quadruple Helix and Quadruple Helix structures represent here an interdisciplinary, and trans-disciplinary, linkage that connects research in quality-of-democracy with innovation concepts.

2. This same conceptual framework will be used and will be tested for comparing and measuring quality of democracy in the different OECD (Organization for Economic Co-operation and Development) and EU (European Union) countries. This comparison is more exploratory in nature and character and wants to provide further evidence about the usefulness of the developed framework. This framework should inspire and inform future research on quality of democracy but

---

1 Michael J Sodaro, *Comparative Politics. A Global Introduction*. (Boston: Mc Graw Hill, 2004); David F. J. Campbell, "Wie links oder wie rechts sind Österreichs Länder? Eine komparative Langzeitanalyse des parlamentarischen Mehrebenensystems Österreichs (1945-2007)". *SWS-Rundschau* 47, no. 4 (2007): 381-404.

2 David F. J. Campbell, Elias G. Carayannis, 'Explaining and Comparing Quality of Democracy in Quadruple Helix Structures: The Quality of Democracy in the United States and in Austria, Challenges and Opportunities for Development', in: *Cyber-Development, Cyber-Democracy and Cyber-Defense. Challenges, Opportunities and Implications for Theory, Policy and Practice.* Elias G. Carayannis, David F. J. Campbell, Marios Panagiotis Efthymiopoulos, (New York, NY: Springer, 2014), 117-148.

also future research in reference to knowledge and innovation systems.[3]

3. Finally, and based on the international comparison, different propositions and recommendations for an improvement of quality of democracy reform in Austria are being developed and suggested. By this, Austrian democracy qualifies as a case study for democracy enhancement.[4]

In our analysis presented here, quality of democracy should be compared mutually between all member countries to the OECD and all the member countries to the EU, thus leading to a country-based comparison of democratic quality. However, most, if not all, member countries of the EU are also member countries to the OECD (For a further general reading on this complex, see also Carayannis, Elias G. / David F. J. Campbell [5] and Helms).[6]

There is naturally not only a single democracy theory (theory about quality of democracy), but the field of democratic theories is rather

---

3 David F. J. Campbell, Die österreichische Demokratiequalität in Perspektive [The Quality of Democracy in Austria in Perspective], 293-315, in: *Die österreichische Demokratie im Vergleich*,,ed. Ludger Helms, David M. Wineroither (Baden-Baden: Nomos, 2012). David F. J. Campbell, Elias G. Carayannis, "Quality of Democracy and Innovation, 1527-1534", in: *Encyclopedia of Creativity, Invention, Innovation and Entrepreneurship.* Elias G. Carayannis (Editor-in-Chief), Igor N. Dubina, Norbert Seel, David F. J. Campbell, Dimitri Uzunidis (Associate Editors): (New York: Springer, 2013); David F. J. Campbell, Elias G. Carayannis, *Epistemic Governance in Higher Education. Quality Enhancement of Universities for Development,* (New York: Springer, 2013); David F. J. Campbell, Elias G. Carayannis Scheherazade S. Rehman, "Quadruple Helix Structures of Quality of Democracy in Innovation Systems: the USA, OECD Countries, and EU Member Countries in Global Comparison",*Journal of the Knowledge Economy* 6, no. 3 (2015) 467-493.

4 David F. J. Campbell,"Reformvorschläge für Österreichs Demokratie: Diskussionspunkte zur Demokratiequalität", in: *Direkte Demokratie und Parlamentarismus. Wie kommen wir zu den besten Entscheidungen?* Theo Öhlinger / Klaus Poier (Vienna: Böhlau, 2015), 43-56, David F. J. Campbell,"Verbesserungsmöglichkeiten und Reformvorschläge für Demokratiequalität in Österreich". *SWS-Rundschau* 55, no. 2 (2015) 219-239, David F. J. Campbell, Elias G. Carayannis, "Explaining and Comparing Quality of Democracy in Quadruple Helix Structures: The Quality of Democracy in the United States and in Austria, Challenges and Opportunities for Development", in: *Cyber-Development, Cyber-Democracy and Cyber-Defense. Challenges, Opportunities and Implications for Theory, Policy and Practice,* ed. Elias G. Carayannis, David F. J. Campbell, Marios Panagiotis Efthymiopoulos :(New York: Springer, 2014). 117-148.

5 David F. J. Campbell, Elias G. Carayannis, *Mode 3 Knowledge Production in Quadruple Helix Innovation Systems. 21st-Century Democracy, Innovation, and Entrepreneurship for Development* Volume 7, (New York: Springer, 2012).

6 Ludger Helms, *Die Institutionalisierung der liberalen Demokratie. Deutschland im internationalen Vergleich,* (Frankfurt: Campus, 2007).

pluralistic and heterogeneous. Various theories and models co-exist about democracies.[7] Metaphorically, based on these (partly contradictory) different theories, democracy theory could also be constructed as a *meta-theory*. Theoretically, democracy can be understood as *multi-paradigmatic*, meaning that there is not only one (dominant) paradigm for democracy. Therefore, we have to state pluralism, competition, co-existence, and co-development of different theories about democracy. *Our analysis is based on the additional assumption, which does not have to be shared necessarily, that between democracy theory on the one hand and democracy measurement on the other hand, important, and also conceptual, cross-references (and linkages) take place.* Just like there is no "perfect" democracy measurement, there is also no "perfect" democracy theory.[8] Theories about the quality of democracy are partly already further developed than it is often (in popular research) being assumed. One of the most important theory models about the quality of democracy that permits an empirical operationalization comes from Guillermo O'Donnell[9]. The field of the quality of democracy is no longer a vague one, especially not for OECD-countries.

The further structure of this contribution is divided into the following sections: In Sections 2 and 3, different conceptualizations of democracy, quality of democracy, and knowledge democracy are being presented, followed in Section 4 by the concrete empirical comparison of quality of democracy in the OECD countries and the member countries to the European Union. In the conclusion (Section 5), the focus is to engage in

7 Gerardo L. Munck, "What is Democracy? A Reconceptualization of the Quality of Democracy. Political Concepts: Committee on Concepts and Methods. Working Paper Series" (Working Paper 60, May 2014).

8 David F.J. Campbell, Thorsten D. Barth, "Wie können Demokratie und Demokratiequalität gemessen werden? Modelle, Demokratie-Indices und Länderbeispiele im globalen Vergleich," *SWS-Rundschau* 49, no. 2 (2009): 208-233; Brigitte Geissel, Marianne Kneuer, Hans-Joachim Lauth, "Measuring the Quality of Democracy: Introduction". *International Political Science Review* 37, no. 5 (2016) 571-579.Hans-Joachim Lauth, *Demokratie und Demokratiemessung. Eine konzeptionelle Grundlegung für den interkulturellen Vergleich,* (Wiesbaden: VS Verlag für Sozialwissenschaften, 2004); Hans-Joachim Lauth,"Möglichkeiten und Grenzen der Demokratiemessung," *Zeitschrift für Staats- und Europawissenschaften* 8, no. 4 (2010): 498-529; Hans Joachim Lauth, "Qualitative Ansätze der Demokratiemessung," *Zeitschrift für Staats- und Europawissenschaften* 9, no.1 (2011): 49-77; Hans-Joachim Lauth, "The Internal Relationships of the Dimensions of Democracy: The Relevance of Trade-Offs for Measuring the Quality of Democracy," *International Political Science Review* 37, no.5 (2016): 606-617; Gerardo L. Munck, *Measuring Democracy,* (Baltimore: The Johns Hopkins University Press, 2009); Gerardo L. Munck, "What is Democracy? A Reconceptualization of the Quality of Democracy. Political Concepts: Committee on Concepts and Methods. Working Paper Series" (Working Paper 60, May 2014).

9 Guillermo O'Donnell, "Human Development, Human Rights, and Democracy", in: *The Quality of Democracy. Theory and Applications,* ed. Guillermo O'Donnell, Jorge Vargas Cullell, Osvaldo M. Iazzetta (Notre Dame: University of Notre Dame Press. 2004), 9-92.

propositions and recommendations for a further and innovative quality of democracy reform in Austria. Furthermore, the "Quadruple Helix" is being emphasized as an interdisciplinary and trans-disciplinary approach for bringing democracy-discourses and innovation-discourses closer together.

2. Conceptualizing Democracy and the Quality of Democracy: Freedom, Equality, Control, and Sustainable Development (Model of Quadruple Helix Structures)

How can democracy and the quality of democracy be conceptualized? Such a (theoretically justified) conceptualization is necessary in order for democracy and the quality of democracy to be subjected to a democracy measurement, *whereby democracy measurement, in this case, can be examined along the lines of the definition of democracy (thus democracy measurement to be utilized to improve the democracy theory).* Hans-Joachim Lauth[10] suggests in this context a "three-dimensional concept of democracy," which is composed of the following (conceptual) dimensions: *equality, freedom, and control* (See Figures 1 and 2) (See also several publications by Lauth.[11]) *These dimensions we want to interpret as "Basic Dimensions" of democracy and of the quality of democracy.* Lauth[12] underlines that these dimensions are "sufficient" to obtain a definition of democracy. The term "dimension" offers a conceptual elegance that can be applied "trans-theoretically," meaning that different theories of democracy may be put in relation and may be mapped comparatively in reference to those dimensions. Metaphorically formulated, dimensions behave like "building blocks" for theories and the continuing development of theory. In the following analysis (See later), we furthermore propose to introduce "sustainable development" as a further basic dimension for democracy and quality of democracy. *To do this, was (first) explicitly*

10 Hans-Joachim Lauth, *Demokratie und Demokratiemessung. Eine konzeptionelle Grundlegung für den interkulturellen Vergleich*, (Wiesbaden: VS Verlag für Sozialwissenschaften, 2004), 32-101.

11 Hans-Joachim Lauth, "Möglichkeiten und Grenzen der Demokratiemessung," *Zeitschrift für Staats- und Europawissenschaften* 8, no. 4 (2010): 498-529; Hans-Joachim Lauth, "Qualitative Ansätze der Demokratiemessung," *Zeitschrift für Staats- und Europawissenschaften* 9, no.1, (2011): 49-77; Hans-Joachim Lauth, "The Internal Relationships of the Dimensions of Democracy: The Relevance of Trade-Offs for Measuring the Quality of Democracy," *International Political Science Review* 37, no. 5, (2016): 606-617; Hans-Joachim Lauth, Oliver Schlenkrich, "Making Trade-Offs Visible: Theoretical and Methodological Considerations about the Relationship between Dimensions and Institutions of Democracy and Empirical Findings," *Politics and Governance* 6, no. 1, (2018): 78-91.

12 Hans-Joachim Lauth, *Demokratie und Demokratiemessung. Eine konzeptionelle Grundlegung für den interkulturellen Vergleich*, (Wiesbaden: VS Verlag für Sozialwissenschaften, 2004):96.

suggested by Campbell.[13] With the adding of sustainable development, possible relationships between *democracy, development, and economic growth* can also be analyzed more directly (See the following publications in footnote fourteen).[14]

Figure 1: The Basic Quadruple-Dimensional Structure of Democracy and the Quality of Democracy

Basic Dimensions of Democracy and the Quality of Democracy:

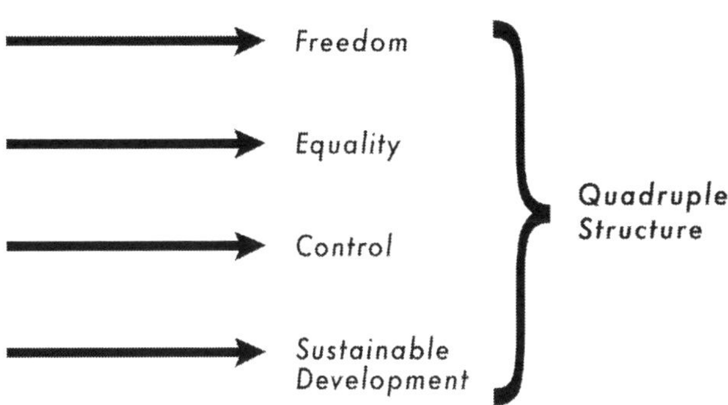

Source: Authors' own conceptualization and visualization based on Campbell (2008, p. 32; 2012, p. 296), Campbell and Carayannis (2013a), and for the dimension of "control" on Lauth (2004, pp. 32-101)

---

13 David F. J. Campbell,"Die österreichische Demokratiequalität in Perspektive", in *Die österreichische Demokratie im Vergleich,*,ed. Ludger Helms, David M. Wineroither (Baden-Baden: Nomos, 2012). 301-302, (here 296).

14 David F. J. Campbell, *Global Quality of Democracy as Innovation Enabler. Measuring Democracy for Success.* (New York: Palgrave Macmillan, 2019); David F. J. Campbell, Thorsten D. Barth,"Wie können Demokratie und Demokratiequalität gemessen werden? Modelle, Demokratie-Indices und Länderbeispiele im globalen Vergleich," *SWS-Rundschau* 49, no 2 (2009):208-233; David F. J. Campbell, Elias G. Carayannis, "Quality of Democracy and Innovation, 1527-1534", in: *Encyclopedia of Creativity, Invention, Innovation and Entrepreneurship.* Elias G. Carayannis (Editor-in-Chief) Igor N. Dubina, Norbert Seel, David F. J. Campbell, Dimitri Uzunidis (Associate Editors): (New York: Springer, 2013); David F. J. Campbell, Elias G. Carayannis, Epistemic Governance in Higher Education. Quality Enhancement of Universities for Development, (New York: Springer, 2013); Adam Przeworski, Michael E. Alvarez, José Antonio Cheibub, Fernando Limongi,"Democracy and Development. Political Institutions and Well-Being in the World, 1950-1990," (Cambridge: Cambridge University Press, 2003).

Figure 2: Dimensions (Conceptual Dimensions) for the Measurement of Democracy and the Quality of Democracy

Neutral line of a left/right balance?

Sustainable Development

Equality Freedom

Europe *left* *right*

North America *liberal* *conservative*

Equality Freedom

Control

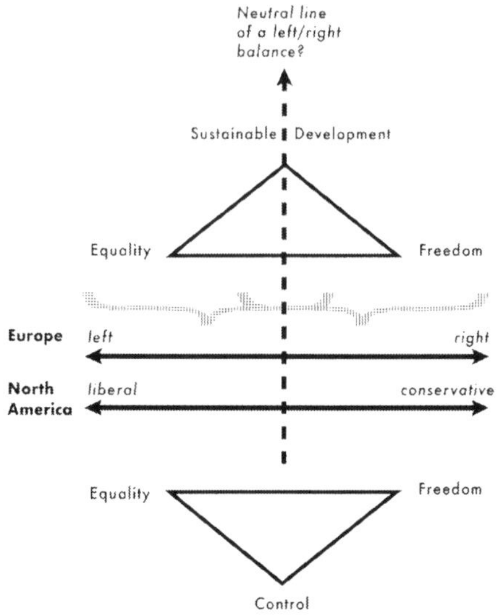

Source: Authors' own conceptualization and visualization based on Campbell (2008, p. 32; 2012, p. 296) and (for the lower triangle) on Lauth (2004, pp. 32-101)

Empirically, it should also be added that the traditional public perception of Western Europe indicates that individuals with a more-left political orientation prefer equality, and individuals with a more-right (conservative) political orientation have preferences for freedom.[15] The European left/right axis would translate itself well for the North American contexts by using a liberal/conservative axis, with left = liberal and right = conservative.

With regard to democracy and the quality of democracy, we are confronted with the following point-of-departure question: whether (1) democracy as a key feature or criterion exclusively refers, or should refer, to the political system, or whether (2) democracy should also include social (societal), economic, as well as ecological contexts of the political system. This produces implications on the selection of indicators to be used for democracy measurement (See footnote sixteen).[16]

15 Stephen Harding, David Phillips, Michael Fogarty, *Contrasting Values in Western Europe. Unity, Diversity and Change. Studies in the Contemporary Values of Modern Society*, (London: MacMillan, 1986), 87.

16 David F. J. Campbell, *The Basic Concept for the Democracy Ranking of the Quality of Democracy*, (Vienna: Democracy Ranking, 2008); Elias G. Carayannis, Thorsten D. Barth, David F. J. Campbell, "The Quintuple Helix Innovation Model: Global Warming as a Challenge and Driver for Innovation," *Journal of Innovation and Entrepreneurship* 1 no.1 (2012): 1-12; Gerardo L. Munck, *Measuring Democracy*, (Baltimore: The Johns Hopkins University Press, 2009); Michael J. Sodaro, *Comparative Politics. A Global Introduction*, (Boston: Mc Graw Hill, 2004).

Over time, democracy theories are becoming more complex and demanding in nature regardless of whether the understanding of democracy refers only to the political system or includes also the contexts of the political system. This also reflects on the establishment of democracy models or models of politics (See footnote seventeen for an overview).[17] Furthermore, this refers additionally to attempts of conceptualization of democracy and of quality of democracy (For examples, see footnote eighteen).[18] Asserting different, perhaps ideal-typical, conceptual stages of development for a further quality increasing and progressing of democracy, we may put up for discussion the following stages: *electoral democracy*, *liberal democracy*, and *advanced (liberal) democracy* with a *high quality of democracy*.

In *Polyarchy*, Robert A. Dahl (See pages 2-9)[19] comes to the conclusion that mostly two dimensions suffice in order to be able to describe the functions of democratic regimes: (1) *contestation* ("public contestation" and "political competition"), as well as (2) *participation* ("participation," "inclusiveness," and "right to participate in elections and office"). We propose to interpret these two dimensions, introduced by Dahl, as "Secondary Dimensions" for describing democracy and democracy quality for the objective of measuring democracy. Also relevant are Anthony Downs's eight criteria in *An Economic Theory of Democracy*[20] defining a "democratic government," but it could be argued that those are affiliated closer with an electoral democracy. In the beginning of the twenty-first century is the conceptual understanding of democracy and the quality of democracy already more differentiated. It can be said that crucial conceptual further developments are in progress. Larry Diamond and Leonardo Morlino[21] have come up with an "eight dimensions of democratic quality" proposal. These include: (1) *rule of law*, (2) *participation*, (3) *competition*, (4) *vertical accountability*, (5) *horizontal accountability*, (6) *freedom*, (7) *equality*, and (8) *responsiveness*. Diamond and Morlino[22] further state: "The multidimensional nature

---

17 David F. J. Campbell, Elias G. Carayannis, *Epistemic Governance in Higher Education. Quality Enhancement of Universities for Development*, (New York, NY: Springer, 2013).
18 Marc Bühlmann, Wolfgang Merkel, Lisa Müller, Bernhard Weßels, "The Democracy Barometer: A New Instrument to Measure the Quality of Democracy and Its Potential for Comparative Research", *European Political Science* 11, no.4 (2012), 519-536; David F. J. Campbell, *Global Quality of Democracy as Innovation Enabler. Measuring Democracy for Success*, (New York: Palgrave Macmillan, 2019).
19 Robert A. Dahl, *Polyarchy. Participation and Opposition*, (New Haven: Yale University Press, 1971).
20 Anthony Downs, *An Economic Theory of Democracy*, (Boston: Addison-Wesley, 1957), 23-4.
21 Larry Diamond, Leonardo Morlino, "The Quality of Democracy. An Overview," *Journal of Democracy* 15, no.4, (2004): 22-8.
22 Ibid,.22.

of our framework, and of the growing number of democracy assessments that are being conducted, implies a pluralist notion of democratic quality." The "eight dimensions" of Diamond and Morlino may be interpreted as "Secondary Dimensions" of democracy and the quality of democracy for the purpose of democracy measurement.

Guillermo O'Donnell[23] developed a broad theoretical understanding of democracy and the quality of democracy. In his theoretical approach, quality of democracy develops itself further through an interaction between human development and human rights: "True, in its origin the concept of human development focused mostly on the social and economic context, while the concept of human rights focused mostly on the legal system and on the prevention and redress of state violence."[24] The human rights differentiate themselves in civil rights, political rights, and social rights in which O'Donnell[25] assumes and adopts the classification of T. H. Marshall.[26] Human development prompts, "...what may be, at least, a minimum set of conditions, or capabilities, that enable human beings to function in ways appropriate to their condition as such beings?" O'Donnell,[27] therefore, is in accordance with human dignity and, moreover, the possibility of participating realistically in political processes within a democracy. O'Donnell also refers directly to the *Human Development Reports* with the *Human Development Index (HDI)* that are being released and published annually by the United Nations Development Program (UNDP) (For a comprehensive website address for all Human Development Reports that are publicly accessible for free downloads, see: http://hdr.undp.org/en/reports/global/hdr2011/). Explicitly, O'Donnell[28] points out: "The concept of human development that has been proposed and widely diffused by UNDP's *Reports* and the work of Amartya Sen was a reversal of prevailing views about development. ... The concept asks how every individual is doing in relation to the achievement of 'the most elementary capabilities, such as living a long and healthy life, being knowledgeable, and enjoying a decent standard of living.'"[29] *If the implementation of O'Donnell is reflected upon the initial questions asked in this contribution for the conceptualization of democracy and the quality of democracy, it can be interpreted, but also convincingly argued, that "sustainable development" can be suggested as an additional dimension ("Basic Dimension") for democracy,*

23 O'Donnell, "Human Development, Human Rights, and Democracy" (2004), 9-92.
24 Ibid., 12.
25 Ibid., 47.
26 T. H. Marshall, *Class, Citizenship, and Social Development. Essays.*, (New York: Doubleday, 1964).
27 O'Donnell, "Human Development, Human Rights, and Democracy" (2004) 12.
28 Ibid., 11-12.
29 Ibid.

which would be important for the quality of democracy in a global perspective (See Campbell,[30] and compare with Campbell.)[31] For a systematic attempt of empirical assessment on possible linkages between democracy and development, see Przeworski.[32] As a result of the distinction between dimensions (basic dimensions) for democracy and the quality of democracy, the following proposition is put up for debate: In addition to the dimensions of *freedom, equality, and control* as being suggested by Lauth,[33] *the dimension of sustainable development should be introduced as a fourth dimension* (See again Figure 1).

As already mentioned, equality is often associated closer with left-wing political positions and freedom with right-wing positions. *A measure of performance of political and non-political dimensions in relation to sustainable development has the advantage, especially in the case where sustainable development is understood comprehensively, that this procedure is mostly (often) left/right neutral. Such a measure of performance as a basis of the assessment of democracy and quality of democracy offers an additional reference point ("meta-reference point") outside of the usual, ideologically-based conflict positions.*[34] It can be argued in a similar manner that the dimension of control mentioned by Lauth[35] positions itself as left-right neutral as well. The definition developed by the "Democracy Ranking" for the quality of democracy is: "Quality of Democracy = (freedom & other characteristics of the political system) & (performance on the nonpolitical dimensions)." *The definition is interpreted as a further empirical operationalization step and as a practical application for the measurement of democracy and the quality of democracy respectively, which is based on the theory about the quality of democracy by Guillermo O'Donnell.* However, the conceptual democracy formula of the Democracy Ranking has been developed independently.[36]

There exist several global initiatives that commit themselves to a regular empirical democracy measurement. One example for this is Freedom

30 David F. J. Campbell, Die österreichische Demokratiequalität in Perspektive [The Quality of Democracy in Austria in Perspective], 293-315, in: *Die österreichische Demokratie im Vergleich,*,ed. Ludger Helms, David M. Wineroither (Baden-Baden: Nomos, 2012), 296.
31 Campbell,"Die österreichische Demokratiequalität in Perspektive"(2012). 293-315.
32 Adam Przeworski, Michael E. Alvarez, José Antonio Cheibub, Fernando Limongi, "Democracy and Development. Political Institutions and Well-Being in the World, 1950-1990," (Cambridge: Cambridge University Press, 2003).
33 Hans-Joachim Lauth, *Demokratie und Demokratiemessung. Eine konzeptionelle Grundlegung für den interkulturellen Vergleich,* (Wiesbaden: VS Verlag für Sozialwissenschaften, 2004).
34 David F. J. Campbell, *The Basic Concept for the Democracy Ranking of the Quality of Democracy,* (Vienna: Democracy Ranking, 2008), 30-32.
35 Lauth, *Demokratie und Demokratiemessung. Eine konzeptionelle Grundlegung für den interkulturellen Vergleich,* (Wiesbaden: VS Verlag für Sozialwissenschaften, 2004),77-96.
36 David F. J.Campbell, Miklós Sükösd, *Feasibility Study for a Quality Ranking of Democracies,* (Vienna: Global Democracy Award, 2002).

House.[37] Another example is the Democracy Ranking. Again, examples for other initiatives are: Vanhanen's Index of Democracy,[38] Polity IV,[39] Democracy Index,[40] and the Democracy Barometer.[41] For a comparison of different initiatives, see Pickel and Pickel[42] and Campbell and Barth,[43] as well as Campbell, Carayannis, and Barth.[44] The Democracy Barometer provides a "Concept Tree" *("Konzeptbaum")* for the quality of democracy, which also consists of the three dimensions of freedom, control, and equality (See: http://www.democracybarometer.org/concept_de.html). A strong resemblance with the three (basic) dimensions of democracy by Lauth[45] is evident in which the talk is also about equality, freedom, and control (Figure 1). Besides those more globally-reaching initiatives of a comparative assessment of quality of democracy, other studies prefer focusing on the democracy of a particular country. The International Institute for Democracy and Electoral Assistance (International IDEA), established in Stockholm, Sweden, dedicated itself to the approach of the Democratic Audit by assessing the quality of democracy (See: http://www.idea.int/). IDEA uses its own State of Democracy (SoD) Assessment Framework for this purpose, which is built on the following two principles: "popular control over public decision-making and decision-makers" and "equality of respect and voice between citizens in the exercise of that control."[46]

---

37 Freedom House, Freedom in the World Methodology. (Washington, DC: 2011).

38 Tatu Vanhanen, A New Dataset for Measuring Democracy, 1810-1998. *Journal of Peace Research* 37, no. 2 (2000). 251-265 http://www.prio.no/CSCW/Datasets/Governance/Vanhanens-index-of-democracy;

39 http://www.systemicpeace.org/polity/polity4.htm (accessed March 1, 2019).

40 Economist Intelligence Unit (2010). Democracy Index 2010. Democracy in Retreat. (London: Economist Intelligence Unit, 2010) http://www.eiu.com/public/topical_report.aspx?campaignid=demo2010 (accessed March 1, 2019).

41 Marc Bühlmann, Wolfgang Merkel, Lisa Müller, Bernhard Weßels, "The Democracy Barometer: A New Instrument to Measure the Quality of Democracy and Its Potential for Comparative Research", *European Political Science* 11, no.4 (2012).

42 Susanne Pickel,/Gert Pickel, *Politische Kultur- und Demokratieforschung. Grundbegriffe, Theorien, Methoden*. (Wiesbaden: VS Verlag für Sozialwissenschaften, 2006), 151-277.

43 David F. J. Campbell/ Thorsten D. Barth,"Wie können Demokratie und Demokratiequalität gemessen werden? Modelle, Demokratie-Indices und Länderbeispiele im globalen Vergleich," *SWS-Rundschau* 49, no 2, (2009),214-18.

44 David F. J. Campbell, Elias G. Carayannis, Thorsten D. Barth, George S. Campbell, "Measuring Democracy and the Quality of Democracy in a World-Wide Approach: Models and Indices of Democracy and the New Findings of the "Democracy Ranking", *International Journal of Social Ecology and Sustainable Development* 4, no. 1 (2013),1-16.

45 Hans-Joachim Lauth, *Demokratie und Demokratiemessung. Eine konzeptionelle Grundlegung für den interkulturellen Vergleich*, (Wiesbaden: VS Verlag für Sozialwissenschaften, 2004), 32-101.

46 David Beetham, Edzia Carvalho, Todd Landman, Stuart Weir, *IDEA/International Institute for Democracy and Electoral Assistance, Assessing the Quality of Democracy. A Practical Guide.* (Stockholm: International IDEA, 2008), 28;

Austria represents the type of an advanced small-sized country democracy in Europe, also being a member country to the European Union. To summarize the current status of research and studies regarding the quality of democracy in Austria, the mid-1990s provide a useful starting point. The *Die Qualität der österreichischen Demokratie* (*Quality of Democracy in Austria* by Campbell et al., 1996) represented the first attempt to analyze the Austrian quality of democracy, at least from an academic (and sciences-based) point of view. The next and once again systematic approach of evaluation of the Austrian quality of democracy took place in the *Demokratiequalität in Österreich* (*Quality of Democracy in Austria* by Campbell and Schaller, 2002; see also Campbell, 2002). Later studies have already started preferring a comparative approach.[47]

3. Quality of Democracy and Knowledge Democracy

There are different theories, conceptual approaches, and models for knowledge production and innovation systems. In the Triple Helix model of innovation,[48] a conceptual architecture for innovation was developed where they tie together the three helices of academia (higher education), industry (business), and state (government). This conceptual approach was extended by Carayannis and Campbell[49] in the so-called Quadruple Helix model of innovation systems by adding as a fourth helix the "media-based and culture-based public," "civil society," and "arts, artistic research and arts-based innovation."[50] *The Quadruple Helix, therefore, is broader than the Triple Helix and contextualizes the Triple Helix* by interpreting Triple Helix

47 Robert A.E. Beck,Christian Schaller, *Zur Qualität der britischen und österreichischen Demokratie,*(Vienna: Böhlau, 2003).; Erich Fröschl, Ulrike Kozeluh, Christian Schaller, Democratization and De-democratization in Europe? Austria, Britain, Italy, and the Czech Republic – A Comparison, (Innsbruck: Studienverlag, 2008).; Anton Pelinka, Democratization and De-democratization in Austria, in: *Democratization and De-democratization in Europe? Austria, Britain, Italy, and the Czech Republic – A Comparison,* ed. Erich Fröschl et al (Innsbruck: Studienverlag, 2008), 21-36.

48 Henry Etzkowitz, Loet Leydesdorff, "The Dynamics of Innovation: From National Systems and "Mode 2" to a Triple Helix of University-Industry-Government Relations," *Research Policy* 29, (2000):109-123 (here 112).

49 Elias G. Carayannis, David F.J. Campbell, "Mode 3 Knowledge Production in Quadruple Helix Innovation Systems. 21st-Century Democracy, Innovation, and Entrepreneurship for Development," (New York: Springer, 2012),14.

50 Elias G.Carayannis , David F. J. Campbell, "Developed Democracies versus Emerging Autocracies: Arts, Democracy, and Innovation in Quadruple Helix Innovation Systems," *Journal of Innovation and Entrepreneurship* 3, no.12 (2014).

Gerald Bast, Elias G. Carayannis, David F. J. Campbell, "Arts, Research, Innovation and Society", (New York: Springer, 2015).

as a core model that is being embedded in and by the more comprehensive Quadruple Helix. *Furthermore, the next-stage model of the Quintuple Helix model of innovation contextualizes the Quadruple Helix by bringing in a further new perspective by also adding the "natural environment" (natural environments) of society.* The Quintuple Helix represents a "five-helix model" "where the environment or the natural environments represent the fifth helix" (See page 61).[51] In trying to emphasize and compare and contrast the focuses of those different Helix innovation models, we can assert that the Triple Helix concentrates on the knowledge economy, the Quadruple Helix on knowledge society and knowledge democracy, while the Quintuple Helix refers to socio-ecological transitions and the natural environments.[52] *For explaining and comparing democracy and the quality of democracy, we propose a "Quadruple-dimensional structure" of four different "basic dimensions" of democracy that are being called freedom, equality, control, and sustainable development* (Figure 1 offers a visualization on these). Here, we actually may draw a line of comparison between concepts and models in the theorizing on democracy and democracy quality and the theorizing on knowledge production and innovation systems. This also opens up a window of opportunity for an interdisciplinary and trans-disciplinary approaching of democracy, as well as of knowledge production and innovation. *In conceptual terms, the Quadruple dimensional structure of democracy could also be re-arranged (re-architectured) in reference to helices by creating a "Model of Quadruple Helix Structures" for democracy and the quality of democracy.* The metaphor and visualization in reference to terms of *helices* emphasizes the fluid and dynamic interaction, overlap, and co-evolution of the individual dimensions of democracy. As basic dimensions for democracy, we propose to identify freedom, equality, control, and sustainable development. With respect to further characteristics and trend developments in and of *knowledge democracy*, see also the conceptual framings and discussions in In't Veld.[53]

---

51 Elias G. Carayannis, David F. J. Campbell, "Triple Helix, Quadruple Helix and Quintuple Helix and How Do Knowledge, Innovation and the Environment Relate To Each Other? A Proposed Framework for a Trans-disciplinary Analysis of Sustainable Development and Social Ecology," *International Journal of Social Ecology and Sustainable Development* 1, no. 1 (2010) 41-69.

52 Elias G. Carayannis, Thorsten D. Barth, David F. J. Campbell, "The Quintuple Helix Innovation Model: Global Warming as a Challenge and Driver for Innovation", *Journal of Innovation and Entrepreneurship* 1, no. 1 (2012) 1-12, (here 4).

53 Roeland J. In 't Veld, *Knowledge Democracy. Consequences for Science, Politics, and Media,* (Heidelberg: Springer, 2010).

4. The Quality of Democracy in International Comparative Perspective: Comparison of the Years 2011-2012 and 2014-2015

The Democracy Ranking (http://democracyranking.org/wordpress/) represents an approach that tries to measure and compare quality of democracy in a global format by applying a scientific model. For that purpose, quality of democracy refers to different dimensions (with different weights), and to those different dimensions, different indicators are being assigned. All indicator scores are transformed into a value (score) range of 1-100, where 1 implies the lowest and 100 the highest value (for quality of democracy). Normally, the Democracy Ranking compares two intervals of double-years where average values are being drawn for every double-year segment.[54]

More specifically, the Democracy Ranking 2016 compares the development of quality of democracy in 112 countries for the (two double) years 2011-2012 and 2014-2015. It is based on the following dimensions: politics (weighted with 50%), economy (10%), ecology and environment (10%), gender equality (10%), health and health status (10%), and knowledge (10%). The possible values that a country can achieve extend from 1 (the observed empirical minimum) to 100 (the observed empirical maximum). The entire scale is thus 1-100.

The following key results of the Democracy Ranking 2016 should be emphasized:[55]

The ten top-ranked countries for 2014-2015 are: Norway (100.00), Switzerland (99.49), Sweden (98.45), Finland (98.04), Denmark (96.61), the Netherlands (93.41), New Zealand (90.26), Germany (90.30), Ireland (89.57), and Australia (88.74).

1. *Improvement Ranking, the increase of quality of democracy:* A relatively large progress, although often resulting from a lower level, was in several African countries—Ivory Coast, Madagascar, Senegal, and Burkina Faso—while in Latin American, it was in Nicaragua and Columbia, as well as in Tunisia. Tunisia is the only country of the Arab Spring that could realize a positive—and by tendency, stable—path to more democracy.

2. *Improvement Ranking, the decrease of quality of democracy:* A decrease can be observed for all the other countries of the Arab

54 David F. J. Campbell, *The Basic Concept for the Democracy Ranking of the Quality of Democracy,* (Vienna: Democracy Ranking, 2008).
55 David F. J. Campbell, Paul Pölzlbauer, Thorsten D. Barth, *Democracy Ranking,* (Vienna: Democracy Ranking Organization, 2016).

Spring (for example, Libya and Egypt), as well as for Venezuela (in contrast to Columbia) and within the EU for Hungary. Furthermore, the decrease of democracy in Turkey is remarkable and obvious. In Russia and China, the quality of the political systems has also decreased.

3. *Austria:* Austria increased its scoring from 86.54 (2011-2012) to 87.76 (2014-2015) but slipped down slightly from rank 12 (2011-2012) to rank 13 (2014-2015). In international comparison, Austria ranks very high (rank 13 from 112 countries). However, during the last years, a few of the other top-rated countries developed a faster dynamic than Austria. Freedom House rated the political rights for Austria during 2014-2015 as stricter than for 2011-2012.

4. *Possibly approaching problem region of the Balkans:* The results of the Democracy Ranking also can be used in the sense of an early warning system for possibly arising problem situations. Serbia achieved an increase in quality of democracy—in the areas of politics, economy, and society—yet apparently not enough to improve its negotiation position for an EU membership. In Bosnia-Herzegovina and Macedonia, the scoring for economy and society improved, but in the area of politics, there was a decrease. Albania could increase its scoring for politics and society, but there was a decrease in economy. These recent trends in Bosnia-Herzegovina, Macedonia, and Albania require a more intensive international attention and observation.

Selected results of the Democracy Ranking 2016 (for the OECD and EU member countries) are summarized in Tables 1 and 2. Value scores have been adjusted to a value spectrum from "0" to "100," where "0" represents the lowest observed empirical value and "100" the highest observed empirical value (for the completely covered time period of 2011-2012 and 2014-2015). Also, changes in the quality of democracy scorings are indicated (improvements but also decreases).

Table 1: Quality of Democracy in OECD and EU Member Countries, the Years 2011-2012 and 2014-2015 in Comparison. Countries ranked alphabetically (Part A).

	Years 2011-2012	Years 2014-2015	*Changes in Scores*
Australia	88.02	88.74	0.72
Austria	86.54	87.76	1.22
Belgium	86.23	88.44	2.22
Bulgaria	58.64	61.82	3.18
Canada	86.92	87.62	0.71
Chile	72.70	74.26	1.56
Cyprus	69.77	69.22	-0.55
Czech Republic	71.81	74.11	2.30
Denmark	94.96	96.61	1.65
Estonia	70.89	74.91	4.02
Finland	97.60	98.04	0.44
France	81.80	85.10	3.30
Germany	88.92	90.30	1.38
Greece	64.70	63.40	-1.30
Hungary	63.12	61.11	-2.01
Iceland			
Ireland	86.80	89.57	2.77
Israel	73.41	74.85	1.45
Italy	70.59	73.06	2.47
Japan	75.97	80.34	4.37
Korea	70.84	71.73	0.89
Latvia	67.64	72.20	4.56
Lithuania	71.70	75.17	3.47
Luxembourg			
Malta			
Mexico	45.48	47.78	2.30
Netherlands	92.26	93.41	1.15
New Zealand	89.89	90.26	0.38
Norway	99.55	100.00	0.45
Poland	70.94	73.14	2.20
Portugal	77.52	78.75	1.23
Romania	60.22	62.69	2.47
Slovak Republic	67.09	67.42	0.33
Slovenia	77.25	81.18	3.93
Spain	81.33	79.85	-1.48
Sweden	96.89	98.45	1.56
Switzerland	97.81	99.49	1.68
Turkey	44.20	39.55	-4.65
UK (United Kingdom)	84.78	87.33	2.55
U.S. (United States)	82.13	82.22	0.09
Mean (unweighted, and without Syria)	**77.48**	**78.92**	**1.43**
Syria	4.27	0.00	-4.27

Methodic note: Scoring extends from 0 (the lowest observed democracy value) to 100 (the highest observed democracy value). In the country sample, Norway (2014-2015) ranks highest, and Syria (2014-2015) ranks lowest.
Source: Authors' own calculations based on the Democracy Ranking 2016 (Campbell, Pölzlbauer and Barth, 2017).

Table 2: Quality of Democracy in OECD and EU Member Countries, the Years 2011-2012 and 2014-2015 in Comparison. Countries ranked based on Scores (Years 2014-2015) (Part B).

	Years 2011-2012	Years 2014-2015	*Changes in Scores*
Norway	99.55	100.00	0.45
Switzerland	97.81	99.49	1.68
Sweden	96.89	98.45	1.56
Finland	97.60	98.04	0.44
Denmark	94.96	96.61	1.65
Netherlands	92.26	93.41	1.15
Germany	88.92	90.30	1.38
New Zealand	89.89	90.26	0.38
Ireland	86.80	89.57	2.77
Australia	88.02	88.74	0.72
Belgium	86.23	88.44	2.22
Austria	86.54	87.76	1.22
Canada	86.92	87.62	0.71
UK (United Kingdom)	84.78	87.33	2.55
France	81.80	85.10	3.30
U.S. (United States)	82.13	82.22	0.09
Slovenia	77.25	81.18	3.93
Japan	75.97	80.34	4.37
Spain	81.33	79.85	-1.48
Portugal	77.52	78.75	1.23
Lithuania	71.70	75.17	3.47
Estonia	70.89	74.91	4.02
Israel	73.41	74.85	1.45
Chile	72.70	74.26	1.56
Czech Republic	71.81	74.11	2.30
Poland	70.94	73.14	2.20
Italy	70.59	73.06	2.47
Latvia	67.64	72.20	4.56
Korea	70.84	71.73	0.89
Cyprus	69.77	69.22	-0.55
Slovak Republic	67.09	67.42	0.33
Greece	64.70	63.40	-1.30
Romania	60.22	62.69	2.47
Bulgaria	58.64	61.82	3.18
Hungary	63.12	61.11	-2.01
Mexico	45.48	47.78	2.30
Turkey	44.20	39.55	-4.65
Iceland			
Luxembourg			
Malta			
Mean (unweighted, and without Syria)	**77.48**	**78.92**	**1.43**
Syria	4.27	0.00	-4.27

Methodic note: Scoring extends from 0 (the lowest observed democracy value) to 100 (the highest observed democracy value). In the country sample, Norway (2014-2015) ranks highest, and Syria (2014-2015) ranks lowest.
Source: Authors' own calculations based on the Democracy Ranking 2016 (Campbell, Pölzlbauer and Barth, 2017).

5. Conclusion

5.1 Comparative Assessment and First Evaluation of Quality of Democracy in OECD Countries and the EU Member Countries: Recommendations for Innovative Quality-of-Democracy Improvements in Austria

The following three research questions governed the analytical procedure of this analysis: (1) to develop—in fact, to proto-type—a conceptual framework of analysis for a global comparison of quality of democracy. This framework will also reference to the concept of the Quadruple Helix innovation systems; (2) in a second step, to use and to test this same conceptual framework for a comparative measurement of quality of democracy in the different OECD and EU twenty-seven member countries; and (3) in a final step, innovative quality of democracy propositions for a democracy reform are being developed for democracy in Austria.

In theoretical and conceptual terms, we referred to a Quadruple-Dimensional structure, also a Quadruple Helix structure (a "Model of Quadruple Helix Structures") of the four basic dimensions of freedom, equality, control, and sustainable development, for explaining and comparing democracy and the quality of democracy.

What comes to mind, when looking at quality of democracy in reference to OECD and EU member countries, is the comparatively high ranking and positioning of the Nordic countries in Europe, particularly Norway, Sweden, Finland, and Denmark (See also on the web the newest and most recent scores of the Democracy Ranking 2016: http://democracyranking.org/wordpress/2016-full-dataset/). Also, Switzerland places very high. The Nordic countries and Switzerland are likewise a good example for sustainable development because they achieved and realized a development across different dimensions and indicators, so their progress is well balanced. Of course, from a philosophical perspective, we always could speculate "how high is the high" of quality of democracy in the Nordic countries and in Switzerland from a "really timeless viewpoint." But in "relative" empirical terms, no country or no democracy places higher than the Nordic countries and Switzerland (so far). So they define a practical and pragmatic benchmark for quality of democracy that already is accomplishable by countries. "The Nordic democracies (and Switzerland) demonstrate in empirical terms and in practice, which degrees and levels of a quality of democracy already can be achieved at the beginning of the twenty-first century."[56]

56 David F. J. Campbell, *Key Findings (Summary Abstract) of the Democracy Ranking 2011 and of the Democracy Improvement Ranking,* (Vienna: Democracy Ranking, 2011),6.

We want to focus now more specifically on Austrian democracy. *For an assessment (evaluation) of the quality of democracy in Austria, we set up for discussion the following propositions in context of a dynamic thesis-formulation:*[57]

1. *Comparatively, Austria's quality of democracy yields good results in:* political rights and civil liberties (dimension of freedom), income equality (dimension of equality), and within both indicators for the dimension of sustainable development.

2. *Comparatively, Austria's quality of democracy yields less good results in:* freedom of press and economic freedom (dimension of freedom), gender equality (dimension of equality), and corruption (dimension of control).

3. *Comparatively, Austria's quality of democracy yields lower-ranking results in:* Both indicators used in the Migrant Integration Policy Index (MIPEX) show a problematic positioning.[58] Austria's comprehensive rank in the MIPEX is only at 26 out of 33 (Here, Austria is behind only by Bulgaria, Lithuania, Japan, Malta, the Slovak Republic, Cyprus, and Latvia), and in the category of access to citizenship, Austria ranks only at 30 out of 33 (Here, only Lithuania, Estonia, and Latvia perform poorer than Austria). However, in relation to this observation, it must be noted that the poor performance of Austria in the MIPEX is not negatively reflected by the Freedom House's freedom rating in the category of political rights and civil liberties. One proposition would be that the integration of foreigners and of non-citizens (but being born and living exactly in the country, where they are) is not given enough weight (by Freedom House).

The comparative strengths and weaknesses of the Austrian quality of democracy blend themselves differently along the dimensions of freedom and equality. Regarding sustainable development, Austria's quality of democracy finds itself ranked highly, and its position remains robust. Taking the ratings of the Democracy Ranking during the years 2009 and 2010 under consideration

---

57 David F.J. Campbell,"Reformvorschläge für Österreichs Demokratie: Diskussionspunkte zur Demokratiequalität", in: *Direkte Demokratie und Parlamentarismus. Wie kommen wir zu den besten Entscheidungen?* ed. Theo Öhlinger, Klaus Poier (Vienna: Böhlau.2015), 43-56.

David F. J. Campbell,"Verbesserungsmöglichkeiten und Reformvorschläge für Demokratiequalität in Österreich". *SWS-Rundschau* 55, no. 2 (2015) 219-239.

58 David F. J. Campbell, *Key Findings (Summary Abstract) of the Democracy Ranking 2011 and of the Democracy Improvement Ranking,* (Vienna: Democracy Ranking, 2011).

(Democracy Ranking, 2011), countries like Norway, Sweden, Finland, and Switzerland find themselves worldwide on top in the category of sustainable development. *Therefore, currently, the Nordic countries provide the global empirical benchmark for democracy development (for a comprehensive and sustainable democracy development). The Nordic countries have impressively demonstrated the level-for-the-quality-of-democracy that is empirically already possible to achieve.* "The Nordic democracies (and Switzerland) demonstrate in empirical terms and in practice, which degrees and levels of a quality of democracy already can be achieved at the beginning of the twenty-first century."[59]

As compared with the OECD countries, the quality of democracy in Austria is ranked high to very high but not in all dimensions and for all indicators. *Evidently, for the purpose of a further learning with respect to the quality of democracy in Austria (so the proposition), the identification of the potentially problematic areas appears to be relevant above all since, naturally, those areas require democratic and political reform.* In Austria, necessity for innovation and *democracy innovation* is drastically needed in freedom of press, gender equality, and in fighting and containing corruption. However, the most urgent action plan for Austria's quality of democracy needs to be implemented, particularly in the improvement of integration of immigrants and of non-EU citizens, as well as a better access to citizenship. Integration policy is also linked, interlinked, and cross-linked with other policy fields such as asylum policy (See Rosenberger[60] and Valchars).[61] Austria's citizenship law knows no *jus soli* but is directed and steered by a pure *jus sanguinis* policy. Automatic acquisition of Austrian citizenship still only takes place through the Austrian citizenship of the parents (*jus sanguinis*), whereas birth in Austria (*jus soli*), and also residence during childhood and youth, are being completely ignored. Persons who are not Austrian citizens of course can always apply for Austrian citizenship (when specific conditions are being met and fulfilled), but this is something else than an automatic acquisition of citizenship. *Therefore, descent—in essence, also a biological principle—actually decides about political rights and automatic political participation in Austrian democracy. This only can be hardly balanced with the developed quality standards of a democracy in the twenty-first century and, when given further thought, stands finally in contradiction to fairness and universal equality of people and the general application of human rights.* According to Pelinka,[62] there is a need in

59 Ibid. 6.

60 Sieglinde Rosenberger, *Asylpolitik in Österreich. Unterbringung im Fokus*, (Vienna: Facultas, 2010).

61 Gerd Valchars, *Defizitäre Demokratie. Staatsbürgerschaft und Wahlrecht im Einwanderungsland Österreich*, (Vienna: Braumüller, 2006).

62 Anton Pelinka, "Democratisation and De-democratisation in Austria", in: *Democratisation and De-democratisation in Europe? Austria, Britain, Italy, and the Czech Republic – A Comparison*, ed. Erich Fröschl et al (Innsbruck: Studienverlag, 2008).

Austria for a more systematic conceptual reflection on the *demos* in the sense of: "Who are the People?" ("*Wer ist das Volk?*"). This reflection should definitely encourage more inclusion. Reforms in citizenship law in other European countries, such as in Germany, in recent years did not enter into Austrian politics and were not taken up by the Austrian mainstream political discourses. Should Austrian politics continue the blocking of an introduction of a *jus soli* component into its citizenship law during the course of the coming years, then it cannot be ruled out completely that the pure *jus sanguinis* design will finally be challenged legally at a "constitutional court"—nationally, supranationally, or even internationally. Here, we can quote also from an original source: "*Bedenklich für Demokratiequalität ist, wenn ein bedeutender Anteil der Wohnbevölkerung nicht im Besitz der Staatsbürgerschaft ist beziehungsweise sich dieser Anteil sogar vergrößert: Denn das könnte dazu führen, dass manche Parteien, die an Wahlstimmenmaximierung interessiert sind, den StaatsbürgerInnen 'auf Kosten' der Nicht-StaatsbürgerInnen Wahlversprechen geben. ... Je größer der Anteil der Nicht-StaatsbürgerInnen, desto höher fällt das populistische Potenzial für den Parteienwettbewerb aus. Soll gegen Populismus ein effektiver Riegel vorgeschoben werden, müsste der Anteil der Nicht-StaatsbürgerInnen an der Wohnbevölkerung möglichst verringert werden.*"[63]

For the purpose of improvement of quality of democracy in Austria, the following propositions are being set up for discussion (See furthermore Campbell;[64] see also Jankowitsch,[65] Öhlinger and Poier,[66] and Wineroither).[67] *These reforms refer to an innovative improvement and reform of quality of democracy in Austria:*

1. *Citizenship*, jus soli*:* Currently, you are only automatically an Austrian citizen if your parents are also Austrian citizens (*jus sanguinis*). So biological descent decides on citizenship, and this clearly is an undemocratic principle from pre-democratic times. Therefore, in addition to the already practiced *jus sanguinis*, every person who is born in Austria should also automatically be an Austrian citizen

63 David F.J.Campbell,"Zur Demokratiequalität von politischem Wechsel, Wettbewerb und politischem System in Österreich, in *Demokratiequalität in Österreich.* ed. David F. J. Campbell, Christian Schaller, (Opladen: Leske + Budrich, 2002),19-46.

64 Campbell,"Reformvorschläge für Österreichs Demokratie: Diskussionspunkte zur Demokratiequalität" (2015) 43-56.

65 Regina Maria Jankowitsch, *Tretet zurück! Das Ende der Aussitzer und Sesselkleber.* (Wien:Carl Ueberreuter, 2013).

66 Theo Öhlinger, Klaus Poier, *Direkte Demokratie und Parlamentarismus. Wie kommen wir zu den besten Entscheidungen?* (Vienna: Böhlau, 2015).

67 David M. Wineroither, *Kanzlermacht – Machtkanzler? Die Regierung Schüssel in historischen und internationalen Vergleich,* (Vienna: LIT-Verlag. 2009).

(*jus soli*). Because if you are born in a society and grow up in a society, you are a member of the "political people," which is a core idea of democracy (It is the population of a country or territory that participates or is participating in a democracy).

2. *Citizenship, dual, and multiple citizenship:* Austria should introduce systematically a dual (multiple) citizenship agenda or regime. So if you, as an Austrian citizen, apply for another citizenship, you should also be able to keep the Austrian citizenship. Consequently, if someone from outside applies for Austrian citizenship, then she or he should also be able to keep his or her other citizenship(s). This should support diversity and global responsibility in a balanced and trustworthy way. Furthermore, this also can support innovation in a knowledge democracy because it opens up opportunities for individuals but also for society as a whole. In reference to migrants, this also means not to emphasize assimilation but really integration.

3. *Term limits for leading executive political functions:* All leading executive functions of government should have a term limit. Currently, only the federal president (*BundespräsidentIn*) is facing a two-function term limit in Austria. This is certainly not enough or sufficient. Term limits should also be extended to the federal chancellor (*BundeskanzlerIn*) and also to the regional governors (*Landeshauptleute*). Term limits could be either two functional periods or a period of eight-to-twelve years. The rationale here is to avoid power concentrations and to support a dynamic flexibility and elasticity for the political system.[68] It is also a protection for the politicians themselves against over-long executive political functions.

4. *More direct democracy:* There are arguments against more direct democracy but also good arguments for more direct democracy. Among the good arguments is to allow for issue politics (issue policy) independently (in an independent mode) of party politics, the innovative experimentation with and elaboration of new forms of politics, further political participation, and a broader understanding of political activity and democracy (democracy inclusion). There should be a specific and sophisticated division of labor between

68 John Emerich Edward Dalberg Acton, first Baron Acton (1834–1902), has put forward on this a famous quote: "Power tends to corrupt, and absolute power corrupts absolutely. Great men are almost always bad men." See again Regina Maria Jankowitsch, *Tretet zurück! Das Ende der Aussitzer und Sesselkleber*. (Wien:Verlag Carl Ueberreuter. 2013).

direct democracy and representative (indirect) democracy. So for local, regional, and non-constitutional national issues, there could be installed a direct-democracy tool in the sense that every petition with a minimum of signatures would be forwarded to a public referendum. However, constitutional issues (constitutional law and also the human rights) and European Union issues (EU law) would be excluded from such a mechanism, i.e. here, the established mechanism of representative democracy (parliamentarism) still would apply and prevail.

5. *Comprehensive democracy education at Austrian schools:* Knowledge and access to knowledge is a key resource for citizens in a democracy to make well-informed political decisions (for example, in the context of elections). Therefore, "democracy education" (civic education) should be introduced comprehensively at all levels of school (also already in the kindergarten system) in Austria. At least at the level of all secondary schools in Austria, democracy education should furthermore represent an independent subject. A further step to be tested is whether there is also more of a need for a good professional qualification of journalists in Austria who want to report on politics.

6. *"Democratic Audit" of Austria:* The political system of Austria, its democracy and quality of democracy, so far have not undergone a systematic *democratic audit*. Attempts by the Austrian political science community to convince Austrian politics and Austrian politicians to support such a democratic audit of Austria were not successful. For this purpose, for example, the procedure of IDEA could be used and applied (See IDEA[69] and Beetham).[70] However, it would also be possible to hybridize or pool different procedures.

5.2 Further Outlook on the Knowledge Democracy

The following final propositions, in the context of our current analysis here, can be put forward for a further discussion of the additional development of discourses that are interested to intertwine ("*Inter-Helix*") quality

69 IDEA (International Institute for Democracy and Electoral Assistance, David Beetham, Edzia Carvalho, Todd Landman, Stuart Weir), *Assessing the Quality of Democracy. A Practical Guide*, (Stockholm: International IDEA, 2008).

70 David Beetham, "Key Principles and Indices for a Democratic Audit", in *Defining and Measuring Democracy*, ed. David Beetham, (London: Sage, 1994), 25-43.

of democracy with innovation and innovation systems *where there are processes of a co-evolution between quality of democracy and knowledge democracy, also emphasizing the idea of democracy as an innovation enabler:*[71]

1. *The basic Quadruple-dimensional structure of democracy and quality of democracy:* The Quadruple Helix structure of quality of democracy identifies four basic (conceptual) dimensions: freedom, equality, control, and sustainable development (Figure 1). *Particularly sustainable development marks here a new and innovative contribution to the theory of democracy.* Sustainable development also helps to avoid the models of measurement of democracy that are biased toward a left-leaning or right-leaning ideological pole of political preferences. Sustainable development adds the important contribution of a more "neutral left/right balance" (Figure 2). *For sustainable development, knowledge, and innovation play an important role, thus fostering the coming together of knowledge society, knowledge economy, and knowledge democracy.* Components of knowledge can be research, education, and innovation.[72]

2. *Quadruple Helix of quality of democracy and of innovation systems:* Quadruple Helix qualifies as a concept with interdisciplinary and trans-disciplinary capacities and capabilities. Quadruple Helix refers to the basic (conceptual) dimensions of democracy and quality of democracy. Quadruple Helix also represents the architecture of Quadruple and Quintuple Helix innovation systems, demonstrating how knowledge and innovation processes in mature and advanced innovation systems are being progressed. Quadruple Helix fulfills here at least two crucial functions: (a) *Knowledge and innovation are being defined as key for sustainable development and for the further evolution of quality of democracy.* Knowledge and innovation are receiving an additional meaning and importance for democracy and theory of democracy. How to innovate, and re-invent, knowledge democracy? Democracy-discourses and innovation-discourses develop further in mutual cross-reference. (b) The other crucial function of the Quadruple Helix is that it demonstrates that the context of

71 David F. J. Campbell, *Global Quality of Democracy as Innovation Enabler. Measuring Democracy for Success,* (New York: Palgrave Macmillan, 2019).
72 David F. J. Campbell, Elias G. Carayannis, Thorsten D. Barth, George S. Campbell, "Measuring Democracy and the Quality of Democracy in a World-Wide Approach: Models and Indices of Democracy and the New Findings of the Democracy Ranking", *International Journal of Social Ecology and Sustainable Development* 4, no. 1 (2013):1-16.

society and of democracy are important for innovation systems. *The unfolding of an innovative knowledge economy also requires, at least in a longer perspective, the unfolding of a knowledge democracy.* So there is also a "perspective of democracy" for advancing innovation systems. "Democracy of Knowledge"[73] plays in both ways.

3. *There is no Quadruple or Quintuple Helix innovation system without a democracy:* Pre-Quadruple Helix innovation systems, such as the Triple Helix, can be applied in very different political environments. Triple Helix is possible in combination with democratic or non-democratic political regimes. The Quadruple Helix is here more specific and concrete. *The architectures of Quadruple Helix and Quintuple Helix innovation systems demand and require the formation of a democracy, implicating that quality of democracy provides for a nurturing of innovation and innovation system so that quality of democracy and progress of innovation mutually "Cross-Helix" in a connecting and amplifying mode and manner.* In a win-win scenario, quality of democracy and innovation systems both cross-link and co-evolve. "The way how the Quadruple Helix is being engineered, designed, and architected clearly shows that there cannot be a Quadruple Helix innovation system without democracy or a democratic context."[74] This relates research on quality of democracy to research on innovation (innovation systems) and knowledge economy.[75] The one matters for the other. *"Cyber-Democracy"*[76] receives here a new meaning. *Quality of democracy moves in favor of a knowledge democracy, with democracy as an "innovation enabler."*[77]

---

73 Elias G. Carayannis/David F.J. Campbell,"Mode 3 Knowledge Production in Quadruple Helix Innovation Systems. 21st-Century Democracy, Innovation, and Entrepreneurship for Development," (New York: Springer, 2012).

74 Elias G. Carayannis, David F. J. Campbell, "Developed Democracies versus Emerging Autocracies: Arts, Democracy, and Innovation in Quadruple Helix Innovation Systems", *Journal of Innovation and Entrepreneurship* 3, no.12 (2014).

75 Elias G. Carayannis, David F.J. Campbell, Marios Panagiotis Efthymiopoulos, *Handbook of Cyber-Development, Cyber-Democracy, and Cyber-Defense* (New York : Springer, 2018).

76 David F. J. Campbell, Elias G. Carayannis, "Developed Democracies versus Emerging Autocracies: Arts, Democracy, and Innovation in Quadruple Helix Innovation Systems". *Journal of Innovation and Entrepreneurship* 3, no.12 (2014).

77 David F. J. Campbell, *Global Quality of Democracy as Innovation Enabler. Measuring Democracy for Success*, (New York: Palgrave Macmillan, 2019) "finally, as a last note and thought: perhaps the economic successes of non-democracies or autocracies (authoritarian and semi-authoritarian regimes) are being overestimated anyway, because autocracies are also benefitting from the knowledge production and innovation systems of democracies and semi-democracies, *so in that sense autocracy is depending on democracy and the knowledge and innovation of democracy in a global system.*"

Austria's Year of Memory and Commemoration 2018 – A Review

Dirk Rupnow[1]

The year 2018 was observed in Austria as an official "*Gedenk- und Erinnerungsjahr*," a year rich in, even overloaded with, memory and commemorative events. The historical events to be remembered and commemorated included the foundation of the First Austrian Republic in 1918, the "Anschluss" and the November Pogrom in 1938, the Universal Declaration of Human Rights in 1948 (and the ratification of the European Convention on Human Rights by Austria in 1958), as well as the global protest movements of 1968. Even the 1848 revolutions were peripherally included, as they were cited as the beginning of parliamentary and democratic developments in Austria. This was at least the summary presented on the official website of the responsible committee, which was established in the Federal Chancellery and chaired by the former Federal President Heinz Fischer.[2] However, this year also marked the 85th anniversary of the dissolution of the Austrian parliament by Federal Chancellor Engelbert Dollfuß in March 1933, which was not included in the official commemorative roster for the year.

These anniversaries were commemorated in countless events and exhibitions in Vienna and in the federal states, accompanied with exuberant coverage by the ORF and by extensive reports in all other media, newspapers, and magazines, not to mention publications in the form of books, catalogues, and edited collections. The sheer volume of this coverage precludes a complete overview and a comprehensive appraisal here, especially so soon after the commemorative year ended. The highly official commemorative events attended by government representatives are nevertheless deserving of special attention considering that only two weeks prior to the beginning of the commemorative year, a new right-wing populist federal government took office consisting of the conservative People's Party ÖVP (who had by then recast themselves as the "*türkis*," or turquoise party, and were no longer the traditional black party) and the far-right Freedom Party FPÖ (the blue party). This new government represents more or less a generational revamp of the Schüssel I government that was formed between the ÖVP and the

1 This text has been translated from German into English by Tim Corbett.

2 Republik Österreich, "*2018 – 100 Jahre Republik*", http://www.oesterreich100.at, accessed Feb. 14, 2019.

FPÖ in February 2000 and resulted in widespread protests at home and abroad. Not surprisingly, such large-scale protests against the current coalition have so far been absent as the global political scene has changed so much in the past years and right-wing populism, in Europe and worldwide, has become just about mainstream.

It is precisely these political circumstances that make 2018 as an Austrian year of memory and commemoration such an interesting test case: How were the legendary "8s"—democracy in 1918, human rights in 1948, and an open society in 1968—celebrated, and how were their abrogation, loss, or total destruction leading to expulsion and genocide (1938) remembered in a political environment in which liberal democracy and human rights are by no means considered sacrosanct anymore? And how did the FPÖ position itself in this memorial constellation, a party that had originally been founded by former Nazis and was characterized by constant oscillation between *Deutschnationalismus* (a far-right, *völkisch* form of ethnic German nationalism) and a chauvinistic patriotism to Austria; characterized, too, by repeated belittlements of the Nazi regime and its mass crimes, as well as perennial antisemitic and racist diatribes?

Before the commemoration of the 1938 "Anschluss" had even got going in March, the year opened in January with a completely unexpected but thematically pertinent scandal: the so-called "*Liederbuch-Affäre*" (songbook affair). Only a few days before the Lower Austrian state election, the Viennese weekly *Falter* published a songbook from the *deutschnationale* fraternity "*Germania*" in Wiener Neustadt, whose deputy chairperson was the frontrunner of the FPÖ. Alongside other embarrassing and scandalous texts belittling the crimes of the German Wehrmacht, the song "*Es lagen die alten Germanen*" ("There Lay the Old Germanic Peoples") includes the line, "*Da trat in ihre Mitte der Jude Ben Gurion: 'Gebt Gas, ihr alten Germanen, wir schaffen die siebte Million.'*" ("Then the Jew Ben Gurion came amongst them and said: 'Step on the gas, you ancient Germanic peoples, we'll nail the seventh million.'")—an obvious play on (and by no means a denial of) the Holocaust, if not an implicit incitement to mass murder. Apart from anything else, this scandal raised the question of how close a relationship the incumbent Austrian FPÖ maintains to *deutschnationale* and Nazi ideology and, consequently, what its stance towards Austria was generally in this year of memory and commemoration. Some intermittent to and fro aside, this case essentially drew no repercussions, whether on the Lower Austrian or on the federal level. The only consequence was that the FPÖ saw itself compelled right at the beginning of this historic year of memory to make a "red-white-red" proclamation, ceremoniously professing its loyalty to the

Republic of Austria, as well as to democracy, parliamentarianism, and the rule of law, while distancing itself from violence, totalitarianism, racism, and, above all, antisemitism. It moreover appointed a "historians' commission" tasked with examining the party's history. Both the composition and methods of this commission remain the object of uncertainty, while in contrast to all initial promises, no final or even preliminary report has yet been published. At the time this article was written, all indications pointed to the commission consisting of a group of FPÖ-friendly historians and journalists who will only peripherally address core topics, such as the party's relationship to the *deutschnationale* fraternities, if at all, and who will moreover likely try to marginalize long-established foundational findings and serious historical research on the party's history. The intention is presumably to present the FPÖ as a normal party in the Second Austrian Republic since, so the argument goes, former Nazis and anti-Semites were present everywhere after 1945. This perspective naturally obscures the fact that the FPÖ actually constituted a reservoir for former Nazis and *deutschnationale* (the so-called "third camp") in Austria after 1945, while antisemitism constitutes a core element of this party's ideology.[3]

In any case, the Lower Austrian "songbook affair" set the stage right from the outset for regular radical right-wing statements and actions by politicians that would follow throughout the rest of the year. Thankfully, the Austrian daily *Der Standard* published a summation at the end of the year detailing fifty such incidents, so about one for every week of the year, including the summer break.[4] Almost all of these can be attributed to the FPÖ, almost all were played down and decried as "isolated incidents," and not a single one came even remotely close to causing a crisis for the governing coalition. These incidents became the order of the day in this year of memory and commemoration, as in the following examples: The FPÖ-friendly, radical right-wing magazine *Aula* described the Austrian contestant in the Eurovision song contest as a "token Moor" on account of his skin color; the local FPÖ in Vöcklamarkt in Upper Austria demanded in a social media post to "protect your race, it is your ancestors' blood!"; an FPÖ city councilor in Amstetten in Lower Austria ranted online about "*Schwuchtel und Neger*," derogatory terms for gay and black men respectively, in response

3 Kantor Center for the Study of Contemporary European Jewry / Tel Aviv University, *Antisemitism Worldwide 2017. General Analysis / Draft*, ed. Dina Porat, 2018, 61–64. See also recently Margit Reiter, "Anton Reinthaller und die Anfänge der Freiheitlichen Partei Österreichs. Der politische Werdegang eines Nationalsozialisten und die ‚Ehemaligen' in der Zweiten Republik," *Vierteljahrshefte für Zeitgeschichte* 66, no. 4 (2018): 539–575.

4 Colette M. Schmidt, Fabian Schmidt, and Sebastian Fellner, "Das war doch nur ein Einzelfall," *Der Standard*, Dec. 7/8/9, 2018.

to an ad campaign by the Austrian Federal Railways; swastikas were posted online; racist caricatures were shared online; and so forth. In a related development, the FPÖ Minister of the Interior, who was responsible for numerous racist election campaigns on behalf of the party in the past, demanded that asylum seekers be kept "concentrated" in one place, while the FPÖ party whip claimed that there were "substantive rumors" that the Hungarian-American philanthropist George Soros "supported the migrant flows to Europe"—a classic antisemitic conspiracy theory in reference to Soros as a Jewish puppet master.

Of course, "migration" (and with it the fear of diversity), which had been exhaustively exploited by both the ÖVP and FPÖ in their election campaigns the year before, remained the actual topic of the year. All the diverse commemorative days of the year could effectively have been related to this topic in order to highlight the fundamental significance of human rights and asylum, as well as perhaps the issue of historical responsibility in this regard. Instead, the discursive illegalization and criminalization of migration and all migrants, especially from outside of Europe, were systematically perpetuated throughout the year, including accusations leveled against NGOs—all of which were naturally carried out in an appropriate European and international context. In the summer, a Member of Parliament of the ÖVP posted on her Facebook profile, "Neither African nor Muslim culture is compatible with our culture," in reference to the ostensibly well-known propensity in these cultures to violence and their high potential for aggression.

Australia continued to serve as a model for the sealing of the borders, including internment of migrants outside of the state territory in order to circumvent asylum applications there (known in Australia by the ambiguous term "Pacific Solution"), for which camps were envisioned in North Africa under various designations (e.g. "disembarkation platforms"). In September, the FPÖ's parliamentary representative on matters of defense suggested in an interview that land in North Africa be occupied with the use of "military forces" in order to create such facilities. A further (and very broad) historical context opens up here, which resonates in practically every field (historical as well as contemporary) but is hardly ever explicitly discussed in public and political discourse: the history of European colonialism, its exploitative and violent character, and its deeply enduring consequences, none of which have to date been adequately explored and all of which remain practically absent in public consciousness and in political debates.

This is the context in which the official ceremonies during this Austrian year of memory and commemoration need to be viewed. The ÖVP and

FPÖ here held sway over a unique political stage for an entire year, from which the Social Democratic Party SPÖ was moreover effectively excluded. It was only represented once, during the state ceremony to commemorate the foundation of the republic in the Vienna State Opera, at which the SPÖ governor of the Burgenland spoke in his capacity as chair of the Provincial Governors' Conference. The former Federal President Heinz Fischer (SPÖ) only appeared at the opening ceremony of the House of Austrian History, although he was otherwise very present in the media throughout the year. Of course, the incumbent Federal President Alexander Van der Bellen (Green Party) was one of the main actors that year.

The dramaturgy of the year began with the commemoration of the so-called "Anschluss" of Austria to Nazi Germany. Not only was Austria's co-responsibility in the crimes of National Socialism addressed here, which is in any case essentially undisputed these days (at least in official stances and speeches), but also the character of the (para-)fascist Dollfuß-Schuschnigg regime that preceded the "Anschluss" from 1933 to 1938. However, Kurt Schuschnigg, with his final exclamation of "God protect Austria!" on the eve of the German invasion, was thereby ultimately remembered as more of a helpless victim—the second helpless victim after Engelbert Dollfuß, who was murdered by Austrian Nazis. In his speech during the commemoration ceremony at the *Hofburg* in Vienna on March 12th, Federal President Van der Bellen emphasized the endangerment of democracies and their susceptibility to populism and demagogy.[5] Federal Chancellor Sebastian Kurz meanwhile focused entirely on the Jewish fate under National Socialism.[6]

Once again, the victims of National Socialism were commemorated on the anniversary of the liberation of the Mauthausen concentration camp on May 6th, which was marked in Vienna with the laying of a wreath at the Memorial against War and Fascism on the Albertinaplatz. While the Federal President here very specifically presented the guarantee of human rights and freedoms, as well as European reconciliation as the pertinent lessons of this history,[7] the Federal Chancellor spoke much more generally

5 Alexander van der Bellen, "Rede anlässlich des Gedenkens an den 12. März 1938," *bundespraesident.at* (March 12, 2018), accessed Feb. 14, 2019, https://www.bundespraesident.at/fileadmin/user_upload/Anschluss_1938_final_formatiert_DOWNLOAD.docx.pdf

6 Sebastian Kurz, "Rede zum Gedenkjahr 2018," *bundeskanzleramt.gv.at* (March 12, 2018), accessed Feb. 14, 2019, https://www.bundeskanzleramt.gv.at/-/rede-von-bundeskanzler-sebastian-kurz-anlasslich-des-gedenkens-an-den-12-marz-1938.

7 Alexander van der Bellen, "Worte bei der Kranzniederlegung am Mahnmal gegen Krieg und Faschismus," accessed Feb. 14, 2019, *bundespraesident.at* (May 6, 2018). https://www.bundespraesident.at/aktuelles/detail/news/achten-wir-darauf-dass-grund-und-freiheitsrechte-einschliesslich-der-medienfreiheit-nicht-schritt/.

about understanding among nations and justice.[8] Vice Chancellor Heinz-Christian Strache (FPÖ) meanwhile traced the multifaceted symbolism of Alfred Hrdlicka's memorial and closed his speech with a poem by Erich Fried—the former a staunch communist and the latter persecuted as a Jew under National Socialism, a salient irony considering Strache's and the FPÖ's political orientation.[9]

The second focal point of this year of memory and commemoration lay between the Austrian national holiday on October 26th and the anniversary of the foundation of the republic on November 12th. On the national holiday, Federal Chancellor Kurz invoked the solidarity and unity of Austria in reference to then Federal Chancellor Leopold Figl's Christmas address in 1945: "I cannot give you anything for Christmas. I can only ask of you: Believe in this Austria!"[10] During the state ceremony on the anniversary of the foundation of the republic in the Vienna State Opera, the federal president, pleading on behalf of liberal democracy and the commitment to democracy, also focused on the quest for common ground and on consensus as the Austrian recipe for success, at least in the Second Republic.[11] Sebastian Kurz picked up this theme in his speech but came back to speak about Austria's co-responsibility for National Socialism, finally addressing a group of Jewish Holocaust survivors who had been invited specially from Israel.[12] The event was also marked with speeches by the president of the Austrian parliament Wolfgang Sobotka and Vice Chancellor Strache.

The official commemorative speeches by representatives of the state, with their repeated invocations of democracy and unity, ultimately contained few surprises and virtually no highlights. However, they become

8 Sebastian Kurz, "Rede bei der Kranzniederlegung beim Mahnmal gegen Krieg und Faschismus," *bundeskanzleramt.gv.at* (May 6, 2018), accessed Feb. 14, 2019 https://www.bundeskanzleramt.gv.at/documents/131008/455732/BK_rede_albertina_060518_de.pdf/21614f30-449b-4059-817f-7ed6d6059763.

9 Heinz-Christian Strache, "Rede Albertinaplatz," *bundeskanzleramt.gv.at* (May 6, 2018), accessed Feb. 14, 2019, https://www.bundeskanzleramt.gv.at/documents/131008/455732/VK_rede_albertina060518_de.pdf/155e24d3-ba5f-4680-a200-ed55ef699bbc.

10 Sebastian Kurz, "Rede zum Nationalfeiertag," *bundeskanzleramt.gv.at* (Oct. 26, 2018), accessed Feb. 14, 2019, https://www.bundeskanzleramt.gv.at/-/rede-des-bundeskanzlers-sebastian-kurz-zum-nationalfeiertag.

11 Alexander van der Bellen, "Ein Plädoyer des Bundespräsidenten für liberale Demokratie und demokratisches Engagement beim Staatsakt »100 Jahre Republik Österreich« am 12. November 2018 in der Wiener Staatsoper," *bundespraesident.at* (Nov. 12, 2018), accessed Feb. 14, 2019, https://www.bundespraesident.at/aktuelles/detail/news/staatsakt-100-jahre-republik-oesterreich/.

12 Sebastian Kurz, "Rede des Bundeskanzlers beim Staatsakt anlässlich „Hundertjähriges Bestehen der Republik Österreich"," *bundeskanzleramt.gv.at* (Nov. 12, 2018), accessed Feb. 14, 2019, https://www.bundeskanzleramt.gv.at/-/bundeskanzler-sebastian-kurz-beim-staatsakt-anlasslich-hundertjahriges-bestehen-der-republik-osterreich-bka-dragan-tatic.

more interesting when viewed in light of the prevailing political conditions and of the various political positions of the protagonists, set in relation to the otherwise populist, antisemitic, or racist statements, the strict anti-migration policies, and the constant smear campaigns against Muslims in Austria, as well as the simultaneous attack on welfare state institutions and accomplishments. The guest speakers invited to the various commemorative events, who were significantly (for the most part) artists, largely broke ranks with the official commemorative routine.

Probably the most important speech of the year was held by the writer Michael Köhlmeier at the Memorial Day Against Violence and Racism on May 4th, to which he had been invited by the president of the parliament.[13] The speech was not even seven minutes long, yet Köhlmeier here trenchantly exposed the hypocritical philosemitism above all of the FPÖ, as well as the culture of consternation surrounding the commemoration of the Holocaust, particularly against the background of inhumane anti-migration policies and racist anti-Muslim agitation. At the opening of the annual Bruckner Festival in Linz in September, the writer Daniel Kehlmann adopted a similar stance, particularly with regards to the restrictive refugee politics of the federal government. He reminded the audience that, eighty years earlier, refugees had also left Austria in search of help, those same refugees who are today commemorated and mourned while simultaneously a politics of seclusion is practiced.[14] At the commemoration of the "Anschluss" on March 12th, the universal artist André Heller described the fate of his father, spoke about Austrian Nazi perpetrators, liberation, and resistance, and, from this vantage point, drew an arc to the fight against racism and xenophobia in the present, among other things pointing out that it was not Auschwitz and the Holocaust that stood at the beginning of Nazi rule but the exclusion of people derided as objectionable and harmful. Following some remarks on political populism, on the current state of refugeedom, and on global justice, he closed with a plea for a recognition

13 Michael Köhlmeier, "Rede beim Gedenktag gegen Gewalt und Rassismus im Gedenken an die Opfer des Nationalsozialismus,", *erinnern.at* (May 4, 2018), accessed Feb. 14, 2019 http://www.erinnern.at/bundeslaender/oesterreich/gedenktage/5.-mai-gedenktag-gegen-gewalt-und-rassismus-im-gedenken-an-die-opfer-des-nationalsozialismus/michael-koehlmeiers-gedenkrede-die-dinge-beim-name-nennen/Rede%20Michael%20Koehlmeier.pdf.

14 Daniel Kehlmann, "Im Steinbruch: Festrede zur feierlichen Eröffnung des Internationalen Brucknerfestes Linz 2018," *OÖNachrichten* (Sep. 9, 2018), accessed Feb. 14, 2019, https://www.nachrichten.at/nachrichten/kultur/Daniel-Kehlmann-Im-Steinbruch;art16,3001741; on the expulsion of Jews from Vienna after the „Anschluss", see also the review essay by Günter Bischof in this volume.

of diversity and empathy.[15] During her speech at the state ceremony in the Vienna Opera House commemorating the foundation of the republic, the Carinthian Slovene writer Maja Haderlap greeted the audience first in German and then in her native Slovenian. Following a summary of the last hundred years, she spoke about the dangers of the increasing economization of life and the integrative potential of democracy—not least of all for the incorporation, as well as protection, of minorities: "Democracy is also the only form of government that incorporates the others and the minorities and is the only order capable of including the people who for various reasons have come to us from different countries and traditions, including them as co-responsible for the community and the values of democracy."[16]

On November 10th, shortly before the state commemoration of the foundation of the republic on November 12th, the "House of Austrian History" (*Haus der Geschichte Österreich*) was opened in the Neue Hofburg on the Heldenplatz in Vienna. Initiatives to found a museum of Austrian history date at least as far back as the reestablishment of the republic after World War II, not least of all because the multiethnic, dynastic Habsburg Empire had left behind no institution whatsoever which could serve as the foundation for such a museum, even in reconceived form. The Habsburg legacy consisted solely of art collections and a museum of military history alongside the (universal) museums in the federal states.[17] Following decades of discussions and numerous concepts and (preliminary) projects, a concentrated effort to realize a museum as a division of the Austrian National Library was made in 2015 under the federal government Faymann II (when Josef Ostermayer served as Minister of Culture). However, shortly after a presentation of the realization strategy in September 2015, the Faymann II government collapsed, leading to yet another delay and moreover to a re-dimensioning of the entire project. What remained unchallenged at least was

15 André Heller, "Gedenkrede zum 80. Jahrestag des 12. März 1938," *bundespraesident.at* (March 12, 2018), accessed Feb. 14, 2019, http://www.bundespraesident.at/fileadmin/user_upload/Gedenkrede_Andre_Heller.pdf.

16 Maja Haderlap, "Festrede: Im langen Atem der Geschichte," *bundespraesident.at* (Nov. 12, 2018), accessed Feb. 14, 2019, https://www.bundespraesident.at/fileadmin/user_upload/Festrede_von_Maja_Haderlap_-_Staatsakt_100_Jahre_Republik_OEsterreich.pdf.

17 Dirk Rupnow, "Nation ohne Museum? Diskussionen, Konzepte und Projekte," in *Zeitgeschichte ausstellen in Österreich. Museen – Gedenkstätten – Ausstellungen*, ed. Dirk Rupnow and Heidemarie Uhl (Vienna: Böhlau 2011), 417–463; Dirk Rupnow, "Staatsmuseum im Schatten. Die merkwürdige Geschichte des Museums Österreichischer Kultur 1945–1994," in *Beruf(ung): Archivar. Festschrift für Lorenz Mikoletzky* (= Mitteilungen des Österreichischen Staatsarchivs 55/2011), 635–650; Charles Maier, "In the Museum of Austrian History," *Austrian Studies Today*, ed. Günter Bischof and Ferdinand Karlhofer (Contemporary Austrian Studies 25) (New Orleans-Innsbruck: UNO Press-Innsbruck university press, 2016), 25–35.

the agreed location of the museum at the Neue Burg on the Heldenplatz. The appointment of the historian and museologist Monika Sommer-Sieghart as museum director in February 2017 finally set the race in motion for the inauguration of a first exhibition, scheduled for November 10, 2018, entitled "*Aufbruch ins Ungewisse. Österreich seit 1918*" ("Into the Unknown: Austria Since 1918").

The amendment to the *Bundesmuseen-Gesetz* 2002 (Federal Museum Law) of April 13, 2016 stipulates that the House of Austrian History should "convey the contemporary history of Austria from the second half of the nineteenth century onwards with thematic flashbacks to the Enlightenment era and beyond and with a particular emphasis on the period from 1918 to the present in its European and international context. The House of Austrian history should be a forum for active and public debate regarding issues of contemporary history as well as topics relating to the history of the present and should be dedicated to the objective representation of historical developments and events."[18] To be sure, some institutions already dealt with contemporary Austrian history, especially during the Nazi period, such as the Mauthausen Memorial, the Museum for Contemporary History in Ebensee, and the Documentation Centre of Austrian Resistance in Vienna. However, no institution existed hitherto that addressed the entire contemporary history of Austria and the Austrian republic, including the creation of a related collection of objects. The exhibitions in Austria's federal state museums treat the entire twentieth century rather marginally, if at all. In Vorarlberg, the restructuring of the state museum in 2013 was used to increase the focus on contemporary history. Lower Austria in particular tried to fill the vacuum on the federal level with the opening of the House of History in the Lower Austria Museum in St. Pölten's administrative district in September 2017—by reference to the central location and significance of Lower Austria for the general history of Austria. The media were particularly vocal in portraying a competitive aspect to the projects in Vienna and St. Pölten, which was nevertheless a non sequitur from the word go: A state museum can hardly stand in for a federal museum. What is moreover interesting is that the Federal Museum Law explicitly conceived of the Viennese House of History as a site of dissemination and a discussion forum, while it evidently appeared necessary to commit the project to an objective scholarly representation of the subject matter. Not only does this reflect questionable notions of scholarship and objectivity, but it is also especially revealing of extant fears of (party) political instrumentalization.

18 BGBl. I, Nr. 14/2002; BGBl. I, Nr. 20/2016.

International media reactions to the recently opened House of Austrian History in Vienna were extremely positive. By contrast, the reactions in Austria itself were thoroughly ambivalent: Following the resignation, in the summer, of two members of the academic advisory board in protest against the ostensible lack of an overall concept and of a narrative to the exhibition, the House of Austrian History was already labeled a "*Problembär*" (in reference to an exhibit, essentially meaning a "problem child") before it had even opened. Other labels soon followed, such as "House of Overly Intellectualized History," "*Häuschen*" (a diminutive belittlement of "house"), and "Closet of the Republic."[19] The positive reviews praised what had been achieved in such a short time, especially given the scale of the project, but they also remarked on the dissatisfactory spatial situation and the obviously provisional nature of the exhibition. The museum director, Monika Sommer-Sieghart, referred repeatedly to the fact that the House of Austrian History was conceived as a discussion forum and that it did not offer only one reading of history, but that it also emphasized important aspects of its subject matter (especially with regards to precisely those years in which Austria was not a republic or a democracy and in part was not even Austria, including the related cultures of denial and/or remembrance). She moreover repeatedly called for clarity from the government concerning the mid- and long-term perspectives for the museum.

One aspect that remains unresolved to date is the question of what to do with the "Führer balcony" from which Adolf Hitler proclaimed the "Anschluss" of Austria to Nazi Germany in front of a cheering crowd on the Heldenplatz on March 15, 1938. This historically contaminated part of the building—which is, architecturally speaking, actually a terrace since it stands above the entrance portal to the Hofburg—cannot presently be put to use or opened to the public due to safety regulations, but there are insufficient funds for its modification. Moreover, a good concept for how this feature could be used is needed as it would permanently alter the entire ensemble of the Heldenplatz. The speech against xenophobia held by the Holocaust survivor and Nobel Peace Prize laureate Elie Wiesel from the terrace in 1992 did not result in an enduring reinterpretation of the site and is only tentatively embedded in collective memory. The House of Austrian History attempted to set a further precedent with the sound installation "The Voices" by the Scottish artist Susan Philipsz, which ran from March to November 2018. Twice a day, the Heldenplatz was filled with sounds

19 Thomas Trenkler, "Das Haus der Geschichte, ein kleiner Problembär," *Kurier*, July 6, 2018; Anne-Catherine Simon, "Haus der verkopften Geschichte," *Die Presse*, Nov. 8, 2018; Hans-Werner Scheidl, "Endlich – ein Häuschen!," *Die Presse*, Nov. 10, 2018; Stefanie Panzenböck, "Im Abstellraum der Republik," *Falter* 46/2018 (Nov. 14, 2018).

created by rubbing the rims of variously filled crystal glasses. Moreover, the area behind the terrace was renamed the Alma Rosé Plateau during the opening of the House of Austrian History, which was where the museum's first temporary exhibition was hosted, a retrospective on the life of the Jewish musician and head of the women's orchestra in Auschwitz-Birkenau, the daughter of the long-term concertmaster of the Vienna State Opera Orchestra and the Vienna Philharmonic Arnold Rosé, on the seventy-fifth anniversary of her death. Thereby, the history of Austria on display one floor below was coherently linked to the historically contaminated terrace, as well as to the collection of old musical instruments on display on the upper floor.

The future of the House of Austrian History remains unclear. The current exhibition will be on display until May 2020. Whether the museum will remain in its current location is also unclear. It is difficult to say at present whether a new building is realizable, perhaps even on the Heldenplatz itself, where the Austrian parliament is currently housed in temporary quarters while the parliament building on the Ringstraße is renovated. In another twist, on the national holiday just before the opening of the museum, the president of the parliament and the minister of culture announced a possible constitutional linkage of the museum to the parliament, with the former to be renamed "House of the Republic." Then, at the beginning of 2019, an "expert committee" was created in order to evaluate and further develop the newly opened museum. It remains totally unclear what organizational, but also content-related, changes this will entail. As cited above, the Federal Museum Law stipulates that it should "convey the contemporary history of Austria from the second half of the nineteenth century onwards with thematic flashbacks to the Enlightenment era and beyond and with a particular emphasis on the period from 1918 to the present in its European and international context." So how would the years when Austria was not a republic—which were not few in number and certainly not without significance—be dealt with in a "House of the Republic?"

After all of these developments, there was no energy left for a worthy commemoration of the Universal Declaration of Human Rights by the United Nations on December 10, 1948, even though this had been explicitly cited as a point of reference for the Austrian year of memory and commemoration (as had the 1968 movements, which also ended up being neglected). This is hardly surprising when considering the frontal assault on human rights and the rule of law by the FPÖ Minister of the Interior Herbert Kickl at the beginning of 2019, who described human rights as "some bizarre legal constructions that are in part many, many years old, that were developed under entirely different circumstances, and that today hold us back from doing what is necessary."This he followed up with the dictum: "The law is to subordinate itself to politics, not politics to the law."

Probably the most disconcerting development in Austrian memory culture is the appropriation and instrumentalization of the commemoration of the Holocaust for the racist, Islamophobic, and anti-migrant positioning of right-wing and right-wing populist parties—albeit that this development is not limited to Austria. This should not come as a surprise considering the fact that the commemoration of the Holocaust in the past years and decades, certainly since the beginning of the new millennium, has shifted from a marginal position to become a government-sponsored, hegemonic, state-run, and state-legitimizing form of memory. The current development may well reflect a consistent evolution of this trend in times of growing right-wing populism and not least of all of right-wing populist governments, as well as of increasingly racist, Islamophobic, and anti-migrant attitudes. This development also reveals that the unique transnational institutionalization of Holocaust commemoration in recent years has resulted in the crystallization of this historical event in collective memory as something exceptional, while the more nuanced questions concerning potential lessons that this past has to teach the present have, by contrast, been marginalized. If Holocaust memory previously underwent a process of globalization and universalization, it is now undergoing a re-ethnicization. Holocaust memory is thereby taking on a decidedly exclusive character while, simultaneously, Jewish history is uncritically appropriated into hegemonic discourse through the catchphrase of the "Judeo-Christian West." This is accompanied by the repeated downplaying and belittlement of the colonial mass crimes of European states committed in the rest of the world. Indeed, European colonial crimes remain a blind spot within Europe. How this will affect the outsider perspective of Europe and, above all, Europe's relationship to other regions in the world is difficult to predict.

The Holocaust is cited less and less as a reason to offer protection and aid to refugees and increasingly as a justification not to allow migrants to enter the country (or Europe generally) because they allegedly import antisemitism, while simultaneously the homegrown, indigenous forms of antisemitism are increasingly belittled and blocked from view.[20] Warnings against the "imported" or "new antisemitism" of Muslims and other immigrants run like a leitmotif through the speeches and statements of the turquoise blue federal government of the past year, from the "red-white-red"

20 Sina Arnold, "Der neue Antisemitismus der Anderen? Islam, Migration und Flucht," in *Neuer Antisemitismus? Fortsetzung einer globalen Debatte*, ed. Christian Heilbronn, Doron Rabinovici, and Natan Sznaider (Berlin: Suhrkamp, 2019), 128–158.

proclamation of the FPÖ in February in which the party actually had to distance itself from antisemitism but ended up projecting it onto Muslims, through the speech of the Federal Chancellor on the anniversary of the "Anschluss" in March, to the anniversary of the November Pogrom of 1938. Beyond the legitimate question of how Muslim antisemitism should be dealt with, Holocaust memory is being repurposed as an ethnic ideology of seclusion and as an argument for double standards and racism—not as a lesson against racism and seclusion and in support of empathy and inclusion.

The situation has indeed become confusing. While in many instances right-wing populist slogans and symbols have incited memories of the 1930s (despite obvious differences between then and now), radical and right-wing populist parties try to distance themselves from their past while proclaiming a newfound friendship with Israel and while claiming to fight antisemitism. This strategy, which is also practiced by the FPÖ in Austria, is related to the hope for international recognition and a united front against Muslim immigrants. However, this superficially proclaimed philosemitism is repeatedly belied by patently antisemitic diatribes and signals from precisely these parties, including the FPÖ.[21] Of special significance here is the observation of the report from the year before that the generally worsening atmosphere of xenophobia, racism, and populism carries the potential of becoming antisemitic at any time.[22]

The turquoise-blue federal government is trying to shape Holocaust memory in Austria beyond the year of memory and commemoration in 2018 through the creation of a so-called "wall of names" in Vienna as a "memorial to the Jewish children, women, and men of Austria who were murdered in the Shoah." The initiative for this memorial stems from the Austrian-Canadian Karl Yakov Tutter, who was born in Vienna in 1930, fled with his family in 1939, and survived the Holocaust in Belgium. He has been campaigning for a memorial site including the names of the 65,000 murdered Jewish Austrians in a central location in Vienna since 2000.[23] After discussions focusing on the Grete Rehor-Park in front of the Justizpalast, between the parliament and the Palais Epstein on the Ringstraße, as a possible location for the memorial, the Ostarrichi-Park in front of the National Bank and beside the university campus was chosen.

21 Kantor Center for the Study of Contemporary European Jewry / Tel Aviv University, *Antisemitism Worldwide 2017. General Analysis / Draft*, ed. Dina Porat, 2018, 6–7.

22 Kantor Center for the Study of Contemporary European Jewry / Tel Aviv University, *Antisemitism Worldwide 2016. General Analysis / Draft*, ed. Dina Porat, 2017, 8–9.

23 *Gedenkstätte für die in der Shoah ermordeten jüdischen Kinder, Frauen und Männer aus Österreich*, accessed Feb. 14, 2019, http://www.shoah-namensmauern-wien.at.

The federal government agreed to fund the memorial in a statement made in relation to the commemoration of November 9, 1938.

The wall of names would be the third central project of its kind in Vienna, following the "Memorial against War and Fascism" by the Austrian sculptor Alfred Hrdlicka that was created on the Albertinaplatz during the so-called "*Bedenkjahr*" (year of mindfulness) in 1988 and the memorial to the Jewish Austrian victims of the Shoah on the Judenplatz by the British artist Rachel Whiteread created in 2000. As had been the case in the much criticized memorial on the Albertinaplatz in 1988, which portrayed the persecution of Jews through the image of a kneeling, street-washing Jew through which their denigration was uncritically perpetuated, it was decided not to stage a competition for the wall of names but rather to promote an already existing, private initiative. In terms of content, the wall of names merely repeats the memorial on the Judenplatz, which was dedicated "to the memory of more than 65,000 Jewish Austrians who were murdered by the Nazis between 1938 and 1945." On the other hand, this means that other groups of victims are once again being excluded in Austria's hegemonic politics of memory. Most crucially, it means that the Austrian victim myth is only being transformed, and not rejected, much rather perpetuated once more. What is to be commemorated here are the Jewish Austrians who became the victims of the Nazis but not the entire collective of Jews across Europe who became the victims of Austrian perpetrators during the Holocaust. There appears to have been no space in the Austrian year of memory and commemoration for this latter perspective.

Non-Topical Essay

"The duty to express value judgments" Charles Adams Gulick, Interwar Austria and the Question of Political Neutrality As A Scholarly Virtue

Florian Wenninger

Historiographical Context

Since the 1990s, contemporary historical research in general and research on memory politics in particular have had a strong focus on National Socialism.[1] While academia largely agrees on its approach to National Socialism and the modes in which it is societally reappraised after 1945, it is becoming increasingly clearer that there is no such consensus concerning the "smaller" European dictatorships.

Austria is a prototypical example for this situation. The "Reder-Frischenschlager-scandal,"[2] the Waldheim-debate,[3] and finally the 50th anniversary of the "Anschluss"[4] in the 1980s led to a public debate on the country's National Socialist past. Subsequently, not only the state of Austria had changed its position towards the compensation of victims of the Nazi terror[5] by the end of the twentieth century, but the public perception of the period from 1938 to

1 For Austria compare recently e.g. Cornelius Lehnguth, *Waldheim und die Folgen: Der parteipolitische Umgang mit dem Nationalsozialismus in Österreich* (Frankfurt/Main: Campus, 2013). For Germany, compare especially the pertinent standard work by Norbert Frei, *Vergangenheitspolitik: Die Anfänge der Bundesrepublik und die NS-Vergangenheit* (Munich: Beck 2012).

2 Barbara Tóth, "Der Handschlag. Die Affäre Frischenschlager-Reder" (PhD diss., Vienna University, 2010).

3 Georg Tidl, *Waldheim: wie es wirklich war: Die Geschichte einer Recherche* (Vienna: Löcker, 2015); Hans Safrian, "Wehrmacht, Deportationen von Juden und Jüdinnen aus Griechenland und die Waldheim-Debatte," in: *Bananen, Cola, Zeitgeschichte. Oliver Rathkolb und das lange 20. Jahrhundert*, Vol. 1, ed. Dreidemy, Lucile et al. (Vienna: Böhlau, 2015), 417-429.

4 See Heidemarie Uhl, *Zwischen Versöhnung und Verstörung: Eine Kontroverse um Österreichs historische Identität fünfzig Jahre nach dem "Anschluß"* (Vienna: Böhlau, 1992).

5 Of special importance in this context was the establishment of the Nationalfonds der Republik Österreich für die Opfer des Nationalsozialismus in 1995, the foundation of the Historikerkommission der Republik Österreich in 1998 and finally the Washington Agreement 2001 which led to the establishment of the Allgemeiner Entschädigungsfonds für Opfer des Nationalsozialismus in the same year, see Ursula Kriebaum/Ernst Sucharipa, "Das Washingtoner Abkommen. Die österreichische Restitutionsvereinbarung vom 17. Jänner 2001," in: *Raub und Rückgabe: Österreich von 1938 bis heute*, Vol. 1, ed. Verena Pawlowsky and Harald Wendelin (Vienna: Mandelbaum, 2005), 164-185.

1945 had changed in general. The second post-war generation finally reached a new common understanding that although Austria as a state had been a victim of German aggression, this aggression was welcomed by considerable parts of the Austrian population and that many Austrians later became perpetrators within the Nazi regime. An important trigger for this shift is to be found on cultural levels, especially in films dealing with the Shoah, such as the TV series *Holocaust* and Steven Spielberg's movie *Schindler's List,* as well as the so-called "*Wehrmachtsausstellung,*" an exhibition about the systematic involvement of the German Wehrmacht in the regime's genocide program.[6] Public sympathy thus shifted from the perpetrators to the victims.[7]

The significant changes in public opinion during the 1980s and 1990s led to a widely shared consensus among the research on Austrian memory politics. What was in fact a hegemonial shift was instead often interpreted as the "end of silence," as the collapse of the Austrian grand delusion. According to those interpretations, the major taboo—the most divisive topic since 1945, both popular and scientific—had been National Socialism.[8] In my opinion, there are good reasons to doubt this assumption. The elephant in the room was not so much National Socialism. It was the time before, namely the First Republic and the dictatorship that followed until 1938. Just a few years ago, the controversial comments in regard to the 80th anniversary of the clashes in February 1934 highlighted how much the assessments of the dictatorship under Engelbert Dollfuß and Kurt Schuschnigg still diverge.[9]

It was the opposing sides of the civil war in February 1934 that together reestablished the democratic republic after 1945. They could only do so because they invented a historical teleology to legitimize the cooperation

6 Hamburger Institut für Sozialforschung, ed., *Vernichtungskrieg. Verbrechen der Wehrmacht 1941 bis 1944,* exhibition catalog (Hamburg: Hamburger Edition, 1996).

7 Walter Manoschek and Thomas Geldmacher, "Vergangenheitspolitik," in *Politik in Österreich: Das Handbuch,* ed. Herbert Dachs et al. (Vienna: Manz, 2006), 577-604.

8 For Austria compare e.g. the contributions in Gerhard Botz and Gerald Sprengnagel, eds., *Kontroversen um Österreichs Zeitgeschichte: Verdrängte Vergangenheit, Österreich-Identität, Waldheim und die Historiker,* 2nd ed. (Frankfurt/New York:Campus, 2008).

9 See the debate in the Austrian daily newspaper Der Standard: Kurt Bauer, "Schwieriges Vermächtnis," *Der Standard,* Feb. 8, 2014; Peter Huemer, "Das 34er Jahr: Widerstand und Heroismus," *Der Standard,* Feb. 12, 2014; Johannes Koll, "Kollateralschäden und Verantwortung. Einige Anmerkungen zum Februar 1934 und seinen Folgen," *Der Standard,* Feb. 12, 2014; Kurt Bauer, "Die vielen Wahrheiten des Februar," *Der Standard,* Feb. 19, 2014; Gerhard Botz, "Irrwege einer historischen Schuld"-Suche zum "Februar 1934. Entgegnung auf zwei Zeitungskommentare von Kurt Bauer," http://www.lbihs.at/Botz_Irrwege.pdf (2014), accessed Dec. 12, 2018; Gudula Walterskirchen, "Die drei Fehler im Blick auf den 12. Februar," *Die Presse,* Feb. 12, 2014. Not by coincidence, a separate, well-attended panel at the Austrian Historikertag 2015 in Linz addressed the disputed questions of the controversy, see the contributions in *Historicum* III-IV (2017).

with the former enemy of their own supporters. It is known as the "myth of the camp road" and, in a nutshell, argues that the First Republic was condemned to fail because, as Ernst Fischer would put it, "the Republicans were not patriotic while the Patriots were not democratic."[10] According to this interpretation, both sides had to learn their lesson and overcome their differences in the Nazi concentration camps. Reality had been different. The post-war political elite—with few exceptions such as Leopold Figl, Karl Seitz, or Alfons Gorbach—did not consist of former detainees, and there is no proof of such reconciliations between socialists and conservatives behind barbed wire. This legitimizing public interpretation was also contrasted by internal party narratives along the original fronts. The Socialists, and also the minor Communist Party, claimed to have been (and, hence, to still be) the only really democratic, antifascist movement in the country, not only resisting Nazism but also Austrofascism before that.[11] While the SPÖ itself had become much more pragmatic and depoliticized, the antifascist past was essential for the political identity of many of their activists.

The conservatives, in turn, rejected sole responsibility for the overthrow of the republic and the establishment of the dictatorship under Dollfuß and Schuschnigg, and they insisted that the coup had either been the result of foreign pressure imposed mainly by Benito Mussolini, an act of pure self-defense against a radical Bolshevik left, or a necessary dictatorship needed to confront National Socialism.

Thus, until the 1970s, the discourse of domestic politics in Austria was strongly influenced by the experiences of the dictatorship from 1933 to 1938. In a severely pillared society,[12] electoral campaigns mainly aimed to mobilize one's own milieu, not to reach out to others and convince them.[13] Fear of the political opponent played a major role in these campaigns—a fear that on the one hand was deliberately stoked but on the other hand corresponded to the historical-political consciousness of the parties' bases.

Under such circumstances, contemporary historical research was inevitably highly politicized in Austria until the 1990s and partly until today. The fact that the interwar period was an ideological minefield strongly limited the domestic scientific preoccupation with it for

10 Ernst Fischer, "Österreichischer Patriotismus," *Neues Österreich. Organ der Demokratischen Einigung*, Apr. 27, 1945.
11 Cf. Norbert Hölzl, *Propagandaschlachten. Die österreichischen Wahlkämpfe 1945-1971* (Vienna: Verlag für Geschichte und Politik, 1974), 15-28.
12 Rudolf Steininger, *Polarisierung und Integration. Eine vergleichende Untersuchung der strukturellen Versäulung der Gesellschaft in den Niederlanden und in Österreich* (Meisenheim/Glan: Hain, 1975).
13 Norbert Hölzl, *Propagandaschlachten. Die österreichischen Wahlkämpfe 1945-1971* (Munich: Oldenbourg 1974).

decades.[14] Since Austrian historians could hardly defy immediate political categorization, which would immunize parts of the auditorium against their argument regardless of however convincing it might have been, foreign historians became of special importance to the debate. Mainly authors from the US and Great Britain, who early created important contributions to the historiography of the Dollfuß/Schuschnigg dictatorship, were—on both sides of the divide—addressed as "neutral" authorities[15] whose assessments allegedly "objectively" proved each position.

Apart from two British journalists, Gordon Brook-Shepherd and G.E.R. Gedye, two US historians were of especial importance to the inner-Austrian debate. Conservatives preferably referred to R. John Rath, who became the founder and editor of the *Austrian History Yearbook* and "Mr. Austrian History" in the US. Instead, left-wingers were clearly in favor of Charles Adams Gulick, who, as a professor for economics at UC Berkeley, wrote to this day the most detailed book about interwar Austria in 1948[16] and caused harsh public criticism there when it was released in German just a few months later.

While Rath had already established close contacts with Austrian conservatives in the 1930s, which he reactivated after 1945, he participated in a central historiographical debate on the question of whether the term "fascist" was appropriate to describe the Dollfuß/Schuschnigg Regime and finally was nominated by the ÖVP as a member of the Körner-Kunschak-Kommission. Gulick did not do anything like that. He was no public intellectual, neither in the US nor in Austria, and would not interfere in historical debates. Little is known about his social, scholarly, or political network within Austria and even less about his beliefs and positions in a more general perspective. Although in the preface of his book

14 The first systematic attempt to scientifically examine the history of the First Republic was the Wissenschaftliche Kommission des Theodor Körner-Stiftungsfonds und des Leopold Kunschak-Preises zur Erforschung der österreichischen Geschichte der Jahre 1927 bis 1938, which was established on the initiative of Chancellor Bruno Kreisky in 1970. For the history of the Kommission as well as for the inter-Austrian historiography see the contributions of Rudolf Neck, Ludwig Jedlicka and Karl Haas in: Ludwig Jedlicka and Rudolf Neck, *Vom Justizpalast zum Heldenplatz. Studien und Dokumentationen 1927 bis 1938* (Vienna: Österr. Staatsdruckerei, 1975), 15-16, 17-20, 156-168.

15 Florian Wenninger, "Austrian Missions – Das Problem der politischen Äquidistanz der Forschung am Beispiel Austrofaschismus," in Ilse Reiter, Christiane Rothländer and Pia Schölnberger, eds., *Österreich 1933-1938: Interdisziplinäre Bestandsaufnahmen und Perspektiven* (Vienna: Böhlau, 2012), 257-272.

16 Charles Adams Gulick, *Austria: From Habsburg to Hitler*. With a Foreword by Walther Federn, Vol. 1: *Labor's Workshop of Democracy*; Vol. 2: *Fascism's Subversion of Democracy* (Berkeley and Los Angeles: University of California Press, 1948).

he strongly emphasized the duty of historians to express value judgments in their work—and did so resolutely himself when writing about the First Austrian Republic—Gulick's personal convictions remained vague. The SPÖ honored Gulick in various ways, and yet the laudations about him never highlighted his biography as scholar and citizen but would let him appear as a variation of Mr. Pim, a figure of a prominent socialist propaganda movie from the 1930s about an American capitalist who visits Red Vienna and is so enthusiastic when he learns about all its achievements that he finally converts to socialism.[17]

Thanks to a grant by the Marshall Plan Foundation, I was not only able to follow Gulick's traces in Austria but also in the US. I went through his relief and his personal file, which are kept at Bancroft Library at UC Berkeley, spoke to former colleagues and friends, and interviewed Gulick's grandson, Paul Perasso, who kindly shared his memories with me and provided not only a lot of valuable information about his grandfather but also plenty of photos of almost every period in Charles Gulick's life.

A Biographical Outline[18]

Charles Adams Gulick Jr. was born as the oldest son of Charles Adams Gulick (1864-1934) and Jackella (Lena) Parks Gulick (1868-1930) in Dallas, Texas on September 13, 1896. The family was not originally Texan. Charles's mother Jackella had come from a cotton plantation near Monroe, Louisiana and had moved to Texas as a child, while his father had been born in Connecticut into a family with Dutch roots whose first members had apparently already come to the US during the eighteenth century.

17 Mister Pim's trip to Europe/Das Tagebuch des Mr. Pim (1930). The 76-minute silent film was commissioned by the Sozialdemokratische Arbeiterpartei Österreichs and directed by Frank Ward Rossak http://www.stummfilm.at/Mister_Pims_trip_to_Europe.html (accessed Dec. 22, 2018).

18 I owe great thanks for information, material and hints provided to me – especially to Charles and Esther Gulick's grandson Paul Perasso, to his former colleagues Clair Brown and Benjamin N. Ward and to Oliver Rathkolb.

The Gulick family, about 1904. Charles Jr. standing in the background.
© Paul Perasso

The family belonged to the WASP middle class. Charles Sr. worked as an insurance clerk,[19] while his wife was the organist of the local Episcopal Church and ran an Episcopal Sunday school in Oak Cliff.[20] Three years after Charles Adams Jr., Jackella gave birth to her second son, John Chase (1899-1963). Hardly any detailed information is available about Charles's youth since he more or less cut his personal ties to Texas, including those with his family, after the death of his first wife. According to his grandson, Paul Perasso, Gulick hardly ever talked about his origins to anyone.[21] Nevertheless, it seems very likely that it was not New York or Berkeley that formed the intellectual Charles Gulick, but Texas. First, of course, that applies to his character, his way of talking and behaving. Unanimously, people who knew him personally described Gulick with attributes usually regarded as being "typical southern US." He was an old-school gentleman with a distinctive Texan accent, slenderly built, always well dressed in a suit and tie, conservative manners, courteous towards students and faculty members alike but holding strong convictions, judging sharply, and, though being very polite, lacking any sort

19 https://www.findagrave.com/memorial/71834637/charles-adams-gulick (accessed Dec. 2, 2018)
20 https://www.findagrave.com/memorial/71834420 (accessed Dec. 2, 2018)
21 Interview with Paul Perasso, Feb. 13, 2018 [further on: Interview Perasso].

of bonhomie. At UC Berkeley, Gulick seemingly did not mingle a lot with people but rather stayed on his own, personally and scientifically a maverick.

Not only his personality but the *zoon politikon* of Charles Gulick was also shaped by his experiences during his youth in Texas. Whoever entered his office at the University of California-Berkeley (Cal) would instantly identify two Texan mementos: a horse bridle and a riding crop made from leather. But in contrast to what his visitors might have assumed, Gulick did not keep these items as nostalgic souvenirs in the classical sense. During his high school years, he had been sent to a relative's cattle ranch in northern Texas to work for several summers. The teenager was not fond of the seclusion of the farm in general, but what disgusted him in particular was the way the Mexican-American ranch hands were treated by the owners of the farm. Charles sympathized with the hands, and they must have cherished his empathy because at the end of one summer, they gave him those two objects they had made themselves as a farewell present. For Gulick, bridle and crop hence did not represent the "good old" Confederate Texas. On the contrary, they were mementos of both inequality and solidarity.[22]

After completing high school in the spring of 1914, Charles went on to the University of Texas at Austin, where he received his bachelor's degree and had his first experiences teaching as a tutor in medieval history in his final BA semester. After the United States had entered World War I, he was drafted in February 1918. During his basic training he, like many of his comrades, contracted Spanish flu and was hospitalized. Since his recovery took time, Charles was lucky enough not to be sent overseas. Instead, after his release from the hospital and his return to the military, he served as an instructor in maps and aerial gunnery at the School of Military Aeronautics in Austin, Texas.[23] Meanwhile, the war had ended, and Charles was finally discharged the following year. He left the military in 1919 not as a pacifist but "with an instinctive mistrust of the military establishment."[24]

In March of 1919, Gulick returned to the University of Texas to complete his MA in modern European history.[25] As an MA candidate, he was given a project position to edit the papers of 19th century Texan President Mirabeau Buonaparte Lamar in four volumes for the state library of Texas.[26]

22 Interview Perasso.
23 Personnel Record Charles A. Gulick, CV-form. Berkeley University Archive, Bancroft Library [heretofore: PRCAG).
24 Interview Perasso.
25 Report on Charles Adams Gulick, Jr., undated [appr. 1929/30], PRCAG.
26 Biography, February 14th, 1941. The result of his work was first published by A. C. Baldwin and Sons, Austin 1921-22 and twelve years later, in 1934, reprinted again by Boeckmann-Jones Co., Austin, as well as in 1973 by AMS Press, New York (six vol.), PRCAG.

From September 1919 to June 1921, he again worked as a tutor—first in English, later on in Economics—at his alma mater and was admitted to Phi Beta Kappa.[27] Those who knew Gulick personally agree that his years at the University of Texas at Austin were formative for his convictions and beliefs. "It was the progressive era and he became committed to central themes of that movement—that a larger measure of social justice must be won for the less privileged members of society."[28] It is very likely that at that time, Gulick also broke with the religious tradition of his family. For the rest of his life, he would feel "that religions, in general, were silly or worse"[29] and kept a jealous watch over religious attempts to influence the public, about which he, already in his late 70s, reported to his friends sarcastically: "The educational authorities of California appear determined to make themselves the laughingstock of the civilized world. Specifically, they are yielding to pressure from 'Creationists' who wish the concept of the evolution of man from lower forms of life to be present in textbooks and classrooms strictly as a theory. Equal prominence is to be given to the Adam and Eve version. So far no one has demanded equal space for the idea that the world is flat; that will come about 1976, that is, on the 200th birthday of the US (A glance back at this makes me realize I possibly should have used quotation marks around the words civilized and lower)."[30]

The early 1920s were the only time in Gulick's life that saw him as kind of an activist. During the presidential election campaign of 1920, he publically supported socialist candidate Eugene V. Debs, who served a jail sentence at that time for his previous anti-war activities. Reportedly, Charles gave speeches in Debs's favor on the university campus.[31] Four years later, he voted, as he would later state himself, "with unqualified enthusiasm" for the progressive candidate Robert M. La Follette, who he hoped would start "what Keir Hardie and Viktor Adler actually did,"[32] which obviously meant the foundation of a labor party. The existing two-party system in the US frustrated Gulick massively: "As early as 1912 I came to the firm conviction, that 'at the bottom line' the difference between Republicans and Democrats is scarcely more, if any, than that between Tweedledee and Tweedledum."[33] In each case, they were likely to be an annoyance: "Since the nominating

27 Phi Beta Kappa (ed.), Alpha of Texas [list of members], University of Texas, 1920, 53.
28 Obituary (draft), 1, PRCAG.
29 Interview Perasso.
30 Kreisky Archiv, Best. Bruno Kreisky, Korrespondenzen/Prominenten-Korrespondenz/ Box 22/Charles Gulick, [heretofore: Kreisky Archiv/Gulick], Charles Gulick, Circular letter, February 7th, 1973; all emphasis taken from the original.
31 Interview Perasso.
32 Charles Gulick, Letter to Bruno Kreisky, September 16th, 1976 Kreisky Archiv/Gulick.
33 Ibid.

conventions of our major parties [1976] I have thought more often of an early passage in Othello and wished that I could help to 'put in every honest hand a whip to lash the rascals naked through the world.'"[34] While holding strictly contained sympathies for Democrats and Republicans alike, the two politicians the old Charles Gulick really became furious about were Ronald Reagan[35] and Richard Nixon. About the re-election of the latter, he expressed "bitter feelings" which were further "increased many times by the 'Xmas Bombings' [in Vietnam 1972]. And nearly every week, sometimes on several consecutive days that bitterness becomes more intense [...] Nixon is concerned only with his own aggrandizement and that of the plutocrats who gave him election campaign funds."[36]

Charles A. Gulick Jr. as a student in Austin during First World War. © Paul Perasso.

34 Ibid.
35 Interview Perasso.
36 Charles Gulick, Circular letter, February 7th, 1973, Kreisky Archiv/Gulick.

Gulick's student years in Texas were also influential in two other regards: his scholarship and private life. Benjamin N. Ward, prominent Professor for Economics at Cal and a student himself at that time, worked as a part-time research assistant for Gulick in 1954. The reason why Gulick chose Ward for the position was for his German language skills that enabled him to support Gulick's research on the ideology of Austrian socialism. Ward remembers his former supervisor being popular at the department due to his modest, charming character. On the other hand, Ward states—and Clair Brown, another former student and later professor for economics at Cal, agrees in principle—"most of his colleagues did not consider Gulick as a 'real' economist, more as a labor historian. His scientific tool set was indeed first and foremost historical."[37]

As for the private developments, Charles befriended two female fellow students: the sisters Marie and Katie Brougher. Though Katie claimed to have been his first sweetheart,[38] Charles finally married her younger sister, Marie. In 1921, the couple left Texas for New York after Charles had been accepted as a graduate student in economics at Columbia University. There, the young PhD candidate met his most important teacher: Professor of Political Economy Henry Rogers Seager (1870-1930). Seager was a dedicated advocator of social reform, especially of social insurance and minimum wages.[39] His economical approach was strongly influenced by the Austrian school of economics around Carl Menger, which he became familiar with when he had spent two years in Europe at the end of the nineteenth century during which he had also visited Vienna for a longer period of time. Under the influence of Seager, Gulick, who quickly started to work at the University of New York as an instructor in economics in 1922 and later on at Columbia University, focused on industrial relations in various fields, as well as on employment. Apparently it was also Seager who introduced Gulick to the welfare systems that had been established after the foundation of the republics in Germany and Austria after World War I.[40] As a consequence, Gulick started to learn German to be able to study them himself.

37 Interview with Benjamin N. Ward, September 22nd, 2016 [further on: Interview Ward].

38 Interview Perasso.

39 See Henry Rogers Seager, "The Theory of the Minimum Wage," *American Labor Legislation Review* 3 (1913): 81-91; For the beliefs and impacts of Seager see the obituaries published by Samuel McCune Lindsay, *Columbia University Quarterly* 22, no. 4 (Dec. 1930): 428-431 and by Samuel McCune Lindsay/H. E. Hoagland/Charles A. Gulick, *American Economic Review* 2, no. 4 (Dec. 1930): 794-797.

40 For the significance of the welfare reforms especially in central Europe to American left-wingers see Axel R. Schäfer, *American Progressives and the German Social Reform, 1875-1920: Social Ethics, Moral Control and the Regulatory State in a Transatlantic Context* (Stuttgart: Steiner, 2000). For the group Seager belonged to see especially 168.

In 1924, Gulick published his PhD thesis on the labor policy of US Steel,[41] which received significant attention due to the permanent conflicts between management and unions in the country's biggest corporation. Economists of various backgrounds unanimously considered Gulick's book a "brilliant" piece of work.[42]

Postdoc, Gulick spent two more years at Columbia before he was appointed Assistant Professor of Economics at Berkeley in 1926. The reasons to leave Columbia for Berkeley were not only of an academic nature but also a result of the poor health conditions of both Charles and especially of his wife, Marie. "[Otherwise] we would not have allowed him to leave Columbia," as Seager wrote.[43] The hope for recovery on the West Coast at first seemed to be fulfilled. Just one year after their move to Berkeley, Mary gave birth to their only child, Elizabeth Anne.[44]

As an Assistant Professor of Economics at Berkeley, Charles continued working on the problems of huge economic power in democratic systems[45] and labor policy in corporations. In 1929, Gulick and Seager together published a book entitled *Trust and Corporation Problems*, which at that time for both of them, it presumably was their most cited and recognized work—although Gulick at least did not regard it to be his most important one. Since he had studied the European welfare states from a distance for quite some time and his German skills had improved a lot,[46] Charles decided in 1930 to take advantage of his first sabbatical leave to visit Europe. Mainly located in Munich, he also travelled to Vienna and spent three months in the city, from April to July 1930,[47] while Marie and Elizabeth stayed in Berkeley. During his residence in Vienna in 1930, Gulick lived as a subtenant in a little flat in Palais Trautson, Museumstraße 7 in the 7th district of Vienna owned by the Viennese Collegium Hungaricum.[48] How the contact between him and the Collegium, resp. the lecturer and radio journalist Otto Polzer, who he listed as a contact, was established remains unclear. But the contact obviously lasted, and even six years later, during

41 Charles Adams Gulick, *Labor Policy of the U. S. Steel Corporation* (Columbia Studies in History, Economics and Public Law) (New York: Columbia University Press, 1924).
42 Report on Charles Adams Gulick, Jr., undated [appr. 1929/30], PRCAG.
43 Excerpt from Promotion Committee Report, Feb. 26, 1929, PRCAG.
44 Elizabeth Anne Gulick, married Perasso (09.12.1927 to 06.09.2011).
45 Charles Adams Gulick, "Holding Companies in Power", *New Republic*, May 26th 1926, 25-28.
46 Joseph T. Simon, *Augenzeuge* (Vienna: published by Maria Dorothea Simon, 1979), 262.
47 Application for Sabbatical or Semi-Sabbatical Leave, December 6th, 1961, resp. the statement of his Department from December 8th 1961, 2, PRCAG.
48 Bundespolizeidirektion Wien, Historische Meldeunterlagen, Meldezettel Charles A. Gulick, 1. April/6. Juli 1930, Wiener Stadt- und Landesarchiv.

his second stay in Austria, Gulick would ask colleagues at Berkeley to use Polzer's address if they wanted to write to him.[49]

According to his Austrian friends, Gulick had originally come to Vienna for the first time because "he wanted to get to know to the city in which Johann Strauß had lived, since his mother had a foible for music and was a great fan of the King of Waltz,"[50] but that seems more like an anecdote without great reliability. Much more likely is that Seager's reports about his experiences in Vienna and the Austrian welfare system, as well as Viennese community socialism, drew his interest, since both of these tried to realize ideas he and his mentor Seager represented in the US.

Whatever the case, it certainly was in that spring of 1930 that Gulick decided to focus his future scientific work on Austria.[51] First, his main interest had apparently been drawn to the trade unions, since from his American background, he in any case regarded unions as the backbone of a labor movement. But his perspective broadened when he better got to know the Social Democratic Party and her huge net of organizations, as well as the social institutions of Red Vienna and the welfare state established shortly after World War I. His opus magnum, *Austria: From Habsburg to Hitler*, but especially the first volume, *Labor's Workshop of Democracy* published almost twenty years later, describes all of that in detail and communicates a lot of admiration for all these aspects. Nevertheless, it has to be stated that Gulick's analysis (in contrast to what some of his critics said) did not ignore problems and insufficiencies of social democratic policies. Hence, it was not a simple defensive maneuver, meant to keep up the appearance of a distant relationship between the SPÖ and the author, when Jacques Hannak stressed that several points in Gulick's book would not reflect the point of view of the party but rather the opposite.[52]

After Gulick left Austria in early July of 1930 with many new impressions (among which the huge rally in Vienna on May 1st was one of the most formidable ones to him),[53] various circumstances caused a delay of several years before he would be able to realize his plot to write the book he planned.

---

49 MS 3 B 3, Vollmer August, Box 13: Letter from Charles Gulick to August Vollmer, August 24, 1936, Bancroft Library.

50 Simon, *Augenzeuge*, 262.

51 Ibid; Ernst Winkler, "Ch. A. Gulick – Der Historiker der Ersten Republik," in *Die Zukunft: Sozialistische Zeitschrift für Politik, Wirtschaft und Kultur* 25, no 18 (1971): 28-30 (here 29).

52 See fn 111.

53 Winkler, "Ch. A. Gulick," 28.

First, shortly after his return to the US, Gulick learnt that his friend and teacher Henry R. Seager surprisingly had passed away during a research trip to the Soviet Union in August 1930. As an intellectual memorial, "a labor of love and a very fine piece of editorial work,"[54] Gulick edited a selection of unpublished papers by Seager the following year.[55]

Secondly, the physical condition of Charles's wife, Marie, severely worsened in 1931.[56] It finally led to a lingering illness that lasted for another two years before Marie finally passed away on April 21, 1933 at the age of only thirty-five. She was survived by her thirty-nine-year-old husband and her sick, six-year-old daughter, Elizabeth.[57]

Marie's death was a hard blow. Though he just took two weeks off after the funeral, it seemed clear to his superior that "Professor Gulick needs a complete change and rest."[58]

While his academic career had advanced during the years before—in 1930, Gulick had been given a tenure track position and promoted to an associate professorship—after Marie's death, a lot of his energy was gone. In the fall of 1933, he—apparently unsuccessfully—applied for an academic exchange that would have allowed him to spend some months in New York while being replaced by one of Marie's brothers, who was a lecturer at NYU.[59] Whereas his prior evaluation had been outstanding, due to a significant lack of productivity, a confidential report by his department opposed Gulick's advancement in 1936, arguing that "his failure to continue his excellent scholarly work, it should be noted, is due to severe handicaps, among which should be mentioned the illness of his wife prior to her death, and continued illness of a child. We are of the opinion, that he simply has had no opportunity of late to show what he can do."[60]

After her mother passed away, Elizabeth was sent to her father's family in Texas for several months to recover. When she returned to

54 Report on Charles Adams Gulick, Jr., undated [appr. 1929/30], PRCAG.

55 Charles Adams Gulick, ed., *Labor and other Economic Essays of Henry R. Seager* (New York: Harper & Brothers, 1931).

56 Memo to Dean Monroe E. Deutsch by Albert H. Mowbray, chairman of the Department of Economics at UC Berkeley, February 5th, 1931, PRCAG.

57 Application for Special Leave of Absence, May 1st, 1933 and report by the promotion committee to President Gobert G. Sproul, March 5, 1936, PRCAG.

58 Statement on the Application for special Leave of Absence, submitted by Mowbray on April 28, 1932, PRCAG.

59 Correspondence on Professor Gulick's request for exchange professorship, November/December 1933, PRCAG. The author bio in the book states that Gulick served as visiting professor at Columbia, Cornell and Colorado, see Charles A. Gulick 1976: Österreich von Habsburg zu Hitler, Wien, Umschlag.

60 Recommendations of the promotion committee to President Sproul, March 5, 1936, 2, PRCAG.

Berkeley, Charles introduced her to a young woman whom he had met as one of his students at Cal two years before[61] and whom he married in 1934, one year after Marie's death, in Reno, Nevada: Esther Kaufmann.[62] Decades later, in her fifties, Gulick's spouse would appear to a young student, who visited the couple at their dapper home at Grizzly Peak Blvd., as a "WASP urban matron."[63] While there are other references that describe Esther as a charming, polite, and open-minded lady, bare of characteristics usually associated with a "WASP matron," this characterization might have been caused by the commonly shared impression that she was more communicative and outgoing than her husband. Anyhow, the description of Esther's character was neither indicated by her social background nor by her personal convictions. She was born in 1911 in Oakland as the daughter of a Jewish butcher from San Francisco and his English-born wife.[64] Esther had grown up in Fresno and completed her BA at UC Berkeley. All available sources agree on the very fortunate, loving relationship between Charles and her (and also between Esther and her step-daughter, Elizabeth) in which Esther not only decisively took care of the social life of the couple but was also intellectually important to Charles. She would actively support his work throughout their marriage, share his strong interest in politics, and inspire his attention for the feminist movement, as well as for environmental matters. Together with others, Esther became a leading figure of the Save The Bay movement in the 1960s,[65] which made Charles very proud of her. As he reported to his Austrian friends: "The big event in recent weeks for me is the recognition my wife is receiving for her part in preserving San Francisco Bay from the assaults of environmental rapists."[66]

---

61 August 25, the day Gulick saw Esther for the first time in 1931, remained special to him until the end of his life, cf, Charles A. Gulick, Circular Letter, September 22, 1981, Kreisky Archiv/Gulick.

62 Esther Kaufmann (29.03.1911-31.05.1995), Biography, February 14, 1941, PRCAG.

63 Interview Ward.

64 For autobiographical information on Esther Gulick see "Save San Francisco Bay Association and the Courts", an oral history conducted in 1986 by Malca Chall, in Save San Francisco Bay Association, 1961-1986, Regional Oral History Office, Bancroft Library, University of California at Berkeley, 1987.

65 Esther Gulick/Catherine Kerr/Sylvia McLaughlin, "Saving San Francisco Bay: Past, Present and Future," XXVIII. *Horace M. Albright Lectureship in Conservation*, Berkeley, California, April 14, 1988 (Berkeley: University of California, College of Natural Resources, Department of Forestry and Resource Management, 1988).

66 Charles A. Gulick, Circular Letter, September 22nd, 1981, Kreisky Archiv/Gulick,.

The Research on Austria

In July 1936, the Gulick Family—Charles, Esther, and Elizabeth—left Berkeley for Vienna where they rented a flat at the Cottagegasse in the city's 19th district, Döbling, a noble, quiet area. In the residential registration form back in 1930, Gulick had stated to be unaffiliated with any religion,[67] but this time he declared himself as being Episcopal.[68] This was apparently a precautionary measure to avoid suspicion by the regime—the same obviously applied to the fact that Esther's Jewish background was not mentioned. The fact that anti-Semitism was not only an ideological privilege of Nazism but also a programmatic basis of Catholic conservatism was, despite all other reservations, surely not helpful for the Gulicks in developing any sympathies for the political right in Austria.

Nevertheless, Charles and Esther liked their new surroundings very much. For Elizabeth, however, who attended a boarding school just outside the city, it must have been quite tough to get along in completely new surroundings without any language skills and confidants. But she coped with the situation, learned German within a few months (for the rest of her life, Elizabeth spoke German fluently[69]), and seemed to have also felt comfortable after the rough beginning.

About the start of Gulick's research in Austria, one of his later friends reported: "On the first day of his stay in Vienna, he [Gulick] went to the nearest tobacconist [...] When Gulick said 'I want all the newspapers,' the tobacconist presented all daily papers he had, but Gulick wasn't satisfied. 'But these aren't all the newspapers,' he insisted. When the salesman assured him that there were no other papers available in Austria at that time, the professor said confidingly '[...] I also want the illegal ones—you can sell them to me, I am not linked to the police.' [...] The tobacconist [...] didn't want to disappoint him. 'Of course I don't have any [illegal papers]. But an old social democrat lives in this building, his son is in jail; he can probably help.'"[70]

In fact, this old social democrat was indeed able to arrange regular delivery of illegal media from that day on. And he did more than that. He—and his son after being released from jail—introduced Gulick to their personal political network. During the following year, Gulick had "hundreds of conversations with politicians, professors, businessmen, union

67 Ibid., Bundespolizeidirektion Wien, Historische Meldeunterlagen, Meldezettel Charles A. Gulick, 1. April/6. Juli 1930, Wiener Stadt- und Landesarchiv.
68 Bundespolizeidirektion Wien, Historische Meldeunterlagen, Meldezettel Charles A. Gulick, 14. September 1936/ 31. Mai 1937, Wiener Stadt- und Landesarchiv.
69 Interview Perasso.
70 Simon, *Augenzeuge*, 262f. In the preface to Simon's book, Gulick confirms the anecdote, ibid, 3.

operatives, waiters, tramway conductors, clerks, public officials and factory workers."[71] The social democrats Gulick was repeatedly in contact with included high ranks like Karl Renner, Robert Danneberg, Hugo Breitner, and Max Adler.[72] In his Czech exile in Brno, Gulick also met with Otto Bauer.[73] Furthermore, he corresponded in particular with Julius Deutsch and Heinrich Schneidmadl, as well as with Rudolf Löw and Josef Afritsch.[74] Characteristic for Gulick's methodological approach was the fact that he was not only interested in the perspective of the party's leadership but also in the opinions and sentiments of ordinary people, might they be activists or not. Therefore, he also spoke to a broad variety of workers, clerks, and employees.[75] Several of the contacts he established lasted for decades. It is evident from a mailing list for circular letters from the 1970s that Gulick at that time was in constant contact with Karl and Josefine Ausch, Paul Blau, Alfred Dallinger, Heinz Fischer, Kurt Heller, Elfriede Kranister, Alfred Magaziner, Karl Mark, Karl Przibram, Annette Richter, Philipp Rieger, Friedrich Scheu, Karl Waldbrunner, Stefan Wirlandner, Christian Broda, Eduard März, Karl and Gina Stadler, as well as Anton Tesarek. Certainly not all of these contacts were already established during his stay in Austria in 1936/37, but since several of the above-mentioned people had belonged to the socialist underground during the Austrofascist period and knew Gulick's contact, Josef Simon, well, Gulick presumably got to know them during that time. However, it is rather unlikely that he met them during World War II, since nobody save Eduard März had been a US exile, while most (Ausch, Magaziner, Rieger, Scheu, Stadler, and Wirlandner) had either fled to the UK or remained in the country (Blau, Mark, Tesarek, and Broda). At least the contact with Karl Waldbrunner must have been dated post-1945, since Waldbrunner had been in the Soviet Union from 1932 to May 24, 1937, while the Gulicks left Vienna on May 31, 1937, so the time they would have both spent in Vienna would have just been a week.[76] At the end of the list, Gulick noted: "I am uncertain about Kreisky and Jonas [whose names on the list he had marked with a question mark]. Both have been extremely kind, but there is not the same close relationship as with most of the [above mentioned] others. If you think it is not presumptuous

71 Winkler, "Ch. A. Gulick," 29.
72 Gulick, Bd. 1, XVI.
73 Winkler "Ch. A. Gulick," 29.
74 Gulick, *Austria*, Vol. 1., XVI.
75 Ibid., XVII.
76 Gulick's Meldezettel, FM 67, and Manfred Zollinger, "Karl Waldbrunner – Schnittstellen eines Lebens zwischen Industrie und Politik", in: Hannes Androsch/Anton Pelinka/Manfred Zollinger, eds., *Karl Waldbrunner: Pragmatischer Visionär für das neue Österreich* (Vienna: Gerold, 2006), 13-184:36.

to send them a letter of this sort, send it to them!"[77] More than with all the others, the contact with Karl Stadler, who became the major social democratic historian during the 1970s, definitely included professional elements, for it was Stadler who initiated and enabled the abridged edition of Gulick's book in 1976.[78]

But during his stay in Austria, Gulick not only met members of the opposition. He also established ties with prominent representatives of the regime, such as Christian trade unionist Franz Hemala; the later diplomat Walter Peinsipp, who at that time worked for the official propaganda service of the regime, hosted by the chancellery; Leopold Kunschak, founder of the Christian Workers Association; Eugen Margarétha, vice president of the industrial association; and with regime officials, such as the vice mayor of Vienna, Ernst Karl Winter, or Georg Blocher, an executive of the *Vaterländische Front*.[79] It may well be that during conversations with the regime officials, Gulick was suggestive of being rather open minded towards the Austrian "new order" and hence was also supported in his research by regime loyalists. This part of the book's background might have been a reason for the harshness of the reaction it faced from that side of the political spectrum. It was not only a matter of opposing opinions but also of a feeling of having been sold out.

His research in Austria provided Gulick with enormous quantities of material (although he himself regarded the corpus as incomplete),[80] which he, with the support of Esther and various assistants, structured and analyzed for years. Although Gulick's compilation of 481 documents, today kept at Bancroft Library at UC Berkeley, contains just a fractional amount of his original collection of sources and unfortunately does not include any personal notes,[81] it certainly still is one of the top collections on the Austrian labor movement during the First Republic and certainly the most important collection in North America today. From today's point of view, not only is the amount of documents he collected remarkable but also his interdisciplinary methodological approach, which was quite uncommon for a historian of his generation. As already mentioned above, Gulick did not only rely on written sources but also on interviews and participant

77 Charles A. Gulick, Circular Letter, Feb. 7, 1973, Kreisky Archiv/Gulick; also ibid., attached handwritten list for Philipp Rieger, passed on to Alfred Reiter on March 21, 1973.
78 The extensive correspondence of Stadler and Gulick: Box 14, Korrespondenz II, Karton 3, correspondence Stadler –Gulick 1969-85, Nachlass Karl R Stadler, Österreichisches Volkshochschularchiv.
79 Winkler, "Ch. A. Gulick", 29.
80 Gulick, *Austria*, XV.
81 Easily verifiable when the content at Bancroft Library is compared to the references in his book and explicitly mentioned in the Bancroft catalogue.

observation. His skepticism towards information released by the regime itself or reported by the loyal media sometimes may have turned into a certain willingness to accept interpretations provided by the underground as factual information, although he could not double check it. But while this made his work error-prone in various details, it was undoubtedly a presupposition for his general analytical depth of field.

Aside from the professional aspects of his stay, it may well be that it was no exaggeration when his friend and eventual assistant Ernst Winkler wrote that Gulick had fallen in love with "the Austrian way of life, the Viennese commodity and the natural beauty of our country."[82] Though they had constantly been short of money throughout their stay, as Esther would claim years later,[83] the Gulicks left Austria in the autumn of 1937 after they had spent (as they had done a year before) the summer months at the Achensee in Tyrol with a deep feeling of connectedness with the country for the rest of their lives. "As you know," Gulick would write more than thirty years later to then chancellor Bruno Kreisky, "there are many times when I feel more Austrian than American."[84] And the Gulicks would not only take their memories with them but also an Austrian housekeeper and governess for Elizabeth. That woman lived with the Gulick family in Berkeley for almost ten years before she married and moved to a house nearby.[85]

Just half a year after the Gulicks returned to the US, the German Reich incorporated Austria, causing a second, much bigger wave of refugees than the one in 1934. As the situation in Austria became increasingly threatening not only for opposing political activists but especially for people who did not meet the racist criteria of the new regime, people heading for the United States were desperately looking for US citizens willing to provide affidavits as preconditions to be accepted as visa applicants. Together with a local YMCA secretary, a Roman Catholic priest, the Rabbi of the university community, and representatives of several Protestant denominations, Charles and Esther organized a committee in support of refugees. They managed to bring nine people to Berkeley, most but not all of whom were of Austrian origin.[86] In a letter to his friends, Gulick described an event that highlighted the relationship to one of these refugees, the later

82 Winkler "Ch. A. Gulick," 28.
83 Interview Perasso.
84 Charles A. Gulick to Bruno Kreisky, Sept. 16, 1976, Kreisky Archiv/Gulick.
85 Interview Perasso. Although I made considerable efforts to identify this housekeeper, whose first name was supposedly Rosserl and who would later on marry an Austrian emigrant, Mr. Jäger, I unfortunately failed in doing so.
86 Charles A. Gulick, Circular Letter, Sept. 22, 1981, Kreisky Archiv/Gulick.

prominent psychiatrist at San Francisco, Wolfgang Lederer,[87] whom the Gulicks had met in Vienna for the first time in 1936 and had enabled him to immigrate to the US in the summer of 1939 via France:[88] "The meeting on September 18 was a pre-nuptial dinner, about forty guests, for his [Lederer's] elder daughter, to be married the next day. Between soup and entree her father called for silence and announced he intended to propose four toasts: [...] The third was: 'To Esther and Charles Gulick, without whom we should not be here. Without them there would not be a wedding, nor a daughter, nor a father named—. Without them I should have been a puff of smoke from the chimney of a Nazi extermination camp, or a lump of soap in some Hausfrau's kitchen. For decades they have been my second parents. I ask you to join me in a toast to Esther and Charles.'"[89]

For at least three of the nine refugees, Gulick successfully provided employment at UC Berkeley. The historian and economist Alexander Gerschenkron,[90] whom he had met at the *Konjunkturforschungsinstitut* in Vienna,[91] was the only scientist among them. As Gulick writes in the preface to his book: "of all my debts the greatest by far is to Dr. Alexander Gerschenkron [... whose] intimate knowledge of the economic and political problems of the first Austrian republic, his analyses and interpretations of complex relationships [...] are integral parts of the book."[92] The other two, Ernst Winkler and Karl Heinz, were political activists and party officials closely linked to the dominant circle around Otto Bauer and Julius Deutsch within the Social Democratic Party. Winkler, a journalist and party official from Lower Austria, had organized the smuggling of propaganda material for the socialist underground from Czechoslovakia to Austria after 1934. He was a loyal supporter of Otto Bauer and often visited Austria illegally until 1938, by order of the Foreign Bureau of the Austrian Social Democratic

87 Wolfgang Lederer (April 19, 1919 – January 3, 2015), obituary published in San Francisco Chronicle on January 11th, 2015, online available at https://www.legacy.com/obituaries/sfgate/obituary.aspx?n=wolfgang-lederer&pid=173720343 (accessed Dec. 14, 2018).

88 Lederer's autobiographical remarks at http://www.tankdestroyer.net/people/honorees/349-lederer-wolfgang-702nd (accessed Dec. 14, 2018).

89 Charles A. Gulick, Circular Letter , Sept. 22, 1981, Kreisky Archiv/Gulick.

90 Henry Rosovsky, "Alexander Gerschenkron: A Personal and Fond Recollection," in *The Journal of Economic History* 39, no. 4 (Dec. 1979): 1009-1013; Karl H. Müller, „Die Idealwelten der österreichischen Nationalökonomen", in Friedrich Stadler , ed., *Vertriebene Vernunft I: Emigration und Exil österreichischer Wissenschaft 1930-1940* (Vienna: Jugend und Volk, 1987), 238-275 (here 247, 266).

91 Johannes Feichtinger, *Wissenschaft zwischen den Kulturen. Österreichische Hochschullehrer in der Emigration 1933-1945* (Frankfurt/Main: Campus, 2001), 251f.;

92 Gulick, *Austria*, Vol. 1, XVI.

Party (ALÖS) in Brno.[93] Presumably, Gulick knew him from his time in Austria in 1936/37, since Winkler was a close friend of Joseph Simon. Karl Heinz had been president of the Social Democratic Youth organization (SAJ) until 1930, became a prominent figure within the social democratic militia "*Republikanischer Schutzbund*," was a close staffer of Julius Deutsch, and was a member of the Austrian Parliament in 1930.[94] Like Winkler, Heinz also fled to the CSSR after February 1934 and worked for the ALÖS in Brno.[95] After the beginning of World War II, both of them moved to Sweden and finally reached the US in 1941 through the Soviet Union. Winkler and especially Heinz continued their political work here, were linked to the New York-based Foreign Representation of Austrian Social Democrats (*Auslandsvertretung der* Österreichischen *Sozialdemokratie*) led by Friedrich Adler, and together with others in June of 1942 founded the Austrian Union in California as a left-wing organization for Austrian exiles on the West Coast.[96] A prominent person in their group was the widow of Otto Bauer, Helene, who would stay with Heinz and his wife, Ella, for the last months of her life.[97] When she passed away in December 1942, it was Alexander Gerschenkron who gave the eulogy at the funeral.[98]

Although Gerschenkron, the economist and former editor of the Österreichische *Volkswirt* Walther Federn, and the jurists Hans Kelsen and Bruno Schönfeld surely had the biggest impact on Gulick's study,[99] it is highly likely that the later SPÖ-Nationalrat Ernst Winkler, who worked as his assistant until his return to Austria in 1950,[100] also influenced Gulick's perspective to a certain extent. Gulick supported the political work of the exiles and, for example, spoke on a "really excellent radio program" about the Austrian Union on the occasion of the 24th anniversary of the First Republic

93 Werner Röder et al., eds., *Biographisches Handbuch der deutschprachigen Emigration nach 1933: Politik, Wirtschaft, Öffentliches Leben*, vol. I, [published by the Institut für Zeitgeschichte, München and the Research Foundation for Jewish Immigration, New York] (Munich: Saur, 1980), 822.

94 Karl Heinz's biography on the website of the Austrian Parliament https://www.parlament.gv.at/WWER/PAD_00560/index.shtml (accessed Dec. 22, 2018).

95 Ibid., 281f.

96 Dokumentationsarchiv des Österreichischen Widerstandes [DÖW], ed., *Österreicher im Exil USA 1938-1945, Vol. 2*, (Vienna: Österreichischer Bundesverlag, 1995), 533.

97 Simon, *Augenzeuge*, 270.

98 DÖW, *Exil USA*, 588.

99 They are all acknowledged in Gulick's preface to *Austria from Habsburg to Hitler*. His article on "Administrative and Judicial Processes as Instruments of Clerical Fascism in Austria," published in *California Law Review* 32 (1944): 161-184, Gulick dedicated the article to Schönfeld.

100 Röder et al, *Biographisches Handbuch*, 822; Heinz Kienzl, Susanne Kirchner, *Ein neuer Frühling wird in der Heimat blühen. Erinnerungen und Spurensuche* (Vienna: Deuticke 2002), 28.

on November 12, 1942, as Heinz reported to Julius Deutsch. According to him, even Helene Bauer thanked Gulick for his passionate commitment.[101] Privately, Gulick was also in touch with several Austrian emigrants in the bay area, such as the Götz family. Alfred Götz had been the chief physician of the tuberculosis center and a close associate of Julius Tandler, his son Franz Rudolf being Gulick's personal physician.[102]

While Gerschenkron left Berkeley first for Washington in 1944 to work for the Federal Reserve Board and, later on, became a prominent professor at Harvard, Winkler returned to Austria in 1950 to become a politician for the SPÖ and an operative of the *Arbeiterkammer*. Among Gulick's little Austrian group at Berkeley, only Karl Heinz decided to stay in California, passing away in Berkeley in 1965. His son, Otto, received a PhD in physics at UC Berkeley in the 1950s and had a considerable career as a scientist and weapons engineer.[103]

Besides his support of left-wing Austrian refugees, which also included contributions for the socialist exile press,[104] Gulick was also interested in the activities of the right-wing exile in the US, which consisted of former proponents of the Austrofascist regime, the *Heimwehr*, and various groups of monarchists. When former *Heimwehr* leader Ernst Rüdiger Starhemberg published his memoirs in New York in 1942, Gulick wrote a highly political review for *The New York Times*, accusing the author of being a political relative to National Socialism and warning allied officials that after Austria was liberated, it would be "fatal to give any position of importance to the *Heimwehr* and quasi-fascist Christian Social personalities who were dominant in the Dollfuß and Schuschnigg regimes. The former deserve no more consideration than Hitler."[105] This comment was prominently reflected in the socialist exile press and in a way marked the beginning of Gulick's role as a socialist chief witness: "Apart from [GER] Geyde [sic], [John] Gunther and [William L.] Shirer hardly anything so correct has been written on Austrian politics as Gulick's masterpiece of a review, which in fact provides a summary of the Austrian history before and after February 1934. Gulick determines responsibility for February and arrives at the conclusion that February 1934 was not only a private agenda of [Emil] Fey—although he personally bears a considerable part of the blame for

101 Karl Heinz, letter to Julius Deutsch, Feb. 7, 1943, DÖW, *Exil USA*, 593f.
102 Charles A. Gulick, letter to Bruno Kreisky, Aug.18, 1970, Kreisky Archiv/Gulick.
103 https://calhoun.nps.edu/bitstream/handle/10945/53221/RESUME_OF_OTTO_HEINZ_1981.pdf?sequence=1 (accessed Dec. 19th, 2018).
104 *Labor Information* 11 (1943): 5.
105 Charles A. Gulick, "The Fascist Prince of Austria," *New York Times*, Nov. 8, 1942, 36f.

the systematic provocation of the workers—but a matter of the *whole* Dollfuß-Government."[106]

The *Opus Magnum*: Austria from Habsburg to Hitler

Finally, after almost thirteen years of research and writing, Charles Gulick published his two volume book of almost two thousand pages, *Austria from Habsburg to Hitler*, in 1948. The first volume, *Labor's Workshop of Democracy*, dealt with the history of the Austrian labor movement, the establishment of the republic in 1918, and the social and labor legislation of the first two years of the republic. The most important part of the first volume, however, was dedicated to Red Vienna, its municipal housing, the welfare work, and education and cultural activities. The second, even more extensive volume, *Fascism's Subversion of Democracy*, analyzes the growing polarization of the political spectrum from 1927 on, the enforcement of a dictatorship in 1933/34, and the development of the latter until its collapse in 1938.

In the US, Gulick's book was mostly positively received (in contrast to Great Britain, where A. J. P. Taylor argued that the dimension of the book would just prove the common exaggeration of the importance of Austrian politics).[107] In particular, reviews stressed the encyclopedic character of Gulick's work and his detailed description of both political actors and legacy on the one hand and cultural and intellectual questions on the other.[108] Critical remarks unanimously referred to the allegedly partisan agenda in favor of the Social Democrats and against the Christian Socialists, as well as to the fact that Gulick gave "his work shape of a concluding statement made by counsel for the defense in some sort of world history trial."[109]

---

106 "*Es ist – mit Ausnahme Geyde's, Gunther's und Shirer's – noch selten so Richtiges über die oesterreichische Politik geschrieben worden wie in der meisterhaften Kritik Gulicks, die in Wirklichkeit eine Uebersicht über die österreichische Geschichte vor und nach dem Februar 1934 gibt. Gulick stellt die Verantwortung für den Februar fest und kommt zu dem Ergebnis, dass der Februar 1934 keine Privatangelgenheit Feys war, obwohl er persönlich ein voll gerüttelt Mass von Schuld an der systematischen Provokation der Arbeiter hatte, sondern eine Angelegenheit der gesamten Regierung Dollfuss*," see *Austrian Labor Information* 8 (1942): 3.

107 A. J. P. T[aylor], "Review" in *The English Historical Review* 65, no 254 (Jan. 1950): 143; Less critical than Taylor is James Joll, "Review", in International Affairs (Royal Institute of International Affairs), 25, no. 2 (Apr. 1949): 223-224.

108 Paul R. Sweet, "Democracy and Counterrevolution in Austria", in *The Journal of Modern History* 22, no 1 (Mar. 1950): 52-58, and the reviews by Walter Galensonm in *American Economic Review* 39, no. 3 (Jun., 1949): 761-765 and by Arthur Freud in *Industrial and Labor Relations Review* 4, no. 3, (Apr. 1951), 471-472.

109 Review by George W. F. Hallgarten in *The American Historical Review* 54, no. 1 (Oct, 1948): 122-124 (here 123), as well as the only damning US review by Walter C. Langsam, in *Political Science Quarterly* 64, No. 2 (June 1949): 288-289.

While the recognition in the US had a clear positive tendency, this was not the case in Austria. Supposedly on the initiative of Vice-Chancellor Adolf Schärf, a team of former Social Democratic exiles,[110] led by SPÖ Party historian Jacques Hannak, translated the volumes within only eight months and quickly published them in a five volume version in late 1948 at the Danubia publishing house, which belonged to the SPÖ.[111] Although the preliminary remark of the German version of the book noted that "it obviously does not need to be pointed out, that the Socialist Party does not always agree with the author on many passages in the book, neither in principle nor in detail,"[112] and although this was not just a charade to cover up Gulick's close ties with the party—because he was indeed harshly criticized by left-wingers[113]—it clearly was the conservatives who unanimously rejected the book. The problem was not so much Gulick's elaborate examination of social politics on a federal, as well as on a Viennese, level—though the fact that he discussed the established welfare state in such detail was clearly interpreted by conservatives as evidence for his left-wing agenda on its own. Instead, socialists and conservatives alike focused on Gulick's openly and sometimes harsh judgment on responsibilities for the destruction of the First Republic, for which he blamed the Christian Socialists and their allies.

While socialists repeatedly highlighted Gulick as a perfectly unbiased chief witness for their retrospective point of view,[114] the conservatives saw him as being clearly on the socialist side and thus untrustworthy as a historian.[115] Gulick himself addressed this problem in his introduction: "[...] it is almost needless to add that I hold that whenever possible the social scientist has not only the right but the duty to draw conclusions from, and express value judgments on, the factual evidence available. In other words, I have no patience with the intellectual contortionist who apparently thinks he is 'unscientific' unless he tries to get a part of each foot on each side of every question that is faintly controversial. [...] To some readers the conclusions and judgments may, at times, seem to read more like a bill of indictment. As a matter of fact, they sum up to a bill of indictment. Moreover, no apology is required or offered for indicting Fascists [...]."[116]

110 The translators were Josefine Ausch, Anny Deutsch, Inge Deutsch, Grete Helfgott, Bettina Hirsch, Minna Lachs, Gertrude Magaziner, Lilly Speiser and Josefine Weissel.
111 Charles A. Gulick, Österreich von Habsburg zu Hitler, Vol. 1 (Vienna: Danubia-Verlag, 1948), preliminary note.
112 Ibid.
113 John T. Lauridsen, *Nazism and the Radical Right in Austria 1918-1934* (Copenhagen: The Royal Library/Museum Tusculanum Press, 2007), 30 (esp. fn 38).
114 Jacques Hannak, *Vier Jahre Zweite Republik: Ein Rechenschaftsbericht der Sozialistischen Partei* (Vienna: Verlag der Wiener Volksbuchhandlung, 1949), 16.
115 See the review published in the Catholic newspaper *Die Furche*, Aug. 5, 1950.
116 Gulick, *Austria*, Vol. 1, 11.

Charles Jr. at the time of the publication of his main work "Austria from Habsburg to Hitler", 1948. © Paul Perasso

Gulick had a clear opinion and would not make any attempts to hide his sympathies. Not only regarding his historiographic position, he was also—contrary to statements from the Socialist Party, which described him as having been "always a progressive and supporter of Roosevelt's New Deal, but was never known as a socialist"[117] back home in the US—clearly partisan for the social democratic side in which he saw the representative of liberal democratic values, as well as a social agenda he had been committed to himself already before he entered Austria. The FBI, which denied to hold individual files about Charles or Esther,[118] characterized Gulick in a report on the Austrian exile activities in San Francisco Bay in late 1944 as a "liberal-thinker and mild pink" but stated that his "propensities are known and not considered serious enough to be termed vicious."[119] However, it was Gulick who would describe himself decades later as an "Austromarxist in the 1926-Linz-program-sense."[120]

As a consequence of the divided reception of Gulick's book in Austria, he as a person was honored by the socialists[121] and widely ignored by the conservatives. Within academia, his work was given more credit from the late 1960s onwards, when a generation of younger and more left-leaning historians entered the field.[122] Even though scholars ignored Gulick's opus for almost twenty years, it remained "an important landmark of historical consciousness within the socialist camp,"[123] where it was regarded as the only reliable overall view on the First Republic and Austrofascism.

After the publication of the German version of "the Gulick" in 1948, the Austrian conservatives were massively alerted that Gulick's book might cause misleading interpretations of their own past—and hence present—role in and outside the country. This apprehension might have been triggered by the fact that not only the SPÖ but especially the umbrella organization

117 Jacques Hannak, *Karl Renner und seine Zeit: Versuch einer Biographie* (Vienna: Europaverlag, 1965), 474f.

118 FOIA Request No. 1363152-000 on Gulick, Charles Adams.

119 FBI report by David C. Spencer, December 2nd 1944, quoted in DÖW, *Exil USA*, 624. On the question of his personal political views, Gulick's paper "The Spirit and Ideology of Austrian Socialism" announced in 1960 but never published, would have eventually been insightful, see Amerikanisches Komitee zum Studium der Geschichte der Donaumonarchie, "Eine Amerikanische Österreich-Bibliographie", in *Der Donauraum* 4 (1960), 122-132 (here 131).

120 Charles A. Gulick, Circular Letter, Sept. 22, 1981, Kreisky Archiv/Gulick.

121 He received the price for humanities of the City of Vienna in 1950, cf. https://www.geschichtewiki.wien.gv.at/Charles_Adams_Gulick#tab=Auszeichnungen (accessed Dec. 16,.2018).

122 Gerhard Botz, "'Eine neue Welt, warum nicht eine neue Geschichte?' Teil I: Österreichische Zeitgeschichte am Ende ihres Jahrhunderts" in *Österreichische Zeitschrift für Geschichtswissenschaften* 1, no. 1 (1990): 49-73 (here 53-54).

123 Ibid., 54.

of the trade unions, the Österreichische *Gewerkschaftsbund* (ÖGB), pushed the systematic distribution of Gulick's book via corporate libraries while there was no alternative that would support "the inner pacification."[124]

Even before he had finished reading Gulick's book, Karl Cornides, publisher and owner of the publishing house *Verlag für Geschichte und Politik* in Vienna, and his father, Wilhelm, decided to initiate a counter-book to "Gulick's pamphlet," which aimed to "prove in a scholarly fashion that the socialist historical interpretation was untenable and make an important contribution to a nationwide conception of history that is not tarnished by the ideology of class warfare."[125] Later Karl Cornides would explain that this project was originally animated by the Minister for Industrial Affairs Josef Böck-Greissau, ministry official Friedrich Maurig, and the founder and the chief editor of *Die Presse* Ernst Molden.[126] Since the financial support of such a book, "written by 'bourgeois' historians"[127] and "which consciously endeavors to re-establish the connection with the traditions of the old Austrian politics [that] can surely be considered a national achievement,"[128] was financially ambitious, Karl Cornides addressed various potential donors (mostly successfully), such as ÖVP-led ministries, the Austrian Industrial Association, banks, and the Chamber of Commerce, to subsidize the project.[129] The "*Antigulick*"[130] was finally published in 1954 as *Geschichte der Republik Österreich* by a group of authors under the supervision of Viennese Historian Heinrich Benedikt. Although it was meant to correct "the one-sided red delineation in five volumes by Gulick," co-initiator Wilhelm Cornides sen. was discontented with the outcome of his project. It would have turned out that eventually, "the previous results of our various, perennial efforts do not set aright Gulick as far as was expected."[131] It might not have improved Cornides's mood when the *Arbeiterzeitung* came to the same result in its review of the publication. The conclusions drawn in Benedikt's book, the newspaper

---

124 ZPH 1765, Karton 1, Konvolut Benedikt, Geschichte der Republik Österreich, [further on: ZPH 1765] Karl Cornides, Letter to the Industriellenvereinigung, Mar. 19, 1955, Archiv des Verlages für Geschichte und Politik, Wienbibliothek im Rathaus/ Handschriftensammlung,.

125 Karl Cornides, letter to the *Industriellenvereinigung* [draft], December 19th, 1950, ZPH 1765.

126 Karl Cornides, Letter to the *Industriellenvereinigung*, Mar. 19, 1955. ZPH 1765.

127 Cornides, Letter to the *Industriellenvereinigung*, Mar. 28, 1955, ZPH 1765.

128 Karl Cornides, letter to the *Industriellenvereinigung* [draft], Dec. 19, 1950, ZPH 1765.

129 Ibid.

130 So called by the publisher Karl Cornides himself, see Memo, Nov. 24, 1954, ZPH 1765.

131 Ibid.

wrote, might often differ from Gulick's assumptions in detail, but when it came to the important questions—which especially meant who was responsible for the overthrow of democracy in 1933/34—the answers by Benedikt and his colleagues would only differ by their tentativeness, and they would not prove it with so much evidence.[132] The problem was the facts, and compromises could be found here and there—the seriousness especially of the author, whom dealt with the coup of 1933/34, Walter Goldinger. As Cornides explained to Carl Karwinsky, secretary of state for security affairs in the Dollfuß government and one who had intervened against too critical assessments by Goldinger against the role of the federal army during the clashes of February 1934: "Nobody could be more unburdened than me, if we would have succeeded to justify the Dollfuß-Schuschnigg-era against all offenses. You may be well assured, that envoy [Stephan] Verosta, who is part of our team, already tried everything possible to provide the opus with a positive character in that sense. But from a certain point on he faced adamant resistance by the people in charge of the case, who—as scientists—take the position, that whatever was true had to be said."[133]

Gulick himself did not intervene in the dispute his book caused in Austria years before and did not comment on Benedikt's book, maybe partly because he was troubled by other things at that time back home in the USA. With great concern, Gulick took notice of McCarthy's conspiracy theories against suspected left-wingers. As such, Gulick felt increasingly isolated in his department at Berkeley. In 1950, the university would demand its faculty sign a loyalty oath stating that they would not become members of the Communist Party, believe, or advocate the overthrow of the US Government.[134] Gulick reportedly signed a petition against the oath, but since the university threatened to dismiss refusers, in contrast to others, Gulick "held his nose and signed" as he explained years afterwards.[135] Nevertheless, the incident obviously concerned him deeply. He remained anxious concerning a "Neo-McCarthyism" coming up[136] and held fierce sympathies for the free speech movement,[137] as well

132 Review in *Arbeiterzeitung*, Nov. 21, 1954, 3.
133 Karl Cornides, Letter to Carl Karwinsky, Sept. 24· 1954, ZPH 1765.
134 Bob Blauner, *Resisting McCarthyism: To Sign or Not to Sign California's Loyalty Oath* (Redwood City: Stanford University Press, 2009).
135 Interview with Clair Brown, September 26th, 2016 [further on: Interview Brown].
136 Charles A. Gulick, "Neo-McCarthyismus in Kalifornien," in *Die Zukunft* (Oct 1961): 292-297.
137 Interview Perasso.

as for feminist attempts in and outside the university.[138] At the end of the 1960s, he increasingly turned towards the anti-war movement.[139] At that time, Gulick was already a pensioner. He had retired from the department in July 1963,[140] though it was said to be because of his bad health: "he was thought to retire to die in peace."[141] In fact, Gulick certainly suffered from severe health problems, but against all expectations, he recovered. He kept his office at Cal and continued coming to work almost daily. In 1976, after seventeen months of work financed by the SPÖ,[142] Gulick published a condensed one-volume translation of *Austria from Habsburg to Hitler*, which, as Chancellor Bruno Kreisky assured him, would be "a valuable publication for active members and functionaries of our party."[143] Despite that, the new German version of his book had been a personal issue for Gulick, since, as he wrote to Bruno Kreisky, "the 1950 translation [of my book] was a total disaster [...] I am convinced that in less than 2,400 pages there are 5,000 errors and that at least 100 of them exactly reverse the meaning of the English."[144]

Charles visited Austria at least twice for longer periods of time in the 1950s. He was a visiting professor at the *Institut für Höhere Studien* in Vienna and worked on the political system of the second republic.[145] Whenever he visited the country, Gulick was flattered by SPÖ officials like the presidents Theodor Körner and Franz Jonas or Vice-Chancellor Adolf Schärf.[146] Among the prominent party members, he himself apparently appreciated Hertha Firnberg the most. When she turned sixty-five and—due to the SPÖ's own regulative—would not have been able to serve as minister, Gulick intervened with Chancellor Kreisky in her favor (who, Gulick might have not known, had invented the rule himself to get rid of his rival, Bruno Pittermann) and urged "as strongly as possible that the Party take whatever steps are necessary to suspend, abrogate or disregard this rule for the benefit of Dr. Firnberg."[147] A final sabbatical leave, during

138 Interview Brown.
139 Ibid.
140 UC Berkeley, Change in Employment Status, approved in Feburary 1963, PRCAG,.
141 Interview Ward.
142 Charles A. Gulick, Letter to Bruno Kreisky, Sept. 3, 1974, Kreisky Archiv/Gulick.
143 Bruno Kreisky, Letter to Charles A. Gulick, Oct. 28, 1975, Kreisky Archiv/Gulick.
144 Charles A. Gulick, Letter to Bruno Kreisky, July 15, 1975, Kreisky Archiv/Gulick.
145 Charles A. Gulick, "Austria's socialists in the Trend Toward a Two-Party-System: An Interpretation of Postwar Elections," in *The Western Political Quarterly* 11, no 3 (Sept. 1958): 539-562.
146 Simon, *Augenzeuge*, 264.
147 Charles A. Gulick, Letter to Bruno Kreisky, Sept. 3, 1974, Kreisky Archiv/Gulick.

which he wanted to finalize his studies on the ideological development of the Austrian Labor Movement in 1962, was not approved by his university. What followed instead were several short stays and a permanently attentive observation of the political developments in Austria. When the SPÖ won the elections of 1970, Charles and Esther Gulick congratulated Bruno Kreisky warmly and had only two regrets: "that you did not secure an absolute majority[, and secondly] we wished that we might have been in election headquarters when the returns came in. The comparable evening in 1959 was one of the most exciting events of our lives."[148] After the snap election a year later in which the SPÖ finally did secure the absolute majority, a seemingly enthusiastic Charles Gulick wrote to Karl Waldbrunner: "Frankly, I had not expected to live long enough to see that majority; consequently, my solid satisfaction is all the greater."[149] Having come to power, the SPÖ did not forget Gulick. On the initiative of Bruno Kreisky,[150] he was awarded the Grand Decoration of Honor for Services to the Republic of Austria in Gold,[151] and a few years later, during one of his last stays in Vienna, Gulick received the Medal of Honor in Gold of the City of Vienna in February 1978.[152]

From the late 1970s onwards, Gulick's physical condition deteriorated more and more, though he kept intellectually agile. In his last circular to his Austrian friends in 1981, he wrote, "as most of you know I feel more and more often that I have had ten, or fifteen too many birthday anniversaries [...] Often I have said that there are DAMN few advantages of becoming old. Esther's honors [for her engagement with environmental issues], [and] your messages and honors [...] prove: I have had more than one man's share of those advantages." His final salute on the letter was the party greeting of Austrian Social Democracy: "Once more: thank you a lot and *Freundschaft*. Charles."[153]

In 1984, Gulick died at the age of eighty-seven. Esther, who had lovingly taken care for him until the very end, survived him by eleven years until she too passed away in 1995.

---

148 Charles A. Gulick, Letter to Bruno Kreisky, Aug. 18, 1970, Kreisky Archiv/Gulick.

149 Charles Gulick to Karl Waldbrunner, November 8th, 1971, quoted from Zollinger, *Waldbrunner*, 135.

150 Bruno Kreisky, undated memo [1971] to Hertha Firnberg; Positive answer by Firnberg on Nov. 24, 1971, Kreisky Archiv/Gulick.

151 Bruno Kreisky, Telegram to Charles A. Gulick, May 26, 1972, Kreisky Archiv/Gulick.

152 https://www.wien.gv.at/wiki/index.php/Charles_Adams_Gulick#tab=Auszeichnungen (accessed Dec. 22nd, 2018)

153 Charles A. Gulick, Circular Letter, Sept. 22, 1981, Kreisky Archiv/Gulick

One of the last shots: Charles Jr. at the end of the 1970s, presumably in Vienna.
© Paul Perasso

Roundtable: On Manfred Flügge's *Stadt ohne Seele: Wien 1938*

Manfred Flügge, *Stadt Ohne Seele: Wien 1938* (Berlin: Aufbau, 2018)

Günter Bischof

Introduction

The papers in this roundtable on Manfred Flügge's *Stadt Ohne Seele: Wien 1938* were first delivered in by the four authors during the German Studies Association's annual meeting in Pittsburgh, Pennsylvania in late September 2018. We are grateful to Quinna Shen of Bryn Mawr College for organizing the Flügge panel. Manfred Flügge was scheduled to be a respondent in the panel. We regret to say that in the end he could not make it to Pittsburgh.

Flügge's riveting account came on the occasion of the 80th anniversary of the "Anschluss" in March 2018. The invasion and annexation of Austria by Nazi Germany in March 1938 has rightly been commemorated as a turning point in Austrian history.[1] In previous commemorations, many of the eyewitnesses to these events were still alive. The 50th anniversary in 1988 was a particularly poignant one as it signaled the end of the official postwar "victims doctrine."[2] After the heated debates and the election of Kurt Waldheim as President of Austria in 1986, it was hard to maintain the myth that Austria had been "the first victim of Hitlerite Germany" as the Allied Moscow Declaration of October 30, 1943 had proclaimed and as the postwar Austrian governments had eagerly latched on to.[3] The record of Austrians serving the Wehrmacht and the many formations of Hitler's killing machine in the euthanasia and Holocaust crimes were simply too overwhelming. In 1988, the formula of Austrians "as victims and

---

1 Oliver Rathkolb, "The Anschluss in the Rear-View Mirror, 1938-2008: Historical Memories between Debate and Transformation," in: *New Perspectives on Austrians and World War II*, ed. Günter Bischof, Fritz Plasser, and Barbara Stelzl-Marx (Contemporary Austrian Studies [CAS] 17) (New Brunswick, NJ: Transaction, 2009), 5-28.

2 See the extensive documentation of 1988 50th anniversary discourses in Heidemarie Uhl, *Zwischen Versöhnung und Verstörung: Eine Kontroverse um Österreichs historische Identität fünfzig Jahre nach dem "Anschluss"* (Vienna: Böhlau, 1992).

3 Günter Bischof, "Die Instrumentalisierung der Moskauer Erklärung nach dem 2. Weltkrieg," *Zeitgeschichte* 10 (Nov.-Dec. 1993: 345-366; Heidemarie Uhl, "Das 'erste Opfer' Österreich: Der Österreichische Opfermythos und seine Transformationen in der Zweiten Republik," *Österreichische Zeitschrift für Politikwissenschaft 30*, no 1 (2001): 19-34; . Stefan Karner and Alexander O. Tschubarjan, eds., *Die Moskauer Deklaration 1943: "Österreich wieder herstellen* (Vienna: Böhlau, 2015).

perpetrators" of/in National Socialism came into usage and has since been the core of Austrian World War II memory.[4]

Flügge is less interested in the trajectory of Austrian memory of the *Anschluss*.[5] His story is a fast-paced account of the events surrounding the "Anschluss": the invasion by the German Wehrmacht of Austria on March 12, 1938 and the subsequent absorption of the country into Hitler's "Third Reich." The "Anschluss" marks the beginning of Hitler's expansion in Central Europe and the incorporation of the German-speaking populations of Austria and Czechoslovakia ("Sudenten Germans") into Nazi Germany. Hitler clearly outlines such a program of expansion—"the need to expand German 'living space'"—to his chiefs of staff in the Reich Chancellery on November 9, 1937 and is remembered in history by the name of the notetaker Colonel Hossbach ("Hossbach Protocol").[6] The Great Powers did not respond to the "Anschluss" but met it with appeasement.[7] Flügge is not much interested in the diplomacy of the Great Power politics in interwar Europe but rather into the human factor of the "Anschluss."

Flügge is particularly interested in what happened to the Jews of Vienna given that Hitler's well-known anti-semitism had already been put to the test in Nazi Germany ("the *Altreich*") since his seizure of power in late January 1933. Hitler's persecution of Austrians who opposed him, like the officials of the *Ständestaat* such as Chancellor Kurt Schuschnigg, are also in Flügge's purview. Flügge portrays the drama of the "amputated lives" (Hans Thalberg coined this term, cf. p. 419) of those who were forced to flee the "Ostmark" after the "Anschluss" (pp. 295-346). Flügge calls "the civil war against the Jewish segment of the population the core element of [the Nazi] political ideology" (p. 275) and not Hitler's expansionism and

4 Cornelius Lehnguth, *Waldheim und die Folgen: Der parteipolitische Umgang mit dem Nationalsozialismus in Österreich* (Studien zur historischen Sozialwissenschaft 35) (Frankfurt am Main: Campus Verlag, 2013); Katrin Hammerstein, *Gemeinsame Vergangenheit – getrennte Erinnerung? Der Nationalsozialismus in Gedächtnisdiskursen und Identitätskonstruktionen von Bundesrepublik Deutschland , DDR und Österreich* (Göttingen: Wallstein Verlag, 2017).

5 There is a rich historiography of Austrian World War II memory after the "Anschluss", see Günter Bischof, "Victims? Perpetrators? "Punching Bags" of European Historical Memory? The Austrians and Their World War II Legacies," *German Studies Review* 27 (Feb. 2004): 17-32; Ina Markova, "Austrian Victims and Austria as Victim in the Short' 1940s: Visual Representations of the Nazi Past 1945-1947," *Austrian Federalism in Comparative Perspective*, ed. Günter Bischof and Ferdinand Karlhofer (CAS 24) (New Orleans-Innsbruck: UNO Press-Innsbruck university press, 2015), 151-171.

6 Ian Kershaw, *Hitler 1936-1945: Nemesis* (New York: W.W. Norton, 2000), 46-48; Volker Ullrich, *Hitler: Ascent 1889*-1939, trans. Jefferson Chase (New York: Vintage, 2016), 696f.

7 Stefan Karner and Peter Ruggenthaler, eds., *1938: Internationale Reaktionen auf den "Anschluss"* (Graz: Leykam, 2019).

the Nazi-German need for "living space." In his reading, the "Anschluss" was "part megalomania and part destructive obsession" ("*Grössensucht und Vernichtungswahn*"). The "Anschluss" was not "an embarrassing accident in Austrian history" ("*peinlicher Betriebsunfall in der* österreichischen *Geschichte*") (p. 275). Only a military intervention by the Western powers or Italy or the "heroic resistance" of the Austrian Army could have saved the country and shown to the world that Austria was indeed "the first victim of National Socialism" as claimed by the Austrian government after the war (pp. 251f). This "demise of Austria without a fight" ("*kampfloser Untergang*") had a devastating effect on all enemies of an "Anschluss" (p. 276).

Flügge pooh-poohs the *Ständestaat* as "a form of preventive collaboration" (p. 251). The *Ständestaat* was "colossally misguided" ("*ein kolossaler Irrweg*") since it destroyed the Republic, weakened its will to resist, delegitimized the state, and failed to protect the country against the "*Zugriff*" of the Nazis (p. 251). Still, Flügge brings none of the partisan animus to his discussion of the *Ständestaat* (1933-38) and Schuschnigg's role in the demise of Austria that has been part and parcel of Austrian historiography since the 1930s. Here his detachment as a German looking at these Austrian events is welcomed and perspicacious.

It was the German writer Carl Zuckmayer who found exile in Austria before the "Anschluss" and who called Vienna "a soulless city" ("*Stadt ohne Seele*") (pp. 235f). The night of March 11/12, when the Schuschnigg government resigned and the Viennese started their depredations against their Jewish neighbors, "all people lost their face." Zuckmayer wrote in his memoirs: a mass of Jews "bludgeoned into a bloody mess, spit upon and abused, Jews with broken rips, bloodied heads, and missing teeth, came to the emergency room of the Jewish hospital [...] old women and men, well-respected rabbis, doctors, and lawyers were forced to clean the streets and cars" (p. 236). So much for the notion of the "golden heart of the Viennese" ("*das goldene Wienerherz*"). These horrific nights of the *Anschluss* events unleashed the great flight of Jews and antagonists of the Nazis, like Socialists, Communists, conservative Christian Socials and Austrian fascist supporters of the *Ständestaat*, and monarchists, like the Habsburg pretender Otto. Flügge's book is about the "amputated lives" of well-known people that were forced into exile—many of them never to return to Austria.[8]

8 Herbert Lackner's *Die Flucht der Dichter und Denker: Wie Europas Künstler und Wissensschaftler den Nazis entkamen* (Vienna: Ueberreuter, 2017) is about the same story of famous Austrian (and German) refugees from Hitler's Germany and their "amputated lives"; see my review of the book in this volume.

The four perspectives presented here in this "Roundtable" give credit to Flügge's deep immersion into these events, his erudition and writing skills, and stress various aspects of his book. Burri lays weight on the drama in Flügge's presentation, Fetz the biographical approach to the "amputated lives," Lerner the Viennese Jewish studies side of Flügge's story, and Wasserman Flügge's missing historiographical embeddedness in the extant literature. Fetz and Wasserman also note that Flügge concentrates on well-known life stories and fails to address the thousands of ordinary people who were forced into exile or perished in the Holocaust. Micro-histories of such ordinary lives do exist for Vienna. A group of young researchers have tried to establish all the Jews kicked out of their apartments in the *Servitengasse* in Vienna's 9th district, very close to the *Berggasse* in the 9th district, where Freud lived. One quarter of the population of the 9th district ("*Alsergrund*") was Jewish. Of the 377 Jewish residents of *Servitengasse*, 160 managed to escape from Austria, 133 were deported, 8 survived the camps, and the rest perished in the Holocaust. The fate of 65 people remains unknown. Altogether 462 people who lived and worked in the *Servitengasse* were victims of persecution.[9] Such micro-histories bring the biographies of ordinary people into focus and heighten the tragedy of the *Anschluss* in Vienna, producing a "*Stadt ohne Juden*" as Hugo Bettauer had speculated in his satirical novel (1922). Lerner suggests that "*Stadt ohne Seele*" is a play on words of Bettauer's "*Stadt ohne Juden,*" suggesting that the Jews were the "soul of the city," and with their absence, "the city has lost its pulse."

Flügge's account ignores the international history of the "Anschluss."[10] He does not deal with the complex history of Austrian "Anschluss" memories.[11] Historiographically he relies on older histories of the *Anschluss.*[12]

9 Birgit Johler, Katharina Kober, Barbara Sauer, Ulrike Tauss, Joanna White, "A Local History of the 1938 'Anschluss' and Its Memory: Vienna Servitengasse," in: *1914: Austria-Hungary, the Origins, and the First Year of World War I*, ed. Günter Bischof, Ferdinand Karlhofer, and Francis R. Williamson, Jr. (CAS 23) (New Orleans-Innsbruck; UNO Press-Innsbruck university press, 2014), 293-317; for more detail, see Birgit Johler and Maria Fritsche, eds., *1938 Adresse: Servitengasse, Eine Nachbarschaft auf Spurensuche* (Vienna: Mandelbaum, 2007).

10 Alexander Lassner, "The Foreign Policy of the Schuschnigg Government 1934-1938: The Quest for Security," in: *The Dollfuss/Schuschnigg Era in Austria: A Reassessment*, ed. Günter Bischof, Anton Pelinka and Alexander Lassner (CAS 11) (New Brunswick, NJ; Transaction 2003), 163-186; idem "Peace at Hitler's Price: Austria, the Great Powers, and the Anschluss, 1932-1938," PhD diss. Ohio State University, 2001..

11 Meinrad Ziegler and Waltraud Kannonier-Finster, *Österreichs Gedächtnis: Über Erinnern und Vergessen der NS-Vergangenheit*, rev. and expand. ed. (Innsbruck: StudienVerlag, 2016).

12 Chief among them Norbert Schausberger, *Der Griff nach Österreich: Der Anschluss* (Vienna: Jugend & Volk, 1978); Erwin Schmidl, *Der "Anschluss" Österreichs: Der deutsche Einmarsch im März 1938* (Bonn: Bernhard & Graefe, 1994).

More recent basic works have not been consulted.[13] As well as the Flügge book is written and as absorbing a tale it is, it will not be the last word on this crucial event in Austrian history.

13 Gerhard Botz, *Nationalsozialismus in Wien: Machübernahme, Herrschaftssicherung, Radikalisierung 1938/39 rev. ed.* (Vienna: Mandelbaum, 2008); Dokumentationsarchiv des österreichischen Widerstandes, ed., *"Anschluss" 1938: Eine Dokumentation* (Vienna: Bundesverlag, 1988); Hans Petschar *Anschuss – "Ich hole euch heim" – Eine Bildchronologie* (Vienna; Brandstätter, 2008).

The Poetics of the "Austrian Tragedy"

Michael Burri

The Classical Drama of 1938

Stadt ohne Seele: Wien 1938 by Manfred Flügge arrived upon the 80th anniversary of the "*Anschluss*" of the Republic of Austria by the German Reich[1]. Unlike previous 10-year anniversaries, however, the 2018 memorialization in Austria had largely been marked not by the testimony of those who lived through 1938, but by being remembered by those who did not. To be sure, many Austrians still recall when these anniversaries featured the passionate and often moving testimony of witnesses. Contemporary forms of commemorating 1938 express this sense of living during an odd interval when witnesses can be remembered but are themselves no longer present. From February 27 to March 21, for example, the state broadcaster ORF carried short spots under 30 seconds each on all its channels in which actors read excerpts from diary entries, press reports, and other sources from February through March 1938 in an emotional style that aimed to mimic the intensity of the period[2]. The website www.zeituhr1938.at, a shared project among historians and institutions, echoed the desire to re-live March 1938. Visitors could experience almost minute-by-minute the 24-hours of March 11-12 by clicking points on a clock-like image.

Stadt ohne Seele, a book its author described as the product of "30 years of thinking on a particular topic," does not aim to keep pace with such new forms of memorialization. Its concern is rather the sweep of events that culminated in the *Anschluss* of 1938. As Flügge put it in an ORF radio interview, themes "converge in Vienna in 1938 in a unity of time and place that one normally only encounters in classical drama."[3] This conceptual framework is flexible. Thus, *Stadt ohne Seele* is also attentive to recent research emphases, treating, for example, the *Anschluss* not only as

1 Manfred Flügge, *Stadt ohne Seele- Wien 1938*. (Berlin: Aufbau, 2018).

2 Österreichischer Rundfunk, "ORF-Programmschwerpunkt 1938: Vor 80 Jahren – Zeitzeugnisse zum 'Anschluss'" accessed Dec. 15, 2018, http:www.ots.at/presseaussendung/OTS_20180301_OTS0177/orf-programmschwerpunkt-1938-vor-80-jahren-zeitzeugnisse-zum-anschluss

3 Manfred Flügge, interview by Judith Hoffmann, *Morgenjournal* ORF, March 12, 2018, oe1.orf.at/artikel/643350

the "humiliation of Austria by Germany, but as the product of Austria's own road to barbarism" (13).

And yet, the traditional metaphor of "drama," with respect to the years between 1918 and 1938, has always been chased by questions. One is the scope of the tragedy. Just how many acts does the "Austrian tragedy" have? One act? Three? Five? Another is the time frame. Where does the tragedy of 1938 begin? 1919? 1927? 1934? 1848? In what follows here, I do not propose a novel answer to such questions. Instead, I wish to indicate three issues raised by the use of the First Austrian Republic as a backdrop for the staging of the "Austrian tragedy" of 1938 (89).

II. Culture as Politics

One. The story of Vienna, the "city without a soul," gains its dramatic force in part from its large cast of characters. In a powerful synthesis, *Stadt ohne Seele* places the lives and works of notable Viennese figures in the context of the years down to 1938. Chapter 5, "The Novel of the Soul," brings forward Franz Werfel, Robert Musil, and Hermann Broch, while substantial chapters are devoted to Sigmund Freud and a shorter section to numerous other figures, from Anton Kuh to Egon Friedell. The accounts of these cultural figures furnish a parallel dynamic that corroborates political events. They also bestow a particular serenity upon the book, an approach that may help explain its success on the Austrian bestseller list last spring. *Stadt ohne Seele* is not looking for someone to blame[4]. Earlier generations of historians may have excited debate by providing accounts that second-guessed the actions of the Austrian Chancellor and others in February and March 1938. "The crisis of March 1938," as A.J.P. Taylor concluded, "was provoked by Schuschnigg, not by Hitler.[5]" By placing political and cultural figures side by side, *Stadt ohne Seele* relieves politicians from this degree of accountability. Cultural figures already tell us that Austria was gripped by a spiritual decline. Vienna, the symptom of all that was wrong with Austria, had no soul.

Of course, inviting cultural figures to answer whether we live in a time of crisis is rather like asking an evangelical minister if we should prepare ourselves for the final judgment. Crisis is their business. In the concluding scene of the Epilogue to *The Last Days of Mankind*, Karl Kraus suggests that a cosmic catastrophe, accompanied by the intonations of God, would

4 "Bestseller," *Profil*, March 19, 2018, 113.

5 A.J.P. Taylor, *The Origins of the Second World War* (1961: New York: Simon & Schuster, 1983), 149.

look very much like Vienna being destroyed[6]. Then again, it was probably cultural and literary voices, like those of Kraus, who in the First Republic delivered the most consistent and forceful denunciation of Vienna and Austria. As Wendelin Schmidt-Dengler once pointed out, among writers, there was no positive image of contemporary Vienna in the 1920s. Writers of all political conviction, in both serious and popular literature, presented it in predominantly dark, virtually post-apocalyptic terms[7].

A number of forces propelled this dark vision. Material circumstances were one. Middle-class professionals—physicians, engineers, bureaucrats, and others—rather than manual laborers, experienced the most drastic drop in living standards in the immediate postwar period. In 1921-22, hundreds of faculty from the University of Vienna and other local institutions needed the food aid administered by the American Relief Administration through the "Professor's Round Table," where serving portions at five sites across Vienna were regulated according to the same nutritional principles of Clemens von Pirquet as the more celebrated European Children's Fund in Austria (*Amerikanische Kinderhilfsaktion*)[8]. It is this broad social and earnings disenfranchisement that unites the dark visions of early-1920s Vienna in two such different writers as Karl Hans Strobl, the German national author of the Vienna novel, *Gespenster im Sumpf* (1920), and the liberal Hugo Bettauer, author of *Der Kampf um Wien* (1923) and *Das entfesselte Wien* (1924), and the most popular writer of the First Republic. In 1920, like many others, Bettauer struggled with poverty and sought work as an intermediary for the "American Relief Committee for Sufferers in Austria," one of the many international relief agencies operating in Vienna[9].

In fact, the widespread representation of Vienna as a showplace of social disintegration also served as a republican answer to the long-term reign of Habsburg ideas, in which, as Fritz Wittels put it in a 1919 article, "That's how they raised us. The Empress Maria Theresia is the matrilineal progenitor of Frau Sopherl of the Naschmarkt... The kind-hearted bearer of legitimate children, the economical, clerical, and parochial woman on the throne lives in hundreds of thousands of Viennese women to this day[10]." In other words, writers of the 1920s found in a style of confrontational realism the literary means to reject the Habsburg pieties they had endured for so

6 Karl Kraus, *Die letzten Tage der Menschheit* (1926: Frankfurt am Main, 1986), 761-770.

7 Wendelin Schmidt-Dengler, "Wien 1918: Glanzloses Finale," *Paradigmen der Moderne*, ed. Helmut Bachmaier (Amsterdam: John Benjamins, 1990); 131-157, (here 149).

8 Der Professorentisch, *Mitteilungen der American Relief Administration*, ed. Friedrich Reischl (46-50: Vienna, 1921), 235-254.

9 Murray Hall, *Der Fall Bettauer* (Vienna: Löcker Verlag, 1978), 16.

10 Avicenna [Fritz Wittels], "Nachruf für Habsburg," *Der Abend* (Vienna) March 26, 1919, 3.

long. Of course, already prior to the war, Robert Musil and others believed that these pieties shackled them intellectually, creatively, and professionally. As Musil wrote of the Austrians in December 1912, "Their religiosity is not credible, nor their childlike loyalty to the Emperor, nor their anxieties; they wait somewhere behind these. They have the passive fantasy of spaces left unfilled, and jealously grant a person everything except his claims, which are so prejudicial spiritually, for the seriousness of his work[11]." In a meaningful sense, 1918 set Musil free.

An account inspired by the Austrian writers, critics, and other intellectuals who retailed fantasies of chaos and peddled narratives of decline in the years after 1918 might be said to present, as a registry of fact, attitudes that are better described as intellectual and emotional positions within the First Republic. Strolling with his student, Alfred Schutz, on the well-paved Ringstraße in the mid-1920s, the economist Ludwig von Mises gravely prophesied that "grass will grow right here where we are standing.[12]" That the context for such attitudes is not easily recollected today cannot be attributed solely to the ever-rising waters of forgetfulness. After 1945, as Adam Kożuchowski has noted, the Cold War ensured that such strongly felt positions of the 1920s—the "entire hodgepodge of Central European political ideologies, national rivalries, and animosities"—melted into two opposing camps: the pro-West and the pro-Communists[13].

That's not to say that only Viennese cultural figures should be acknowledged for their passionate vision of the looming disaster. The 1920s themselves were the high point of catastrophist visions of the decline of Western civilization. In different ways, Lenin, Spengler, and Toynbee were among its most powerful prophets.

III. The Return of "*Lebensunfähigkeit*"

Two. First Republic cultural figures proposed that Austria and Vienna were fighting a losing battle against the forces of history that would sweep Austria from the face of the globe. Into this gloomy echo chamber, politicians also shouted. From Otto Bauer to Ignaz Seipel, nearly every major postwar Austrian political figure, though never all at the same time, declared that the Republic of (German-) Austria was a state "incapable of surviving." Karl

11 Robert Musil, "Politics in Austria," *Precision and Soul*, trans. and ed. Burton Pike and David S. Luft (Chicago: University of Chicago Press), 17-21, (here 18).
12 Peter Kurrild-Klitgaard, "The Viennese Connection: Alfred Schutz and the Austrian School" *Quarterly Journal of Austrian Economics* 6, no.2 (Summer 2003): 35-66, (here 55).
13 Adam Kożuchowski, *The Afterlife of Austria-Hungary. The Image of the Habsburg Monarchy in Interwar Europe*. (Pittsburgh: Pittsburgh University Press, 2013), 18.

Renner and many others rightly complained that Habsburg successor states conspired against Austria, while Austria itself was both severed from its old economic partners and isolated internationally. But their complaints also had a strategic dimension. For one group, they helped fuel the hope, which was widely shared until at least 1933, that Austria would be permitted to join Germany. For another group, they kept alive the dream of many a Vienna-led Danube confederation. Since neither option was realistic, as Nathan Marcus has noted, the Austrian leaders could broadcast their misery, believing Britain and France might simply finance Austria for the foreseeable future since it was their creation and the economic malaise therefore their fault[14].

After 1945, debates around the "viability" (*Lebensfähigkeit*) of *Kleinstaat* Austria ceased. Their disappearance, as Oliver Rathkolb suggests, may well be related to how closely the rhetoric of viability was connected to arguments for annexation to Germany. But in fact, Second Republic elites retold this story while also giving it a new title. For the historian and journalist Hellmut Andics, who repackaged the "viability" narrative in a book that held second place in an Austrian bestseller list in 1963, the First Republic was *Der Staat, den keiner wollte* [15]. Martin Reisacher has discussed how quickly this phrase, *"der Staat, den keiner wollte"* entered the public vocabulary, finding here a confirmation of linguistic theories of how successful "political slogans communicate both mental historical and contemporary historical aspects.[16]" Others have noted that the title of Andics's book recalls that of *Der Staat wider Willen*, a dismissive book account of the First Republic published in 1940 by the National Socialist historian Reinhold Lorenz[17]. In the early Second Republic, the First Republic words of Karl Renner may have been reformulated, but the sentiment still flourished.

In the early Second Republic, the claim that First Republic Austria was the state that "no one wanted" branded the First Republic a failure in order to declare the present a success. The Second Republic became the "state that

---

14 Nathan Marcus, *Austrian Reconstruction and the Collapse of Global Finance 1921-1931* (Cambridge: Harvard University Press, 2018), 223-256; Norbert Schausberger, "Österreich und die Friedenskonferenz: Zum Problem der Lebensfähigkeit Österreichs nach 1918," *Saint-Germain 1919*, ed. Isabella Ackerl and Rudolf Neck (Vienna: Verlag für Geschichte und Politik, 1989), 229-264.

15 Oliver Rathkolb, *Die Paradoxe Republik. Österreich 1945 bis 2015* (2005; Vienna: Zsolnay, 2015), 114.

16 Andrea Stangl, "Mythen und Narrative: 'Der Staat wider Willen' und 'Der Staat, den keiner wollte,'" ww1.habsburger.net/de/kapitel/mythen-und-narrative-der-staat-wider-willen-und-der-staat-den-keiner-wollte. Hellmut Andics, *Der Staat den keiner wollte. Österreich 1918-1938* (Vienna: Herder, 1962).

17 Martin Reisacher, "Die Konstruktion des 'Staats, den keiner wollte'" (MA thesis, University of Vienna, 2010) 11. accessed Dec. 15, 2018, http://othes.univie.ac.at/10190/1/2010-06-07_0252520.pdf

everyone wanted." Of course, as Tony Judt once argued, the government's "future-oriented vocabulary of social harmony and material improvement" served in Austria, as it did elsewhere in Europe, "to avoid the more painful examination of myths of victimization[18]." But more than elsewhere in Europe, the social and material well-being of Austria was directly linked to maintaining the status of victim. Here, the claim that First Republic Austria was "the state that no one wanted" provided historical cover for the celebrated "victim myth" regarding the actions of Austria and its citizens in the Second World War. After 1918, the argument went that the victory-drunk Allies created a First Republic Austria that had no realistic chance of surviving. This Austria did what it could but was ultimately helpless in the face of the onslaught of a National Socialist Germany in the 1930s. The First Republic did fret over its viability, but the story that the First Republic ended in a tragedy that began in 1918 is a powerful creation of the Second Republic. And while socialist historiographies may have circled 1934, and conservative historiographies 1938, as the critical juncture, they shared the view that at Saint Germain, the Allies had already created an Austria fated to become "the first victim of fascism."

IV. Too Big to Fail?

Three. Lacking the benefit of historical hindsight, Austrian politicians of the First Republic knew that their country could survive. Their doubts, as Peter Thaler writes, "did not concern its *viability* but its *desirability*.[19]" Their target audience was international, not domestic. Prior to the war, the Viennese had made up around 4 percent of the dual monarchy's total population but had produced and consumed at least three times their demographic share in services and output[20]. When politicians invoked *Lebensunfähigkeit*, they meant that the new Austrian state would not be able to pay for the high standard of living that Austrian elites wanted and to which they felt entitled. This sense of entitlement greatly shaped not only politics, ideology, culture, and science in the First Republic, but attitudes and behavior. For elites, Austria was not "a" successor state to Habsburg Austria, but together with Hungary, "the" successor state.

---

18 Rudolf Neck, "Das Jahr 1918 - Einleitende Bemerkungen," in Österreich November 1918. Die Entstehung der Ersten Republik, ed. Isabella Ackerl (Vienna: Verlag für Geschichte und Politik, 1986) 11-17, (here 13).

19 Tony Judt, "The Past is Another Country: Myth and Memory in Postwar Europe," *Daedelus* 121, no 4 (1992): 83-117, (here 83).

20 Peter Thaler, *The Ambivalence of Identity. The Austrian Experience of Nation-Building in a Modern Society* (West Lafayette: Purdue University Press, 2001), 70.

Here, the recent history of the First Republic, *Die Gescheiterte Republik* by Anton Pelinka, provides a helpful way of framing the densely-woven presentation of politics and literature, philosophy, sociology, and psychoanalysis of *Stadt ohne Seele* [21]. With a scope that surpasses his previous scholarship, Pelinka describes the political culture of the First Republic, in which a silo mentality (*Lagermentalität*) gripped all parties, as a determination to exist side-by-side but not together, an all-or-nothing approach that turned domestic political opponents into "enemies."

This "silo mentality," it might be added, also fairly describes literary, intellectual, and scientific culture across the First Republic, even if some sought to avoid "politics." The aloof Stefan Zweig, Hannah Arendt once acidly observed, could not bring himself to mention the word "unemployment.[22]" The period was, as Pelinka writes, "full of future-oriented projects, full of noble values, including quasi-religious ones. But none of these projects were shared by all camps.[23]" Where political parties are concerned, what fueled this accommodation with "irreconciliability" was that "the political ideological camps were imbued with an intensity that simply did not correspond to the realities of a country of six million.[24]" A politician of the format of Otto Bauer or Ignaz Seipel felt entitled to more, and like many others, they struggled to internalize the smallness, the narrowness of the First Republic within whose borders they now functioned. In the Empire, political leaders understood themselves as one party among others; after 1918, it was all or nothing. The embarrassment of riches that *Stadt ohne Seele* brings forth in the intellectual sphere testifies to the experiences of the past and the dreams for the future that far outstripped the demographic, geographical, and political realities of First Republic Austria.

21 Marcus, *Austrian Reconstruction*, 30.
22 Anton Pelinka, *Die gescheiterte Republik. Kultur und Politik in Österreich 1918-1938* (Vienna: Böhlau, 2017),
23 Pelinka, *Die gescheiterte Republik*, 165.
24 Pelinka, *Die gescheiterte Republik*, 165.

A Cultural History of the Austrian Exodus after the "Anschluss"

Gerald Fetz

As a teacher and scholar who has been keenly interested in and committed to studying the connections, interdependencies, and differences between the fields of history and literary studies for several decades, I read, studied, and made a presentation at the 2018 German Studies Association's annual conference during a session on Manfred Flügge's book, *Stadt ohne Seele: Wien 1938* (City without a Soul: Vienna 1938), which appeared on the 80th anniversary of the *Anschluss* (Annexation). My initial impression of the book was, and in most ways still remains, that it is a compelling, informative, thought-provoking, and important book. It is, in part, a tad quirky, and it's clearly not your ordinary history book. After the first fifty pages or so, one recognizes that it's a hybrid text—part political history, part literary and cultural history, and part biography, especially of Sigmund Freud—that lacks a consistent, chronological line and includes what appears to be a couple of digressions, but more about that below. The discussion that followed the GSA roundtable—moderated by Professor Günter Bischof, with Michael Burri, Paul Lerner, and Janek Wasserman as the other participants—was lively and led to a good discussion among the presenters and with the audience. Most of what I will assert about the book below was already included in my informal presentation, but some of this "review" was also influenced by the other presenters and the discussion, as well as by a third reading.

Stadt der Seele is a weighty but very readable book of some 479 pages, including the extensive "*Anhang*" (Appendix) with 20 chapters, 931 endnotes, and 14 pages of bibliography. The text does, despite my assertion above, read at times much like what one expects of a traditional history book, but at others, it reads like a dramatic novel in which days, times, and certain characters aren't always presented in a chronological order. That shouldn't, however, impede the reader's ability to follow the stories that all revolve around what Flügge terms in his title of the first chapter, "*Anschluss, Ausschluss, Abschluss*" (Annexation, Exclusion, Finale). The first lines of the book read: "*Sigmund Freud verließ Wien am Samstag, dem 4. Juni 1938. Das goldene Wiener Herz hatte jeden Glanz verloren, als der Vater der modernen Seelenkunde den Weg ins Exil antrat*" (p. 9) (Sigmund Freud left Vienna on

Saturday, the 4th of June 1938. The Heart of Vienna had lost its glow when the father of modern psychology took his path into exile). Flügge, with assistance from the work of writers and writings from the 1920s and 1930s prior to the *Anschluss*, makes clear that a "*Stadt ohne Juden*" (City without Jews, the title of a 1922 novel by Hugo Bettauer), in which a future Vienna without Jews had been envisioned and perhaps even anticipated almost two decades before the events and actions in 1938, sought to make it come true. Flügge also mentions in this context Karl Lueger, the mayor of Vienna during the first decade of the 20th century, and the subsequent anti-Semitic movement via his Christian Social Party as a prelude to the anti-Semitism that flares up again in the late 1930s. In Chapter 6, "*In Freuds Welt*" (In Freud's World), and in the next chapter, "*Der Mann Freud und der Mythos Moses*" (The Man Freud and the Myth of Moses), following the initial five chapters that discuss the beginnings of Austro-fascism and the *Ständestaat*, the author's focus is on, in somewhat of a digression, Freud, his work, his theories, his circle, and his fame, while he also discusses the major role the world-famous psychiatrist plays in defining and exemplifying the "Soul of Vienna." The next-to-last chapter of the book eventually returns to Freud after abandoning him for a long stretch and focuses not only on him but also on his wife, daughter, and others close to him during the almost two months following the *Anschluß* before their departure from Vienna and then, subsequently, their arrival and early weeks in London.

The first of what I would term the two main sections in the center of the book deals first with the historical characters, tensions, and events that lead, dramatically, from Austria being an independent European country to its rapid devolution into the *Ostmark*, a rather small part of the Nazis' growing German empire. The second section deals with numerous individual Jews (and others) who were forced to flee. In the first section, Flügge also focuses on important individuals, but this time they're the political and church leaders of the *Ständestaat*, Austria's sad experiment with authoritarian fascism that lasted a little more than four years (1934-38) before being swallowed by the Third Reich. Here, the reader follows the dramas and melodramas involving such players as Kurt Schuschnigg, Seyss-Inquart, Miklas, Cardinal Innitzer, and even Otto von Habsburg and both Hitler and Göring, who was the actual designer of the *Anschluss*. These chapters—starting with chapter 8, "*Hitler's Wien-Lüge*" (Hitler's Vienna Lie), and ending with chapters 12 and 13, "*Ohne Gnade*" (Without Mercy) and "Ehrenhäftling Schuschnigg" (The Honorable Prisoner Schuschnigg)—replay for the reader the chaotic and fateful events leading up to March 11th and 12th. Just a few days after that, the *Anschluss* is more or less completed.

For anyone desiring a close-up view of the tensions and details involved in Hitler's take-over of Austria, as well as the ineffective attempts by some of the *Ständestaat* officials to ward it off, these chapters are fascinating and wonderfully informative.

One of the many strengths of the book, in my opinion, resides in the author's willingness in this section and the next to let many of the actors speak for themselves through citations. Flügge also adds his own conclusions about these individuals and the events that threaten them, along with those of other scholars. He, those he cites, and the actors themselves prove to be excellent storytellers. The tone is one of seriousness, of chaos, and ultimately of tragedy—a tone quite fitting for putting on display a number of Austrian characters that are not quite evil but certainly incompetent (when compared to Hitler and his henchmen) and who have both together and against one another led Austria, in its form as the Austro-fascist Regime, to the unfortunate point where no other country would come to its aid. Flügge terms these last weeks before March 11th, which include the tragi-comic meeting between Schuschnigg and Hitler in Berchtesgaden. Neither Schuschnigg nor the other last leaders of the *Ständestaat* are a match for Hitler and the German Nazis, who were sometimes in clandestine fashion, or sometimes openly, supported by a fairly significant number of Austrian Nazis and Hitler sympathizers. It is in this segment of the book, a kind of prelude to the no-shots-fired *Anschluss*, that the weaknesses and untenable future of the *Ständestaat* Austria as a sovereign state becomes sadly obvious. Hitler and Nazi Germany had already inserted themselves and Austrian partners into that government prior to March 11th, as it turns out, and most Austrians showed, in the final analysis, that they were not willing to put up any real resistance to the annexation.

Flügge places a good deal of attention in this section on the plans by Schuschnigg and his government to hold a referendum on the possible annexation and its forced cancellation just hours before it was to take place on March 11th. The government, or at least Schuschnigg, had been perhaps naively certain that Austrians would vote in the majority to remain a separate state, but the threats by Hitler and the amassing of German troops on the border were too frightening, and Schuschnigg called off the vote in order to avoid violence. These were, in Flügge's detailed but dramatic telling, tension-filled days and hours, almost a Shakespearean set of events. As it turned out, even if a majority of Austrians had not wanted to become a part of Germany—who knows?—they certainly were not inclined to resist when the Nazi troops crossed the border and moved across the country to Vienna. Less than a month later, the Nazis, now joined by a significant number of Austrians, called for a new referendum, the results of which were now not in doubt: 95.73 percent of those who went to the polls voted to merge with Nazi Germany. The extent to which the capitulation and even the jubilation of a high percentage of Austrians—as evident from the many photos of them wildly cheering on the Nazi soldiers on their victory march across the country, or of the throngs of Viennese gathered gleefully on the *Heldenplatz* once the German soldiers reached Vienna—seemed to provide clear proof that a large portion of the Austrian people fully supported the annexation. Whatever resistance some may have desired or even planned remained at this point essentially quiet and, as one can read below, most real resisters were soon arrested and put out of commission. Others, along with many Jewish Austrians, tried to flee the country for safer havens and, if successful, new lives.

The second major section in the center of the book, as I read it, then focuses on what follows the rapid takeover of virtually all aspects of government, society, business, media, police, and the army. This *Gleichschaltung* (forced synchronization) that had taken place in Germany over months and even a couple of years after 1933 took far less time in Austria and was essentially completed within weeks. Some Austrians who immediately attempted to flee the country, both Jews and non-Jews, succeeded, but it didn't take long for the Nazis to close the borders, and many more who attempted to escape failed and suffered harsh consequences. Among the Jews who fled were a significant number of writers, artists, musicians, journalists, and scientists. A number of non-Jews who were clear-eyed enough to realize that they, too, because of their wealth, political stances, or social status, were in danger, also made an effort to flee. Flügge does an excellent job not only in following the paths and ultimate fates of many famous Austrians who attempted to leave what had been their homeland, but he also shows how quickly Austrian anti-Semitism reached a frightening pitch and how quickly many Austrians began harassing and assaulting Jews of all walks of life—on the streets, in their shops, and in their homes. Flügge's major interest here is to describe, mostly through biographical sketches or vignettes, what happened to a large number of famous Austrian Jews. As a scholar and teacher of German and Austrian literature, art, and culture, I found this section of the book quite compelling. Some of what he relates about the challenges faced by many of these individuals is not new, but these stories, linked together in the context of this life-and-death period, provide a useful, and often terrifying, picture of how difficult it was for most of them to escape and save their lives. Several, of course, ultimately did not succeed. For readers interested in understanding just how many of these famous writers, artists, musicians, journalists, and scientists were Jews with whom the newly installed Nazis wanted to purge from Austria, they simply have to read their stories as Flügge tells them.

Who are they? Here's a partial list: Jewish writers who had lived in Austria after fleeing Nazi Germany earlier in the 1930s, like Carl Zuckmayer and Walter Mehring; home-grown Austrian writers, such as Alfred Polgar, Franz Werfel and his famous wife, Alma Mahler Werfel, Anton Kuh, Stefan Zweig, Joseph Roth, Egon Friedell, Felix Salten, Robert Breuer, Friedrich Torberg, Jura Soyfer, Karl Kraus, Eugen Kogon, Hermann Broch, Robert Musil, and Hans Weigel; non-Jewish writers who had openly opposed the Nazis before the annexation, such as Franz Theodor Csokor and Ödon von Horvath; musicians and stars of the theater, like Bruno Walter, Max Reihnardt, Ernst Lothar, Hertha Pauli, Richard Tauber, Lotte Lehmann, and Karl Farkas; academics and scientists, like Victor Hess, Erwin Schrödinger, Otto Loewi, and Eric Kandel; plus many others, such as Bruno Kreisky, who perhaps was not yet famous at the time but certainly became famous in postwar Austria as the Socialist Chancellor of the restored Austria between 1970 and 1983. And, of course, Sigmund Freud and his family. As suggested above, not all of these people survived: Egon Friedell, for instance, committed suicide by jumping out a window when he saw SA-men approaching his apartment; Jura Soyfer died in the Buchenwald concentration camp; Ödon von Horvath died in Paris, crushed by a falling branch during a storm in Paris shortly after his arrival there; and Stefan Zweig later committed suicide in South America. About Friedell and his death, Flügge writes: "*Sein Fenstersturz ist das Symbol für den Untergang der Wiener Seele, die er auf seine Weise retten wollte.*" [Catapulting himself out the window is the symbol for the demise of the Soul of Vienna which he, in his own way, wanted to save]. The author also points out, however, that Friedell's suicide was no exception: in the first six days after the "takeover" by the Nazis, 600 Austrians committed suicide. And as proof of how dangerous things became for Jews and opponents of the Nazis, Flügge notes that 14,000 were arrested in those same 6 days, and by the end of March that number rose to 70,000. Many of them, of course, were sent to concentration camps. The author notes as well that plans for what would become the largest and most deadly camp within the borders of Austria, Mauthausen, on the Danube near Linz, were already well underway prior to the *Anschluss*. And before the Allies conquered the *Ostmark* in May 1945, Mauthausen concentration camp had some 60 sub-camps spread across what had been and would again be Austria.

I think a further strength of the book is that Flügge doesn't neglect mentioning several writers, musicians, stars of the theater, and scientists, none of them Jewish, who remained in the so-called German *Ostmark* and accommodated themselves and their professions to Nazi rule: Bruno Brehm, Karl H. Waggerl, Josef Weinheber, Karl Böhm, and several members of the most famous Austrian theater family, including Attila Hörbiger and his wife, Paula Wessely. World-renowned scientists Lisa Meitner and Wolfgang Pauli went into exile to Sweden and the U.S. from their German and Swiss research posts. Konrad Lorenz stayed and experienced, after the war, at least minor stains on their reputations. I do wonder, however, and find it to be a missing piece of these stories in the book, why Flügge did not include any discussion to speak of about the thousands of Austrians, Jews, and non-Jews alike who were not famous but who also tried to flee, yet were caught, punished, mistreated, arrested, deported, and suffered many resulting horrors, including death in the camps. For anyone interested in reading more about those unsung Austrians, there are numerous studies in print that deal with them. But for those readers who would like to read more about them in less academic ways, I would strongly recommend two novels that present rather amazing but realistic pictures about how those anonymous Austrians also suffered in a myriad of ways, including torture and death. These novels, from different decades, are: Gerald Szyszkowitz's *Puntigam oder Die Kunst des Vergessens* (1988) and Robert Seethaler's recent work, *Der Trafikant* (2012).

The final chapter of the book should be of interest to film buffs, especially those who are interested in the film *Casablanca*. Here, Flügge tells the story of a young, Jewish, New York City teacher, Murray Burnett, who decides in 1938 to travel with his wife to Vienna, where many of his relatives had come from. Their experiences in Vienna, where they were discriminated against as Jews, and then their experiences in southern France, where they met numerous Jewish exiles from Germany and Austria, led him, once back in New York, to write a novel entitled *Everybody Knows Rick*, which became the basis for the famous film. Giving his readers one more "unusual" but fascinating piece of information related to the overall topic of *Stadt ohne Seele*, Manfred Flügge manages to wrap up his study in a way that may inspire us to look for additional pieces of and stories about the "Annexation, Exclusion, and Finale" history in places we may not tend to look.

Manfred Flügge's *Stadt ohne Seele: Wien 1938: Strolling through the Crisis*

Paul Lerner

In his 1978 memoir, the Vienna-born architect and urban planner Victor Gruen (née Grünbaum) recounts his "ninety days in the Third Reich," the three months between the *Anschluss* and his torturous immigration to New York (via Zürich, Paris, and London), as a period marked by uncertainty, terror, and its share of irony. He depicts a deeply divided society and a spectrum of attitudes and behaviors from convinced Nazis through sympathetic anti-Fascists.[1] Although Gruen, who went on to have a distinguished career in commercial architecture and urban redevelopment, is not mentioned in Manfred Flügge's magisterial *Stadt ohne Seele: Wien 1938*, his tone and several of his anecdotes succinctly capture the spirit of Flügge's project, and Gruen's trajectory—from Vienna to New York to Los Angeles and back to Vienna—evokes some of the broader contours of the Austrian-American relationship over the past eight decades. Eighty years on, as democracy and minority rights are challenged again by a rising tide of xenophobia and authoritarianism on both sides of the Atlantic and throughout the world, this reexamination of the months around the *Anschluss* appears at a timely moment indeed.

On the 14th of March 1938, the day of Hitler's arrival in the Austrian capital, Gruen was working on a retail building on the *Mariahilfer Straße*, which was then, as it is today, an upscale shopping street in Vienna's seventh district, only a stone's throw from the *Haus der Literatur* where one of the two available copies of his memoir is currently housed. Gruen was curious to witness Hitler's entry into the city and granted his workers permission to take part of the day off to watch the procession. They declined his offer, however, and kept working. So did Gruen. This, the most momentous of days in the Nazi imagination, was then met with a typical, world-weary Wiener shrug.

One day Gruen was riding the bus when a man wearing a uniform bumped into him. Gruen excused himself with a "pardon," to which the

1 Victor Gruen, "Ein Realistischer Träumer: Rückblicke, Einblicke, Ausblicke," unpublished manuscript (1979), N1.EB-82 Gruen, Victor Typoskript, Exilarchiv, Literaturhaus Wien.

man angrily replied, "We Germans say '*Verzeihen Sie*'." Gruen paused and then quickly shot back with, "*Je suis Francais,*" to which the man retreated and took his leave. The anecdote points to the understudied Austrian-French connections that constitute one of the great many subthemes and vectors that run throughout Flügge's book, but beyond that it signals the absurdity of the Nazi narrative of "Germanizing" Austria, which Gruen mocked through his appropriately absurd response.

Gruen, like thousands of other Viennese Jews and anti-Nazis, had to tread cautiously in those terrifying days. Even as he needed to scramble around the city to get his finances in order and to obtain transit papers and visas, one false step, or walking on the wrong side of the street, could mean falling into the hands of the authorities. One day Gruen was arrested by two stormtroopers and taken to the Liebenberg Memorial near the university where around 100 Jews had been rounded up. He waited there as more and more were brought in. Within an hour the number of amassed Jews had nearly doubled. Then suddenly a young man in uniform jumped out and released all of the captive Jews, exclaiming: "*Ihr habt's a 'Massel'. Wir haben heut schon zu viel Juden.*" ["You guys are lucky. We already have too many Jews today."] The man, Gruen adds, had no idea that *Massel* was a Yiddish word (mazel), and without this mazel, he adds, he would not have survived to write these lines. Viennese culture was so saturated and intertwined with Jewishness that the Austrian Nazi was completely unaware of the Jewish origins of the slang expression he had used derisively with his Jewish victims.

Austrian Nazis, in Gruen's memoir, appear as bumbling fools, but they were nonetheless deadly for it, embodying the dichotomy of Hollywood film tropes—the idiotic, *Hogan's Heroes*-like Nazi and the coldhearted and calculating Nazi perpetrator of countless films—and this was only one of several close calls in those fateful months. As the historian Lisa Silverman has pointed out in her study of Jews and Vienna's urban geography, the decision of which route to take through the city, even which side of the street to walk on, could have life and death consequences.[2] Moreover, for this secular, social-democratic Viennese Jew, Germany and Austria were self-evidently distinct countries and cultures—Gruen writes about his German mother's struggles to adapt to life in Vienna, recounting how for years she had to take a native interpreter along with her to shop at the *Naschmarkt*—and Austrian language and culture were inextricably interwoven with Jewishness.

2 On Jews, walking and urban space in Vienna, see Lisa Silverman, "Jewish Memory, Jewish Geography: Vienna before 1938," in *Making Place: Space and Embodiment in the Modern City* ed. by Arjit Sen and Lisa Silverman (Bloomington: Indiana University Press, 2014), 174-97.

Interweaving is perhaps the appropriate metaphor for a discussion of *Stadt ohne Seele*, a book which at times reads like a *Spaziergang* through the interconnected networks of Viennese writers, thinkers, and political figures at home and abroad, in French retreat, than in British or American exile. Its title, of course, is a play on Hugo Bettauer's *Die Stadt ohne Juden*, and the replacement of "Juden" with "Seele" suggests that in some way Jews were the soul of the city. In their absence, as in Bettauer's parable, the city has lost its pulse, its vibrancy, its status as a cosmopolitan crossroads, a center of cultural and intellectual ferment. Vienna without Jews then was a soulless outpost, a semi-reluctant Nazi province.

And at the center of the Jewish entanglement with Vienna, and at the center of Flügge's account, lies Sigmund Freud, *Seelenarzt*, doctor of the soul, perhaps the single figure most closely identified with pre-Nazi Vienna. Indeed, Freud is wrapped around this entire history, at times in counterpoint to Hitler: in Berchtesgaden, where the Freuds (and later Hitler) liked to vacation and where Hitler humiliated Chancellor Kurt Schuschnigg and brought Austria close to the brink of capitulation, and in Vienna. The book begins with Freud's departure in early June 1938 (the symbolic loss of the city's soul) and ends back where it began, with Freud's departure in early June 1938, except for a brief coda that concludes with Austrian-American Eric Kandel's Freud-inspired project of uniting neuroscience and psychology.

Part literary rumination, part probing political-historical investigation, *Stadt ohne Seele* offers a thick description of Vienna in its last gasps before Nazification. It lays bare the Austrian predicament in that fateful year, as the doomed *Ständestaat* hopelessly struggled to stay afloat on its own, having failed to secure the support of Fascist Italy, Britain, or France. Flügge takes his time, in good Viennese fashion, spinning out the threads of this rich tapestry, following chains of association where they lead him. But this relaxed style should not obscure the serious issues at stake. Flügge pulls back the curtain behind the highly choreographed scenes of *Anschluss*-ecstasy to show a much more nuanced reality: an ambivalence and skepticism toward the Germans who quickly subsumed Austria into the infrastructure, if not the upper echelons of the Third Reich. Significantly, he threads the needle between exculpating the Austrians for their inability to thwart the advances of their more powerful neighbor to the north and assuming that the *Anschluss* was inevitable or even desirable to many, if not most, Austrians, thus staking out a kind of third way between Austrian guilt and innocence.

Flügge's portrayal of Hitler stands out as an especially peculiar and unconvincing intervention. For Flügge, Hitler was a latecomer to anti-Semitism and, indeed, an opportunistic, strategic anti-Semite whose relationships with Jews before 1918 were not a source of acrimony and were certainly not the catalysts for his dreadful career. This interpretation disrupts Hitler's own narrative, by which his time in Vienna played a crucial role in his development by exposing him to the twin evils of Jews and Marxism. Flügge thus exculpates Vienna and relieves it of bearing responsibility as the site that generated Hitler's anti-Semitism and the most monstrous crimes of the twentieth century. Perhaps his portrayal is intentionally overdrawn to make a point, namely that our image of Hitler remains based on myths, many of which Hitler himself very self-consciously crafted, and that the historian's job is to peel back myth, unraveling layer after layer of falsehood.

Vienna too, perhaps more than any other city, is shrouded in myth and wrapped up in discourses about itself, and untangling the threads of these myths fills Flügge's pages. Each of the major Vienna narratives—romantic city of waltzes, *fin-de-siècle* modernist hotbed, center of science and medicine, point of origin of political anti-Semitism, and Jewish Vienna, from the "matzah island" to the fiercely integrated bourgeois establishment—comes under scrutiny here. *Stadt ohne Seele*, a tour de force of admirable erudition and insight, guides its readers through these various, competing, coexisting Viennas. In the end, however, one has to ask whether Flügge truly succeeds in extricating himself from these myths in his treatment of the city.

Comparison with Carl Schorske is inevitable. In fact, it's nearly impossible to disentangle Viennese culture from the influence and perspectives of his classic work, and even though Flügge tries to peel back some of Vienna's myths, he often seems beholden to others.[3] Unlike Schorske, however, Flügge has relatively little or nothing to say about music, the visual arts, and architecture. Red Vienna, which is today experiencing a much needed historiographic revival, barely makes an appearance in these pages, and readers will not come away with a sense of the housing, educational, and social welfare programs which for roughly a decade made Vienna a center of Social Democratic experimentation and reform. His treatment of Jews as the city's soul or psyche risks romanticizing the city's Jewish past and essentializing its Jewish inhabitants. Flügge's survey is not aimed at specialists; he does not offer up fresh research, nor does he engage explicitly with the latest historiographic debates, and he makes a notable few missteps, like inflating Vienna's Jewish population by fifty percent (from 200,000 to 300,000).

Significantly, Flügge mostly stays out of the fray concerning Austria's contentious, polarized postwar debates about the *Anschluss* and its legacies

3 Carl E. Schorske, *Fin-de-Siécle Vienna: Politics and Culture* (New York: Knopf, 1979).

and Austria's status as victim or all-too willing co-conspirator in Nazi aggression. Despite these qualifications, Flügge's noteworthy achievement is to capture the spirit and mood, the particular relaxed intensity of Viennese politics and culture on the precipice of destruction. If Weimar German culture has been characterized as a "dance on the volcano," Flügge's Vienna comes across as a relaxed stroll through a zone of crisis.[4]

4 Thomas Kniesche and Stephen Brockman, eds., *Dancing on the Volcano: Essays on the Culture of the Weimar Republic* (Columbia, SC: Camden House, 1994).

Popular History and the Anschluss

Janek Wasserman

With the eightieth anniversary of the Anschluss falling in March 2018, a number of books have appeared that reconsider the ramifications of that world historical event. Manfred Flügge's *Stadt ohne Seele* contributes to that ongoing conversation, offering an articulate and compelling narrative. Focusing on the experiences of Austrian political and cultural elites, *Stadt ohne Seele* tells a tale of a flourishing metropolis cut down by the barbarity of the National Socialists. The departures of Sigmund Freud, Kurt Schuschnigg and thousands of others represented more than a humanitarian crisis or a brain drain, it stood for the loss of Vienna's—and, by extension, Austria's—soul. Understandably the book has already enjoyed a positive reception from the press and lay public alike, attaining best seller status. Whether *Stadt ohne Seele* has much to add to scholarly conversations about the *Zwischenkriegszeit* or the Anschluss, or whether it adds meaningfully to our understanding of the politics of memory or *Vergangenheitsbewältigung* in Germany or Austria, is more doubtful.

For a book about the horrors and depredations of the Anschluss, *Stadt ohne Seele* is paradoxically rather comforting. It paints a warm, nostalgic picture of modernist, interwar Vienna. As reviews and the GSA roundtable comments highlighted, Flügge's work is as much an impressionistic tableau as it is a systematic, analytic historical treatise. "Panorama", "novelistic", "pastiche", and many other aesthetic descriptors appear in summaries; these characterizations are apposite. The book offers a history in the form of feuilletonistic essays about leading Viennese personages as the city descended into darkness. After spending four chapters setting the scene with a cursory timeline of events leading up to 1938, Flügge turns to his preferred mode—evocative set pieces and biographical vignettes—to wrestle with the major questions haunting Austrian politics, pre-Anschluss: identity, constitutional, and Jewish. To tackle these overlapping issues, Flügge turns to exemplary figures. Sigmund Freud is the subject of four (out of twenty) chapters, and he becomes Flügge's representative man because he grappled with all of the core issues that inflected Austria's twentieth century fate—psychoanalysis tackled identity issues; *Moses and Monotheism* addressed Jewish identity and antisemitism; his later works confronted authoritarian leadership and the pathologies of human societies. Flügge conveys the brilliance of Freud's intellectual meditations and the anguish of his interwar experience masterfully. Freud's story of escape poignantly encapsulates the flight of Austrian spirit at the time of the Anschluss.

Before returning to Freud's story in the closing chapters, Flügge uses dozens of biographical tales to capture the atrocity of the Anschluss. In the longest—by far—chapter, „*Amputierte Lebensläufe*," Flügge offers twenty life stories of authors, composers, playwrights, publishers who experienced the rupture, which forced them to live lives sharply divided into separate phases: before and after the Anschluss. Reading more like a litany than a systematic analysis of Austrian emigration, this chapter, which should have been one of the most evocative, instead bogs down in a welter of detail.

It took a barbarian invasion to drive Austrian culture into exile, where it continued to thrive until a possible postwar return. Flügge draws clear fault lines between the bad German Nazis and the good Austrian victims. The first Hitler capsule serves this end clearly. Flügge includes a lengthy reflection on the young Hitler and Vienna, drawing on the work of Brigitte Hamann, in order to dispel the self-stylized "Hitler myth" that the Nazi leader received his antisemitic political education in the Habsburg capital. By exculpating Vienna, Flügge enjoins the reader to search for the roots of National Socialism elsewhere than in the ideas of Karl Lueger or Georg von Schönerer.

In dismantling one myth, however, Flügge strengthens another—the Austrian victim myth—which the example of Kurt Schuschnigg demonstrates. In telling the political story of the Anschluss, Flügge relies (too?) heavily on two sources: Schuschnigg's post-WWII memoirs and the reminiscences of the conservative French diplomat (and Schuschnigg sympathizer) Gabriel Puaux. Predictably, Schuschnigg emerges as the main protagonist in the political chronicles at the center of the book. Confronted by scheming National Socialist leaders, Schuschnigg ultimately cannot forestall German annexation in March 1938. In return for standing up for his beliefs and his country, the Nazis incarcerated Schuschnigg in a concentration camp, where he languished for years. In these tautly written chapters, Flügge transports the reader to the heady hours and days that led up the German invasion, and he conveys the tension and uncertainty of those moments well. That said, Schuschnigg's many failings—his active role in undermining the First Republic, his German nationalist sympathies and antisemitism, his belated, half-hearted consideration of "popular front" opposition to National Socialism, among many others—are glossed over in giving the Austrian Chancellor a sympathetic place in the Anschluss drama.

Stadt ohne Seele evinces Flügge's wide-ranging interests and his extensive reading on every page. As one of the GSA roundtable participants noted, it is rare that a *Sachbuch* has such an extensive apparatus of notes and such a long bibliography. With around one thousand notes and 250 bibliographic entries, the book attests to Flügge's erudition, but it also raises significant problems, too. While Flügge has stayed abreast of recent biographical works on his central intellectual figures, his historiographical references are decidedly out of date. *Stadt ohne Seele* is a book that could just as easily have been written to celebrate the fiftieth anniversary of Anschluss as the eightieth. None of the extensive scholarship on Austrian emigration, starting with the Friedrich Stadler-edited, two-volume *Vertriebene Vernunft* (1987/1988) and including dozens of significant publications, is mentioned. This is troubling, because it restricts Flügge's story of the Anschluss to a very narrow subset of the Anschluss's "victims": mostly male intellectuals and Catholic conservative politicians and thinkers. The reliance on post-Anschluss sources also colors this account: how reliable are Schuschnigg's postwar reflections, for example, when he is trying to rehabilitate his image and burnish his legacy? We will return to these points at the conclusion of this essay.

Flügge also fails to engage the growing scholarship on interwar Vienna and the Austrofascist *Ständestaat*, which challenges his somewhat sanguine approach to the end of the First Republic and the subsequent authoritarian government. While Flügge concedes that the First Republic "died" in two phases—1927 and 1934—Flügge is uninterested in assigning blame to any participants. This allows him to take a more benign view of the *Ständestaat*: it becomes the only viable alternative to National Socialism and therefore inspired loyalty from most Austrians. That a figure like Othmar Spann, perhaps the most significant intellectual of the interwar period and a vital defender of authoritarianism and fascism, could be portrayed as the "theoretician of the *Ständestaat*" (which is not accurate, he hated it) and as an unfortunate, if problematic, victim of the National Socialists, is disappointing given the scholarship on him. Recent work on Seipel (the last chapter of John Boyer, *Karl Lueger*), Dollfuss (Lucile Dreidemy, *Der Dollfuß-Mythos*), and Schuschnigg (Lucile Dreidemy/Florian Wenninger, eds., *Das Dollfuß/Schuschnigg Regime*) would have enhanced his discussion enormously. The uncritical use of Schuschnigg's and Puaux's memoirs as his primary eyewitness accounts of the Anschluss leaves much to be desired at this remove from actual events.

The desire to cover his canvas with bold brushstrokes, vivid colors, and clear lines does not work well for a story of such historical complexity and moral ambiguity. Flügge's portrayal of generally "bad" Germans and "good"

Austrians required much greater nuance. As extensive English-language work by Evan Burr Bukey, F.Parkinson, and Bruce Pauley, and German-language scholarship by Klaus Taschwer have shown, not only was antisemitism rampant in Austrian society and culture, but the Austrian Nazi movement had significant adherents throughout the interwar era. Moreover, many notorious "German" Nazis—not just Hitler but Eichmann, Globocnik, Kaltenbrunner, Franz Stangl and others—had Austrian roots. This list does not even include figures like Arthur Seyss-Inquart, whose treatment in *Stadt ohne Seele* is too cursory. It also fails to account for the thousands of Austrians who happily participated in the Nazi regime, post-Anschluss. As a consequence of this lack of attention to the complicity of Austrians in National Socialist atrocities, the book occasionally has a *Sound of Music* feel to it—true Austrians were the noble patriots who resisted or fled Nazi incursions, not those who implemented the Nazi regime in the Ostmark.

From class and gender perspectives, too, *Stadt ohne Seele* restricts its vision too severely. The experience of the Viennese *Bildungsbürgertum* and political elite was not representative of the city's experience as a whole. To suggest that Vienna lost its soul because a few hundred (or even thousand) prominent figures emigrated grossly undersells the contributions of "ordinary" Austrians to their own culture. In the past several decades *Alltagsgeschichte* has enriched our knowledge of the National Socialist era, whether in Detlev Peukert's pioneering work or Peter Fritzsche's or Marion Kaplan's recent studies of Germans and Jews, respectively. More attention to everyday experience during the Anschluss would have added a lot. For example, the Jews of Vienna numbered at least 170,000 in 1938, with many residing in penury in Leopoldstadt. There were also at least 25,000 *Ostjuden* living in Vienna after the Great War, and they receive no discussion. There are too few accounts of women (did they not contribute to Vienna's soul?) Where are other ethnic minorities—Poles, Czechs, Sinti and Roma? There are no stories of socialists or communists. In other words, there is no use of Fritzsche's "people's archive" to expand our focus.

Given that Flügge's narrative privileges escape, exile and survival, the chilling brutality of the Anschluss—and the subsequent Holocaust—is perversely minimized. The place where this narrowness is most evident is in the closing chapters on Freud. Freud is arguably the most famous Austrian émigré and likely the most popular. Whether this justifies dedicating one-fifth of the book to him is an open question. In the final pages of the chapter "Freud geht fort," there is a brief moment where it appears Flügge may open up his narrative to a new range of experiences. He turns to the fellow residents in Berggasse 19, where Freud lived, to offer additional biographies.

This is a welcome pivot, since Freud's story is not at all representative of Vienna 1938. Unfortunately, neither are those of his neighbors. A textile factory owner, a grocer and fruit importer, and a director of a major insurance company were his neighbors. We learn more about the Viennese *Bürgertum* but little about people without means or connections—for example, the domestic servants that likely served those families. While the John family met a grisly fate in the Lodz ghetto (or elsewhere in the East), their story gets a laconic paragraph. In comparison to recent work by Kurt Bauer (*Die dunklen Jahren*), Flügge's panorama seems rather myopic.

To point out these shortcomings is not meant to diminish *Stadt ohne Seele*'s contributions. This book is not intended as a major historiographical intervention; it is a work of popular history. It evokes a familiar image of Vienna, popularized by Stefan Zweig, Robert Musil, Carl Schorske, Kurt Schuschnigg and many others. It captures the tragedy that befell Vienna as a result of the Anschluss, especially for intellectual and political elites. Flügge deserves credit for overcoming the conservative/socialist divisions in his writing that typically plague Austrian scholarship of the twentieth century—perhaps this owes to his German nationality. Unfortunately, this measures "apoliticism" also produces a somewhat uncritical and conservative interpretation of the Anschluss. While *Stadt ohne Seele* succeeds in dispelling certain myths about the interwar era—especially about Hitler—it struggles to critically assess the Austrian victim myth and the often uncritical politics of memory of the Second Republic. In *Stadt ohne Seele* most Austrians become victims, and the Second Republic becomes a success story, since conservatives and socialists rebuilt a flourishing democracy that avoided the problems of the First. Ironically, many Austrian émigrés—including ones mentioned by Flügge—were not invited back to their homeland after WWII, and more had no desire to return, as Friedrich Stadler's and Christian Fleck's research on Austrian émigrés has shown. These details muddy the picture of a harmonious, soulful Vienna, both before the Anschluss and after 1945. In the search for a coherent and comforting narrative—the final chapter highlights the successes of the Viennese around the world and the rejuvenation of postwar Vienna using the case of the Nobel Prize-winning Austrian-American neuroscientist Eric Kandel as an example—the possibility of an equally vibrant, yet sadder and more ambiguous, narrative was lost. Ultimately, *Stadt ohne Seele* is a compelling narrative about Zweig's "Welt von Gestern," Kraus's "die letzten Tagen der Menschheit," or Bettauer's "Stadt ohne Juden," but it is a limited account of Vienna 1938.

Review Essays

Exile Studies in Austria

Evelyn Adunka, Primavera Driesen-Gruber, Simon Usaty with Fritz Hausjell and Irene Nawrocka, eds., *Exilforschung: Österreich. Leistungen, Defizite & Perspektiven* (Exilforschung heute vol. 4) (Vienna: Mandelbaum Verlag 2018)

Herbert Lackner, *Die Flucht der Dichter und Denker: Wie Europas Künstler und Wissensschaftler den Nazis entkamen* (Vienna: Ueberreuter, 2017)

Günter Bischof

Austrian exile studies experienced a slow start in the 1970s but picked up speed and vigor in the 1980s. Among the first generation of scholars most intensely promoting the study of Austrian exile during the World War II era have been Friedrich Stadler, Christian Fleck, Evelyn Adunka, Konstantin Kaiser, Helene Maimann, and Peter Roessler.[1] The Adunka et al. volume under review here introduces a young and engaging new generation of exile scholars such as Siglinde Bolbecher and Irene Nawrocka. Austrian exile studies, ever since the first conference was organized on this subject matter in 1975, have been driven by such conferences in the late 1980s and beyond. A number of organizations have been crucial to developing the field of exile studies in Austria. Among the more important ones are the *Österreichische Gesellschaft für Literatur* (since 1961), the *Dokumentationsarchiv des österreichischen Widerstandes*'s (DÖW) multi-volume documentary series, *Österreicher im Exil* (since 1984), the *Theodor Kramer Gesellschaft* (1984), the *Österreichische Exilbibliothek*

1 As a result of a conference in the late 1980s, Friedrich Stadler edited a pathbreaking work of Austrian exile studies, see his massive volumes *Vertriebene Vernunft I-II: Emigration und Exil österreichischer Wissenschaft 1930-1940*, 2 vols. (Vienna: Jugend & Volk, 1987-1988); Peter Weibel/Friedrich Stadler, eds., *Vertreibung der Vernunft: The Cultural Exodus from Austria* (Vienna: Löcker, 1993).

(1993) in the *Literaturhaus* with their concentration on literature, and the *Österreichische Gesellschaft für Exilforschung* [öge] (2002). The öge organized the 2013 conference on the presentations of which the Adunka et al. volume is based. There also is a more recent branch of "exile studies," namely refugees who seek asylum in Austria, which is not under review here.[2]

Here we have two very different volumes under review: Evelyn Adunka et al.'s deep and very scholarly essays on every imaginable aspect of the flight and exile of Austrians after the "*Anschluss*" and Herbert Lackner's popular history of the flight from Nazi German by some of Central Europe's finest minds, written in a breathless journalistic style. Perhaps the Jewish historian Heinrich Graetz's distinction between *Geschichtsforscher* and *Geschichtsschreiber* may be helpful here.[3] Adunka et al. have compiled a volume full of ambitious young researchers in exile studies who have been in the archives, a sort of summa of the field, whereas Lackner's book is that of a writer who summarizes the research of other scholars.

Christian Fleck, a leading mind in Austrian exile studies, has also reminded us that the trend in Austrian (and German) exile studies has been to research the more prominent protagonists among those who left Central Europe before 1938 or were expelled after the "*Anschluss.*" He sees the reason for this in the "intellectual wasteland" ("*intellektuelle Öde*") that was Austria after the war. Looking for "role models" during the postwar years, one often found them amongst those "*Altösterreicher*" that had been driven out of the country.[4] While Lackner follows this old trend by concentrating on a handful of the most famous protagonists being forced out of Central Europe by the Nazis before World War II, the Adunka et al. volume brings many of the less-famous exiles to light.

2 For a good introduction to this field, see *Aufnahmeland Österreich:* Über den Umgang mit Massenflucht seit dem 18. Jahrhundert, ed. Börries Kuzmany and Rita Garstenauer (Vienna: Mandelbaum, 2017), see my review in Habsburg https://na01.safelinks.protection.outlook.com/?url=https%3A%2F%2Fwww.h-net.org%2Freviews%2Fshowpdf.php%3Fid%3D51659&data=01%7C01%7Cgjbischo%40uno.edu%7C5c5c731588334d9c225508d6028de632%7C31d4dbf540044469bfeedf294a9de150%7C0&sdata=kil1r%2BvDex2cJH5ihajho5MT5JGqdrdkMMmogsv%2FCtk%3D&reserved=0.

3 Graetz's distinction is cited in Raul Hilberg, *The Politics of Memory: The Journey of a Holocaust Historian* (Chicago: Ivan R. Dee, 1996), 138.

4 Christian Fleck, "Soziologie und Exilforschung," in *Die Rezeption des Exils: Geschichte und Perspektiven der österreichischen Exilforschung*, ed. Evelyn Adunka and Peter Roessler (Vienna: Mandelbaum, 2003), 177-186 (here 182f); Frank Stern makes a similar point in "Anmerkungen zum österreichischen Gedächtnis: Wandernde Bilder zwischen Wien – New York – Tel Aviv," in *Österreichische Nation – Kultur – Exil und Widerstand: In Memoriam Felix Kreissler*, ed. Helmut Kramer, Karin Liebhart, Friedrich Stadler (Vienna: LIT, 2006), 243-252 (here 243).

Lackner, a former editor of the Austrian news magazine *Profil*, claims that the history of the flight of Central Europe's intellectuals from 1933/38 to 1940 has "never been told in a coherent fashion" (11). Nothing could be further from the truth. Starting with Donald Fleming and Bernard Bailyn in the 1960s, Anthony Heilbut's *Exiled in Paradise* and Lewis Coser's *Refugee Scholars in America* in the mid-1980s, and Christian Fleck, this story has often been told either *in toto* or in parts.[5] Lackner tells the story of the dramatic flight of the best-known Austrian refugees and some German ones from Hitler's "Third Reich," especially after the invasion and incorporation of Austria. These intellectuals and artists barely escaped the clutches of the Nazis by way of Switzerland and France, via Spain and Lisbon, Portugal, mostly to the United States. France, a traditional country granting refugees asylum, tightened its policies once it was at war with Hitler after September 1939. France herded thousands of refugees from Nazi Germany into unspeakable internment camps. When the Nazis invaded France in May 1940, the refugees left these camps for unoccupied Southern France and tried to stay ahead of the Nazis.

Lackner gives ample credit to the American "refugee helper" Varian Fry, whom the "Emergency Rescue Committee" sent to Marseille in 1940 to "save" Central Europe's brightest artists and scholars and financially support the refugees' escape via the Pyrenees into Franco's Spain to neutral Portugal. If they managed to get visas and affidavits to the U.S. and had the means to secure a ticket on a ship or even on an airplane, they headed to the United States. Some did not make it out of France and eventually ended up in Auschwitz or other Nazi-killing centers; others like Walter Benjamin committed suicide along the way. Lackner compares this dramatic story of flight and rescue with the mass exodus of refugees via the Mediterranean to continental Europe in the summer of 2015 when, again, tens of thousands of refugees were on the move and the world was as unwelcoming of them as in 1939/40.

5 In the 1960s already Donald Fleming and Bernhard Bailyn edited a pathbreaking collection of essays on refugee scholars, see *The Intellectual Migration: Europe and America, 1930*-1960 (Cambridge, MA: Harvard University press, 1969); the pace of exile studies picked up in the 1980s, see Anthony Heilbut, *Exiled in Paradise: German Artists and Intellectuals in America from the 1930s to the Present* (Boston: Beacon Press, 1983), and Lewis A. Coser, *Refugee Scholars in America: Their Impact and Their Experiences* (New Haven: Yale University Press, 1984); more recently University of Graz sociologist/historians have made vital contributions, see Christian Fleck, *Transatlantische Bereicherungen: Zur Erfindung der empirischen Sozialforschung* (Frankfurt a. M.: Suhrkamp, 2007), idem, *Etablierung in der Fremde: Vertriebene Wissenschaftler in den USA nach 1933* (Frankfurt a. M.: Campus, 2015); Johannes Feichtinger, *Wissenschaft zwischen den Kulturen: Österreichische Hochschullehrer in der Emigration 1933-1945* (Frankfurt a. M.: Campus, 2001).

Lackner is very critical of American immigration policies in the 1930s based on the 1921/24 "quota system." Similar to the current incumbent in the White House, for domestic, political reasons, President Franklin D. Roosevelt failed to challenge the restrictive American immigration policy to allow more refugees into the country once the war broke out in Europe (16-20 and *passim*). Meanwhile, FDR's wife, Eleanor, persistently tried to aid the refugees and influence her husband, the President, in getting more refugees out of France. She was never "sidelined" ("*kaltgestellt*", 162), as Lackner asserts. It is an irony that in the end, most of the refugees traced by Lackner ended up in the United States in spite of the U.S. quota system. Lackner fails to reference any of his quotations and has an anemic bibliography at the end of his book (199-204; all the books cited in the footnotes of this review essay have not been consulted by him).

On the other hand, the reviewer finds it hard to do justice to the rich 39 essays collected in *Exilforschung: Österreich*, a volume that can be seen in the succession as an update to the earlier volume edited by Evelyn Adunka and Peter Roessler, *Die Rezeption des Exils.*[6] Almost all of them are meticulously researched and footnoted, with all of them offering select bibliographies at the end of the essay. The volume is subdivided into six sections: 1) "countries of refuge" ("*Zufluchtsländer*"; 2) professions and scholarly disciplines; 3) Austrian musicians in exile; 4) aid organizations and networks; 5) generations and exile; 6) new sources and approaches. Many of these essays—some of them pithy, all of them engaging—touch on new aspects of "exile studies." In the very first essay of the volume, Georg Pichler presents a typology of French internment camps and their various levels of repressiveness. Whereas these camps are portrayed as uniformly miserable in Lackner's book, in Pichler's essay they emerge as a system of camps where life was more (*Les Milles*) or less (*Les Vernet*) acceptable.[7] Essays on little known Austrians in Palestine (Victoria Kumar), Yugoslavia and Spain (Ute Sonnleitner), Belgium (Frank Caestecker), Sweden (Irene Nawrocka), Canada (Andrea Strutz), Australia (Christine Kanzler/Elisabeth Lebensaft), and Hungary (Sándor Komáromi) add

6 *Die Rezeption des Exils: Geschichte und Perspektiven der österreichischen Exilforschung*, ed. Evelyn Adunka and Peter Roessler (Vienna: Mandelbaum, 2003).

7 Felix Kreissler, an Austrian refugee in France who experienced 3 different camps (Stade de Colombes, Meslay du Maine, and Récébrdou) before he was shipped to Buchenwald, confirms Pichler's point, see his well-known essay "Von Lager zu Lager nach Österreich" (first published in 2002) and reprinted in *Österreichische Nation – Kultur – Exil und Widerstand*, 35-49; now the French camp system is analyzed in exhaustive detail within the larger context of shifting French emigration policies, see Vicki Caron, *Uneasy Asylum: France and the Jewish Refugee Crisis, 1933-1942* (Stanford Studies in Jewish History and Culture) (Stanford: Stanford University Press, 1999).

much knowledge to our understanding of the varieties of Austrians in exile during World War II. None of these countries were particularly welcoming to refugees. Georg Deutsch, in the final essay of section 1, writes about a considerable number of Austrians, like Alfred Polgar and Anton Kuh, who left provincial Vienna for the more exciting cultural metropole of Berlin in the 1920s and returned to Vienna after Hitler's seizure of power in 1933. They left their new "*Heimat*"land to return to their old *Heimat*land, Austria. Was the return to Austria "exile" (171)? Ernst Bloch's wife put it this way: "Politically speaking emigration to Austria was not very smart [...] But life was pleasant there. Nobody bothered us, Jews were not persecuted, and one got used to the illegal Nazi- demonstrations" [my translation].

Section 2 offers many fascinating case studies of lesser-known professional organizations and people and their exile experiences. Viennese gardeners and landscape architects went to Palestine and literally managed to make the desert bloom (Ulrike Krippner/Iris Meder). Many Jews working in the theater were forced to leave Austria (Peter Roessler), including most of the talented people working in Yiddish cultural institutions (Brigitte Dalinger), dancers (Andrea Amort), as well as art and antiquities dealers, some of which, like Franz Kurt Lévai, almost single-handedly cornered the international art market after the war (Gabriele Anderl). And then there are the fascinating individual life stories like the Viennese psychoanalyst A.J. Storfer, who started the highly-intellectual *Gelbe Post* journal in Shanghai (Thomas Pekar), or of the exceedingly-productive classicist Ludwig Bieler, who, with his profound knowledge of Medieval Latin, found a new home in Dublin and became one of the world's great experts on the Irish patron saint, St. Patrick (Franz Römer).

Section 3 deals with musicians in exile, with two essays on Argentina, and section 4 with aid organizations and networks. Anne Klein's contribution on "transatlantic and local asylum networks" of Austrians in exile treads some of the same ground Lackner does in his book but with more depth. She notes that the U.S. since the 1920s indeed could no longer be considered a traditional place of asylum ("*Zufluchtsland*") without blaming President Roosevelt personally (160). In his memoirs, Raul Hilberg, the founder of Holocaust studies and also of Viennese-Jewish background, tells how the weird quota system affected him and his family. With affidavits from Raul's mother's relatives in New York, they managed to get on a boat to Havana, Cuba after their flight from Vienna to Paris in early April 1939. Crossing the Rhine at Kehl, Hilberg noted that from one minute to the next, "we were free" but had become rootless and poor refugees. After four months in Havana, as a former Austrian citizen, 13-year-old Raul left on the German quota for the U.S. to stay with relatives in New York. His parents, both born in Galicia in the late Habsburg Monarchy, were allowed to enter only ten months after their son on the Polish quota (even though their place of birth was in what would later become Ukraine—such is the serendipity of Central European history). The Austrian quota was much smaller than the German one and was incorporated into the German quota after the "*Anschluss*".[8]

Beyond the work Varian Fry did for the "Emergency Rescue Committee" (ERC) in Southern France, Klein also presents the concept of the Austrian "*Fluchthelfer*," which included, for instance, Joseph Buttinger and his wealthy American wife, Muriel Gardiner, who helped dozens of Austrian Jews and Socialists with exit visas, affidavits, and apartments once in New York.[9] Klein credits Buttinger/Gardiner and former Austrian Communist Karl B. Frank, along with Eleanor Roosevelt (and two others), for initiating the ERC. Because of their contact with the President's wife, this connection was then used to put pressure on the President's immigration policies.[10] Without presenting any sources, Lackner, however, credits Thomas Mann for the founding of the ERC (97). Klein also mentions the Galician Jew Max Diamant, a leftist Socialist who built up a coordination network in Montauban, Southern France to help German and Austrian Socialists escape (466-72). Thus, Varian Fry was not the only rescuer of Central European refugees in Southern France.

Olena Komarnicka deals with the formation of the "Austrian Forum" in New York and the role it played during and after the war in helping Austrians maintain contact with their old "*Heimat*," which they missed so much, as well as their partial integration into American society (480). In 1968, the Austrian Forum commemorated the 30th anniversary of the "*Anschluss*." Forum President Irene Harand gave a speech about the

8 Hilberg, *The Politics of Memory*, 42-47 (paragraph on the quotas, 47).

9 Buttinger/Gardiner also supported Thomas Lachs' family's flight – Lackner includes an interview with Lachs at the end of his book (187-93). I have written on Buttinger/Gardiner also, see Günter Bischof, "Busy with Refugee Work": Joseph Buttinger, Muriel Gardiner, and the Saving of Austrian Refugees, 1940–1941, in: *Zeithistoriker – Archivar – Aufklärer: Festschrift für Winfried R. Garscha*, ed. Claudia Kuretsidis-Haider and Christine Schindler in Auftrag des Dokumentationsarchivs des österreichischen Widerstandes und der Zentralen österreichischen Forschungsstelle Nachkriegsjustiz (Vienna: DÖW, 2017), 115-126; see also Philipp Strobl, "Thinking Cosmopolitan or How Joseph Became Joe Buttinger," in *Austrian Lives*, ed. Günter Bischof, Fritz Plasser and Eva Maltschnig (Contemporary Austrian Studies 21) (New Orleans-Innsbruck: UNO University Press-Innsbruck University Press, 2012), 92-122.

10 On Eleanor Roosevelt, see the definitive 3-volume biography by Blanche Wiesen Cook, *Eleanor Roosevelt: The War Years and After*, vol, 3: *1939-1962* (New York: Penguin Books, 2016), 288-289.

psychological consequences of the "*Anschluss*" and the "shameless Nazi crimes" of Austrians (485).

Section 5 deals with the generational differences of dealing with exile abroad. Philipp Mettauer interviews some of the 2,300 Austrians who found asylum in Argentina and investigates how the traumatic experience of exile is remembered in the generations of the exiled and their children. Whereas the refugees never could get beyond the feeling of being uprooted in "eternal emigration" and "never having arrived" (544), their children wanted a new start in life. "Hanging on to their old culture and maintaining their familiar life style" (551) were crucially important for the refugees to master their trauma.

Section 6 offers the most "meat" in this collection of essays. Katharina Prager ruminates about new biographical approaches to exile studies. Many prominent and not-so-prominent refugees, as this book richly demonstrates, have become the subject of biographical study.[11] Biographies of those in exile have to deal with the "self-in-translation" (567), the long history of waiting for papers to reach a place of exile, but also of the failure to do so (In that sense, Lackner's book is also a collective biography of prominent refugees in transit). While in postwar Austria people did not want to be reminded of the neighbors they persecuted and drove into exile, biographies of refugees—females included—have become fashionable, especially if women and children are included.[12]

Vida Bakondy presents a study of the visual history of exile via two picture albums Fritzi Löwy left behind. Löwy was a champion swimmer in the Jewish sports club Hakoah before she was driven into exile in Italy and finally Switzerland. Bakondy's close analysis of this visual history of one refugee offers new avenues for understanding the trauma of Nazi

11 See also Bernhard Fetz, "Biographical Narrative between Truth and Lies, Production and Authenticity," in *Austrian Lives*, 19-28; for another book of biographical case studies of Austrians in the U.S. and with an essay on theory of biography by Volker Depkat, see *Quiet Invaders Revisited: Biographies of Twentieth Century Austrian Immigrants to the U.S.*, ed. Günter Bischof (TRANSATLANTICA 11) (Innsbruck: StudienVerlag, 2017); for an analysis of the autobiographical writings of two prominent Austrian emigres to the U.S., see Dominik Hofmann-Wellenhof, *Autobiographische Darstellungen von Identitätskrisen im Exil: Frederic Mortons und Ruth Klügers Suche nach Brücken in einer neuen Heimat* (TRANSATLANTICA 9) (Innsbruck: StudienVerlag, 2016); see also the essays on Austrians in World War II exile by Elisabeth Lebensaft/Christoph Mensch and Irene Nawrocka in *Biographie und Gesellschaft*, ed. Ernst Bruckmüller and David M. Wineroither (Vienna: New Academic Press, 2012), 95-127.

12 Notable among female (feminist) Austrian Jewish refugees is the life story of Ruth Klüger, eloquently and profoundly presented in her autobiography *Still Alive: A Holocaust Girlhood Remembered* (New York: The Feminist Press at the City University of New York, 2001).

persecution and the loss of family members in the Holocaust, which is ultimately an unmasterable past (“*Ich kann es nicht verarbeiten, ich kann es nicht verkraften*”, 592). Bakondy thus demonstrates the richness of private photo albums as historical sources.

Anthony Grenville and Charmian Brinson/Richard Dove present findings from a recently opened source in British archives, namely the reports of the MI5, British secret intelligence surveilling the Austrian immigrant community. Great Britain admitted more Austrian refugees than the United States, argues Grenville (597). Not so, says Claudia Kuretsidis-Haider of the DÖW. More than 30,000 Austrians were admitted to the U.S. while only 27,000 to 30,000 to Great Britain (635). Among the refugees in Great Britain were many Communists, such as Eva Kolmer, organizing in the principal refugee organization, “Austrian Centre.” MI5 came to the conclusion: “For anyone who has eyes to see, it is clear that the Austrian Centre with its subordinate organisations is nothing more or less than a camouflage body of the Austrian Communist Party” (615). Among them was the chemist Engelbert Broda, who was working on the atomic bomb project (code name: “tube alloys”) at the Cavendish Laboratories at Cambridge University. MI5 anxieties were justified considering that Broda was passing on vital scientific information to Stalin’s secret service, NKVD, as post-Soviet archival openings have shown (616-17).

Michaela Wolf is looking on authors in exile from the perspective of translation science and comes to the conclusion that migration and exile needs to be seen as a “process of translation” from one culture to the next (665). Of 13,000 Austrian refugees in Latin America, 1,500 found refuge in Mexico, among them Prague-born Alice Rühle-Gerstel, who saw “herself translating” from culture to culture (675).

François Kreissler takes a deep look at the historiography of Austrian exile studies with regard to the Shanghai community. Until the summer of 1939, Shanghai accepted German and Austrian (mostly Jewish) refugees without demanding a visa. Thousands found a refuge there. However, most lived isolated and impoverished in a ghetto-type environment and left Shanghai after the war. Kreissler notes that since the 1980s, Chinese scholars have started to write about this refugee community and have added much depth to the scholarship. Peter Pirker, meanwhile, offers a broad historiography of “political thinking in exile.” Much has been made of patriotism in exile studies, and Pirker sees that paradigm coming to an end (He calls it the “positive legacy of politics and culture in exile—the “*Verdienstparadigma*”, 706). Exile leaders helped shape some of Austria’s postwar, political myths, such as the doctrine of “Austria—the first victim of

National Socialism" (720-21). Austrians, especially the Socialist Party SPÖ, did little to welcome back their countrymen in exile after the war (721).

Given that some 30,000 Austrians found a new home in the United States, it is astounding that neither of these studies are deeply familiar with American immigration policies of the 1930s.[13] President Roosevelt inherited the quota system from his Republican predecessor, William Harding (1920-24). He had to "manage" it through the 1930s and into World War II. Like today, American public opinion was very xenophobic and anti-immigration. Millions of Americans were out of jobs during the Great Depression; incorporating new arrivals into the labor markets was highly unpopular, the academic labor market included.[14] Moreover, there was considerable American anti-semitism at the time, albeit through prejudice rather than the genocidal anti-semitism developing in Hitler's Germany. A keen politician such as Roosevelt, who wanted to be re-elected, followed these public opinion trends and therefore opted not to change immigration law. In spite of such a domestic political climate, the quota system and preferred admission for academics and well-known artists allowed a considerable number of Austrians to find refuge in the U.S.[15] American history

13 On individual life stories of ordinary Austrian refugees to the U.S., see Margarete Limberg und Hubert Rübsaat, eds., *Nach dem 'Anschluss': Berichte österreichischer EmigrantInnen aus dem Archiv der Harvard University* (Vienna: Mandelbaum, 2013); Thomas Trenkler, ed., *Das Zeitalter der Verluste: Gespräche über ein Dunkles Kapitel* (Vienna: Czernin, 2013); for an analysis, see Andrea Strutz, „Split Lives: Memories and Narratives of Austrian Jewish Refugees," in: *New Perspectives on Austrians in World War II*, ed. Günter Bischof, Fritz Plasser, Barbara Stelzl-Marx (Contemporary Austrian Studies 17) (New Brunswick, NJ; Transaction, 2009), 182-199; Gerhard Jelinek, *Nachrichten aus dem 4. Reich* (Salzburg: Residenz, 2008).

14 Melissa Jane Taylor, Family Matters,"The Emigration of Elderly Jews from Vienna to the United States, 1938-1941," in: *Journal of Social History* 45 (2011), 238-260.

15 David S. Wyman has been the sternest critic of the Roosevelt administration, arguing that they were mere "bystanders" during the Nazi persecution and destruction of the Jews, see his *Paper Walls: America and the Refugee Crisis 1938-1941* (New York: Pantheon Books, 1968); *idem*, *The Abandonment of the Jews: America and the Holocaust, 1941-1945* (New York: Pantheon Books, 1984); more recently Richard Breitman and Allan J. Lichtman have tried to salvage Roosevelt's reputation, see *FDR and the Jews* (Cambridge, MA: Harvard University Press, 2013). The numerous Roosevelt biographies also deal with the "refugee crisis." On the specific context of U.S. – Austrian relations and how it affected the refugee situation, see Günter Bischof, "Austria's Loss – America's Gain: *Finis Austriae* – The "Anschluss" and the Expulsion /Migration of Jewish Austrians to the U.S.," in: idem, *Relationships/Beziehungsgeschichten: Austria and the United States in the Twentieth Century* (TRANSATLANTICA 4) (Innsbruck: StudienVerlag, 2014), 57-82; John S. Berteau,"U.S.-Austrian Relations in the Pre-Anschluss Period: FDR's Unwillingness for War," MA thesis, University of New Orleans 2007; on the sudden loss of the comfort and security of Vienna's Jews, see the prize-winning dissertation by Ilana Fritz Offenberger, "The Nazification of Vienna and the Response of the Viennese Jews" (PhD Diss. Clark University, 2010), now also published as a book.

continues to be *terra incognita* among Austrian academics and journalists.

Finally, some of the essays also analyze definitions of categories such as "exile" vis-à-vis "emigration." Georg B. Deutsch reminds us in his essay on "exile in Austria" (1933-1938) that terms such as "exile," "emigration," and "persecution" are not always clearly defined and kept apart. "Persecuted persons" forced to leave their *Heimatland* into emigration, "exiles" in the true sense of the word, share the suffering with those "persecuted" who are forced to leave their *Gastland* (their guest country). This led famous writer Joseph Roth to reverse Cicero's famous "*ubi bene, ibi patria,*" concluding jarringly, "*Wo es mir schlecht geht, dort ist mein Vaterland. Gut geht es mir nur in der Fremde*" (Adunka et al., 177, 179). Christian Fleck also insists that "emigration" and "exile" are often mixed up. While one is forced into "exile", one voluntarily chooses "emigration." Exiles always maintain their "mental ties to their *Heimat*" and want to return home one day. Emigrants, on the other hand, leave for economic or other reasons and are drawn to a new home for economic, political, religious, etc. considerations (the vaunted "push and pull" factors of migration studies) and do not plan to return home. "Exile then is part of migration studies," Fleck concludes.[16] Brigitte Dalinger points to the special place of Yiddish and notes that since it is a "diaspora language," it is difficult to speak of "Yiddish culture in exile" (Adunka et al., 325). Michaela Wolf observes that those who want to socially integrate and "make a country" in their exile also makes a return from their country of exile almost impossible. As Alfred Polgar has described this tricky process: "*Die Heimat ist uns Fremde geworden, und die Fremde nicht Heimat*" (We have become estranged from our home country, but our guest country has not become our new home) (Adunka et al., 664f). But for Jews, the opposite could be true too, as Abish Meisels noted in his unpublished Yiddish play, *Dritte Akt*: "*In meiner Heimat Wien war ich ein Fremder, und hier in der Fremde* [in London] *bin ich heimisch*" (I was a stranger in my home in Vienna, and here abroad I'm at home) (Dalinger in Adunka et al., 335-338 [here 338]).

For many who had been forced to leave after 1933/1938, exile had indeed become unmasterable, and they wanted to return home. But, as has often been noted, remigration to Austria was difficult since the exiles were not invited back to postwar Austria nor welcomed back. The field of exile studies may have been a long time coming, but the study of the complex place of Austrian exiles in the World War II era has come into its own and has reached a level of scholarly maturity as *Exilforschung: Österreich* demonstrates.

16 Christian Fleck, "Soziologie und Exilforschung," in: *Rezeption des Exils*, 178-180.

The Green Party in Austria

Robert Kriechbaumer, *Nur ein Zwischenspiel (?) Die Geschichte der Grünen in Österreich: Von den Anfängen bis 2017* (Vienna: Böhlau, 2018)

Ulrike Lunacek

Over the last fifteen years, the Austrian Greens have been one of the champions among Green parties in Europe. Others successfully copied some of their campaign ideas. No one imagined that on October 15, 2017, the most bitter and shocking end of the federal election campaign made them stay under the 4 percent threshold needed to qualify for parliamentary representation by just 10,000 votes. Therefore, the Austrian Green Party currently is not represented in the main chamber of the Austrian parliament.

Does this electoral defeat—not unique in the history of European (Green) parties (see below)—mean the eventual end of the party? Or is there hope for a return to *Nationalrat*, the principal stage in the domestic political arena?

The Salzburg historian Robert Kriechbaumer published a 650-page volume about the thirty-year history of the Austrian Green Party with the question "just an episode (?)" (*Nur ein Zwischenspiel [?]*) in the main title of the book, intimating that the Green Party might not return into the halls of power. Most members of the Green Party would say, "Not so fast!" The parentheses around the question mark suggests that their comeback is rather doubtful. Yet Kriechbaumer at the end of the book states that "the future is open. It is, especially in politics, not just the result of [...] circumstances, but mostly of the energy of the players and their actions, which should be based on the power of ideas" (633).[1]

Robert Kriechbaumer is a prolific writer about Austrian regional and national political history, along with the history of political parties. In his prologue, he admits that he did not write the 650-page book in the few months after the defeat of the Austrian Greens in the national election of

1 All translations from German are from the author of this review.

2017. He had been working on this history for some time. He had started to take an interest in the history of the Salzburg Green Party. In 1982, the Salzburg Greens were successful in the polls and entered the Salzburg City Government (in a coalition with the Social Democrats). They were to be the first Greens in Europe to occupy an executive function in (local) government.

His expertise on Austrian regional and federal history may explain why Kriechbaumer in this book provides the reader not only with his insights[2] about the Greens on the federal level. He also looks at the genesis of the Green Party at the end of the 1970s, when campaigns of civil society led to the victory in the referendum against the nuclear power plant Zwentendorf in 1978. In the early 1980s, environmentalists and other activists were also successful in the struggle against building a hydroelectric power plant on the Danube in Hainburg between Vienna and Bratislava. Stopping the Hainburg power plant project laid the basis for uniting the different groups and interests, allowing them to enter the national parliament for the first time in 1986.

Kriechbaumer's history of the Green Party is also a more general history of Austrian domestic politics since the end of the 1970s. He provides the reader with insights and analysis on the general political situation and society in the 1970s and 1980s. From 1986 to 2017, the history of the Austrian Greens in the framework of Austrian politics is the subject matter of this book, a detailed investigation on both the federal and the state level (Austrian has nine states—Vienna being both the capital of Austria and one of the nine states). He spends a lot of time with the successful development of the Greens in the Central and Western Austrian provinces of Upper Austria, Salzburg, the Tyrol, and Vorarlberg. Since 2003, the Greens have served for many years as a minority partner in state governments with the Conservative Christian Democrats (the People's Party = ÖVP). Also, the Red-Green coalition government in Vienna, now in its second term, is analyzed deeply.

However, Kriechbaumer shows a clear personal bias in support of the Black-Green governments (i.e. ÖVP coalitions with the Greens) in Western Austria. He shares less sympathy for the Red-Green government (i.e. SPÖ coalition with the Greens) in Vienna. What may be termed the "East-West divide" indeed marks an important trait of the Austrian Greens. In the (more conservative, more rural) central and western regions of Austria, the

2 Kriechbaumer quotes a multitude of published interviews, comments, and articles in media, as well as polls. But no direct interviews with the main political actors were done for this book, which probably accounts for weaknesses and mistakes in his interpretation, particularly when it comes to more recent events.

Green Party has been and still serves in governments with the conservative ÖVP. In Eastern Austria, especially the capital Vienna—the only Austrian metropolis with almost two million inhabitants—the Greens have served in a government coalition with the Social Democrats (SPÖ) since 2010. These different coalitions may seem strange to outsiders; they are a result of the fact that the Austrian Greens have always positioned themselves on the left-liberal, progressive side of the political spectrum. Along with a focus on the environment, they have been champions of human rights and appeal to a segment of the conservative Christian social spectrum. For in the end, "conserving" our planet for future generations, not extracting all the resources from the earth, and protecting the environment can also be viewed as "conservative" issues.

These coalition alliances also are proof for the point long-standing party leader Eva Glawischnig has made. She is quoted in the book arguing that in none of the regions where Greens have taken responsibility in joining a government have they lost votes in the next elections: "We don't disappoint voters, because our demands are serious. And we don't fool people, we stick to the truth. Citizens understand that you have to compromise" (477).

The volume presents an extensive chronology of the trajectory of the Austrian Green Party. It is filled with polling data and election results, voter flow charts, as well as voting behaviour according to age, sex, and other factors. For some readers, this material might be too meticulous and detailed. Readers might prefer the sometimes-missing political analysis, making the blizzards of data more understandable beyond their numerical significance.

The Austrian Green Party (like Greens in many other European countries) united many movements of the 1970s and 1980s. The Greens were constituted, among others, out of both the ecological and the anti-nuclear movements. Part of the Green movement positioned itself at the political right. They had a very conservationist outlook on issues regarding nature and the environment and a very traditional view on social issues such as gender roles—this comes across clearly in a leaflet that is part of the photo section (323, photo nr. 18) of the book. The majority of the Green movement positioned itself on the more progressive left wing of the political spectrum, including those interested in issues of human rights, as well as ethnic and sexual minorities' rights. Others came from both the peace and women's movements, as well as the movement relating to the North-South divide on the globe (what was called the "Third World movement" at that time), while others came from the "alternative scene." Kriechbaumer presents a wealth of details of the various strains in the Green movement at its beginning and their difficult (inter)relationships. He painstakingly quotes many activists from the earlier times of the party. In his introductory chapters, he offers a very useful overview of both the rigidities of Austrian society and its political system. Until the mid-1980s, the two big parties (ÖVP and SPÖ) divided the spheres of power on the federal and state levels, as well as the cities and municipalities among themselves.

The Greens first entered parliament in 1986 under the leadership of the iconic Freda Meissner-Blau, a well-known journalist, ecologist, feminist, and peace activist. She was the only woman in the first parliamentary group of eight MPs.[3] The eight new Green MPs really created a stir in the "*Hohes Haus*."[4] Greens managed to make parliament function more openly vis-à-vis the public and in a more transparent fashion. By the mid-1980s, the time was finally ripe for breaking up the traditional SPÖ-ÖVP power monopoly. The year 1986 was a turning point[5] in Austrian politics: The Greens entered parliament, and the "*enfant terrible*" Jörg Haider took over the right-wing Freedom Party (FPÖ). With his populist and xenophobic message, Haider managed to successfully increase the votes for the FPÖ in subsequent elections.

In the 1990s, the Green Party made the first steps towards becoming more professional on the federal level. It focused on presenting lead candidates in elections. Due to the competition with a new party, the Liberal Forum (LIF), and its charismatic leader, Heide Schmidt, this search for top candidates in national elections became necessary. In 1994, Madeleine Petrovic was the Greens' top candidate. By garnering 7.31 percent of the vote, she came close to doubling their numbers on the polls. In a snap election a year later, the Green Party's vote declined to 4.81 percent of the vote. These losses were both due to competition with the LIF and Madeleine Petrovic losing her charisma as a leader. The Greens' losses at the polls were also the result of the intense struggle between Chancellor Franz Vranitzky (SPÖ) and the increasingly successful right-wing populist Jörg Haider (FPÖ).

In 1997, Alexander Van der Bellen was elected party leader. The retired university professor of economics helped Austrian Greens to again rise in the polls to 7.4 percent of the vote in the 1999 federal elections. Kriechbaumer concedes Van der Bellen's personal appeal in all factions of the Green Party and beyond. Van der Bellen has a good sense of humor and easy-going manners. This and his weighty bearing as a former professor,

3 The next group in 1990 already had a gender quota to prevent such an imbalance.

4 In Austria and Germany, Parliament is also called the "High House."

5 Not mentioned here is the election victory of former UN Secretary General Kurt Waldheim for Federal President of the Republic in 1986, which was the starting point for Austria uncovering and debating the involvement of Austrians in Hitler's Third Reich.

which is uncommon among politicians, helped him and his team to unite the party and open it to a wider spectrum of voters.

In 2003, government negotiations between the conservative ÖVP and the left-liberal Greens were initiated. For the only time in history up to now, there was a majority of seats in the Parliament between one of the mainstream parties, ÖVP or SPÖ,[6] and the Greens. These negotiations and the conflicts within the Green Party are well described by Kriechbaumer. However, here as elsewhere, his partisan bias towards the ÖVP point of view is obvious. He describes the reasons for the failure of this "missed opportunity" ("*Eine versäumte Chance*" is the title of Chapter 5.3). He notes that "[t]he reasons for the failure [of these negotiations] in the end was not due to the utterly rigid attitude of the ÖVP, as the Greens claim, but was the result of the increasingly massive resistance by the Viennese Greens" (268).

Here, Kriechbaumer's analysis demands correction. The author of this review was a member of the negotiating team (as the Greens' expert on foreign and European affairs) in 2003. At the time, she herself was rather sceptical about this coalition option. Had the ÖVP, namely Chancellor Wolfgang Schüssel, been prepared to make concessions to the Greens in two or three of their main demands—and some other minor issues—both Van der Bellen and Glawischnig would have taken these concessions to the Party Congress for a vote. Both these leaders wanted the Greens to join a coalition with Schüssel. They would have been able to win over many sceptical party members, probably this author included, had there been important Green topics included in a coalition agreement. With such an accord, a majority of the party most likely would have been prepared to enter the government in a coalition with the ÖVP. The Austrian Greens in that moment knew that anything would be better for the country (not necessarily for the Greens) than a rerun of a coalition with the right-wing populist and anti-European Union FPÖ, which had been in a coalition with the ÖVP since 2000. However, the Greens had found out on the day before the negotiations ended with the ÖVP that Schüssel's party had already started coalition negotiations with the FPÖ. It had been agreed that such negotiations would not happen as long as the ÖVP sat at the negotiating table with the Greens. The Greens knew full well that a coalition with the ÖVP would be extremely difficult to tolerate for many party members. Nobody wanted to "whitewash" Chancellor Schüssel after he had accepted a coalition with Haider's FPÖ in 2000. The Freedom Party had too many skeletons in the closet when it came to its unresolved relationship with Austria's Nazi past. Most Greens found it difficult to stomach entering a coalition with Schüssel.

6 With the Social Democrats, such a majority never existed.

Under Van der Bellen's and Eva Glawischnig's leadership, the Greens' external communication and appearance was unified and became more professional. The symbol was the "one logo for all" the different Greens in the regions, cities, and municipalities. New strategies of campaigning, such as using humour and puns or even self-irony, were deployed. These two innovative party leaders, supported by the secretary-general, the board, and a marketing agency, intended to reach more voters and maximize the Greens' potential. According to polls, up to 30 percent of the Austrian population could imagine one day voting for the Greens. On the other hand, this also signalled that 70 percent could simply not be reached by the Greens. Therefore, election campaigns had to focus and zoom in on voter segments of these 30 percent potential Green voters, leaving the other 70 percent aside. Not all Green functionaries and party members appreciated such a strategy.

The new campaigning strategy evoked little criticism among the party's faithful as long as election results showed increases in voters. In the national elections of 2013, the Greens reached 12.42 percent of the voters and became the fourth strongest party in parliament. In six out of nine regions between 2003 (Upper Austria) and 2014 (Vorarlberg), the Greens successfully joined governments. During Glawischnig's time as a leader, both the party leadership and the marketing agency promoted a change of attitudes, showing a more optimistic general outlook. Kriechbaumer describes this as simply following the majority of pro-European Green voters who want Greens to be part of governments. During the twenty years of Van der Bellen's and Glawischnig's leadership (1997 to 2017), the Austrian Green Party evolved from a protest party to a constructive parliamentary party. They introduced and shaped important issues ignored by the parties in the federal government, such as the energy transition from fossil fuels to renewables and energy efficiency, ecological-social tax reform (i.e. taxing fossil fuels higher and reducing labour costs for employers), and new mechanisms for party financing, as well as increasing the number of women elected to parliament in the other parties as well.[7]

Kriechbaumer acknowledges the Green Party's constructive role in parliament, but it came at the price of less activism that had shaped the early years of the party. The Greens' board, along with the marketing agency, proposed a change of attitude in the party such as decreasing the perception that the Greens were a bleak and joyless lot and appeared to

7 Greens have a "zipper system" of gender balance—they succeeded in having ratios of 50 percent women and men in the national parliament. No other party in Austria was so successful in increasing the number of women in parliament.

be an "anti-party," seen as agitating against cars and hosting anti-smoking campaigns. Kriechbaumer does not include such attitudinal strategies of the party in his analysis. He should know that successful regional leaders in the Green Party such as Astrid Rössler, regional deputy prime minister in the state government of Salzburg from 2013 to 2018, Georg Willi, now the mayor of Innsbruck, and Johannes Rauch, a regional government minister in the state government of Vorarlberg since 2014, presented themselves as fearless, optimistic, and with a sense of humour, not only focusing on the details of issues.

In the 2014 elections for the European Parliament, the Greens experienced their biggest electoral success. They scored 14.5 percent of the vote and for the first time garnered three seats in the European Parliament (out of a total of eighteen Austrian seats). The author of this review led the Greens to its victory based on her long-standing expertise in foreign policy and European affairs. Kriechbaumer tries to dismiss her as a mere advocate for Lesbian-Gay-Bisexual-Transgender-and Intersex (LGBTI) rights, yet her main achievements in her political career are manifold. She was a co-chair of the European Green Party (2006-2008), the foreign affairs spokesperson both of the Austrian Greens and the Greens in the European Parliament, the European Parliament's rapporteur for Kosovo,[8] the co-chair of the LGBTI-Intergroup, and—the highest position of an Austrian in the EU—Vice-President of the European Parliament (2014-2017).

Kriechbaumer's book also features an extensive photo section. However, it is odd that he includes no photos on the Green Party's biggest political success stories to date, namely Glawischnig's excellent results in the 2013 national elections, as well as the Greens' great gains in the 2014 election to the European Parliament. Yet Peter Pilz, a founding father of the Green Party in 1986 and a long-time member of parliament, is included in nine of the fifty-one photos in the book. Does Kriechbaumer feature Pilz so prominently because he tried to wreck the Green Party in 2017, when he decided to blackmail the party and – when this did not work out – founded his own party against the Greens?

The European Green movement experienced its biggest success to date in the 2016 Austrian presidential elections. The Austrian people directly elected former Green Party leader Alexander Van der Bellen as their president as a result of the two mainstream parties, ÖVP and SPÖ, failing to find promising candidates. Norbert Hofer, from the right-wing populist FPÖ, competed against Van der Bellen in the run-off elections. Even

8 Ulrike Lunacek, *„Frieden Bauen heißt weit bauen": Von Brüssel ins Amselfeld und retour: Mein Beitrag zu Kosovos/Kosovas Weg in die EU* (Klagenfurt: Wieser, 2018)

though Van der Bellen laid down his party membership by running as an independent, he was originally the candidate of the Green Party. Yet his team succeeded in building a platform of many people beyond Green Party loyalties who supported him. Due to the FPÖ demanding a rerun from the Constitutional Court after they had lost the first run-off on May 22nd, along with serious administrative and organizational flaws of the election machinery, Van der Bellen ultimately won the election in the final December 4, 2016 ballot after a year of campaigning. The Green Party provided lots of funding to the endless election campaign and contributed considerable staff resources. All over the European Union, Van der Bellen's victory was seen as a triumph against nationalist, xenophobic, and hate-mongering, right-wing forces gaining influence in Europe, trying to destroy progress in European integration and undermining the European peace project.

Van der Bellen's signal 2016 electoral victory in the race for president ironically weakened the political agenda of the Austrian Greens. Van der Bellen's team had asked the Greens to tamper down their critical positions on the SPÖ-ÖVP coalition government's anti-asylum and migration policies during the big inflow of refugees and migrants from the Near East and Africa in the summer of 2015. These events, along with infighting in the Green Party (the Pilz affair), contributed to the election shock on October 15, 2017 when the writer of this review ran as the top candidate for the Greens.[9]

Kriechbaumer's account reveals some flaws. When he presents the facts, he is prone to using qualifying adjectives and nouns, usually revealing his personal bias. He talks, for example, about "saying good-bye to the mono-maniacal fixation on the ecological theme" (232), as if the Greens have been focusing since the very beginning on ecological topics alone. He qualifies the so-called "EU-sanctions" against the Austrian national-conservative government (with the right-wing FPÖ) in 2000 as "totally inappropriate" (263), indicating his disapproval of these "sanctions." Yet he fails to explain what the reason for these "EU-sanctions" was. With the formation of the Schüssel government in January 2000, for the first time in Europe, the taboo of the so-called "*cordon sanitaire*" against a right-wing populist (some even call it "extremist party") was broken. The Green Party and many progressive forces in Austria and Europe welcomed the "EU-sanctions." At the same

9 In March 2017, the Young Greens were ousted from the party after inner-party conflicts could not be resolved. This created a major upheaval. On top of it, Peter Pilz—accused of sexual harassment after the elections—created his own party list. He had tried to publicly blackmail the Party Congress at the inner-party elections and decided not to continue running after losing the seat he wanted to a young Green. (He most probably would have won the next possible seat on the list.) Moreover, many Green and "Red-Green" voters cast their ballots in October 2017 for the Social-Democrats, hoping that the SPÖ still had a chance to win the election, or at least come in in second place, pushing the FPÖ into third place.

time, they criticized the EU for not having prepared an exit strategy from the "sanctions."

Kriechbaumer facilely dismisses the long-lasting protests against the ÖVP-FPÖ government in 2000 as "*Erregungskultur*" (253f), implying hysteria rather than intense criticism and even fear motivating the protesters. Kriechbaumer consistently ignores the fact that Greens "elect" their candidate lists for parliament in a democratic process unlike the traditional parties in Austria. Instead, he prefers to use the terms "nominate" and "designate," failing to acknowledge the deep democratic culture that characterizes the Austrian Green Party. Moreover, Kriechbaumer describes Johannes Voggenhuber as the party's "Savonarola" (205), thus insinuating an inquisition-type attitude by this long-standing national and European parliamentarian (Voggenhuber stepped down after losing the role as lead candidate for the 2009 European elections to the author of this review).

Kriechbaumer is also prone to showing a male gender bias. He describes Eva Glawischnig as "attractive" (347), but would he care to characterize the looks of male politicians? The Greens' support of two referenda in 2007—one against genetically modified organisms (GMOs) and the other one in favour of more equal rights for women—betrays similar gender bias. Kriechbaumer devotes five pages to the former and a mere two pages to the latter, characterizing it as "aggressive lobbying" (225) on behalf of women's affairs. He argues that its demands for "quota and positive discrimination" were "deviating from EU law." This argument is false. No EU law prohibits a member state or a party or company from instituting quotas and/or "positive discrimination."[10] Kriechbaumer also tries to dismiss the agenda of the women's referendum as being "obviously part of class struggle" and "having a clear tendency towards state regulation" (226).

What runs through Kriechbaumer's text as a constant refrain is their positioning on the left side of the political spectrum. Time and again he frets about the Greens' "turn to the left" in the course of their thirty years of existence. He keeps referring to the Green Party's Marxist and/or Communist/Anti-capitalist positions. Such repetitiousness is sheer fear-mongering. If Austrian Greens had done all the left turns Kriechbaumer mentions, they would have been ideologically totally outside of any political spectrum for a long time. He ought to ask himself, "is the Austrian electorate turning to the left when it elects Greens?" The Greens in Austria, and in most other parts of Europe, have become a left-liberal force in the political spectrum and are represented in many parliaments and governments with their constructive attitude and progressive policies.

10 What in the United States is called "affirmative action" and has a long history.

Kriechbaumer is no friend of "multiculturalism" and characterizes such a Green position as "naïve" (614). He dismisses the big successes the Greens have had in twelve years of Black-Green governments (i.e. ÖVP-Green) in Upper Austria with their creation of "Green jobs." He calls such job creation a "soft topic," contesting the real influence it has on people's lives, as analyzed by long-standing Green, Upper Austrian minister Rudi Anschober in his signal book, *Das grüne Wirtschaftswunder.*[11]

The major question raised in the title—*Just an Episode (?)*—remains unanswered. However, the coming electoral cycles for the EU parliament in May 2019, the Vienna municipal elections in 2020, and the Austrian national elections in 2019 will answer the questions raised by Kriechbaumer. Alexander van der Bellen's election as president would suggest that the Greens have arrived in the mainstream of Austrian politics. Issues such as the environment, the climate crisis, gender equality, ethnic and sexual minorities' rights, tax justice, youth unemployment, and peace in Europe and the world will not go away, especially as long as the parties in the government do not address them forthrightly.

To his credit, Kriechbaumer does remind the reader about important historical precedents. In 1994, the (then West-) German Greens did return to the German *Bundestag*, the German main chamber of parliament, after having failed to pass the 5 percent threshold in 1990, while the East-German *Bündnis 90* remained in the *Bundestag* throughout those four years. He also refers to the German liberal party FDP ousted from the *Bundestag* in 2013 but managed to return to the German parliament in 2017. He might have cast his analytical glance beyond the German-speaking EU member states and enriched his analysis with more recent examples of Green Party successes in Europe. One of the earliest European Green Parties, the Belgian "*Groen*" Party (in the Flemish part of the country), missed the threshold of 5 percent in 2003 after having been one of the first Green parties in Europe to be included in a national government coalition in 1999. The Belgian *Groens* returned to the national Belgian Parliament in the 2007 elections and are one of the strongest Green parties in Europe today. The Dutch *Groen Links* Party went through a similar trajectory as the Belgian Greens. In 2012, they lost almost one third of their votes and went down to 2.3 percent of the national vote. They were only able to be awarded four seats in the national parliament because there is no minimal threshold (as the 4 percent in Austria and the 5 percent in Germany) in Dutch election law. In 2017, they more than quadrupled their votes to 9.1 percent and had a realistic chance to enter the government.

11 Rudi Anschober, *Das grüne Wirtschaftswunder: Wie die Energierevolution funktioniert und wie jeder davon profitiert* (Vienna: Ueberreuter, 2011).

A reviewer also has to point out sloppiness in the final editing of Kriechbaumer's book as quite a few names are misspelled. Yet that is minor business when considering that the author, to a large extent, has approached the history of the Austrian Green Party from a biased and partisan political perspective. One is left to suspect wishful thinking on his part, namely that what he views as the "left-wing" Green Party would only vanish from the Austrian political arena and leave the field open to the current conservative-nationalist consensus on the right of the political spectrum.

Book Reviews

Helmut Rumpler and Ulrike Harmat, eds. *Die Habsburgermonarchie 1848-1918, Band XII: Bewältigte Vergangenheit? Die nationale und internationale Historiographie zum Untergang der Habsburgermonarchie als ideele Grundlage für die Neuordnung Europas* (Vienna: Verlag der Österreichischen Akademie der Wissenschaften, 2018).

Gary B. Cohen

This book stands as the last numbered volume in the large-scale collective history of the Habsburg Monarchy after 1848, which began in 1973 with the publication by the Austrian Academy of Sciences of their first volume on economic development. One installment remains to be published: the long-delayed volume X on cultural history. The editors of volume XII on the historical legacy and historiography of the dissolution of the monarchy and its aftermath, Helmut Rumpler and Ulrike Harmat, wrote the foreword in November 2017, just a few months before Rumpler's sudden passing. The foreword explains that the first impulses for this volume came during a 2010 planning workshop for the series volume devoted to World War I. It was soon realized that the issues of the legacy and historiography of the monarchy's fall were too significant and complex to fit within the volume devoted to the war. In May 2014, the Austrian Academy of Sciences then proceeded to stage, in cooperation with several other Austrian institutions, a large international conference to discuss that legacy and historiography, and the chapters in this volume represent edited papers from that meeting.

The editors are to be commended for bringing this volume, with its twenty distinct contributions, to publication in four years after the conference, a shorter gestation than a number of other volumes in the series. That relative speed is particularly important for the value of the historiographical essays included, which can quickly become outdated. The purposes and chosen format of this volume, however, have created some significant challenges, which are met with varying degrees of success. A collection of edited conference papers, seven in English and the rest in German, represents a significant departure from previous volumes in the series. As with many conference volumes, there is considerable variation in the length and scholarly significance of the individual contributions. Several chapters, such as those by Pieter Judson, Raoul Motika, Erwin Schmidl, Martin Schulze Wessel, and Gianluca Volpi, are informative and learned, but at around ten pages each, they read like pithy, short conference papers. Other chapters are more ambitious and considerably longer. The editors argue with good reason that the historiography of the dissolution of the Habsburg Monarchy and its aftermath should be considered as integral to the legacy and memory of those events in the successor states and elsewhere in Europe, but the combining of chapters, which directly address events with those that discuss historiography and historical memory, has created problems of integration.

The volume begins with Rumpler's introductory chapter, presented unusually for him in English. His contribution assesses in general terms the Habsburg Monarchy's political legacy to Europe and its potential to serve in later times as a model for a polity uniting different nationalities. Rumpler's analysis leads naturally into some discussion of the historiography of the monarchy, particularly in the Austrian Republic and the United States. The political legacy of the monarchy comes up again in Jana Osterkamp's cogent final chapter on the evolution in the successor states of ideas for federal polities, which were first bruited before 1918. No concluding essay follows Osterkamp's to sum up the findings and implications of the individual contributions.

Strong chapters by Harmat and Ernst Hanisch take up, respectively, scholarly understandings of what led to the downfall of the Habsburg Monarchy and its legacy for political thought and national identity in the Republic of Austria. Harmat adroitly juxtaposes the differing visions of Austrian, Hungarian, British, and American contemporary observers and later historians about the weaknesses of the imperial polity and what led to its final dissolution. In a brief chapter, Hanisch offers insights on the challenges that the first and second Austrian republics faced in defining national identity and in trying to construct viable political systems given the heritage of the monarchy's institutions and the long-term political and ideological conflicts.

World War I and the development of international relations are the focus of chapters by Alan Sked, Wolf Gruner, Catherine Horel, B. J. C. McKercher, Raoul Motika, and Mark von Hagen. Sked presents a lively review of the varying accounts on the significance of World War I in international historical scholarship—with little direct reference to the Habsburg Monarchy or its successor states. Gruner, a distinguished historian of modern Germany, presents an incisively argued overview of historians' treatments of Germany's place in European politics and international relations from the late nineteenth century to 1918. Unfortunately, he says nothing about relations between the Imperial German government and the Habsburg Monarchy before and during World War I or about German attitudes and expectations regarding the monarchy. This is surely a missed opportunity. Horel's chapter addresses French efforts to create a new diplomatic equilibrium in Central Europe after 1918, providing a clear-sighted synthesis on the challenges and ultimate failure of those efforts by the mid-1930s. Her chapter is paired with McKercher's on the development of British policies toward Central and Eastern Europe between 1918 and 1925. Impressively researched and cogently written, von Hagen's chapter treats the diplomacy dealing with the Eastern Front at the end of World War I and the efforts to gain international support for an independent Ukraine. Motika offers a brief but thoughtful overview of the Ottoman Empire's troubled legacy to the Near East. The chapters by Sked, Gruner, Horel, McKercher, Motika, and von Hagen all present valuable scholarship, but one can reasonably question whether a volume in the Austrian Academy's series on the history of the Habsburg Monarchy is the most appropriate publication venue for them.

Chapters on historiography in various European countries dealing with World War I, the dissolution of the Habsburg Monarchy, and the emergence of the successor states take up the rest of the volume. Readers seeking well-informed and insightful introductions to various national historiographical traditions on these subjects will appreciate the contributions by László Szarka on Hungarian writings, Martin Schulze Wessel and Ota Konrád on Czech scholarship, Holm Sundhaussen on Serbian memory culture, Wlodzimierz Borodziej and Maciej Górny on Polish memory culture, Răzvan Pârâianu on Romanian writings, and Alexander Medyakov on Russian scholarship dealing with the Habsburg Monarchy.

The 2014 Vienna conference and the resulting volume have gathered together a group of accomplished scholars, and when taken individually, their contributions offer much value. The strengths and weaknesses of the volume as a whole are largely what one might expect from a collection of edited conference papers. Given the subject matter and format of this volume, perhaps it might be best considered as an addendum to *Die Habsburgermonarchie 1848-1918* rather than as the volume of concluding thoughts for which one might have hoped as the final installment for the series.

Kurt Bednar, *Der Papierkrieg zwischen Washington und Wien 1917/18* (Innsbruck: Studienverlag, 2017)

Roger Chickering

This is an odd book—hard to characterize, hard to read. Its subject is not what its title suggests: a history of relations between the United States and the Habsburg monarchy during the final two years of the First World War. The bulk of the book comprises, instead, a detailed survey of reports by American observers of Austro-Hungarian affairs. Most of these observers were associated with agencies that were called to life during or just after the war in order to advise the Wilson administration on peace negotiations. The emphasis in the survey falls on the "Inquiry" under "Colonel" Edward House, the American Commission to Negotiate Peace, and the so-called Coolidge Mission, whose representatives toured central Europe in the aftermath of the war and reported on the situation there. On the basis of these reports, the author argues that the Wilson administration began in the spring of 1917, months before the United States declared war on Austria-Hungary, to plan the dismemberment of the Habsburg Empire into autonomous or independent national units. The object was strategic: to weaken Germany.

Bednar has produced a mountain of information about the reports of these observers. The difficulty lies in his failure to fashion the details into a coherent narrative. The organization of the book is less chronological than randomly thematic, but the treatment of the themes produces less narrative than extended bibliographical lists, and because the author's pervasive neglect or defiance of chronology extends even into these lists, the exposition verges on turmoil. "The American press confronted events in Europe with no comprehension," begins a chapter on George Creel. The following sentence reads: "O'Keefe covered [*nahm sich an*] the press in New York, the city in which nearly all immigrants first stepped onto American soil" (124). The footnote reveals that the O'Keefe in question had nothing to do with George Creel but was the author of a dissertation in 1971 on the press in New York City. Another section of the same chapter treats "War Crimes and Propaganda." Its five pages survey a list of studies of this subject, devoting a paragraph each to works that appeared (in order) in 1929, 1920, 1978, 1941, 1971, 1920, 1928, and 1934. The chapter on the Coolidge Mission rests on reports sent by its representatives to Paris, including those that Coolidge himself sent from Vienna, eleven of which (which range from number five to number 192), are rehearsed over four pages of text (the reports themselves, the reader learns, comprised thirty pages).

Teasing out analytical generalizations is no simple matter in these circumstances. A thesis emerges nevertheless, most clearly in an afterword, where it sits next to the acknowledgements. The Habsburg Empire's collapse, writes Bednar, "was for the most part determined externally, initiated and permitted with crude recklessness at the least" (457). This proposition comports with arguments that have increasingly colored the historiography of the Habsburg monarchy, particularly in the United States, where Pieter Judson has given them forceful expression. In this view, the monarchy was a great deal more stable and functional in 1914 than earlier scholarship had allowed, and its collapse was due to the extraordinary domestic circumstances of the war. A more uncompromising version of this argument can be pieced together in Bednar's book. The monarchy might, in this account, well have survived even the pressures of war but for the support that exiles and emigrants in the United States, the disaffected advocates of the national minorities, found among American political elites who, acting in "terrifying ignorance of conditions in Europe," swallowed the "poison pill" of national self-determination (285). Important facets of this argument remain, however, unsupported or unexplored in this book. While Bednar can cite a lot of evidence to buttress his claims of missionary naïveté among the American experts who studied Austria-Hungary, the book leaves questions open about the impact of their work even on Wilson, the "fervent [*begeistert*] lone fighter" (397), let alone on central Europe, which remains largely a passive object throughout the account. Most of the sources the author cites on developments within the Habsburg Empire are the reports of just these American experts, and they hardly suggested stability.

It is a pity that so many problems persist in this work and that the author has so willfully defied the legitimate expectations of his readers for narrative coherence. Bednar has many interesting and smart things to say, and his research has unearthed a lot of neglected scholarship, much of it in American doctoral dissertations. Still, his book reads like a first draft. It begs for reorganization, consolidation, clarification, thematic transitions, and generalization. The work would likely be twice as valuable were it half as long.

Robert Dassanowsky, *Screening Transcendence: Film under Austro-Fascism and the Hollywood Hope, 1933-1938* (Bloomington, IN: Indiana University Press, 2018).

Jacqueline Vansant

Hardly an American Austrianist knows the Austrian and Hollywood film industries as well as Robert Dassanowsky. He has demonstrated his prowess with publications such as *Austrian Cinema: A History* (2005), his editorship of *World Film Locations: Vienna* (2012), and his co-editorship of *New Austrian Film* (2011). In addition to such comprehensive volumes, he has authored numerous articles, some of which serve as the genesis of chapters in *Screening Transcendence*. With this publication, Dassanowsky reaffirms his dedication to introducing and explaining Austrian cinema to English-speaking readers as he follows the unique struggles the Austrian film industry faced during years of the Austro-Fascist regime (1933-1938). For those unfamiliar with Austria, it may be surprising to learn that one of the industry's biggest challenges was pressures and restrictions leveled against it by Nazi Germany. Threatened with boycotts from Germany if film companies included "Jewish" employees on film credits and rosters, mainstream producers accommodated their northern neighbor, who was also their largest film market. The industry crisis was exacerbated by the influx of those working in film who fled to Austria after Hitler came to power in March 1933. Consequently, two parallel film industries emerged in Austria. Alongside mainstream companies, which catered to German demands and "continued to answer to the 'Aryan' laws of two states" (20), the independent *Emigrantenfilm* evolved. "The independent Emigrantenfilm ... would utilize émigré and Austrian 'non-Aryan' talent, coproduce their films with foreign studios in multilanguage versions, and market them across Europe" (20). Dassanowsky argues that this "'new' film industry is particularly interesting as a way to diagnose the enforcement of legal restrictions in a non-governmental segment of the Austrian economy" (20).

In the introductory pages, the author explains that "the 'transcendence' of the book's title refers to the regime's spiritual and geopolitical/cultural desires, as well as the popular desire to overcome the impoverishment that plagued Austria since 1918 in different extents" (x). According to Dassanowsky, the desire for transcendence characterizes film production in Austria. "Attempts to valorize that ethos are obvious in almost all of Austrian films made in the era regardless of genre" (x). He divides his exploration into three main sections: "Structures," "Genres, Narratives, Contexts," and "Locations." In the three-chapters of "Part 1: Structures," Dassanowsky provides necessary information for those unfamiliar with Austria and the era of Austro-Fascism. Impatient and more knowledgeable readers may wish to proceed directly to "Part 2: Genres, Narratives, Contexts," where Dassanowsky deals with a wealth of films. The heart of the book consists of eight chapters, in which the author explores different aspects of the dual film industry. When focusing on mainstream films, he includes productions that comply with German demands while at the same time attempting to appeal to a wide audience. He highlights how the Austrian-made films present their citizens differently from the Austrians of German productions; he explores films compatible with the tenets of the Catholic Austro-fascist regime; and he analyzes films with messages vague enough that they would pass muster with the Nazis and appeal both to German and Austrian audiences. In his discussions of the *Emigrantenfilm*, he explores how they work to bolster an independent Austrian identity and appeal to cosmopolitan audiences through their narrative and filmic innovations.

The ways in which the films of the parallel industries deal with the problems of capitalism serve as a litmus test for the author. For example, he highlights the efforts in two emigrant films, *Singende Jugend* and *Der Pfarrer von Kirchfeld*, to express Catholic values, condemn capitalism, and call for a national unity, which transcends class boundaries. He juxtaposes the films of two female stars, Paula Wessely and Franziska Gaal, and their association within the parallel film industries in such movies as Wessely's films *Maskarade, Episode,* and *Ernte* and Gaal's *Peter-das Mädchen von der Tankstelle* and *Csibi, der Fratz.* Whereas Wessely makes her mark as a film star in these mainstream productions in a way that would be acceptable in Germany as well as Austria by playing the "anti-glamorous" and motherly heroine, the Hungarian actress Franziska Gaal, of Jewish ancestry, imbues her characters in the *Emigrantenfilm* with humanism and agency. Another highpoint includes Dassanowsky's reading of the mainstream film *Leise flehen meine Lieder* where he argues that "The Austrian Viennese Film genre can ... be understood as a cinematic Counter-Reformation of the 1930s positioned against the problems of modern capitalism and the Protestant/National Socialist film culture of Germany" (77). Equally fascinating is his tracing of the career of Erich Engel, who goes from making films with a mythologized Austrofascist ideology to the post-Anschluss film *Hotel Sacher* that reveals him as the consummate opportunist.

This section of *Screening Transcendence* undoubtedly constitutes a major contribution to the study of Austrian cinema. However, the otherwise insightful readings get sidetracked and interrupted by digressions, and the reader is often overwhelmed by facts that could have been placed in footnotes. Because the chapters are so extensive, a clearer overview or roadmap of the argument to follow would have greatly enhanced the author's own arguments. Moreover, the chapters too often end abruptly. A conclusion and reiteration of the ways in which the films discuss screen transcendence would have helped cement the interpretations. Lastly, the quality of the 62 black and white screen shots, which illustrate Dassanowsky's argument, is poor. The exorbitant costs of stills no doubt prevented the inclusion of photos of better quality.

Despite the thorough, in-depth close readings in "Part 2," I found "Part 3: Locations," with its chapter "From Rome to the Hollywood Hope: Shared Aesthetics, the 1936-1937 Vienna-Hollywood Coproduction Plan, and Cine-Economic Brinkmanship with Berlin," the most original contribution and utterly fascinating. Here the author draws on original archival research and clearly presents the Austrians' short-lived cooperation with Rome and failed efforts to establish business deals with Hollywood. After some initial co-productions with Italy, the cross-cultural work fell apart after the Rome-Berlin Pact in 1936. Dassanowsky tells of the unfolding drama of the Austrians' attempt to work with Hollywood studios in an effort to escape German pressure. He pinpoints the seeds of this potential cooperation with a short letter, which Frederic Dormer, the representative of the Austrian Bureau for Foreign Trade in New York City, wrote to Eugen Lanske of the Ministry of Trade in November 1935 in an effort to secure more of Vienna's short culture and tourist-aimed films for viewing in the United States. The next player to enter was Paul Koretz, who represented Hollywood studios in Europe, first from Berlin and then from Austria after he was no longer welcome in Germany. Impressed with the use of Dormer's efforts to inform audiences of postwar Austria, Koretz wrote to Lanske's boss, Minister of Trade Fritz Stockinger, in January 1936, suggesting that there would be an interest for importing Austrian feature films. Over the next two years, including Lanske's visit to Hollywood, this little known episode of film history, which Dassanowsky has uncovered, would be of major interest to trade publications and the potential rescue of the domestic film industry. "Understood in terms of Austrofascism's Catholic political ideology, this match would mean Austria's symbolic transcendence from its material losses, physical reduction, and diplomatic limitations could fulfill the regime's idea of Austria as the better German state, one with a continued mission in leading Central Europe" (352). Austrian hopes were eventually dashed. Dassanowsky reveals how those in Hollywood explained the failure of cooperation away with specious arguments. He attributes the failure of an Austrian-Hollywood partnership to the American industry's commercial interests and its fear of offending German markets, as well as the strong German influence in Hollywood.

In addition to the wealth of information in the book, Dassanowsky has included an outstanding filmography of Austrian produced, coproduced, or completed feature films from 1933-1938. The bibliography is a gold mine for anyone studying film and this era of Austrian history. This section also includes an index of names, which would have been enhanced and eased targeted reading if the author had also included concepts and names of the films.

Overall, *Screening Transcendence* does a great service by introducing this era to English-reading audiences, and it points to the need for further study of this corpus.

Gertrude Enderle-Burcel (ed.), *Berta Zuckerkandl – Gottfried Kunwald: Briefwechsel 1928–1938* (Vienna: Böhlau, 2018)

Theresia Klugsberger[1]

One of the most exciting tasks of academic research is to re-shine the spotlight of public attention on important personalities who have vanished from collective consciousness for decades. Gertrude Enderle-Burcel has edited a correspondence that provides us with new insights into ten years (1928-1938) inside the lives of two such figures, namely Berta Zuckerkandl and Gottfried Kunwald. The two protagonists were of very different dispositions, yet they shared a central political concern about the increasingly endangered independence of Austria during those "fateful years" for the country.

Many facts about Berta Zuckerkandl's life and work are well-known to a wider audience. Her volumes of published memoirs and her innumerable articles in newspapers and magazines are not only generally available, but have, at various times, also been the subject of research and review. Her life and her role as a salonière have attracted increasing interest within the field of women's studies. The fact that the history of the Zuckerkandl family could be recovered from oblivion is due to the debate about the question of restitution, arisen as a consequence of the purchase by the Austrian National Library of the pre-death estate of the renowned evolutionary biologist Emile Zuckerkandl, who was famous not only in America but also beyond (although not in Austria). This material came to Vienna in instalments, some of it as his estate after his death in 2013. Documents and letters from this, many of them written by his grandmother, Berta Zuckerkandl, constantly provide new impulses and perspectives on the academic integration of her cultural, political, and journalistic standing.

The situation is rather different with regard to the sources of this edition's second correspondent. The financial expert Gottfried Kunwald, who had a decisive influence on financial policy after the First World War, is largely unknown in his role as currency expert and financial adviser to the Austrian Federal Chancellor Ignaz Seipel. The extensive biographical introductions to the two personalities, which preface the main part of the

1 This essay was translated from German into English by Peter Waugh.

book, namely the correspondence, prove to be an important supplement to the letters. They reflect the current state of research and, in the case of Gottfried Kunwald, expand it considerably through the analysis of previously unknown biographical sources.

The history of the origin of these sources is yet again evidence of the tortuous journeys taken by the endless amount of material and works that were stolen by the National Socialists. Immediately after annexation, Gottfried Kunwald committed suicide in order to pre-empt his murder in a concentration camp. His private and professional documents were removed by the National Socialists to Berlin. From there they eventually arrived in Moscow, where they were incorporated into the Austrian collections of the Russian Special Archive. Among these "Files Looted from Austria," as they were known in the Moscow collection, the "twice-looted files" (p. 9) on Gottfried Kunwald comprised more than 2,000 bundles. They were among those parts of the Moscow collection that were returned to the Austrian State Archive in Vienna in 2009. It is these documents, which, on the one hand, expand our knowledge of Kunwald's biography enormously and, on the other, also contain the previously unknown correspondence between him and Berta Zuckerkandl, that forms the core of the present publication.

The letters have been edited and placed within their historical framework by the historian Gertrude Enderle-Burcel, a task facilitated by her many years of experience at the Austrian Society for the Study of Historical Sources and as project leader of the edition of the Ministerial Committee Proceedings of the Republic of Austria in the Austrian State Archive. Political events, which recur frequently in the letters, are explained in the footnotes. A Biographical Appendix provides the most important background information, or it at least supplies details that are probably unknown to many readers. Over almost 50 pages, all the people mentioned in the correspondence are documented with not only their biographical data but also, as far as could be ascertained, their professional, political, or private roles. This constitutes a significant aid for understanding the letters. Besides personalities from Austria, Germany, other European countries, and also some Americans, the list contains, above all, people who were influential in French society in the 1930s—politicians, artists, economic experts, and others—whose biographical details facilitate historical contextualization. The volume highlights the value of the historical sources of the letters in relation to both of the authors yet above all with regard to how they were part of a historical and political framework.

A close friendship between Kunwald and Zuckerkandl, both of whom came from assimilated Jewish, upper-middle class backgrounds, began in

1925, at the latest. A few letters, which derive not from the bundles of looted letters but from the part of Kunwald's estate now owned by the Stadlen family in England, can be traced to that date and are quoted here for the very first time. One of them, written by Berta Zuckerkandl to Gottfried Kunwald in April of that year, already enters into details of her work as a translator of French theatre plays. The mediator of their acquaintance was the Christian-Social politician Dr. Ignaz Seipel. On the one side, we have Kunwald, important for Seipel as financial adviser and economic expert during his time as Federal Chancellor and beyond that as his friend, and on the other, we have Berta Zuckerkandl with her contacts to French and American politicians, her commitment to the survival of Austria in the turbulent years after 1918, and her contribution to the efforts to organize financial aid and loans from the League of Nations.

The two protagonists are therefore both public personalities, each in their own different way, and a common basis of understanding may be traced through their correspondence from 1928 to 1938: Kunwald, the fiscal policy maker who went down in history as "Seipel's grey eminence," a man in the background, confined to his wheelchair yet who "with seminal works, articles and lectures on financial policy continued to be in the public eye" (p. 78); and Zuckerkandl, the writer and salonière who (at least until the 1930s) was full of vibrant activity, promoting art and artists and also attempting to mediate between the politicians in Vienna and Paris.

The letters deal with questions concerning aspects of financial policy, Austrian politics, culture and the arts, and social events, as well as personal and private matters. The fact that these fields merge and that their borders are fluid is particularly conspicuous in Berta Zuckerkandl's letters. Indeed, it is typical of her personality. Her writings would also readily lend themselves to analytical examination from a linguistic-literary perspective with regard to the dynamic elements of the style and their dramaturgical potential in general. Not only the salonière but also the letter-writer establishes connections in the discursive web of a (cultural) historical situation and makes the communicative intertwining discernible. The majority of the letters were written by Berta Zuckerkandl, which is in line with the logic of the creation of the collection.

Zuckerkandl addresses her letters to her friend and often encloses texts written by others as a way of documenting something that she has referred to in the respective letter. That is why the edition of the letters begins, rather surprisingly, with a short letter written by (six-year-old) Emil to "Uncle Kunwald" thanking him for his invitation to a theatre performance and with two letters by her sister, Sophie Clemenceau. Included are also letters from Annette Kolb and Ludwig Ullmann—the one a friend and colleague, the other a trusted confidante even during Berta Zuckerkandl's exile, first in France, then in Algiers. Occasionally, a couple of pieces of correspondence are added to the bundle, which serve to compress time in an exemplary way. For instance, there is a letter to Berta Zuckerkandl from Ethel Snowden, a British women's rights campaigner and politician associated with Labour Party circles, as well as Berta Zuckerkandl's reply and a series of letters between Zuckerkandl and Kunwald in which the topic is briefly put into perspective (p. 146 ff.). The content of the letter is about an article entitled "Austria's Plight as I saw it," published by Snowden in the *Daily Mail* in January 1935, and in her extensive letter, which alternates between private and public discourse, Zuckerkandl masterfully pulls out all the linguistic stops, interweaving her analysis (in defence of the Austrian government as a guarantee of independence from Germany) with appeals and emotional elements. Her initial accusation is that her (former?) friend has not written about what she saw but only about what she was allowed to see. Ironically, it brings to mind Karl Kraus, who, as early as 1921, had intensified one of his attacks on Berta Zuckerkandl by claiming that Ethel Snowden was seeing Austria and Vienna through the eyes of Zuckerkandl.

However, Austria's independence is not the only theme running through the letters. That of "financial predicament" is also to be found in the correspondence, which includes a third party. Likewise, in 1935, Gottfried Kunwald writes to request payment from Hans Békessy, alias Hans Habe, the (by this time already ex-) editor-in-chief of the newspaper *Der Morgen*, for the latter having been granted the publishing rights to print a letter by Crown Prince Rudolf, which had formed part of the estate of Zuckerkandl's father, Moriz Szeps. By association, there is something of Berta's youth present here, namely her involvement in her father's work as a journalist and as a confidante of the Crown Prince. At the same time, her reflections on the role of the legitimists in maintaining the independence of Austria become more evident over the further course of the letters.

One thing is certain, namely that Berta Zuckerkandl's letters give us a clear and, to a large extent, previously unknown picture of her financial situation and, above all, of how she experiences it. What is tragic about this situation, according to her presentation of it, is the effect it has on her family: son, daughter-in-law, and grandson. Her son, Fritz, who is only marginally represented, if at all, in her memoirs, plays a prominent role in the letters. There is a surprising intensity expressed in the relationship between the mother and her adult son, which Stekel-experts (Wilhelm Stekel was Fritz

Zuckerkandl's father-in-law) or other psychoanalysts would find well worth examining. Due to his complete incapability (to put it euphemistically) in financial matters, Fritz Zuckerkandl is a source of disaster for her nuclear family. Gottfried Kunwald represents him as his lawyer not only in the case of the sanatorium in Purkersdorf, in which Berta and Fritz Zuckerkandl inherited a share after the death of her brother-in-law, Viktor Zuckerkandl, and his wife in 1927. Kunwald takes over Fritz's official legal representation, and when the latter moves to Paris in 1935 with the intention of having his wife and child follow him there later, the correspondence traces not only how the chemist repeatedly tries to set himself up professionally with the name Zuckerkandl (which was itself famous in the pharmaceutical industry) but also the many requirements and obstacles involved in the process of becoming naturalized in France, even though Fritz avails himself of the renowned name of his uncle, Paul Clemenceau. At first, Fritz Zuckerkandl fails due to the fact that, without professional security, he is not allowed to have his family follow him, which should have been easily solved on account of the existence of his son, Emile. "Because there is a law saying that if a foreign family has a son, then the process of naturalisation is thereby facilitated. Since this son signifies one more soldier for France." (15 Feb. 1935, p. 153). By the time this matter is last mentioned (in June 1937), naturalization has still not been achieved. (In spring 1940, as a soldier of the French army, Fritz Z. is stationed in Bourges, where Berta Zuckerkandl's flight to Algiers begins.)

Nevertheless, Berta Zuckerkandl is able to keep the financial problems of the family separate from her own financial difficulties as an independent and professionally active woman. In the early 1920s, she had begun to do translations of theatre plays from the French; she gradually attempts to expand her work as a mediator of literature. When the National Socialists come to power, she loses the source of income from her theatre royalties in Germany. These professional matters are described time and again in the letters when she refers to contracts, the persons involved, intrigues, and small successes. Particular insight is gained from the exact listing of her revenue, including her "pension as a professor's widow" and her obligations, which Kunwald repeatedly records for the ministry of finance and other institutions, in order to arrange a postponement of payments. Incidentally, it may be gathered, in combination with another letter, that her pension is about 25% higher than the unapproved special monthly payments, which her partner, Paul Stiasny, makes to himself from the budget of the sanatorium in Purkersdorf in order to supplement his salary.

She records her desperation about her professional decline and the insoluble financial situation in her letters to Gottfried Kunwald. The edition thereby clearly brings out an aspect of Berta Zuckerkandl's personality, which only gradually becomes evident but has never been so intensely comprehensible before. The reason for this openness on her part lies not least in her correspondent, who not only repeatedly supports her with his professional expertise and even materially, despite the limitations of his own financial situation, but is above all else an understanding listener. This is shown by her many requests for visits.

Kunwald is a solicitor and economic expert, one who, although he does have an interest in culture, was nevertheless at home in a different intellectual sphere. His use of language in those letters of which refer to private matters exhibits a characteristic aloofness—although in exchanges with his correspondent, he can also create a feeling of closeness. His social life differs considerably from that of Berta Zuckerkandl, not least due to his physical disability. Nonetheless, interestingly enough, they have one thing in common: They each use the rooms of their respective homes for both their private and their public lives.

The roles of giver and taker are not as clearly delineated as the field of private finances might suggest. Their common political activism constitutes a major part of their friendship, and it is here that Berta Zuckerkandl brings to bear her network of contacts in France and her whole commitment. In particular, her efforts to disseminate Kunwald's writings in France become a leitmotif, yet they are apparently not crowned with any great success. Here we find, for instance, considerations about how the economic fields could concretely contribute to agreements with France in order to boost the Austrian economy. The amusing idea of exporting cheese to France, thereby achieving a coals-to-Newcastle effect, is only briefly remarked. However, a more extensive exchange of letters in the summer of 1933 highlights the complications involved in drawing up a preferential agreement for exporting wood.

Alongside the exchange of opinion about her disastrous financial situation and the existential desperation that accompanies it, the correspondence also sheds light on a further aspect of Berta Zuckerkandl's character. In economic discussions covering a wide variety of facets, she proves herself to be proficient in the subject-matter, and her letters relating to this, which always embed the topic in the world of her social contacts, are full of élan. On the basis of how she presents her argumentation, one can understand how she must have tried to mediate between Kunwald and Joseph Caillaux and then the financial expert Charles Rist—whether in monetary questions, Kunwald's international projects, such as the plan for an international air fleet (for which she considered whether to activate her relations to the Rockefeller family), or plans for an international bank in Vienna. Rist emerges as one of Kunwald's most important contact persons in France, although he subsequently proves to be an increasing disappointment, above all in the eyes of Zuckerkandl.

To overcome Austria's isolation on foreign policy is a concern which is repeatedly hinted at in the letters and is not only of significance from the perspective of financial policy. Plans to establish contact between Austrian and French politicians seem to fall through time and again due to the fact that no rapprochement takes place between Kurt Schuschnigg and Otto Bauer or between the Christian-Social Party and the Social Democrats, even though this was demanded as a pre-condition by the French side and could have been initiated by Schuschnigg. The first official contact with the Blum government occurs in 1937 after Schuschnigg, according to a statement by the Austrian diplomat Wasserbäck in Paris, claimed that reconciliation with the Socialists was one of his most important concerns.

The concepts of financial and monetary policy comprise a substantial part of Kunwald's letters. As a vehement opponent of the deflation policy, he expressed his increasing opposition to Kienböck, the president of the Austrian National Bank. In these letters, his style differs considerably from that of his private "settlement reports." A text over 5 (book) pages long, dated June 21, 1936 and written in reply to Berta Zuckerkandl's enquiries about his political evaluation of the situation in Austria, skilfully presents his analysis in a concise and rhetorical manner. An analysis of the connections between the deflationist financial policy and the political mentality in Austria concludes with the inevitability of a referendum, as addressed to a people which is not accustomed to being asked anything. "Therefore, if the Austrian people were presented with the choice of annexation or independence in a referendum today, the Austrian people would not answer with a vote for either annexation or independence, but instead would answer with Hitler or Schuschnigg. … Hitler is the powerful and successful German inflationary economy, Hitler is enthusiasm, Hitler is hope" (p 257). The independence of Austria could, accordingly, only be achieved by pursuing a different economic policy. Politically, Kunwald displays clear sympathies for a backward-looking legitimist policy with a democratic credo, thereby contradicting previous theories, which demanded more independence and responsibility, also on the part of the people.

When the edited correspondence comes to an end in January 1938, there is, on the one hand, a letter from Berta Zuckerkandl to her friend, which seems to be an anticipated farewell complete with heartfelt gratitude; on the other hand, all that follows is a letter from the bank Auspitz Lieben

& Co. to Gottfried Kunwald, who had repeatedly negotiated deferrals of payment for Berta Zuckerkandl: No further allowances would be made for her situation. To a certain extent, a more than atmospheric framework is created by two short notes—one is Emile Zuckerkandl's note of thanks for an invitation to the theatre, and the other is a final demand for the repayment of debts owed to the bank. They contextualize the personal profiles of the two correspondents in a supplementary manner: two characters whose life paths seem at first glance to overlap in their unconditional commitment to the independence of Austria, as well as in a shared basis of emotional openness. The final document records Kunwald's entrenchment and the recurrent theme of financial ruin that continues to the end.

The editor emphasizes the fact that the much earlier end to Berta Zuckerkandl's activities as a salonière becomes articulated in the course of the correspondence, revealing a new, previously unknown aspect of her personality. Nevertheless, despite the passages of desperation in her letters, one still finds an enthusiastic networker even when she is in her seventies. Naturally, these letters provide us solely with excerpts from the lives of the two protagonists. Documents from her estate show, for instance, that Berta Zuckerkandl remained a committed member of the Salzburg Festival scene even in 1937, when she was struggling to survive both professionally and psychologically, and this determined attitude becomes more evident in the present volume.

The edition makes it possible, through extensive and knowledgeable research and through its exemplary treatment of the historical sources, to gain an insight into the penultimate and ultimate segments of the lives of two personalities who were prominent in public life and who have, for a long time now, been too absent from public consciousness.

Hannah Arendt and Günther Anders, *Schreib doch mal* hard facts *über Dich: Briefe 1939 bis 1975*, ed. Kerstin Putz (Munich: C.H. Beck, 2016)

Jason Dawsey

The release of this volume signifies a real "event" in the study of Central European and trans-Atlantic intellectual history. Thanks to the labors of Kerstin Putz, many of the exchanges—philosophical, political, and personal—between Hannah Arendt (1906-1975) and Günther Anders (1902-1992) are available to the Germanophone public. Scholarship on their connections, already enriched by the 2011 *Die Kirschenschlacht: Dialoge mit Hannah Arendt* (The Cherry Battle: Dialogues with Hannah Arendt), will have much to consider with this work.[1] It should find a place in every research library.

Putz, the editor of the volume, is easily one of the world's leading authorities on the life and ideas of Günther Anders. Her extensive work in the Anders *Nachlass*, held at the Literature Archive of the Austrian National Library in Vienna, has already led to a growing series of publications on the Arendt-Anders relationship.[2] Researchers who have investigated Anders's intellectual biography, this author included, owe much to her generous assistance. That debt has ballooned with the work of translation, collation, and annotation she undertook for this publication. The letters stem from three collections: the Anders *Nachlass*, the Hannah Arendt Papers at the Library of Congress, and the Lion Feuchtwanger Papers at the University of Southern California. Among its many helpful features, the work includes Putz's fine afterword, over forty pages of notes to the correspondence, a timetable for both Arendt and Anders, and a list of the many texts they refer to in their communications.

1 Günther Anders, *Die Kirschenschlacht: Dialoge mit Hannah Arendt*, ed. Gerhard Oberschlick (Munich: C.H. Beck, 2011). These dialogues are taken from Anders's private papers.

2 For examples, see "The Letters of Günther Anders: His Correspondence with Hannah Arendt," in *The Life and Work of Günther Anders: Émigré, Iconoclast, Philosopher, Man of Letters*, eds. Günter Bischof, Jason Dawsey, and Bernhard Fetz (Innsbruck: Studien Verlag, 2014); "Hannah Arendt/Günther Anders: (Über-)Lebenszeichen," in *Das Literaturmuseum: 101 Objekte und Geschichten*, ed. Bernhard Fetz (Salzburg: Jung und Jung, 2015) . See also her "Improvised Lives: Günther Anders's American Exile," in *Quiet Invaders Revisited: Biographies of Twentieth Century Immigrants to the United States*, ed. Günter Bischof (Innsbruck: Studien Verlag, 2017).

This collection not only greatly expands our knowledge of the two German-Jewish thinkers, but it also fosters deeper reflection on the experiences of exile and return, solidarity and helplessness, philosophical ambition and hubris, and language and alienation. One can see these binaries throughout *Schreib doch mal* hard facts über *Dich* (Write "Hard Facts" About Yourself), and they, unintentionally, give structure to the book. The pieces Putz chose, of course, also further contemplation on what it meant to survive and then render for others the "dark times," to recall Arendt's ordinary yet so resonant phrase, of the 1930s and 1940s.[3]

Three sets of correspondence make up the core of the volume. The rather leisurely repose exhibited in the book's cover photographs of Arendt and Anders clashes with the apprehension and turmoil revealed in the first set of missives. They consist of twenty-two letters from Arendt to Anders, discovered in the latter's papers, in German and French, with smatterings of English, from September 1939 to November 1941. Anders's letters to her have not been recovered. Putz's afterword provides the prehistory to these wartime exchanges. She describes how Arendt and Günther Stern ("Anders" was a pseudonym he adopted in the early 1930s and used almost exclusively after 1950) first met in Marburg in a 1925 seminar held by Martin Heidegger. They encountered each other again and fell in love in 1929 after Arendt's affair with Heidegger ended. Marrying a few months later, Arendt and Anders, in Putz's words, "formed a—if shortlived—community of philosophical thought and work" (227). The volume contains the fruits of their collaboration: a jointly authored essay on Rainer Rilke's beautiful *Duino Elegies* and their separate critical pieces on Karl Mannheim's *Ideology and Utopia*.[4] The texts show them long before they became the thinkers familiar to us, exploring questions of love, transcendence, and the social embeddedness of knowledge.

With the rise of Hitler and the Nazis, Anders drifted to the radical Left, becoming close to Bertolt Brecht and other intellectuals linked to the Communist Party of Germany (KPD), while Arendt embraced Zionist politics. They fled Berlin in 1933, several months apart, arriving separately in Paris. The strains of exile took their toll on the couple. As their marriage, which, Putz states, "had long only still existed on paper," collapsed, Anders decided in 1936 to leave France for life in the United

3 Hannah Arendt, *Men in Dark Times* (New York: Harcourt, 1968).

4 An English translation of the text on Rilke is available in Arendt, *Reflections on Literature and Culture*, ed. Susannah Young ah-Gottlieb, trans. Colin Benert (Stanford: Stanford University Press, 2007). Arendt's essay on Mannheim can be found in Arendt, *Essays in Understanding 1930-1954*, ed. Jerome Kohn, trans. Robert and Rita Kimber (New York: Harcourt, 1994).

States (236). Divorce came the next year, and Arendt found a long, lasting love with Heinrich Blücher.

The first set of letters from Arendt to Anders, which include a few additional missives from her mother, details her efforts to get out of France, now partitioned between the German occupiers and the Vichy government, as quickly as possible. Both Arendt and Blücher had already experienced internment at the hands of French authorities. Unsurprisingly, questions about paperwork (affidavits, visas), money, and contacts fill these pieces. Arendt powerfully described to Anders "life in the Pyrenees—where we really had nothing to eat" and where they faced "more or less immediate danger. I know now what the Greeks named Hades, the quasi-normal shadow existence" (21). Despite missteps and delays, Anders's relentless work to secure safe passage for them paid off. Right after their arrival in New York via Lisbon in May 1941, Arendt and Blücher sent a telegram to a surely relieved Anders with the simple yet overwhelming message: "are saved" (23). Her other missives in this section detail the transition into American life, the task of learning English, and locking down employment.

If one can only glimpse at Anders through the lines of Arendt's missives in the first section of correspondence, the inclusion of three of his letters from 1941 to the writer Lion Feuchtwanger makes his voice, with its desperation, quite real. "Hannah is in danger," he confided to Feuchtwanger, "and I am afraid her rescue from the unoccupied area of France could fail due to lack of money" (97). His pleas for assistance also conveyed the fright he and Arendt felt for the socialists Rudolf Breitscheid and Rudolf Hilferding, who were in even greater peril. In his final letter, Anders informed Feuchtwanger that a "happy ending" had transpired with Arendt's situation.

More than thirty letters penned between them from 1955-1975 constitute the longest and philosophically most interesting part of *Write "Hard Facts" About Yourself.* There, the divergence of lives, reputations, and outlooks comes through most glaringly. Arendt, already famous for *The Origins of Totalitarianism* yet committed to a career in the United States, and Anders, gaining notoriety for *Die Antiquiertheit des Menschen* (The Obsolescence of Human Beings) while building a new existence in Vienna, engaged in uneasy exchanges. The frustrations, mainly on his part, about seeing one another are compounded by an awareness of his advancing age and illness. In December 1959, in one of the book's more poignant moments, Anders wrote to her, "but I don't feel old, mainly because—one can't help it—completely new tasks have popped up" (80-81). His radical, uncompromising opposition to nuclear weapons and his often prophetic ambition to lead the burgeoning anti-nuclear movement, certainly one of the "completely new tasks" mentioned, deepened Arendt's reluctance to stay in closer touch. There are huge gaps in the correspondence and, according to Putz, they only met twice: in 1961 and then again in 1975, just months before her death from a heart attack in December of that year. These letters, then, throw light on the travails of an emblematic twentieth-century friendship, directly shaped by the century's extremes, which rarely had time for more relaxed contact.

Several luminaries of twentieth-century European thought appear in these pages: Heidegger, Hans Jonas, Karl Jaspers, and Theodor W. Adorno. The memory of Walter Benjamin, however, is a recurring and imposing presence in the exchanges between Arendt and Anders. Benjamin was Anders's cousin and spent considerable time with him and Arendt in shared exile in Paris after the Nazis gained power. Arendt grew close to Benjamin after Anders departed for the United States and, eventually, she would number, along with Adorno and Gershom Scholem, among the principal interpreters of his legacy.[5] As things collapsed in France in 1940, Benjamin entrusted Arendt with taking his recently finished manuscript, *On the Concept of History*, to Adorno and the Institute for Social Research. When his attempt to cross the Pyrenees into Spain in September of that year ran into an unexpected closing of the border, he took his own life. Dutifully, Arendt gave the work to Adorno, but as her letters to Anders record, she worried what would become of the text and its brilliant reflections on Marxism and theology.

After the war, this distrust did not dissipate. In November 1955, the year that Adorno and Scholem published a collection of Benjamin's essays, Anders wrote a concerned letter to Arendt about the legacy of the friend they continued to dub, with affection, "Benji." "That you do not want to write about Benji is sad," he wrote. "Who should, outside of us, if one does not want to leave the monopoly to Adorno?" (57) Putz shows how both had already written about Benjamin, reprinting Anders's eulogistic 1940s poem and Arendt's poem, "W.B.," from two years later, as well as a short, previously unpublished text from 1950 by Anders. In the latter, he lamented, "how I miss him; how each of my sentences miss him" (181). From the materials present in this volume, one could begin to trace the development of the "Benjamin Wars," the conflicts over who held authority to interpret and to transmit Benjamin's legacy after 1940.

These topics only comprise a few of the issues covered in this extremely rich, fascinating, and carefully edited work. Hopefully, readers will find

5 Arendt edited and introduced the most famous anthology of Benjamin's work, *Illuminations*, which appeared with Harcourt, Brace, and World in 1968.

their way from the volume to two subsequent collections of Anders's writings, many of them previously unpublished.[6] The fields and sub-fields in the humanities that will benefit from *Write "Hard Facts" About Yourself* are too numerous to name. It deserves immediate translation into English.

6 See *Musikphilosophische Schriften: Texte und Dokumente*, ed. Reinhard Ellensohn (Munich: C.H. Beck, 2017); *Die Weltfremdheit des Menschen: Schriften zur philosophischen Anthropologie*, ed. Christian Dries, in collaboration with Henrike Gätjens (Munich: C.H. Beck, 2018).

Barbara Serloth, *Von Opfern, Tätern und jenen dazwischen: Wie Antisemitismus die Zweite Republik mitbegründete* (Vienna: Mandelbaum, 2016)

Christian Karner

The renewed prominence of anti-Semitism is among our era's most disconcerting phenomena. There is thus an urgent need for analyses of the conditions of possibility and manifestations of such politics of exclusion and hatred, both past and present. With her detailed examination of the workings of post-war Austrian anti-Semitism, Barbara Serloth's recent book provides one such much-needed discussion.

Serloth's most significant contributions to the wider literature are two-fold. Thematically, she casts light on the darkest side of Austrian politics in the post-1945 era by critically reexamining and looking beyond prominent themes in existing portrayals of the country's period of reconstruction: e.g. paternalistic political structures, the power-sharing (*Proporz*) between Austria's two dominant parties, the long transition from the end of the war until the State Treaty, and an ensuing, decade-long "social peace". Connecting these themes to other, well-known facets of post-war Austrian society and politics, including the country's identity-bestowing victim narrative, the myth-like construction of 1945 as an absolute caesura (i.e. Stunde Null), and well-known manifestations of "secondary anti-Semitism", Serloth demonstrates that these were not separate discursive and political phenomena that merely unfolded in parallel; instead, they are here shown to have been mutually intertwined and partly constitutive of the early Second Republic. Conceptually, and informed by some pertinent political science literature, Serloth's definition of anti-Semitism as the refusal to recognize Jews as equals promises to be of relevance far beyond the field of Austrian Studies.

In order to illuminate what she terms the "political architecture" and the "definition of norms" in operation in Austria post-1945, Serloth pursues a well-chosen, methodological strategy of examining the minutes of parliamentary debates and of ministerial meetings, as well as contributions to wider public discussion. This enables her to show the continuing workings, after the Holocaust, of anti-Semitic stereotypes and strategies of exclusion. Political discourse, as well as social policy—most notably the definition of victims of war entitled to pensions, the political parties' problematic approaches to a purported "de-Nazification", long delays and systematic obstacles faced by Austrian Jews seeking restitution, and a general reluctance to encourage Austrian Holocaust survivors to return from exile—are revealed as key sites of post-war anti-Semitism.

On all these points, Serloth provides new or deeper insights, compellingly underpinned by documentary evidence throughout, and her critical insights into, and responses to, the workings of anti-Semitic rhetoric and political praxis are of far more than "just" historiographical interest. Given the longer historical continuities and the above-mentioned, renewed salience of anti-Semitism today, Serloth's work makes a valuable contribution that enriches our contextual understanding of post-war Austria, whilst also feeding productively into wider and more contemporary debates. All this having been said, there are also a number of areas where further analysis, more extensive historical contextualization, and a (considerably) wider engagement with the existing literature were warranted.

Some of the moderate criticism to be formulated here arises from important points that Serloth makes but does not elaborate on in enough depth. For instance, her conceptual point that anti-Semitisms are always embedded in and complement wider political worldviews (37) is highly suggestive. However, this called for a more systematic comparison of how exactly these ideological articulations worked in post-war Austria. Although Serloth provides evidence of anti-Semitism being articulated across the ideological spectrum, its exact discursive role for ÖVP-, SPÖ-, and VdU- (later FPÖ) politicians respectively—and hence the place of anti-Semitism in the longue durée histories of Austria's three major political "camps" (i.e. the Christian Social Movement, Social Democracy, and pan-Germanism)—needed more extensive discussion. Also, nineteenth-century ideologues such as Karl von Vogelsang or the Linzer Programm of 1882 are mentioned (102) but not explored in their full historical significance.

On a related note: Although Serloth repeatedly (and rightly) stresses some continuities, in terms of political rhetoric and personnel, of Austrian anti-Semitism before and after the Holocaust, important contributions to the international literature on this longer history (e.g. by Beller, Boyer, Schwarz, and Wistrich) are conspicuous by their relative or complete absence. Other important works, for instance by Heinz Wassermann, Maximilian Gottschlich, or Ruth Wodak, whose analyses of discursive "victim-perpetrator reversals" are more relevant to Serloth's discussion than the latter reveals, are mentioned but not explored in all their convergences with the analysis at hand. In yet other cases, attentive readers may wonder why important cross-references were not discussed at all. For example, Serloth herself invokes the distinction between "active" and "passive anti-Semitisms", at one point (21) even mentioning its Hinterbühnen, yet this does not extend to a discussion of Christian Fleck's and Albert Müller's (Goffman-esque) thoughts on Austria's post-war, anti-Semitism's "front- and back-stages" (see Wassermann 2002: 8). Had this analytical thread been developed yet further, with the aid of seminal literature on everyday racism (Essed 1991), then the structural entanglements of ethnic prejudices, political action, and institutionalized exclusions could have been analyzed in yet greater depth.

Serloth's book is at its most compelling when she subjects concrete statements to close scrutiny, thereby revealing the workings of specific stereotypes and their deeply problematic, ideological "logic" at play (e.g. 242ff.). Similarly, her diachronic tracing of anti-Semitic topoi in, for example, Leopold Kunschak's various statements between 1919 and 1946 epitomizes the kind of analysis needed to counter enduring exclusions and injustices. In another instance (i.e. the discussion of critical counter-discourses offered by Helmut Qualtinger and Carl Merz, by Erwin Ringel and by Thomas Bernhard and Claus Peymann, respectively), readers may be both utterly persuaded by their relevance to Serloth's discussion yet puzzled by their exact placing within the analysis.

Overall, however, Serloth succeeds in capturing how enduring anti-Semitic exclusions were part and parcel of the construction of a new "community of solidarity" at a key juncture in recent Austrian history. This acquires additional importance when read against its longer historical backdrop and in light of some of today's worrying political trajectories.

Literature Cited

Essed, Philomena, *Understanding Everyday Racism* (London: Sage, 1991).

Wassermann, Heinz P., "Vorwort", in H. P. Wassermann, ed., *Antisemitismus in Österreich nach 1945* (Innsbruck: Studienverlag, 2002), 7-11.

Paul Miller and Claire Morelon, eds., *Embers of Empire-Continuity and Rupture in the Habsburg Successor States after 1918* (New York: Berghahn, 2019)

Vicko Marelić

The Habsburg Empire lasted for six centuries, ten times longer than the European integration project and three times longer than the United States. It has enjoyed a positive afterlife as its multifaceted legacy, from Brody to Bregenz has been recognized since the beginning of the Habsburg historical revival. Following Franz Ferdinand's 100th birthday, Claudio Magris' work on the Habsburg myth[1] started off a process that would challenge the broken mirror view of the Danube monarchy that was cultivated by anti-Habsburg British[2] propagandists during the First World War.[3] Since then, the sun has been steadily rising on the various facets of the "venerable realm on the Danube."[4] Scholarly re-examination of the K.u.K monarchy has contributed to re-discovering the shining elements of the original empire where the sun never set. Monographs on groundbreaking Viennese culture,[5] the unique, multinational imperial army,[6] and the well-oiled bureaucracy[7] have partially rescued Austro-Hungary from the historical scrap heap. *Embers of Empire* follows this trend and reexamines what remained smoldering in the former realms of the *Doppeladler.*

Published in the prestigious series "Austrian and Habsburg Studies", the major center of Austrian studies at the University of Minnesota, the 22nd edition attempts to walk the historical tightrope between rupture and

1 Claudio Magris, *Der habsburgische Mythos in der modernen österreichischen Literatur* (Vienna: Zsolnay, 1963).
2 Nicole Phelps, *U.S.-Habsburg Relations from 1815 to the Paris Peace Conference-Sovereignty Transformed,* (Cambridge: Cambridge University Press, 2013).
3 For a detailed investigation that traces the historiography of the Habsburg empire since 1918, see John Deak, "The Great War and the Forgotten Realm: The Habsburg Monarchy and the First World War Review," *The Journal of Modern History* 86, no. 2 (2014): 336-380.
4 Arthur J May, "R.W. Seton-Watson and British anti-Habsburg sentiment," *American Slavic and East European Review* 20, (Feb 1961): 40-54 (here 40).
5 Carl Schorske, *Fin de Siècle Vienna-Politics and Culture* (New York: Vintage, 1981).
6 István Deák, *Beyond Nationalism: A Social and Political History of the Habsburg Officer Corps 1848-1918* (Oxford: Oxford University Press, 1990).
7 John Deak, *Forging a Multinational State: State Making in Imperial Austria from the Enlightenment to the First World War* (Stanford: Stanford University Press, 2015).

continuity before and after 1918 in Central Europe. The work includes historians of the Habsburg empire as well as its successor states. Several have recently completed their PhDs and/or published valuable monographs on previously unexplored facets like war veterans,[8] post-war Prague,[9] and the latest assessments of the Habsburg army.[10] Published in November 2018, the book arrives adroitly at the final stretch of the centenary marathon from 1914-1918.

The volume contains four subsections: politics in the the successor states, the army's afterlife through its officers, the post-war fate of the imperial pillars (church, emperor, and aristocracy), and the processing of the empire's memory in the Austrian republic. A wide range of primary sources are used, from Czech newspapers and Polish political memoirs to German language diocesan court journals. An equally broad range of secondary sources draw to the most recent publications. In its opening pages, one of the joint editors, Claire Morelon, guides the reader to think about "continuities in people, institutions and ideas" (p. 4) in order "to better understand the empire's legacy in the successor states political, military and intellectual cultures" (p. 4). The book attempts to go beyond "the Habsburg myth that has been central to scholarship on the persistence of post-1918 Austro-Hungary" (p. 3). Structures, rather than sentiment, are the watchword. Using a comparative methodology taken from previous studies of the Ottoman Empire and its successor states, the chapters present a valid tool of comparison that often yields impressive results in "showing how the Habsburg empire continued to shape the region it had long ruled" (p. 6).

Four chapters focus on national politics in transition features in the first section. Gábor Egry points out accurately that "what is generally lacking in the historiographic literature are comprehensive comparative studies of local level traditions and to what extent was the old elite replaced" (p. 15). In the largest Transylvanian city of Cluj/Kolisz, "village notaries who were expelled and replaced by Romanians were later reinstalled" (p.16). The protracted nature of transition, together with a new legal framework, took time, with the Austrian civil code of 1852 remaining as a foundation of private legal relation until 1930 in the former Habsburg region of Siebenbürgen.

The next chapter by Claire Morelon takes the urban face of Prague as the subject of how the city becomes the center of "de-austrianisation"

8 John Paul Newman, *Yugoslavia in the Shadow of War: 1903–1945* (Cambridge: Cambridge University Press, 2015).
9 Claire Morelon, "Streetscapes of War and Revolution, Prague 1914-1920" (PhD diss., Sciences Po Paris, 2015).
10 Richard Bassett, *For God and Kaiser: The Imperial Austrian Army, 1619-1918* (New Haven: Yale University Press, 2015).

(p. 17) in order to make a clean break with the past. Initially the statue of Habsburg general Joseph Radetzky was first veiled (this image braces the book's cover) and then removed from the Bohemian capital. Like in Bratislava, an embodiment of the new Czechoslovakia, president Thomas Masaryk replaced Kaiser Franz Joseph. Although the removal of the monuments represented a visible rupture and a symbolic reconquest of the public sphere, "to avoid violence and avert the threat of civil war, many of the civil servants in the army and the police kept their jobs" (p. 45) since the "continuity of personnel was necessary for the efficient functioning of the state" (p. 45). The homogenizing unitary framework of the new Czechoslovak state was thus more limited than purged cityscapes attempted to show.

In the same section, a chapter that would certainly justify a full biography on the model of Timothy Snyder's *Red Prince*[11] takes the adaptable government minister, Leon Biliński, as a case study of continuity of political personnel. Biliński served the Habsburg Empire as a finance minister and was to retire in 1918 if not for Joseph Pilsuski's invitation to do the same for the post-war Polish state. His case is instructive as he embodies both the ruptures and continuities of the Habsburg Empire, demonstrating a commitment to both Vienna and Warsaw. The impeccable, *kaisertreu* reputation of Biliński reminds us that there were people who saw no conflict of interest between nationalism and imperial loyalty.

The last article by Martha Filipová in the politics section looks at the fascinating example of showcasing the state through government-sponsored exhibitions, comparing the Prague Jubilee exhibitions in 1891 and Czechoslovakia's "Exhibition of Contemporary Culture in Brno" in 1928. Large scale international fairs had "political and ideological ambitions for the organizers and exhibitors that were used to proclaim political ideas about the states and nations" (p. 91), serving "both as vehicles of modernity and construction of ethno-national identity" (p. 91). Filipovà explores the continuities of the indispensable medium of exhibitions as state legitimation ideologies, which included idealized unity of numerous nations, the state as a bridge between East and West, and the patronage of the head of state—Franz Joseph and Masaryk—both whom would visit and feature as statues in the *ante* and *post-bellum* exhibitions.

The second section examines well-dressed, multilingual mini-Habsburgs, the K.u.K army officers, and their post-1918 fate. The first chapters fire off with a general overview on Habsburg officers through the empire, noting that it was the army that had saved the dynasty both in

11 Timothy Snyder, *The Red Prince: The Secret Life of a Habsburg Archduke* (New York: Basic, 2008).

1619 and 1848 but not in 1918. The former London *Times* correspondent of Central Europe, Richard Bassett, marches the section off with a series of military figures familiar to any Habsburg historian, such as the Hungarian Admiral Miklós Horthy, the "eagle of Trieste" Gottfried Banfield, and the "last Habsburg"[12] Josip Broz Tito. Less familiar but more intriguing to historians are revelations about three Jewish Habsburg officers: Loew, Friedmann, and von Weiss, who later become involved in the precursor to the Israeli defense force, the *Hagenah.* Such insights give the Habsburg empire an additional transcontinental element, which would certainly be of further research interest in the buoyant field of Jewish studies and the Habsburg empire.

The military section marches forward with John Paul Newman's examination of the fate of the Croatian officers in the post-war period. The author attempts to connect the various rejectionists of the unitarist Pan-Slav state, including K.u.K Croatian officers, several of whom would end up with positions in the quisling *Ustaša* state in the 1940s. His bold, unsupported claim argues that the *Ustaša* "conceived their state as no less than a triumphant rupture with Serbian and Yugoslav subjugation in the interwar period and in glorious continuity with the Habsburgs" (p. 160). While the first part of the statement is correct, the second one lacks evidence. The *Ustaša* state prefixed itself as "independent," i.e. a proclaimed rupture from the Habsburg empire. Newman fails to differentiate between the instinctively anti-Serbian of the Croatian-born Habsburg officers, such as Stjepan Sarkotić, and those Croatians radicalized by Greater Serbian state terrorism, like the murder of the Croatian leader Stjepan Radić in the Belgrade parliament. Despite the lack of concrete evidence, the conclusion that "in its origins, the *Ustaša* was the product of a Croat culture of defeat nursed by former officers of the Austro-Hungarian army" (p. 170) is an original interpretation of continuity that will intrigue those interested in this still controversial subject.

Historical analysis of the post-Habsburg constellation frequently leaves out Austria when dealing with the post-bellum states from the Baltic to the Adriatic. The next four chapter dedicated to the Alpine Republic is thus a welcome addition. They start in part three of the book, which begins with a rare insight into the core pillars of the Habsburgs including the church, the aristocracy and the dynasty. The Austro-Hungarian empire, up to its collapse, was the largest Catholic entity in the world. Michael Carter-Sinclair's examination of "one of the staunchest supporters of the Habsburg monarchy" (p. 182) presents the church as "anti-democratic" (p. 181) and "anti-sovereign" (p. 179) due to the strong "alliance of throne and altar" (p.

12 AJP Taylor, *The Habsburg Monarchy 1809-1918* (London: Penguin,1948), 260-1.

181). The author's analysis of the church's position regarding "the republic that no one wanted" argues that "the upper church hierarchy never fully accepted the secular republic, even never gave it a chance" (p. 196) gives a previously unknown insight into a historiographically much neglected yet key institution.

The importance of ecclesiastical recognition re-appears in chapter ten as the decade-long evolution of the process of remembrance of the forlorn Kaiser Karl is revisited. The last ruling was that Habsburg would enjoy a grander legacy in death than in life. His memory ultimately benefitted the Roman Catholic cause more than any other as his partisans lobbied for his beatification on account of his advocacy for peace among nations. The chapter sits well just after the chapter on that most transnational unit, the nobles. The nobility was "most affected by transition from empire to nation state" (p. 203) for they were "a symbol of everything the new states' leader sought to replace; Habsburg imperial institutions, social inequality and German dominance" (p. 203). The last two chapters examine the processing of the empire's passing in post-war Austria. The reader is reminded that Austria, in fact, has an almost forgotten memorial to its fallen in the First World War at the *Heldenplatz* in Vienna. Lastly, the second joint editor, Paul Miller, points out the ambivalent memory in Austria towards Franz Ferdinand, "the first victim of the First World War" (p. 284). The man, whose death was seen by many as a *casus beli* for the First World War, features sparsely in official Austrian memory.

Finishing the book, the reader absorbs on a more erudite level a similar theme as *Kakanische Kontexte*,13 where writers, intellectuals, and journalists from the Habsburg successor states ponder on the legacy of *"Kakanien"* and *"Mitteleuropa"* in 2014. Thus, *Embers of Empire* does for an English-speaking audience what *Kakanische Kontexte* did for a German-speaking public. By mostly dealing with the timeframe of 1918-1938, the book coincidently also echoes the *Time* magazine journalist, Hollywood scriptwriter, but above all Viennese satirist Friedrich Torberg's view that contrary to what "superficial history books recall, the Habsburg empire fell not in 1918 but in 1938."[14] With the benefit of hindsight, at the end of the second decade of the 21st century, the authors show how the embers of empire continued to glow right up to the 21st century as is demonstrated by the mention of the process of beatification of the last emperor Karl I in 2004 or the 2011 funeral of Otto von Habsburg, the last monarch born in *Altösterreich*.

13 Peter Becher, ed., *Kakanische Kontexte: Reden über die Mitte Europa* (Vienna: Otto Müller, 2014).

14 Friedrich Tornberg, "Ein sentimentales Vorwort," in: Ernst Trost, *Das bleib vom Doppeladler: Auf den Spuren der versunkene Donaumonarchie* (Vienna: Goldmann, 1965) 10-11.

Overall, the book argues convincingly against the imagined idea of the 1918 break from the past. As the book correctly shows, there was a plethora of continuities in the post-bellum states of Central Europe. The book reminds historians to step away from the now century old anti-Habsburg narrative that focused on projecting the national to the past and the present. Instead it encourages them to examine the local and regional rather than the national. The major strengths of the work are informed, updated, and ambitious pieces that attempt to span the range of the empire in the style of the *Kronprinzenwerk*. 'Embers of Empire' thus represents a sound start for further research, especially on the biographies of less well-known personalities that appeared on the stage in the wobbly world of the post-bellum states. For these reasons, it should find its place in every Habsburg and Central European historian's shelf.

Kurt Luger and Franz Rest, eds., *Alpenreisen: Erlebnis, Raumtransformationen, Imagination* (Innsbruck: Studienverlag, 2017)

Marc Landry

As editors Kurt Luger and Franz Rest note in the introduction to their sizeable edited volume, *Alpenreisen: Erlebnis, Raumtransformationen, Imagination*, there is scarcely a region in Europe that is simultaneously so yearned for as a destination (far better expressed with the German *Sehnsuchtsort*) and shrouded in myth as the Alps. This is certainly true, and both of these phenomena have fueled the desire to visit these mountains for over two centuries. It is to the relationship between tourism and the Alps that this book dedicates itself. Where Alpine tourism stands today, and where it's headed—these are the broad themes addressed by the thirty-five contributions that make up this interdisciplinary volume. *Alpenreisen* stands as a helpful, state-of-the-field overview of the nexus between the Alps and tourism, particularly for the German-speaking regions of the chain. It also distinguishes itself in its efforts to grapple with the impacts of climate change on the future of Alpine tourism—both from the perspective of the tourist industry and the inhabitants of the mountains who hope to preserve the area as a livable space.

Alpenreisen is a book that bears the influence of a number of dates, events, and anniversaries. The volume itself is the result of the Thirteenth International Salzburg Tourism Forum that took place at the University of Salzburg in November 2016. This tourism conference was also held in the context of Salzburg's 20!6 [sic!] celebration of the two hundredth anniversary of the region belonging to Austria. Finally, as the editors mention, the years 2002 and 2017 also serve as useful bookends. The former was the International Year of Mountains and the latter was the International Year of Sustainable Tourism as declared by the United Nations' General Assembly. The theme of sustainability—of the tourist industry as a crucial economic sector and of Alpine inhabitants' quality of life—is shared by many of the more forward-looking contributions.

Given the Salzburg roots of this project, it is not surprising that a major focus of many of the chapters is the province itself. Still, the editors solicited contributions beyond the initial conference papers, and the result is a work that can plausibly present itself as addressing the entire region. A handful of chapters are framed in circum-Alpine fashion. Switzerland is also well represented. Nevertheless, a focus on the German-speaking Alps is unmistakable. *Alpenreisen* is also a truly interdisciplinary effort; there is something here for almost everyone. Authors stem from the fields of cultural studies, economics and tourism, geography, history, and land use planning, and the contributions range from traditional historical explorations to an abridged version of the editors' conversation with legendary Austrian mountaineer Kurt Diemberger.

For an edited volume, the chapters in *Alpenreisen* cohere rather well. Editors Kurt Luger and Franz Rest, both communications scholars at the University of Salzburg with decades of pioneering research on Alpine tourism, start the proceedings with a brief introduction that highlight some of the common themes. A number of authors make the point about the crucial significance of transport technology and infrastructure in the nexus between tourism and the Alps. Mass tourism of the nineteenth century was only possible with the advent of railways that brought travelers from the cities into the mountains. After the Second World War, the automobile revolutionized the ways that tourists could access the Alps and required the construction of a network of roads as well. Nowadays, ropeways that allow even the less hardy tourists to access the treasures of the high Alps have moved into the foreground. They have become, in the memorable words of one of *Alpenreisen*'s authors, the "alpha dogs" of economic development in the Alpine region. With the aid of these and other technologies, tourism played a key role in transforming the formerly agricultural society that dominated in the Alps to a modern service economy. But the very success of tourism in reshaping the social and physical landscape of the Alps has prompted resistance to touristic expansion, as well as contemporary efforts to make this branch sustainable for humans and nonhuman nature alike. This dilemma animates a large number of the approaches in *Alpenreisen*, particularly in reference to the future challenge of global warming. In the aggregate, *Alpenreisen* presents no real consensus on how a warming planet will affect the future of Alpine tourism apart from the conclusion that higher altitude areas that can better keep their snow cover in winter will be well placed to benefit. In fact, some research shows that fears about the disruptions of global warming might be exaggerated, at least for the near term. Finally, a number of chapters explore the importance of the imaginary, of the mountains of the mind, in the touristic interaction with the Alps.

Still, most interest will likely be drawn by individual contributions. Highlights include the opening chapter, coauthored by Luger and Rest, that orients the reader on the current state of Alpine tourism. Luger and Rest note that nowadays, tourists are driven into the mountains for different reasons than in the past. Whereas the Alps have been a place of yearning in the modern period, modern sociologists now see the mountains as place of "resonance" as well. To the degree that urban and industrial society has alienated humans from nature both internal and external, a landscape like the Alps can provide resonance: a functioning, harmonious relationship to the natural world. Whether this will continue to be the case, they argue, depends on the outcome of the struggle between two future visions of Alpine tourism: one characterized by growth and profit, and one focused on sustainability. An essay by Patrick Kupper on the entangled histories of tourism and national parks in the Alps stands out for its recognition of the global dimensions of these developments—in particular, the connections between early Alpine tourism and the conception of national parks in the United States. Kupper demonstrates that influences went both ways, as the American model of national parks eventually made their way back to the Alps and acted as yet another spur to Alpine tourism. Finally, the chapter by Ingrid Runggaldier on women in Alpine history stands out as an effort to diversify a field that is still dominated by men.

Alpenreisen is an important contribution to our understanding of tourism and its manifold consequences and possibilities in one of the world's most iconic landscapes. It also stands as a reckoning of where the Alpine journey might be headed in an era of shifting societal and natural landscapes.

List of Authors

Petra Bernhardt is a lecturer and researcher at the University of Vienna.

Günter Bischof is the Marshall Plan Chair of History and the Director of Center Austria: The Austrian Marshall Plan Center for European Studies, University of New Orleans.

Michael Burri teaches in the department of German at Bryn Mawr College. He is Vice-President of the Austrian Studies Association.

David F. J. Campbell is an associate professor with the Department of Political Science at the University of Vienna, researcher with the Danube University Krems/Alpen-Adria-University of Klagenfurt as well as a Quality Expert for the University of Applied Arts, Vienna.

Roger Chickering is Professor Emeritus of History, Georgetown University.

Gary Cohen is professor Emeritus of history at the University of Minnesota, Twin Cities, and former director of the Minnesota Center for Austrian Studies.

Jason Dawsey is a Research Historian at the Institute for the Study of War and Democracy, The National World War II Museum, New Orleans.

John Deak is associate professor of history at Notre Dame University, USA.

Martin Dolezal is Senior Scientist at the Department of Political Science at the University of Salzburg and Fellow at the Institute for Advanced Studies (IHS) in Vienna.

Gerhard A. Fetz is Dean and Professor Emeritus at the University of Montana.

Jonathan Gumz is a Senior Lecturer in Modern History and Director of Research, School of History and Cultures, University of Birmingham.

Reinhard Heinisch is professor of Austrian Politics in Comparative European Perspective and chair of the department of political science at the University of Salzburg.

Erin Hochman is associate professor of History at Southern Methodist University.

Christian Karner is a lecturer at the University of Nottingham, where he is associate professor of sociology at the faculty of social sciences.

Theresia Klugsberger is an independent researcher and lecturer at the New Design University in St. Pölten, Austria.

Marc Landry is an assistant professor of Central European History and the Associate Director, Center Austria: The Austrian Marshall Plan Center for European Studies.

Paul Frederick Lerner is Professor of History and Director of the Max Kade Institute for Austrian-German-Studies.

Karin Liebhart is a Lecturer and Researcher at the University of Vienna.

Ulricke Lunacek was a leader of the Austrian Green Party; she served as Vice President of the European Parliament (2014-2017) and member of the European Parliament for the Austrian Greens (2009-2017).

Vicko Marelić is a PhD student of history at the University of Vienna and Austrian Ministry Fellow at the Austrian Marshall Plan Center for European Studies, New Orleans.

Anton Pelinka is retired now after a career as a Professor of Political Science at the University of Innsbruck (1975–2006), and as Professor of Nationalism Studies and Political Science, at Central European University, Budapest (2006–2018).

Hannes Richter serves in the public affairs division of the Austrian Embassy in Washington, D.C.

Dirk Rupnow is a professor at the Institute for Contemporary History and currently Dean of the Faculty for Philosophy and History at the University of Innsbruck.

Jacqueline Vansant is a professor of German at the University of Michigan-Dearborn.

Janek Wasserman is an associate professor of Modern Central European and German history at the University of Alabama.

Florian Wenninger is a post-doctoral student at the Institute of Contemporary History at the University of Vienna.

David M. Wineroither is a senior research advisor at National University for Public Service, Budapest and Senior Research Fellow, Hungarian Academy of Sciences.

Contemporary Austrian Studies

Günter Bischof, Anton Pelinka/Fritz Plasser/Ferdinand Karlhofer, Editors

Volume 1 (1992)
Austria in the New Europe

Volume 2 (1993)
The Kreisky Era in Austria
Oliver Rathkolb, Guest Editor

Volume 3 (1994)
Austria in the Nineteen Fifties
Rolf Steininger, Guest Editor

Volume 4 (1995)
Austro-Corporatism: Past—Present—Future

Volume 5 (1996)
Austrian Historical Memory & National Identity

Volume 6 (1997)
Women in Austria
Erika Thurner, Guest Editor

Volume 7 (1998)
The Vranitzky Era in Austria
Ferdinand Karlhofer, Guest Editor

Volume 8 (1999)
The Marshall Plan in Austria
Dieter Stiefel, Guest Editor

Volume 9 (2000)
Neutrality in Austria
Ruth Wodak, Guest Editor

Volume 10 (2001)
Austria and the EU
Michael Gehler, Guest Editor

Volume 11 (2002)
The Dollfuss/Schuschnigg Era in Austria: A Reassessment
Alexander Lassner, Guest Editor

Volume 12 (2003)
The Americanization/Westernization of Austria

Volume 13 (2004)
Religion in Austria
Hermann Denz, Guest Editor

Volume 14 (2005)
Austrian Foreign Policy in Historical Perspective
Michael Gehler, Guest Editor

Volume 15 (2006)
Sexuality in Austria
Dagmar Herzog, Guest Editor

Volume 16 (2007)
The Changing Austrian Voter

Volume 17 (2008)
New Perspectives on Austrians and World War II
Barbara Stelzl-Marx, Guest Editor

Volume 18 (2009)
The Schüssel Era in Austria

Volume 19 (2010)
From Empire to Republic: Post-World War I Austria

Volume 20 (2011)
Global Austria: Austria's Place in Europe and the World
Alexander Smith, Guest Editor

Volume 21 (2012)
Austrian Lives
Eva Maltschnig, Guest Editor

Volume 22 (2013)
Austria's International Position after the End of the Cold War

Volume 23 (2014)
1914: Austria-Hungary, the Origins, and the First Year of World War 1
Samuel R. Williamson, Jr., Guest Editor

Volume 24 (2015)
Austrian Federalism in Comparative Perspective

Volume 25 (2016)
Austrian Studies Today

Volume 26 (2017)
Migration in Austria
Dirk Rupnow, Guest Editor

Volume 27 (2017)
Austrian Enviromental History
Marc Landry and Patrick Kupper, eds.
Verena Winiwarter, Guest Editor